This is the first collection of essays to explore the wide dimensions and influence of eighteenth-century opera. In a series of fresh articles by leading scholars in the field, new perspectives are offered on the important figures of the day, including Handel, Vivaldi, Gluck, Rameau, and Mozart, and on the fundamental problems of creation, revision, borrowing, influence, and intertextuality. Other essays reinterpret librettos of serious opera in the French and Italian theater during the later eighteenth century. Sister arts, notably painting, the novel, ballet, and the spoken stage are also examined in their relationship to the development of opera. Bracketing the collection are studies of the early pastoral opera and of Prokofieff, which expand our historical view of operatic life during the Age of Reason. The book contains numerous rare illustrations, and will be of interest to scholars and students of opera and theater history.

Opera and the Enlightenment

Opera and the Enlightenment

Edited by

THOMAS BAUMAN and
MARITA PETZOLDT McCLYMONDS

Published by the Press Syndicate of the University of Cambridge
The Pitt Building, Trumpington Street, Cambridge, CB2 1RP
40 West 20th Street, New York, NY 10011–4211, USA
10 Stamford Road, Oakleigh, Melbourne 3166, Australia

© Cambridge University Press 1995

First published 1995

Printed in Great Britain at the University Press, Cambridge

A catalogue record for this book is available from the British Library

Library of Congress cataloguing in publication data

Opera and the Enlightenment / edited by Thomas Bauman and Marita Petzoldt McClymonds.
p. cm.
Includes index.
ISBN 0 521 46172 3
1. Opera – Europe – 18th century. 2. Enlightenment. I. Bauman, Thomas, 1948–.
II. McClymonds, Marita P.
ML1720.3.064 1995
782.1'09'033–dc20   94-11009   CIP   MN

ISBN 0 521 46172 3 hardback

TAG

These essays are dedicated to
DANIEL HEARTZ
*with respect, admiration, and affection
by his colleagues, students, and friends*

Contents

List of plates page xi
Library abbreviations xiii

INTRODUCTION
    THOMAS BAUMAN   1

PROLOGUE

1   GARY TOMLINSON
      Pastoral and musical magic in the birth of opera   7

OPERA AND THE VISUAL ARTS

2   THOMAS BAUMAN
      Moralizing at the tomb: Poussin's Arcadian shepherds in eighteenth-century England and Germany   23

3   KERRY S. GRANT
      Dr. Burney, the bear, and the knight: E. F. Burney's *Amateurs of Tye-Wig Music*   43

4   ANTHONY NEWCOMB
      New light(s) on Weber's Wolf's Glen Scene   61

SERIOUS OPERA

5   REINHARD STROHM
      Sinfonia and drama in early eighteenth-century opera seria   91

6   MARY CYR
      The dramatic role of the chorus in French opera: evidence for the use of gesture, 1670–1770   105

Contents

   7   MARITA PETZOLDT MCCLYMONDS
        Transforming opera seria: Verazi's innovations and their
        impact on opera in Italy   119

HANDEL AND GLUCK

   8   WINTON DEAN
        Handel's *Serse*   135

   9   JOHN H. ROBERTS
        The "sweet song" in *Demofoonte*: a Gluck borrowing from
        Handel   168

  10   BRUCE ALAN BROWN
        Zéphire et Flore: a "galant" early ballet by Angiolini and
        Gluck   189

  11   JULIE E. CUMMING
        Gluck's Iphigenia operas: sources and strategies   217

CONCERNING MOZART

  12   WALTER E. REX
        The "storm" music of Beaumarchais' *Barbier de Séville*   243

  13   JOSEPH KERMAN
        On *Don Giovanni*, No. 2   260

  14   JOHN A. RICE
        Leopold II, Mozart, and the return to a Golden Age   271

EPILOGUE

  15   RICHARD TARUSKIN
        From fairy tale to opera in four moves (not so simple)   299

Index   308

Plates

1	Poussin, *Et in Arcadia ego* (ca. 1630) Chatsworth, Duke of Devonshire	page 25
2	Poussin, *Et in Arcadia ego* (ca. 1638) Paris, Musée du Louvre	27
3	a. Chodowiecki, *Arcadia* Leben, Bemerkungen und Meinungen Johann Bunkels (Berlin, 1778), No. 12 b. Rossmässler, *Auch ich war in Arcadien* Der Kinderfreund (Leipzig, 1781)	30 30
4	Edward F. Burney, *Amateurs of Tye-Wig Music* Yale Center for British Art, Paul Mellon Collection	47
5	Anonymous print, *The Graces* Farmington, Mass., Lewis Walpole Library	50
6	Fantascope invented by Etienne-Gaspard Robertson for producing projections in his phantasmagoria	62
7	Drawing of one of Robertson's presentations	66
8	Slide projection for a phantasmagoria, attributed to Etienne-Gaspard Robertson Jac Remise, *Magie lumineuse* (n. p., 1979)	69
9	Cartoon illustration of Gounod's *La Nonne sanglante* (1854) *L'Illustration* (Paris, 1855)	75
10	Weber's sheet of instructions for staging *Der Freischütz* D-Bds, Sammlung Weberiana, Cl.II A g 2	78
11	Design for the final act of Lully's *Amadis* (1684), drawing by Jean Bérain F-Pn	108

12	Collasse's *Thétis et Pélée* (1689), engraving by J. Dolivart after Bérain F-Po, Réserve 926(3), p. 38	109
13	Costume for a male chorus member in Lully's *Armide*, by Boquet F-Po, D. 216 V A. 2 folio 99	110
14	Costume for a female chorus member "à la Romaine" (1768), by Boquet F-Po	111
15	Costume for a male chorus member in the 1769 revival of Rameau's *La Princesse de Navarre* F-Po, D. 216 VIII	112
16	Machinery for the appearance of demons, drawing by Bérain F-Pn	114
17	*Zéphire et Flore*, No. 5; unattributed drawing from the largely dispersed "Durazzo Collection" University of Salzburg, Institut für Tanzforschung	192
18	Teresa Fogliazzi Angiolini in the role of Psyche, in Hilverding and Starzer's *Psyché et l'Amour* New York, Public Library for the Performing Arts	198
19	a–d "Orage," Antoine Laurent Baudron, *Le Barbier de Séville*, Act 4 F-Pn, Réserve F 1124	252–5
20	Barbara Krafft or Georg Weikert, painting of Gluck with his wife Marianne Vienna, Museum der Stadt Wien	269
21	"Vivat Leopoldus Secundus," allegorical engraving by I. C. Berndt in celebration of Leopold's coronation as Emperor, 1790 Frankfurt am Main, Historisches Museum	273
22	Playbill announcing the debut of Emperor Leopold's opera seria troupe in Sebastiano Nasolini's *Teseo a Stige*, 24 November 1791 Vienna, Nationalbibliothek, Theatersammlung	280

Library abbreviations

A-Wn	Vienna, Österreichische Nationalbibliothek, Musiksammlung
B-Bc	Brussels, Conservatoire Royale de Musique
D-B	Berlin, Staatsbibliothek Preussischer Kulturbesitz
D-Bds	Berlin, Deutsche Staatsbibliothek
D-Mbs	Munich, Bayerische Staatsbibliothek
D-MH	Mannheim, Wissenschaftliche Stadtbibliothek und Universitätsbibliothek
D-Sl	Stuttgart, Württembergische Landesbibliothek
F-Pn	Paris, Bibliothèque Nationale
F-Po	Paris, Bibliothèque-Musée de l'Opéra
F-V	Versailles, Bibliothèque Municipale
I-Bc	Bologna, Civico Museo Bibliografico Musicale
I-Mc	Milan, Conservatorio di Musica Giuseppe Verdi
I-Nc	Naples, Conservatorio di Musica S Pietro a Majella
I-PAc	Parma, Conservatorio di Musica Arrigo Boito
I-Pci	Padua, Museo Civico, Biblioteca Civica e Archivio Comunale
I-Rsc	Rome, Conservatorio di Musica S Cecilia
I-Vcg	Venice, Biblioteca Casa di Goldoni
I-Vgc	Venice, Biblioteca e Istituto della Fondazione Giorgio Cini
I-Vnm	Venice, Biblioteca Nazionale Marciana
P-La	Lisbon, Palácio Nacional da Ajuda
US-NYp	New York, Public Library at Lincoln Center, Library and Museum of the Performing Arts
US-Wcm	Washington, Library of Congress, Music Division

Introduction

THOMAS BAUMAN

The essays included in this volume cover the history of opera from Monteverdi to Prokofieff, from the sinfonia to the finale, from the chorus to the ballet, yet they are anything but a dutiful chronological survey of opera. Rather, they offer examples of some of the multifarious ways we have come to think about what is perhaps the most troubling and rewarding musical genre in the long history of Western art music.

The volume was conceived as a way of honoring one of the major figures in operatic research and criticism during the second half of the twentieth century, Daniel Heartz, who retired this year after over three decades of service on the faculty of the University of California at Berkeley. His work and personality are strongly imprinted on each of the essays in the present volume, contributed by colleagues, students, and friends.

It is perhaps not simply a matter of chance that opera during the Enlightenment forms the focal point of these essays. Today, thanks in no small part to the scholarship and teaching of Professor Heartz, the eighteenth century has re-emerged not only as an area of serious scholarly inquiry, but as an ever more important part of the repertories of our varied operatic institutions. Although Mozart is by no means absent, the emphasis throughout falls on opera during the era of Handel and Gluck – a period once regarded as unknown territory, of interest neither to scholars nor to performers and directors. In this context, one cannot forbear acknowledging the parallel impact of the century's first great champion of the half-forgotten world stretching from Scarlatti to Mozart, Edward J. Dent. The fact that a book like this can center on that world rather than on the one extending from Rossini to Puccini is owing largely to the successive championship of eighteenth-century opera – and especially of eighteenth-century opera seria – by these two gifted writers.

The perspectives provided by the following fifteen essays indicate how varied were the cultural and intellectual crosscurrents within the lifeworld of the eighteenth century – and how varied are the present-day responses they evoke. As Gary Tomlinson's inaugural essay explains, opera's beginnings at the time of Monteverdi were already ambiguous. Its first exemplars were still steeped in the mentality of an era very distant from our own. But opera, unlike the pastoral drama of the Renaissance, found the resources to negotiate the turn to a modern, "scientific" spirit that came to full flower in the Enlightenment.

Three iconographic studies touch on the multi-leveled interconnections of opera, the visual arts, and their audiences during the seventeenth and

Introduction

eighteenth centuries. My essay on the effective history of Poussin's *Et in Arcadia ego*, or more precisely of the ambivalent theme it embodied, examines the intersection of the Horatian concern that a work of art edify with art's innate sensual proclivities in a series of paintings, novels, and operas on the theme of death in Arcadia. Kerry Grant finds abundant, fascinating cultural commentary and innuendo embedded in an engraving by Charles Burney's nephew that confronts the English cult of Handel and "ancient music," and he points up its unhappy consequences for the career of Burney himself in Georgian England. Anthony Newcomb casts an account of the cultural debt owed by Weber's famous Wolf's Glen Scene to a battery of popular spectacles spawned by a combination of technological advances, entrepreneurship, and a coalescing mass audience at the turn of the nineteenth century. The deeper affinity linking Weber's finale to these contemporaneous entertainments (and to the modern cinema as well), Newcomb explains, lies in its realistic rather than symbolic mode of presentation, yet another abiding ambivalence in the history of opera.

The dismissive attitude of earlier eras toward eighteenth-century opera before Mozart was in many ways a direct reflection of their dismissive attitude toward serious opera. In contrast, serious genres occupy a central position here, particularly in a group of essays whose common theme is the reassessment of many received notions. Reinhard Strohm calls into question a traditional source of critical disdain, the tendency of Italian composers such as Pergolesi, Vinci, and Vivaldi to redeploy both arias and overtures from opera to opera in the first half of the century. The practice, he suggests, does not necessarily imply the absence of large-scale cohesion, nor unconcern for dramatic relevance. Mary Cyr offers a related argument reassessing evidence for the reported gestural ineptitude of the French chorus on the tiny stage of the Opéra. And Marita McClymonds delivers the coup de grâce to the withered claim that opera seria ossified into a tired and sententious sterility after Metastasio by examining the innovative librettos of Mattia Verazi and the young Italian librettists who followed his lead during the century's last decades.

In the four studies on Handel and Gluck included here, new discoveries inspire additional layers of speculation on the tangled world of eighteenth-century operatic production and reception. Winton Dean's essay on Handel's *Serse* finds affinities both with its operatic past (in earlier settings by Cavalli and Bononcini) and with Mozart's master comedies. John Roberts and Bruce Brown add new dimensions to our picture of Gluck's early career: Roberts discusses two arias borrowed from Handel, both to reinforce Michael Kelly's testimony on Gluck's veneration for the older master and to bring into relief the creative side of the process of borrowing – including self-borrowing; and Brown's study of a newly identified early ballet by Gluck and Gasparo Angiolini enlarges our understanding of the changes that their collaboration underwent during the years of the Viennese reform operas. Gluck's ripest works and their impact on future operatic practice figure in the essay of Julie Cumming. In assessing the great Iphigenia operas, she shows how Gluck and

Introduction

his French librettists relied not simply on disembodied literary ideals but on the rich stage history of the tales, on Parisian intellectual currents, and on Gluck's own earlier serious operas, ballets, and opéras comiques.

John Rice develops an array of links between Mozart's two valedictory operas and the works of his last years in the employ of Colloredo, paralleling the more explicit links Leopold II sought to forge with a past Golden Age of Habsburg absolutism and artistic patronage. Three Berkeley colleagues of Professor Heartz offer other provocative insights into operas of the post-Gluckian era. Walter E. Rex interprets the storm music to Beaumarchais' *Barbier de Séville* from deep within the character of Bartholo, spinning out strands directly relevant to both Paisiello's operatic version of the play and Mozart's *Figaro*. Joseph Kerman, with characteristic acumen, draws our attention to unsuspected resonances and hidden riches in one of the defining numbers in Mozart's "Oper aller Opern," the duet of Anna and Ottavio in *Don Giovanni*. And by way of epilogue, Richard Taruskin harnesses Prokofieff to the age of Mozart and Goldoni in order to show some of the continuities of eighteenth-century operatic traditions into our own very different era.

The problems and issues raised in the following essays are not matters of interest solely to eighteenth-century specialists; they are broadly typological ones embedded in the nature of opera throughout its varied history. Opera has always confounded neat categorization. And as modern chaos theory is beginning to teach scientists, the rapid development from simple beginnings to dizzying levels of complexity – everywhere discernible, not only in nature but in human culture as well – is not a barrier to understanding but rather one of its most fascinating objects. To approach opera in the interdisciplinary spirit that runs through the essays in this volume is to exonerate its multivalent nature of the compound charges of improbability, unnaturalness, and absurdity with which it has been so often reviled, and to open new insights into the many ways it has enriched our complex and ambivalent world.

Chicago
5 October 1994

Prologue

1

Pastoral and musical magic in the birth of opera

GARY TOMLINSON

Of all our dramatic arts, opera demands the most of us. It asks us to accept it as dramatic representation, to immerse ourselves in a sequence of imitated actions far more specific and complex than those offered by the gestural arts of dance or mime. Yet because it is sung it requires, if it is to be taken seriously as drama, a leap of imagination longer than that needed for spoken theater, a suspension of disbelief more uncompromising. Perhaps this explains why opera is so often not taken seriously: we have all encountered the superficial allegiances of opera buffs, their cults of divas and heldentenors, and we all have also known people who on some visceral and unselfconscious level reject altogether the notion of sung drama. But difficulty in appreciating opera as serious drama is not the burden of sycophants and the naive alone. Instead we each contend with it, reaching our own more or less uneasy compromises with the genre. We struggle in some part of ourselves to restrain the skepticism that can shatter the spell of its music drama. We strive to accommodate the breach of verisimilitude inherent in its singing talk.

This is not a stance unique to the twentieth century. The history of opera could almost be written as a chronicle of such accommodations, of the varying means by which skepticism has been repressed. The frequent reform initiatives in this history (no artistic genre, it seems, has more often called for purgation) amount to little other than repeated readjustments of strategy in the face of the fundamental unbelievability of drama in song. This is as true of Gluck's or Wagner's famous refashionings as it is of countless less marked and less clearly self-proclaimed alterations in the genre. Opera places us, Voltaire wrote, "in a land of fairies," and because of this "we suffer [its] extravagances, and are even fond of them."[1] It sits just beyond the frontier of our rational, scientific world. It inhabits an unverisimilar, unreal, and finally magical realm that Western culture long ago repudiated but cannot quite shake. From this ambivalent mix of forbearance and immersion arises our enduring fascination with the genre.

The frontier itself, the borderline between real and unreal realms, between verisimilitude and its absence, has not shifted much since the mid-seventeenth century, the period of opera's establishment as a more-than-sporadic manner of entertainment. Complaints about the artifice of sung drama sprang up soon after the opening of the first public opera theater in Venice in 1637, as research by Ellen Rosand has shown. They are recorded for us in several librettists' tendency to justify their dramatic procedures, irregular from the perspective of Aristotelian guidelines for spoken drama, by citing the general unreality of the sung drama in which they were collaborating. Francesco Sbarra's defense of a libretto of his from 1651 is typical:

> I know that the *ariette* sung by Alexander and Aristotle will be judged contrary to the decorum of such great personages; but I also know that musical recitation is improper altogether, since it does not imitate natural discourse and since it removes the soul from dramatic compositions, which should be nothing but imitations of human actions. Yet this defect is not only tolerated by the current century but received with applause.[2]

Statements like this one constitute an acknowledgment of the peculiarly emphatic suspension of disbelief that opera required already by the middle of the seventeenth century. And this has been a requisite of operatic appreciation ever since.

But such statements seem not to have emerged much earlier than the 1640s. In particular they are not associated with the works music historians consider the first operas, the music dramas produced from 1590 to 1610 at the courts and in the salons of Florence, Mantua, and other north Italian cities. Historians from Solerti on have amassed hundreds of pages of contemporaneous accounts concerning these works, accounts that range from the fulsome and propagandistic to the vituperative and jealous and that were penned variously by the poets and composers themselves and by members of their audiences. But from all these accounts there seems to emerge no selfconscious acknowledgment of the unreality of sung drama. Their typical tone, rather, is one of unquestioning acceptance, as in this matter-of-fact report from the Estense ambassador to Mantua on Monteverdi's *Arianna* of 1608:

> Then they put on the Comedy in music... and all the well-dressed reciters played their parts very well, but best of all [was] the comedienne Ariadne. The story was of Ariadne and Theseus, [and she,] in her lament in music accompanied by viols and violins, made many weep at her sorrow. There was a [musician named] Rasi who sang divinely, but Ariadne was best, and the eunuchs and the others were awful.[3]

The first operas, in other words, seem to have been received in an atmosphere not noticeably tinged by the skepticism and aesthetic distance that has colored operatic reception almost ever since. They seem to have answered to a different conception of dramatic verisimilitude than the one that has dominated operatic appreciation since around 1650. The border between real and unreal realms seems, in short, to have been set differently for them than for later music dramas.

With this hypothesis of a shifted border in mind we may reconsider one of the arguments Nino Pirrotta advanced in his "Early Opera and Aria," a virtuosic essay that has guided all students of early opera since its first publication in 1968. There Pirrotta noted that the early Florentine and Mantuan music dramas again and again featured legendary musicians among their protagonists (especially Orpheus, in three operas, and Apollo, in two more). He asserted that the creators of these works, in particular the Florentine poet Ottavio Rinuccini, the librettist of most of them, chose such mythical singers in a selfconscious attempt to justify the musical medium of their dramas.[4] In saying this, of course, Pirrotta implied the felt need around 1600 for such justification, the need, in other words, to help the audience along in its suspension of disbelief. But, as I have said, I see no evidence that the audience in 1600 required this sort of justification for music drama. The closest thing I know to such evidence is a passage in *Il corago*, an anonymous Florentine treatise on dramaturgy brought to light since Pirrotta wrote, that recommends ancient gods, heroes, and especially mythical musicians as the most appropriate protagonists for sung drama.[5] Here the issue of the verisimilitude of sung speech is clearly raised. But *Il corago* was written no earlier than 1628, and perhaps, for all we know, some years later.[6] It was written, that is, at least a generation after the early court operas. It can just as easily be adduced as evidence for the emergence of new operatic values – for the emergence of views anticipating those of Venetian librettists of the 1640s and 50s – as it can be linked to the positions of the creators themselves of the first operas some thirty years before.

Pirrotta's contention about the protagonists of the early court operas, in sum, imputes to the creators and audiences of those works reactions for which we have documentation only from later operatic history. (It poses, by the way, the additional difficulty of accounting for *Arianna*, Rinuccini's libretto for Monteverdi that features, like his *Dafne* and *Euridice*, the characters of Ovidian myth but unlike them includes no legendary musicians in its *dramatis personae*.) I will return below to suggest a different interpretation from Pirrotta's for the preponderance of musicians among the protagonists of the first operas.

The broadened view of musico-dramatic verisimilitude around 1600 that I will advocate here may also help to explicate a suggestion I made, I fear somewhat cryptically, in *Monteverdi and the End of the Renaissance*:[7] the suggestion that we rethink our general assumptions about realism in Monteverdi's surviving operas. These operas fall into two pairs, *Orfeo* and the fragmentary *Arianna* presented in Mantua in 1607 and 1608, and *Il ritorno d'Ulisse in patria* and *L'incoronazione di Poppea* staged in Venice in the early 1640s: one pair, in other words, from each side of the shift in operatic perceptions that I am suggesting separates early court opera from later Venetian opera. Received musicological wisdom holds that the later operas (especially *Poppea*) display a sort of dramatic realism not evident in the earlier ones.[8] At one level this is true. Their subjects are historical – if distantly so in the case of Ulysses – instead of mythical, and many of the situations and actions they depict have a down-to-earth, everyday quality not found in earlier court operas. But, keeping in mind the skeptical distance from sung drama that I see emerging by the 1640s, we might well suspect that this superficial realism of subject and action conceals a deeper unreality in Monteverdi's last operas. As I put it in *Monteverdi and the End of the Renaissance*, in these works

> musical speech as a matter of accepted convention, little touched by the demands of verisimilitude, has replaced music as a rhetorical heightening of speech credible in its well-defined mythical context. The humanist ideal of music and poetry as two sides of a single language... has given way to a modern suspension of disbelief in the face of the anti-rational anomaly of characters speaking in song. (p. 218)

In Monteverdi's late operas realistic acts and situations can be seen to accentuate the unreality of the medium in which they are presented. I believe this dilemma was a deeply felt one in the 1640s and that it was symptomatic of a manner of perceiving music drama that was then new. Musical speech had solidified into a convention that could either be considered to stand outside criteria of dramatic verisimilitude or be judged according to those criteria; in the latter case it had either to be accepted as whimsy or to be rejected altogether. In 1600, I think, the situation was different. At that time musical speech and dramatic verisimilitude were not yet mutually exclusive. Musical speech could still be viewed as an authentic representation of some aspect of reality, a mimesis embodied in a world-view that would begin to seem much less credible only a few decades later. In the remainder of this essay I will outline this world-view and suggest how early court opera participated in it.

The dramatic genre practiced around 1600 in which musical speech most naturally pressed its claim to verisimilitude, music historians have long believed, was the pastoral play. Pirrotta insisted upon the ease of music's admission to the pastoral realm.[9] He quoted Giambattista Guarini's words in his *Compendio della poesia tragicomica* of 1601 on ancient shepherds' musical and poetic prowess. Guarini asserted "that the Arcadian shepherds... embellished their speeches with poetic ornaments," that they were all poets, and "that their principal study and their principal activity was music."[10] The Florentine theorist Giovanni Battista Doni echoed this view in his *Trattato della musica scenica*, written in the 1630s. He noted that pastoral dramas "represent gods, nymphs, and shepherds of that most ancient century when music was natural and speech almost poetic." For this reason more than any other, he said, "true song... is suitable to pastoral plays."[11]

But we should tread carefully here. For though it may be true that the pastoral play was uniquely congenial to music among the spoken dramatic genres of the late sixteenth century, this does not warrant a number of further conclusions about early opera commonly drawn in musicological writings and elsewhere. These include the notion that the creators of opera chose pastoral subjects and settings for their works in order to revive onstage the shepherds who had once sung in Arcadia (and thus, again, justify their presentation of drama in music), the simpler idea that opera is a genre derived from late sixteenth-century pastoral drama, and the more grandiloquent idea that early opera represents nothing less than the pastoral play confronting its eternal musical essence (here especially the Hegelianism of De Sanctis lives on: "The word," he wrote of Italian literary history around 1600, "no longer being anything more than music, had lost its *raison d'être* and cedes the field to music and song").¹²

All these conclusions are more than a little questionable. In the first place there is little evidence that the literati who created opera and theorized about it or their audiences believed that shepherds had once spoken in song. Guarini and Doni, after all, said no such thing, but only held that the Arcadians' speech was closer to poetry than present-day talk and that they often sang as well: in Arcadia, as Doni put it, "music was natural and speech almost poetic." The picture of ancient shepherds that emerged from such writings, as we should expect, was not so much an anticipation of Metastasio's singing heroes as it was a recollection of the rustics of Vergil and Theocritus, who had easily enough distinguished their normal if poetic speech from their full-fledged song. Surely no historical belief that shepherds once sang instead of speaking served in any important way to legitimize the continuous song of the first operas. Nor did such a belief provide a decisive impetus for the creators of these works to choose pastoral stories and characters.

Indeed the stories and characters they chose were not pastoral at all, if we define that adjective as they may well have defined it, by reference to the plots and protagonists of spoken pastoral drama in the late sixteenth century. The early court operas, that is, were not pastoral dramas, but rather dramatized myths that happened to be set in the country (and how many myths are set in the city?). This distinction is worth pausing over. Louise Clubb has shown, in one of the few studies that attempts an ecumenical overview of the Italian pastoral play in the decades of its most famous exemplars, Tasso's *Aminta* and Guarini's *Pastor fido*, that the genre depended on regular *cinquecento* comedy for its plot structures and for some of its stock characters. Its typical plot was built of the intertwined multiple love affairs, the disguises and mistaken identities, and the intrigues of comedy. Its typical protagonists were mortal rustics ranging in refinement, often in the same play, from barely countrified nobility to satyr-like bestiality and Bottomed-out buffoonery.¹³

The first operas showed none of these features. Their protagonists were not Arcadian mortals but instead the gods, demigods, and heroes of Ovid's *Metamorphoses*: Orpheus and Euridice, Daphne and Apollo, Ariadne, Theseus, and Bacchus, Cephalus and Aurora. Their plots were utterly straightforward in structure, relating their simple, affective tales without peripeties, disguises, recognitions, or intrigues. For this reason, no doubt, the most common generic designation their authors applied to these works was not the *favola pastorale* or *favola boscareccia* so frequent in the tradition Clubb has described but rather a stripped-down epithet nowhere to my knowledge found on the title-pages of late sixteenth-century pastoral plays: *favola*, meaning simply "myth," "fable," or "story."

Add to all this the fact that the first librettos differ utterly from spoken pastoral dramas in their typical length – much less than half that of even shorter pastoral plays like *Aminta* – and in their characteristically lyric prosody – madrigalian for the most part, interspersed with *ottave*, *terze rime*, and *canzonette* in Gabriello Chiabrera's novel metric arrangements – and the hypothesis of opera's derivation from pastoral drama crumbles. The early operas were not *favole pastorali* "musicked"; on the surface the two genres share little more than their rural settings. If there is a significant connection between them, it lies not in borrowed dramatic techniques or even in broader patterns of intergeneric influence but at a deeper level of cultural substructure and the expressive aspirations arising from it – at what we may call, with Michel Foucault, an archaeological level of meaning.

To unearth this level we need first to realize that in creating the opera libretto Rinuccini looked back not on the pastoral play but instead on an earlier genre foreign to the climate of Aristotelian definition and constraint in which the pastoral play tenaciously grew. This is the mythological *favola* or *fabula* of the late fifteenth century, most famously represented by Agnolo Poliziano's *Fabula di Orfeo*. This *Orfeo*, written probably in the mid-1470s, gave rise to a miniature tradition of mythological plays, barely dramatized versions of stories drawn from Ovid, by such poets as Niccolò da Correggio, author of a *Fabula di Cefalo*, Gian Pietro della Viola, probable creator of a *Representazione di Dafne*, and Antonio Tebaldeo, to whom a revised and enlarged version of *Orfeo* has been ascribed.[14] These works share with the librettos of the first operas all the features in which those librettos differed from late-cinquecento pastoral plays: their Ovidian stories and mythological protagonists, their extreme brevity, their simplicity of plot, their use of lyric verse-forms in a dramatic context, and even, in some cases, their unqualified generic designation, *favola*.

Literary historians have since the eighteenth century routinely described Poliziano's *Orfeo* as music drama, and since the days of Romain Rolland music historians have recognized the general likeness of the work to the Orpheus librettos of the court operas: the Italian title of Pirrotta's classic collection of essays on Renaissance theater music, *Li due Orfei: da Poliziano a Monteverdi*,[15] is only one recent token of this recognition. But musicologists have consistently stopped short of attributing to the early librettists knowledge of Poliziano's work and of the genre it helped to establish. In this their historiographical caution has gotten the better of them. For there can be little doubt that Rinuccini, at least, was cognizant of Poliziano's *fabula* and perhaps of other similar works. I have developed the case for this assertion elsewhere[16] and will retrace only its outlines here.

In the first place, Rinuccini lived in a grand ducal Florence that looked back with nostalgic and self-promoting pride on the city's achievements in the days of Lorenzo the Magnificent, Poliziano, Botticelli, and Marsilio Ficino. In the literary realm Florentine publications like *Tutti i trionfi, carri, mascherate ò canti carnascialesche andati per Firenze, dal tempo del Magnifico Lorenzo vecchio de Medici* of 1559 and the many collections of *Canzone a ballo* by Lorenzo, Poliziano, and their contemporaries printed in the 1550s and 60s bear witness to this retrospective pride.

In the second place, Poliziano's little play was by no means a forgotten work in the sixteenth century. According to Carducci's research a century ago, it was published in some two dozen editions from 1494 into the 1550s. It spawned a semi-popular tradition of Orphic recitations by *cantastorie* that continued to paraphrase it well into the nineteenth century. And it inspired at least three revised versions, including the one ascribed to Tebaldeo, that have come down to us in manuscript.[17] Clearly, some Renaissance E. D. Hirsch intent on superficial indices of cultural literacy could well have doubted the credentials of a Florentine aristocrat of Rinuccini's era who had not heard of Poliziano's *Orfeo*, all the more so if that aristocrat proposed to write an Orphic drama of his own. It is, simply, unthinkable that Rinuccini did not know Poliziano's work in some version or versions. And the case may well be cinched by certain situations and particulars in Rinuccini's dramatization of the story that echo those of Poliziano and his epigones but that seem to have no precedent in ancient sources.[18]

Poliziano's *Orfeo* was conceived in substantial part to be sung, though its music has not come down to us.[19] *Orfeo* exemplifies, in other words, one of the many versions of music-drama practiced at Renaissance courts, and Rolland's famous phrase for it, "l'opéra avant l'opéra," is off the mark only in the teleological premise it embodies. The particular version of music drama *Orfeo* represented was steeped in Neoplatonic musical mysteries. It arose from a Florentine cultural elite captivated by notions of Orphic singing and its effects, an intellectual milieu permeated by a Ficinian Neoplatonism that granted music a fundamental role in the structuring of the cosmos and magical powers in man's interactions with it. Many immersed in this culture, including Ficino and his sometime follower Pico della Mirandola, regarded Orpheus as a supreme magician, a divinely inspired theologian whose most powerful expressions had taken the form of song. And this power could be revived. Pico wrote that "nothing is more effective in natural magic than the Hymns of Orpheus if there be applied to them a suitable music, proper disposition of the soul, and other circumstances known to the wise."[20] And Ficino, who professed to know the proper circumstances and state of the soul, practiced a brand of Orphic astrological chant perhaps not unrelated to the music employed in early performances of *Orfeo*. Against this background, whether or not we accept precise Ficinian readings of *Orfeo* like Richard Cody's that seem to depict Poliziano as a selfconscious purveyor of Neoplatonic ritual in his play,[21] we must see that *Orfeo* told a tale that was magically charged in its original milieu.[22] It was a drama that must have touched in its creators and early audiences chords resonating with occult mysteries of music's power.

The magic of Orphic music persisted in Italian culture a century later. The first operas still played themselves out against a backdrop reminiscent of Poliziano's time, for Ficino's Neoplatonism had not weakened its hold in the intervening years. Instead it had gone underground, achieving in many circles of elite and educated European culture the status of a tacit knowledge guiding patterns of thought in mainly unspoken and often incognizant ways – something on the order of Freudian psychology in the twentieth century, to

Prologue

invoke Panofsky's happy analogy. In the sixteenth century Neoplatonism occupied a central place in what Foucault called the "positive unconscious of knowledge." It contributed decisively to the largely unformulated "rules of formation" by which thinkers came to perceive their objects and artists to conceive their expressions.[23] Neoplatonic thought pervaded countless areas of the courtly culture of the time. It inspired theories of the human psyche and its affects, particularly love; it colored discussions of literary creativity and interpretations of individual works; it prompted idealistic conceptions of beauty in the visual arts; it shaped codes of refined behavior like those in Castiglione's *Courtier*; and – the most direct connection to my subject – it helped stimulate a century-long fascination with the expressive powers of music.[24]

Throughout these years Orpheus remained a singularly malleable symbol of these powers. D. P. Walker put the matter dialectically in a discussion of polemics from around 1600 over the effects of Orpheus' song:

> By discussing the effects of Orpheus' music one could range, with easy suppleness, over every possible practical application of Neoplatonism, from the whitest to the blackest magic, from the most intellectual religion to the most crude superstition, from the beauty of music to the power of a whispered incantation.[25]

But Walker's oppositions here, while rhetorically vibrant, obscure behind twentieth-century values a fundamental truth about late Renaissance culture. This culture knew no distinctions so clear as those we confidently posit today between religion and superstition, between white and black magic, between beautiful song and magical incantation. Precisely the adjacency of each of these paired terms, the proximity and even merging of what we tend to see as distant extremes, generated the passion of disputes over their definition in the sixteenth century. The interstices between these related areas and kinds of thought were narrower then, more easily bridged or obscured, than those that determine our thinking.

Frances Yates came closer than Walker to conveying this in a remark she made about some late sixteenth-century French songs experimenting in musical effects:

> The question as to whether such songs are incantations in the magical sense or incantatory for their artistic quality alone is a very difficult one, for the borderline between magic and art is as hard to trace in this period as the borderline between magic and religion.[26]

Even here, however, the characteristically modern impulse to choose between magic and art or between magic and religion persists. Yates did not quite succeed in projecting the image of a culture in which magic comprised a natural part of everyday sensations and conceptions rather than one of two opposed heuristic means for understanding them. Italians of the late Renaissance believed that hidden or occult forces surrounded them and determined many manifest phenomena that otherwise eluded explanation. They did not perceive "occult and scientific mentalities" – to borrow a phrase from the title of a recent collection of essays that perpetuates Walker's dialectical view – as mutually exclusive ways of comprehending the world. To speak only of the realm of the psychological effects of art, there is little evidence from the period around 1600 of a distinction between an aesthetic explanation for them and a magical one. The much discussed "aesthetic of the marvelous" in Italian art and literature of the time is from one perspective little other than a domesticated reading of the occult psychological effects ascribed to artworks by the magi of the period.

The creation around 1600 of an Orphic musical speech, then – or an Apollonian one, to include the other great musical protagonist Rinuccini borrowed from the Neoplatonic pantheon – was still in some degree the creation of an occult art, the discovery in Neoplatonic theory of magical practice. Rinuccini inevitably (and to some degree, no doubt, unwittingly) emphasized this aspect of the new opera when he fashioned its first librettos in the guise of Poliziano's *Orfeo*. This is not to say that he or his collaborators set out, any more than Poliziano had, to make their works incantatory. Yet incantatory they were, rituals of more or less unconscious making and appreciation rendered magical by virtue of their mythological subjects, their musical means, and the not-yet-disenchanted culture that produced and received them.

From this vantage point the question Pirrotta raised of the preponderance of mythic musicians in the first operas may be seen anew. They did not represent beings who were imaginary in some modern sense and could therefore assuage the unbelievability of musical speech. They were instead imaginary in the Platonic, idealistic sense: tracings in the imagination touching on and capable of revealing higher truths. They were potent musical symbols of their audiences' lingering magical universe, of a cosmos in which music remained an occult ontological and psychological force. They were magicians whose revelatory magic was music, not musicians who could entice their audiences to forget, for a moment, a demystified reality.

My emphasis on the undercurrents of Neoplatonism and its persistent magic that fostered court opera also helps to clarify the relationship of the new genre to the earlier spoken pastoral. To see how it does this we must return to Louise Clubb's views on pastoral drama. In her essay "The Making of the Pastoral Play," Clubb pointed out the large role of magic in pastoral drama of the late sixteenth century, particularly of Ovidian transformations (of the sort, by the way, that would play a major part in the first operas). This magic represented a departure from the verisimilitude, the stricter adherence to "physical law and historical fact," that governed tragedy and regular comedy. It was, Clubb wrote, "part of [a] continued experimentation towards the unverisimilar" in late Renaissance theater (p. 68). In a later essay Clubb carried this reasoning further and, in my reading, altered its terms slightly but significantly. Now she saw the magic of the pastoral and also some of its fundamental, recurring themes as elements in the "mimesis" of an "invisible reality." "In this genre," she wrote,

> we see the effort to give regular drama a new object of *mimesis*. The imitation of reality, the aim of drama throughout the early sixteenth century, remains valid ... but the reality imitated is not only that which presents itself to our eyes or can be grasped by the five senses. The theorists of drama do not state this goal; instead they obscure it, continually holding forth on the "natural" and the "verisimilar." ... The texts of pastoral dramas, on the other hand, manifest the aspiration to a reality not directly accessible to the physical senses.[27]

In this broadened and, it seems to me, just view, the magic of the pastoral did not depart from verisimilitude; instead it played upon a conception of it broader than ours. It offered what we might call a supersensual verisimilitude.

This enlarged conception of verisimilitude, Clubb suggested, was founded in Neoplatonic currents of thought. Pastoral drama presented an ideal, Platonic world that was by no means unreal but that could only be perceived indirectly by the bodily senses. It did so in two ways: in its insistent exploration of human emotions, especially love (which, as I have suggested, remained one of the most fertile grounds for the dispersion of Neoplatonic speculation through the sixteenth century), and in its reference to an invisible external reality, a cosmos guided by harmony in ways unceasingly affecting human beings but never entirely grasped by their reason. "The countryside of pastoral drama," Clubb concluded, "is the place where one can see into oneself, perceive a heavenly design, heal the mind (even if by the path of frenzy or furor), [and] put oneself in harmony with nature and [with] one's own nature" (p. 75). I can think of no more succinct summary of the aims Ficino explicitly stated for his Neoplatonic magic.

Thus the pastoral drama embodied what Richard Cody, writing a few years before Clubb, had called "aesthetic Platonism."[28] He defined this phrase in the terms that Clubb would later elaborate on the basis of her much broadened reading of Italian pastoral dramas. "Orthodox Italian pastoral," he wrote, "brings together the psychology of human love and the mysteries of Neo-Platonic theology in a celebration of the poet's own art" (p. 12). It aims to reconcile "this-worldliness and other-worldliness," to bring about a "Socratic compromise between ... transcendence and immanence" (p. 12). This takes the form of an intersection of three "esoteric traditions": pastoral landscape as sensible universe reflecting divine perfection; Socratic speech, especially the erotic speech of Plato's most pastoral dialog, the *Phaedrus*; and Orphic song (p. 16). Of the intersection of these traditions Cody wrote, in a gnomic utterance worthy of his sources: "It is the voice of Socrates that in Italian pastoral, under the influence of Ficino, emerges as Orphic" (p. 23). In this view Renaissance pastoralism was a most direct expression of Florentine Platonism (p. 6). Ficino's mystical Orphism, a veiled transformation of Platonic reasoning into song, found its appropriate dramatic landscape in the *locus amoenus* of the pastoral. In doing so it rendered pastoral drama magical.

According to Cody, "The makers of Renaissance pastoral, poets and audiences, [were] esoterics" (p. 40). So indeed were the makers of early court opera. This genre, like Cody's and Clubb's pastoral, was drama in a Neoplatonic mode, and it is significant that Cody began his definition of Platonic/Orphic pastoralism by analyzing Poliziano's *Orfeo*, the work the early operas emulated. Both of Clubb's specific means by which pastoral drama imitated the hidden world, the exploration of human sentiment and the manifestation of an occult external reality, were taken up again by the first operas. These were dramas of affect, stories of the inner emotional realm stripped to their merest essentials: Apollo loves Daphne, loses her, and laments; Ariadne loves Theseus, loses him, and laments; Orpheus loves Euridice, loses her, and sings movingly to win her back. The portrayal of the protagonists of these works focused singlemindedly on the psychological states of love and loss. Meanwhile these *favole* vindicated the occult harmony of the cosmos in their outcomes: in the answer of Daphne's just prayers by her magical transformation, in the alleviation of Ariadne's woes by the miraculous descent of Bacchus, in the transformative power of song in Rinuccini's and Alessandro Striggio's Orpheus librettos and the apotheosis of Orpheus in the rewritten end of Striggio's. The occult world harmony spoke also, and more essentially, through the medium itself of these works. Their musical speech affirmed it and rendered it audible; their recitative realized in the most literal way the Orphic song that had long lived at the heart of Renaissance mysticism.

All this is not to reinstate the Hegelian view I rejected earlier of pastoral drama bursting into song in the form of opera. Early opera was not a specific version of pastoral drama; their differences of dramatic technique are too fundamental to admit this view. Rather both spoken pastoral and the nascent opera were renderings in drama of deeper, archaeological impulses of the late Renaissance. Both arose from lingering and pervasive Neoplatonic conceptions. Both manifested the occult forces empowering these conceptions. Both displayed a world where ostensible truth might turn out to be illusory, an inclusive world embracing "this-worldliness and other-worldliness" where "physical law and historical fact" might conceal less transparent realities not accessible to the senses alone.

Early opera, then, was a product of the same vision of reality, broader than ours, that gave rise to pastoral drama. It was a late outgrowth of the esotericism that burgeoned in Renaissance thought in the wake of the fifteenth-century revival of Neoplatonism and related forms of ancient mysticism. It arose from a culture whose world still offered magical realms, and its characteristic locus was the realm of musical speech.

By the early seventeenth century, however, this magical vision was strongly challenged by other views, and by 1650 it would seem decisively less credible than it had a half century before. (Certainly it had little place in the libertine and cynical ruminations of the Venetian literati who practiced opera at that time.) But opera did not die with the waning of magic, as traditional pastoral was to succumb, in Renato Poggioli's view, to the advent of a difficult-to-define but palpably modern "scientific spirit."[29] Instead the magic of music-drama was (in a modern sense) rationalized, concealed behind a willing suspension of skepticism that has persisted in our own response to it. This rationalization marked the most fundamental shift in operatic epistemology that the genre has known.

The magical reading of the earliest operas I have offered here connects these works not only to Poliziano's *Orfeo* and later spoken pastoral plays but also, generally, to the many dramas and court festivals in France and England during the same period that have been seen as involving more or less explicit magical processes and appeals. Such magical interpretations have been offered, in varying degrees of elaboration, by D. J. Gordon, Frances Yates, Stephen Greenblatt, Thomas M. Greene, and others.[30] Also – again generally – the shift in modes of perceiving opera across the early seventeenth century that I have described was, I think, part of broader cultural and epistemological changes that characterize the era; here, as I have argued in *Music in Renaissance Magic*, Foucault's analysis in the first chapters of *The Order of Things* is (with due adjustment) especially apropos.

But this is not the place to dwell on these general topics. Instead I might draw out one final issue, specific to operatic history, that is implicit in my discussion. The emphasis of shifting operatic perceptions across the early seventeenth century encourages a tendency in recent socio-historical approaches to opera to distinguish as independent genres the court opera of Florence and Mantua and the public opera of Venice.[31] For though Venetian opera borrowed from court opera the broadest terms of its musical style, it nevertheless answered the needs of a culture that had left behind the deeper meanings of the earlier genre. The court operas were the predecessors of later opera, then, in many particulars of their musical and poetic styles. But in their embodiment of a still-verisimilar world of musical magic they were an ending, not a beginning, a final homage to the whispered incantations of the Neoplatonic universe. They were, in this fundamental way, the last musical dramas of the Renaissance rather than the first examples of what would become the quintessentially modern genre of opera.

NOTES

An earlier version of this essay was presented at the symposium "The Pastoral Landscape," held at the National Gallery of Art and the University of Maryland at College Park on 20–1 January 1989.

1 Introduction to *Oedipus*; quoted from Ruth Katz, *Divining the Powers of Music: Aesthetic Theory and the Origins of Opera* (New York, 1986), p. 22.
2 Quoted from Ellen Rosand, *Opera in Seventeenth-Century Venice: The Creation of a Genre* (Berkeley, 1991), p. 45; see also pp. 42–4.
3 Quoted from Angelo Solerti, *Gli albori del melodramma*, 3 vols. (Milan, 1905), vol. 1, p. 99.

4 "Early Opera and Aria," ch. 6 of Nino Pirrotta and Elena Povoledo, *Music and Theatre from Poliziano to Monteverdi*, trans. Karen Eales (Cambridge, 1982), pp. 262–4.
5 See Paolo Fabbri and Angelo Pompilio, eds., *Il corago o vero alcune osservazioni per metter bene in scena le composizioni drammatiche* (Florence, 1983), p. 63; quoted and discussed in Lorenzo Bianconi, *Il seicento*, Storia della musica a cura della Società italiana di musicologia, vol. 4 (Turin, 1983), pp. 175–7, and Rosand, *Opera in Seventeenth-Century Venice*, p. 39.
6 See the editors' introduction to *Il corago*, pp. 9–10.
7 (Berkeley, 1987), pp. 217–18.
8 See among others Leo Schrade, *Monteverdi: Creator of Modern Music* (New York, 1950), p. 357, and Jane Glover, "The Venetian Operas," in *The New Monteverdi Companion*, ed. Denis Arnold and Nigel Fortune (London, 1985), pp. 289–90.
9 *Music and Theatre*, p. 264. The insistence might well have obviated his thesis that the early operas needed to justify themselves additionally with protagonists of mythical singing abilities.
10 Ibid., pp. 264–5.
11 Quoted from Angelo Solerti, *Le origini del melodramma* (Turin, 1903), pp. 203, 205.
12 Francesco de Sanctis, *Storia della letteratura italiana*, ed. Benedetto Croce, 2 vols. (Bari, 1925), vol. 2, p. 209.
13 "The Making of the Pastoral Play: Some Italian Experiments between 1573 and 1590," in *From Petrarch to Pirandello*, ed. J. A. Molinaro (Toronto, 1973), pp. 45–72.
14 For these plays see Antonia Tissoni Benvenuti and Maria Pia Mussini Sacchi, eds., *Teatro del quattrocento: Le corti padane* (Turin, 1983).
15 (Turin, 1969; 2/1975).
16 "Rinuccini, Peri, Monteverdi, and the Humanist Heritage of Opera," Ph.D. dissertation, University of California at Berkeley, 1979, ch. 3.
17 See Giosuè Carducci, "Delle poesie toscane di Messer Angelo Poliziano," in *Edizione nazionale delle opere di Giosuè Carducci*, 30 vols. (Bologna, 1939–40), vol. 12, pp. 135–376 (218–71).
18 See Tomlinson, "Rinuccini, Peri, Monteverdi," pp. 160–70.
19 On the precise role of music in the *fabula* see Pirrotta, *Music and Theatre*, pp. 19–36, and Cynthia Munro Pyle, "Il tema di Orfeo, la musica, e le favole mitologiche del tardo Quattrocento," in *Ecumenismo della cultura 2: La parola e la musica nel divenire dell'umanesimo*, ed. Giovannangiola Tarugi (Florence, 1981), pp. 121–39.
20 Giovanni Pico della Mirandola, *Conclusiones sive theses DCCCC*, ed. Bohdan Kieszkowski (Geneva, 1973), p. 80.
21 *The Landscape of the Mind: Pictorialism and Platonic Theory in Tasso's* Aminta *and Shakespeare's Early Comedies* (Oxford, 1969), pp. 30–43.
22 See Gary Tomlinson, "The Historian, the Performer, and Authentic Meaning in Music," in *Authenticity and Early Music*, ed. Nicholas Kenyon (Oxford, 1988), pp. 115–36 (126–34).
23 See Michel Foucault, *The Order of Things: An Archaeology of the Human Sciences* (New York, 1970), p. xi.
24 For elaboration of many of these themes see Gary Tomlinson, *Music in Renaissance Magic: Toward a Historiography of Others* (Chicago, 1993).
25 *Spiritual and Demonic Magic from Ficino to Campanella* (London, 1958), p. 131.
26 *Giordano Bruno and the Hermetic Tradition* (New York, 1969), p. 175.

27 "La mimesi della realtà invisibile nel dramma pastorale italiano e inglese del tardo rinascimento," *Misure critiche* 4 (1974): 65–92 (71).
28 *The Landscape of the Mind.*
29 *The Oaten Flute: Essays on Pastoral Poetry and the Pastoral Ideal* (Cambridge, Mass., 1975), pp. 31–2.
30 D. J. Gordon, *The Renaissance Imagination*, ed. Stephen Orgel (Berkeley, 1980); Frances A. Yates, "Poésie et musique dans les 'Magnificences' au mariage du duc de Joyeuse, Paris, 1581," in *Musique et poésie au XVIe siècle*, ed. Jean Jacquot (Paris, 1954), pp. 241–64; Stephen Greenblatt, "Loudun and London," *Critical Inquiry* 12 (1986): 326–46; Thomas M. Greene, "Magic and Festivity at the Renaissance Court," *Renaissance Quarterly* 40 (1987): 636–59.
31 See especially the excellent account in Bianconi, *Il seicento*, chs. 19–21.

Opera and the visual arts

2

Moralizing at the tomb: Poussin's Arcadian shepherds in eighteenth-century England and Germany

THOMAS BAUMAN

> "I wonder that thou ... goest about to apply a moral medicine to a mortifying mischief."
> *Much Ado About Nothing*, I: 3

Sometime around 1622 the young Giovanni Francesco Guercino completed at Rome a painting that introduced into Western art one of its most enduring and provocative mottos, the Latin inscription "Et in Arcadia ego." Its sources and fortunes formed the subject of an influential essay by Erwin Panofsky, first published in 1936 and later revised and reprinted many times.[1]

Panofsky argued the following points. Arcadia, in fact a poor and inclement area of the Peloponnese inhabited of old by a brutish, ignorant race, had been idealized by Vergil in his *Eclogues* as a region of "luxuriant vegetation, eternal spring, and inexhaustible leisure for love." Vergil's conception lay dormant until the Renaissance, when Jacopo Sannazaro reawakened and deepened its elegiac melancholy in his *Arcadia* (1502), and Torquato Tasso added in his *Aminta* (1573) the element of nostalgia for a beautiful, lost Golden Age.

Little if any of this transpires in Guercino's painting. Instead, it features most prominently an oversize skull with mouse, fly, and worm, symbols of death and decay beholden to the traditions of medieval Christian art. Panofsky claims that, in contrast to popular interpretation, the only philologically correct translation of the Latin inscription "Et in Arcadia ego," seen beneath the skull, should read: "Even in Arcadia, there am I." Guercino's painting makes clear that this rendering can have no other grammatical subject but Death itself, personified in the prominent skull.[2]

But that is not Panofsky's main point. The theme in his view underwent a decisive turn with the second of two *Et in Arcadia ego* paintings by Nicolas Poussin. While retaining Guercino's inscription, Poussin broke with its medieval, moralizing tradition and returned to the elegiac sentimentality of Vergil, Sannazaro, and Tasso. Poussin's famous canvas, now in the Louvre, colored the motto "Et in Arcadia ego" with a new, less literal meaning, one Poussin's imitators and commentators were quick to supply with translations such as "And yet I lived in Arcadia," "I, too, lived in delightful Arcadia," or "I, too, was born in Arcadia."

Opera and the visual arts

Particularly during the Enlightenment, there arose among art critics, artists, and authors active in England and Germany a tendency to misdescribe Poussin's painting. The obviousness of their errors and their remarkable consistency offer an intriguing case history of fruitful misprision, of a great work of art acting not as a painting but as a thematic source, as a pretext for reassessing a broader range of meanings evoked by the theme of Death in Arcadia and for translating them into specifically Enlightenment terms.

That era's most characteristic tendency was to disjoin Youth and Arcadia, hitherto so intertwined that it was hard to think of one without the other. Their separation greatly expanded the opportunities to moralize and enlarge upon the moment captured by Poussin, in which youthful felicity dissolves into melancholy reflection on human mortality. In the post-rococo world of Diderot and Lessing, of Richardson and Hogarth, patent moral meaning was an ingredient no work of art, however humble, could afford to leave at home when it paraded forth. It comes as no surprise, then, that moralizing became the cornerstone of a series of English and German literary works, most notably several opera texts, that explicitly claim Poussin's painting as their inspiration.

The eighteenth century stood heir not only to the visual tradition initiated by Guercino and Poussin, but also to the literary cultivation of Arcadia on which that tradition built. Renaissance writers introduced an important ambivalence over the Arcadian ideal, one that was to inform later works, both visual and literary, that elaborated the *Et in Arcadia ego* theme. Sannazaro on the one hand envisioned a lost Golden Age whose happy inhabitants devoted themselves wholly to love, tripping from meadow to meadow and partner to partner without constraint of custom or jealousy.[3] Such was the age also described by Tasso. The famous passage from his *Aminta* beginning "O bella età dell'oro" laid the groundwork for the dichotomy of uncorrupted nature and decadent civilization so important to eighteenth-century humanists. For Tasso the cardinal reason the Golden Age was "bella" was because

> quel vano
> 670 nome senza soggetto,
> quell'idolo d'errori, idol d'inganno,
> quel che dal volgo insano
> onor poscia fu detto,
> che di nostra natura 'l feo tiranno,
> 675 non mischiava il suo affanno
> fra le liete dolcezze
> de l'amoroso gregge;
> né fu sua dura legge
> nota a quell'alme in libertate avvezze,
> 680 ma legge aurea e felice
> che natura scolpì: "S'ei piace, ei lice".

(that vain name without subject, that idol of error and deceit, later to be called 'honor' by the senseless rabble, which is the wicked tyrant of our nature, did not mix its anxiety with the happy endearments of the amorous flock, nor was

Plate 1 Poussin, *Et in Arcadia ego* (ca. 1630). Chatsworth, Duke of Devonshire.

its hard law noted by those souls accustomed to freedom, but rather the golden and happy law sculpted by Nature: "If it pleases, it is allowed.")[4]

But in his *Pastor fido*, completed three years later in 1584, Battista Guarini pointedly opposed Tasso's formula for unrestrained indulgence. His new Arcadia celebrates not freedom but moderation and control. In a parallel chorus to the one just quoted, Guarini replaces the dictum "If it pleases, it is allowed" with its obverse: "If it is allowed, it should please."[5] This, more than Tasso's phrase, proved grist for eighteenth-century mills of moral ministry.

As we might expect, erotic love did not occupy a central place in Guarini's artistic invocation of Arcadia, and it played no role at all a few decades later in Guercino's painting. On the other hand, Poussin's first *Et in Arcadia ego*, painted around 1630, reintroduced Arcadian eroticism in the form of an alluring shepherdess with bared breast and deliberately exposed thigh (Plate 1). Yet she is all but ignored by the two shepherds absorbed in an intense confrontation with the tomb and more specifically its inscription. This is a much more dramatic rendering than the later Louvre painting. The shepherds seem to rush up to the tomb with the light at their backs. The bearded shepherd deciphering the inscription has reached the word "ego" to which not only his finger but also the strongly articulated shadow[6] his forearm casts on the tomb point. As with several later *Et in Arcadia ego* paintings and drawings, the eye moves naturally from left to right, from light to shade. Here the movement is manifestly dynamic, suggesting the dark, mortal force that pulls the shepherds from the physical pleasures their companion offers to an intense contemplation of the tomb and of their own mortality.

Poussin's earlier version of *Et in Arcadia ego* was not widely known until Ravenet engraved it in 1763. A correspondent who saw a copy in London described it that year to the German readers of Christian Felix Weisse's *Bibliothek der schönen Wissenschaften und der freyen Künste*. The shepherds, he remarks, "are suddenly moved in an instant in which they entertained anything but melancholy thoughts," and he notes in particular the counterpoise of erotic and sober: "From the countenance of the shepherds, whom a shepherdess of exceptionally beautiful form accompanies, there radiates great confusion and disquiet."[7]

In the second and, today, more famous version Poussin painted of the same subject, Panofsky sees nothing of either the moral message or the emotional drama of the earlier picture (Plate 2). Instead there is symmetry, a simple sepulcher, and "mellow meditation on a beautiful past." The inscription, he stresses, can no longer refer to Death, and he also rejects the possibility that the tomb itself may be uttering "Et in Arcadia ego"; rather, these are the words of its unknown occupant (pp. 238–9).

Poussin's painting was quite faithfully engraved by Etienne Picart near the end of the seventeenth century,[8] but it became widely known thereafter only in a more distorted form. This happened through confusion either with an as yet unknown third version of the subject by Poussin or – what appears far more probable – with later imitations that sought to soften the Classical severity of his elegiac vision of the melancholy shepherds, imitations that came to be attributed to Poussin himself.[9]

Some such imitation inspired the eighteenth century's highest and most influential source of critical authority on Poussin's painting, an analysis of its content and meaning in the Abbé du Bos' *Réflexions critiques sur la poësie et sur la peinture*, first published in 1719. Here is the relevant passage from Thomas Nugent's English translation, made from the fifth edition and brought out at London in 1748:

> The picture... exhibits a landskip of that delightful country: In the middle thereof you see the monument of a young maid snatched away in the flower of her age; which appears from her statue lying on the tomb, after the manner of the antients. The sepulchral inscription contains those few latin words, *Et in*

Poussin's Arcadian shepherds

Plate 2 Poussin, *Et in Arcadia ego* (ca. 1638). Paris, Musée du Louvre.

Arcadia ego: And I was once an inhabitant of Arcadia. But this short inscription draws the most serious reflections from two youths and two young virgins decked with garlands, who seem to be struck with their having thus accidentally met with so melancholy a scene, in a place where one might naturally suppose they had not been in pursuit of an object of sorrow. One of them points with his finger to the inscription, to make the rest observe it, whilst the remains of an expiring joy may yet be discerned through the gloominess of grief which begins to diffuse itself over their countenances. Here you imagine yourself listening to the reflections of those youthful persons upon death, which spares neither age nor beauty, and against the attacks of which the most happy climates can afford no sanctuary. Your fancy now suggests to you, the affecting speeches they are going to make to each other upon recovering from their first surprize, which you will naturally apply to yourself, and to those whom you have a concern for.[10]

From a Poussinesque point of view, several things are amiss here, for in neither of his known pictures on the *Et in Arcadia ego* theme did Poussin include a statue of a young maid lying on the tomb, nor a complement of "two youths and two young virgins decked with garlands." What was Du Bos looking at when he wrote this description? The rest of the century did not consider the question any too closely; rather, it welcomed his deviations as inviting avenues in need of further exploration. In one direction, attention began to fix more closely on the tomb's female occupant both as an emblem of pure innocence snatched away in its prime and as an object of deep empathy and personal reflection. In another, the description called to mind Arcadia's traditional amatory activity by pairing the nymphs and swains. Du Bos' deviations, in other words, reevoked the ambivalent Arcadia of Tasso's and Guarini's rival epigraphs.

Du Bos also suggested a transition from visual to verbal treatment of the subject with his observation that the painting impels us to imagine the reflections and affecting speeches of these young persons. The transition was carried out quite literally, seven years after Nugent's translation appeared, by the eccentric Irish novelist Thomas Amory in his semi-autobiographical *Memoirs: Containing the Lives of Several Ladies of Great Britain* (1755). Despite its title, the book's 400 pages do not get past Amory's first subject, Marinda Bruce, the daughter of his friend and tutor. In the novel he meets this gifted young lady in Northumberland, near the Scottish border, in 1739. She is mistress of both the violin and the brush, we learn, and Amory describes in detail a picture she has painted called *Arcadia*. In elaborating on it he can do no better than to pilfer and amplify Nugent's translation of Du Bos, quoted above:

> In the middle of this delightful country, there appears the monument of a beauty, who had been snatched away in her prime. Her statue lies on the tomb, after the manner of the ancients. There is this sepulchral inscription: *And I was once an inhabitant of Arcadia*. The unexpected melancholy scene strikes powerfully some youths and virgins, who had not a thought of meeting with this object of sorrow, and as they gaze upon the image of the lovely maid, they seem to fall into the deepest reflexions. The youngest of the shepherdesses pulls off a garland of flowers, and with a finger of her other hand, points to the short inscription. She ponders with the most serious attention; and in every face a gloomyness of grief may be discerned, through some remains of an expiring joy. They all appear very greatly affected, and seem to have many interesting thoughts of death, as they see it spares not even youth and beauty; and that even the happy climate of *Arcadia* can afford no sanctuary from the grave. The pointing shepherdess is opening her mouth to speak...[11]

Two of Amory's additions to Du Bos' description are significant. First, in the paragraph preceding the one just quoted, he stationed a group of happy Arcadians in the picture's background, "plighting vows, and constant hearts to one another" and "footing it in country measure." Second, among the principal group at the tomb-side, not Poussin's shepherd but a young shepherdess points to the inscription. Amory obliged Du Bos by letting Marinda Bruce herself supply an example of the "affecting speeches" he imagined the chastened shepherdess is about to speak: life is short and death our common lot; it strikes at any time, so we must not limit ourselves to play and idleness but devote time to religion and our ultimate duty so as to prepare ourselves for the Last Judgment. He fashioned this short sermon on the picture's moral, Amory added, for the benefit of "some *fair Arcadians*" who might listen to this shepherdess, though they heed not the divine in the pulpit who says the same things.

Amory's homily represents one of the first and one of the most flagrant eighteenth-century examples of moralizing at the tomb. In his analysis of the Louvre painting Panofsky explicitly ruled out any such tendency in the dispirited shepherds, but such was not the tenor of interpretations during the Enlightenment. Rather, Du Bos' inaccurate but influential description had set in motion a century-long search for an ethical message to the *Et in Arcadia ego* theme that could be imprinted on the minds of heedless youth.

Miss Bruce's *Arcadia* was, as far as we know, an imaginary painting, nor can we identify for certain the picture or engraving Du Bos had before him when describing what he thought was Poussin's *Et in Arcadia ego*. One of the most popular illustrators of the eighteenth century did offer an indirect visual idea of the sort of picture Amory may have had in mind. In 1756 and 1766 Amory had issued a two-volume sequel to the *Memoirs*, called *The Life of John Buncle, Esq*. It appeared in 1778 at Berlin in a German edition that also incorporated Amory's earlier novel. Daniel Chodowiecki supplied the composite work with a series of sixteen engravings, the twelfth of them Miss Bruce's *Arcadia* (Plate 3a).[12]

Chodowiecki's inscription reflects the identification of the tomb's occupant made by Du Bos and Amory: "Auch ich war einst eine Einwohnerin in Arcadia," it reads – "I, too, was once an inhabitant [female] of Arcadia." The plighters and dancers Amory had added to Du Bos' description Chodowiecki represented here by only a single couple in the background, otherwise the picture is quite literal. Around the tomb there are two shepherds and two shepherdesses, and the young Arcadian's statue rests on the tomb "after the manner of the antients"; finally, one young shepherdess kneels and points to the inscription just as Amory had indicated. But Chodowiecki has added sobering details of his own. The light entering from the left casts an especially stark shadow of the young shepherdess on the monument and on the garland she has just removed. No longer a symbol of Arcadian delights, the doffed garland doubles a wreath already on the monument, linking the shepherdess quite pointedly with the unfortunate beauty inside the tomb. For good measure, Chodowiecki has included not one but two skulls on the monument.

Back in England, the moralizing tradition initiated by Amory continued in a dramatic poem published in 1773 by George Keate, called *The Monument in Arcadia*. Keate, though trained as a lawyer, never practiced his profession but devoted himself instead to poetry, painting, natural history, and antiquarian interests. He exhibited regularly at the Royal Academy and in 1760 had secured a commission for the Venetian Francesco Zuccarelli to paint an *Et in Arcadia ego* for an English patron. He also was close to Angelika Kaufmann, who had paved the way for her own arrival in Britain with a painting of Arcadians moralizing at the side of a sepulcher, exhibited in 1766.[13]

Keate himself decided to render the theme with poetry rather than paint. In his preface to *The Monument in Arcadia* he explains why. After quoting Du Bos's reflections on Poussin's painting, he chides him for reading into the picture more than the medium allows: "*Painting* can but half tell the Story,"

Opera and the visual arts

Plate 3a   Plate 3b

Plate 3a Chodowiecki, *Arcadia. Leben, Bemerkungen und Meinungen Johann Bunkels* (Berlin, 1778), No. 12.
Plate 3b Rossmässler, *Auch ich war in Arcadien. Der Kinderfreund* (Leipzig, 1781).

he observes. "The Pencil even under the happiest Guidance, must be confined to a single Action." Narrative power belongs rather to a sister art,[14] and so Keate formed this "little piece" on the subject of Poussin's picture. In fact his "Dramatic Poem" is a species of opera, in two very brief acts that include four arias, two choruses, and a duet. The text was apparently never set to music nor publicly acted in any form, a fate Keate himself had predicted in remarking on its serious cast and sober moral message.

Serious opera in the eighteenth century was loath to embrace a tragic ending where a *lieto fine* could with any plausibility be introduced, and Keate worked one in here. Euphemia has fled Sparta with her beloved, young Lysander, and come to Arcadia. It was the dying wish of her nurse Aranthe, who raised her in Sparta, that she wed nowhere but in Arcadia. Local shepherds greet the strangers and take them before an altar to Pan to swear marital vows. Euphemia and Lysander learn of a gray hermit, Dorastus, living in a cave nearby, cut off from society ever since his only daughter had been stolen from him. Euphemia desires his blessing on their vows. They find him at the tomb he has erected to his lost child; Lysander reads the inscription on it: "I too was an Arcadian." Euphemia is transfixed by the monument, even as the hermit Dorastus gives them his blessing. She explains to Lysander that she now recognizes how deluded she has been in having

>   foul'd my Sense
> With visionary Hope, and now awake to meet my Error.
> ...
> This good Man's Sigh has op'd my Eyes; this Scene
> Of Death has undeceived me. — Blind to think
> That there was any Ground where Mortals tread
> On which Affliction walks not! — Ev'ry Clime
> Engenders human Woe; and fam'd ARCADIA
> Is pregnant with the same disastrous Fortune
> That other regions know. (p. 32)

Yet even in lamenting her vain hopes she chances to breathe her mother's name, and this leads directly to Dorastus' recognizing her as his lost child.

Both in this aragnoresis and in the play's epilogue Keate piles moral upon moral: the virtuous are eventually rewarded with happiness; man must never abandon hope; expecting too much inevitably breeds disappointment; we must curb our wishes and be thankful for what we have. Keate concludes with the remark that unbridled hope that "wildly seeks ideal Plains" will soon discover that "ARCADIA'S ONLY IN THE MIND."

In the mind was precisely where Vergil, Sannazaro, and Tasso had wanted it to be, but this was not good enough for Keate: his Arcadia is no lost Golden Age but a template for the virtuous life as people really ought to live it today. Several of the opera's songs harp on a theme that had distinguished Guarini from Tasso and company – moderation. Even a song in praise of wine speaks of "Joys that wait the *temp'rate* Bowl." Into this world of moderation fits the opera's cardinal departure from the visual cultivation of the *Et in Arcadia ego* theme – the denial of the tomb. The empty monument is no more than a stage prop, a cheap excuse for disabusing the heroine of Arcadian fantasies. Inevitably, both Death and Arcadia come up short when Keate gets down to the moral of the story. Dorastus shouldn't run around building monuments in hopeless despair, and Euphemia shouldn't run around expecting to find an idyllic ideal that never existed. Moderate your despair, but moderate your hopes as well.

In Germany the theme of the Grave in Arcadia received even greater literary attention than in England, and precisely for the reasons that had led Keate to render it poetically rather than pictorially: a narrative not only allows for the discursive description of events a picture can only suggest, it also allows the author to hammer home the moral lessons a picture can only imply.

Paralleling its literary cultivation of the theme, Germany also produced a series of visual interpretations. Best known was a painting by Goethe's drawing master, Adam Friedrich Oeser, done sometime between 1767 and 1777 for a friend and patron at Hamburg.[15] It employs virtually all of the motifs the subject had accumulated over the years – dancers, lovers, a simple square monument with a female statue lying upon it, and a strongly articulated shadow cast across it by light from the left as a beautiful shepherdess points out the inscription, now somewhat pedantically rendered in Greek. Oeser's influence both as a painter and teacher was considerable in Saxony. He seems to have encouraged several of his pupils to essay the same topic, including his most talented and promising protégé, Carl Philipp Emanuel Bach's son Johann Samuel, whose attempt was much admired at the annual Dresden exhibit in 1776, but is unfortunately lost.

The earliest literary traces of the *Et in Arcadia ego* theme in Germany do not come from Saxony, nor do they have much in common with the Classical style Oeser strove for. Instead, they come from young writers with strong leanings toward the sentimental and even precious in their poetry and prose. The first known use of the famous motto in German literature occurs in Johann Georg Jacobi's *Die Winterreise* of 1769, a mixture of prose and verse written under the immediate impression of Laurence Sterne's *Sentimental Journey*.[16]

Two years later a young dilettante-aristocrat set about putting together a German libretto based on Poussin's painting, or rather on Du Bos' description of it. Count Julius von Soden of Ansbach was only seventeen when he published his "Operette" *Lindor und Ismene* in 1771, a more or less brainless piece of adolescent hedonism. Soden dedicated his play to a certain Julie, hoping in his prefatory letter that she would give his work a small, unimportant place on her night table next to "the poets of the Graces, our Jacobi and Wieland." And if she were even to grant it a sacred tear, how splendid were his reward! But let his only laurels in that case be a tender rose entwined in his hair by *her* hands, then even the immortals of poetry will envy him.[17]

These youthful effusions, which Soden himself withdrew in later editions of the libretto, rather naively adumbrate the frivolously amatory conception of Arcadia that Poussin had wholly subdued in his Louvre painting, and that here is linked through the author's own persona to thoughtless youth. It also figures in his play. Soden adopted the two sets of lovers suggested by Du Bos and transferred them to the traditional roles of light and serious pair, long familiar in pastoral drama and opera. The serious couple draws on the myth of Cephalus and Procris. A year earlier Lindor had accidentally shot Ismene with an arrow, and now he is still grieving inconsolably at her graveside. His best friend Bellamis shows up, registers the compulsory shock at finding a grave in Arcadia, and after learning the reason for its existence suggests that his own mother, the sorceress Armide, may have been behind Lindor's misfortune. This assuages Lindor's guilt, but not his grief: he remains determined to join Ismene in death.

Meanwhile, we are treated to a contrasting episode in which Bellamis must explain his long absence to his lover Naïde. He describes how Armide, disapproving of their relationship, had had a dragon bear him away to Queen Mirmide, whom he found lying nude under a scanty covering of foliage. But after a few months he tired of her, and so Armide has returned him to Naïde.

After these lovers make up, Armide herself appears before Lindor, regretful of her misdeed. She cannot overmaster Death, but Fate has decreed, she tells him, that his death will mean life for both him and Ismene. And sure enough, when Lindor stabs himself the grave disappears, Ismene materializes, and Lindor recovers.

One cannot help wondering what, exactly, Soden saw in Poussin's painting. The denial of the grave is pushed here to an extreme, with the help of opera's supernatural heritage: the loyalty even unto death of the *pastor fido* Lindor becomes a restorative to life, youth, and love that literally sends the monument packing. Together, Arcadia and Youth triumph over Death, a triumph confirmed by the refrain of the opera's *divertissement* and its appeal to the Arcadian myth of eternal springtime:

> Lebt glücklich! jeder Eurer Tage
> Sei heiter, wie ein Tag im Mai!
>
> (Live happily! may every one of your days
> be as cheerful as a day in May!) (p. 39)

Soden's rococo dream of Arcadia virtually does away with moralizing on the appearance of Death amidst gaiety, so crucial to the *Et in Arcadia ego* theme in other eighteenth-century versions. Psychologically, the tomb is so closely associated with its female occupant, rather than with the more general concept of Death in Arcadia, that the only inscription it bears is her name – Ismene. Lindor, the *pastor fido*, does not moralize at the tomb but laments the loss of his companion. Like his illustrious predecessor Orpheus, he invokes music's power to express his grief. Equally in keeping with tradition, Soden besought the aid of poetry's sister arts not only here but also in the scenes that celebrate Arcadia's blessings. His preface carries the remark that perhaps his drama "could receive in the theater the advantages it now lacks through the enchanting composition of a Hiller, through decorations, and principally through dances."

Johann Adam Hiller, at the time the most popular composer of German comic opera, did not set Soden's libretto, nor did anyone else until it by chance fell into the hands of Joseph Schmittbauer, Kapellmeister at Karlsruhe, in 1778. His setting achieved great popularity at the court theater in Hannover and elsewhere in Germany, and inspired Soden to revise his text, by then something of an embarrassment to him, in 1779 under the new title *Ein Grab in Arkadien!*[18] Schmittbauer's is the only known music to an eighteenth-century libretto on the *Et in Arcadia ego* theme. Unfortunately, the single manuscript score to survive into this century was destroyed during the Second World War, but prior to that it had been studied by Ludwig Schiedermair.[19] Schmittbauer, he tells us, alternated in his music for the lighter pair of lovers between a frankly Hilleresque Lied style and a more elaborate Italian manner. On the other hand the serious tone of Lindor's lamentations mixes elements of aria and obbligato recitative in ways reminiscent of Jommelli and Gluck. Schiedermair reproduced an example from Lindor's opening G minor lament,

Ex. 1 Schmittbauer, *Lindor und Ismene* (Hannover, 1779), No. 1

shown here as Ex. 1. While the opening eight-bar thought is at most sweetly plangent, the transition to the relative major (B♭) in bars 9–13 introduces at least a hint of Gluckian sobriety. Conventionally, an aria beginning in the minor mode moved directly into the relative major after the opening period, which Schmittbauer could easily have done at bar 9. The diversionary B♮ in the basses sustains the opening's minor coloring where it is most needed. Only begrudgingly does the musical discourse yield to the major mode.

Schiedermair much preferred Schmittbauer's portrayal of Lindor, in whose songs of mourning he detected a German spirit, to that of Ismene. Such was not

Ex. 2 Schmittbauer, *Lindor und Ismene*, No. 12

the judgment of a popular Viennese journal, the *Bibliothek der Grazien*, which singled out her lone aria for reprinting, along with the opera's overture, in 1789. A graceful four-bar idea (Ex. 2) sets this charming aria's tone of pastoral warmth from the outset. Choice of key fell on A major, by operatic tradition long invested with amatory associations (Mozart was to choose the same key for both versions of the love duet in *Idomeneo*, and for Belmonte's "O wie ängstlich, o wie feurig" in *Die Entführung*). Toward the end the compass opens up with gentle scalar descents through the octave, affective downward leaps, and a final *cadence galante* (Ex. 3). Soden's poetry likewise paints Ismene's awareness of her return to life in essentially sensuous terms, for instance with mention of the happy moonlit grove where she so often fell asleep in Lindor's arms.

Hiller, whom Soden had hoped would set *Lindor und Ismene*, was in fact asked to compose quite a different Grave in Arcadia text, the last libretto of his old friend and collaborator Christian Felix Weisse. Weisse's late librettos came to life principally for the sake of a journal he carried on almost singlehandedly from 1776 to 1782, *Der Kinderfreund*. It represents one of the German Enlightenment's last expressions of its abiding practical concern for the moral education of children.[20] The journal follows the ongoing experiences of a stereotypical bourgeois family. Four evenly spaced children aged eleven to five discuss a panorama of moral, social, intellectual, and aesthetic topics with their parents and especially with a set of family friends who pop in from time to time. One of these, Herr Spirit, shows up near the end of the journal's last set of installments with a play he has written, *Das Denkmal in Arkadien*, "A Rural Drama for Young People with Intermixed Songs."[21]

He catches the children at an apt moment: they have just returned from a visit to the grave of Leipzig's beloved poet Christian Fürchtegott Gellert. They agree to listen as Herr Spirit reads his play, though with some misgivings over the possibility of yet another depressing experience. The story, with certain modifications, is George Keate's *Monument in Arcadia*. As a postlude to his reading, Herr Spirit mentions the paintings and drawings by Oeser and his pupil Bach on the same subject. After seeing one of them he had gone home

Ex. 3 Schmittbauer, *Lindor und Ismene*, No. 12

and, recalling a "Dramatic Poem" by a certain Englishman, reconstructed it from his memory and his own imagination. Herr Spirit also mentions the picture by Poussin with its Latin inscription and quotes Du Bos' interpretation of it. He stresses especially the dying joy registered in the faces of the youthful Arcadians as they consider how death does not spare even the young, and he concludes with the hope, "May my little play have the same effect on you and your friends that this art critic ascribes to that painting."[22]

What a killjoy! It is difficult to believe, though undeniably true, that Weisse's play traces its pedigree to the same painting to which young Soden had appealed when publishing his own mongrel offspring a decade earlier. But again, we see that the painting itself was not really the direct source, rather it was Du Bos' interpretation of it. Yet even that scarcely explains the divergent views of these two librettos. In Soden's case, possibly, the adolescent antipathy of a young noble toward the serious reflection his subject demanded colored his libretto, and even more vital were his literary loyalties, which lay with the elegant, playful hedonism of the French and German poets he mentions in his preface. He sees Poussin not just through his own temperament and through Du Bos's *Réflections*, but also through the likes of Gresset's famous poetic tribute to Arcadia, "Le Siècle pastoral." Pious moralizing is out of the question – if anything, it is his mistress's bedside that Soden has uppermost in mind.

Weisse inhabited quite a different world as a father, respected Burger, tax collector, pedagog, eminent playwright and poet, and moralist. Furthermore, Poussin's *Arcadian Shepherds* came to him through different channels – through Du Bos, again, but filtered through the high moralizing of English literature and German painting, both of which he knew first-hand as editor of the most influential German journal devoted to the fine arts.[23]

As mentioned, Weisse modeled his libretto on George Keate, but not without changes. The most important one occurs in the central scene of the story, the one that recaptures the moment Poussin and his successors painted, the scene at the tomb. Here Weisse departed from Keate and indeed from the entire tradition of the *Et in Arcadia ego* theme, which demanded a group of figures around the monument. Perhaps some dim operatic instinct guided Weisse in clearing the stage of everyone but the heroine Daphne for this moment. Her father Palämon, unbeknownst to her, is hiding behind the tomb as she approaches it and reads the inscription, "Auch ich war in Arkadien." An indispensable motif, this: nearly every picture, engraving, and description related to the Grave in Arcadia after Guercino had included a figure pointing to the inscription. In this *scena* Weisse provided his heroine with a remarkably impassioned recitative-like passage in often disjunct prose, then a dolorous aria of disillusionment. There is nothing like these pages in anything else Weisse had ever written for the musical stage – if indeed he ever seriously intended this play to be performed anywhere but in the minds of his young listeners:

Auch ich war in Arkadien! — *Auch ich war in Arkadien!* — In Arkadien? und wurdest vermuthlich in der Blüte deiner Jahre vom Tode hingerafft? und schlummerst hier in diesem Grabe! und ein guter Vater, eine zärtliche Mutter weinen über dir! und dies ist Arkadien? — Arkadien? auf dessen Boden, wie ich wähnte, kein menschliches Elend wüchse! und Seuchen und Krankheit und Unfall, oder welches Unglück dich, holdseliges Mädchen, vor der Zeit hingerissen, wohnen auch hier? mitten in diesen reizenden Fluren? O wie habe ich mich geirrt! Eitle Hoffnung! wie hast du mich getäuscht!

("I, too, was in Arcadia"! — "I, too, was in Arcadia"! — In Arcadia? And you were snatched away, so it seems, by Death in the flower of your years? And you sleep here in this grave! And a good father, a tender mother weep for you! And this is Arcadia? — Arcadia? in whose soil, so I imagined, no human misery could grow! and disease and sickness and accident, or whatever misfortune bore you off before your time, all gracious maid, live here, too? amid these charming fields? Oh, how mistaken I have been! Vain hope! how you have deceived me!)

Hiller's setting of Weisse's lamentation at the tomb does not survive – if he ever actually composed the opera at all. We do have a visual illustration, however, for not surprisingly this was the scene chosen for the engraving that appeared with the libretto in *Der Kinderfreund* (Plate 3b). Weisse, or perhaps his publisher Siegfried Lebrecht Crusius, turned to one of Oeser's students, the prolific illustrator Johann August Rossmässler, for this depiction. What is so fascinating about his engraving is that he failed to illustrate the scene as Weisse had described it; instead, he created his own aggregate of motifs from the drama and from the pictorial history of the *Et in Arcadia ego* theme.

Astonishingly, the heroine is nowhere to be seen. The minor female figure comforting a grieving shepherd to the left and the supine statue atop the tomb Rossmässler borrowed more or less directly from Chodowiecki (see Plate 3a), whom he was especially fond of copying in his illustrations. Equally surprising, none of the figures points or otherwise draws attention to the inscription on the monument – one of the few times since Guercino that this motif had been omitted. Rossmässler does incorporate two novel features of his own, and both relate to Weisse's play and the journal in which it appeared. First, in place of Chodowiecki's two skulls surmounting the tomb he includes two lambs, symbols of young innocence. But they are overshadowed, first by the statue lying on the tomb and second by the engraving's most striking and disturbing feature, the cypress tree thrust into the foreground. Why did he interpose it so abruptly between the tomb and the principal figure on the right, who has removed his garland and ought by rights to be kneeling and deciphering the inscription? And why does the tree cast no shadow, unlike the young shepherd approaching the tomb?

This chilling touch has its counterpart in Weisse's play, which lays heavy stress on classic botanical symbology – myrtle and roses studiously associated with marriage and Arcadian bliss, and the cypress tree with death and mourning. These symbols meet head on in Daphne's aria following the monolog quoted above:

> Nicht Cypressen; Ros und Myrthen
> Sucht' ich bloß bey diesen Hirten –
> Und Cypressen find ich hier?

(Not cypresses, but roses and myrtle were all I looked to find among these shepherds – and I find cypresses here?)

After the reunion scene of father and daughter, Weisse inserted a stage direction telling the Arcadian shepherds to remove the cypress at the monument and replace it with myrtle as Daphne receives a crown of roses from her new husband.

So both in Rossmässler's engraving and in the play itself the shadowless cypress tree's role is provisional. Once it has served its admonitory function, out it goes. The tomb, too, proves in the end to be a provisional, or at least premature, monument. Both these warnings are but a reflex of Weisse's didactic goal in writing the play to begin with: first to impress thoughts and tokens of human mortality on the tender minds of his young readers, then to console their chastened spirits with a scene of reunion and festivity at the end.

From its inception, the motto *Et in Arcadia ego*, like the theme of Death in Arcadia itself, had evoked a variety of responses and interpretations. The phrase's power over Western art was focused most intensely in Poussin's Louvre canvas, but even this great painting could not channel its variety and ambiguity. The eighteenth-century writers we have mentioned here all declared Poussin as their inspiration. Panofsky did not know any of their works, but they are among the beneficiaries of his insight that those who translate the Latin motto, as they all do, with a form of "I, too, lived in Arcadia," rather than Death's admonition, "Even in Arcadia, there am I," are in fact faithful interpreters of their model's spirit. They do violence to Latin grammar, he admits, but justice to the new meaning the theme acquired in Poussin's composition.

Mostly, however, they do equal violence to both, and they do so by restoring the element Poussin had rejected in Guercino's painting – the tradition of moralizing at the tomb. Du Bos had invited them to imagine the affecting speeches Poussin's Arcadian shepherds are about to make to each other; for the most part, they answered not with the melancholy reflections of youth but with the philistine precepts of their elders. Soden, the only youth among them, declined the invitation altogether.

Why the opera libretto became a vehicle for moralizing at the tomb is unclear. The ancient Arcadians were reputed to be a musical people, a trait that pastoral tradition had allied both with the plaints of the bereft *pastor fido* and with dance as an expression of Arcadia's sensual pleasures. It is perfectly fitting, in consequence, that of the three eighteenth-century opera texts inspired by Poussin, only one was actually set to music and put on stage – Soden's celebration of an imagined victory of Youth and Love over Death. The stern sermons to the young created by Keate and Weisse were better left unsung.

NOTES

1 "'Et in Arcadia Ego': On the Conception of Transience in Poussin and Watteau," in *Philosophy and History: Essays Presented to Ernst Cassirer*, ed. Raymond Klibansky and H. J. Paton (Oxford, 1936), pp. 223–54. For revised versions, see "*Et in Arcadia ego*: Poussin and the Elegiac Tradition," ch. 7 in Erwin Panofsky, *Meaning in the Visual Arts: Papers in and on Art History* (New York, 1955), pp. 295–320; and "*Et in Arcadia Ego*," in *Pastoral and Romance: Modern Essays in Criticism*, ed. Eleanor Terry Lincoln (Englewood Cliffs, N.J., 1969), pp. 25–46.

2 Werner Weisbach strenuously opposed Panofsky's interpretation and sought to link Guercino's painting more closely to the spirit of Poussin's two *Et in Arcadia ego*

paintings by reading the Latin phrase as the words of the unfortunate occupant of the tomb, rather than those of the abstraction Death. "'Et in Arcadia ego'," *Gazette des beaux-arts*, ser. 6, vol. 18 (July-December 1937): 287–96. Panofsky replied in the same journal, "'Et in Arcadia ego' et le tombeau parlant," ser. 6, vol. 19 (January-June 1938): 305–6.

3 *Arcadia* (Venice, 1502; 2/1504). Panofsky points out that "Sannazaro's is the first pastoral poem actually staged *in* Arcadia," rather than in a setting tied to contemporary events or persons (p. 230, n. 4). All of the literary works to be discussed below also explicitly locate themselves in Arcadia. But only one of them, as we shall see, can claim any spiritual kinship with Sannazaro's vision of Arcadia.

4 (Venice, 1581), quoted from the edition of Mario Fubini (Milan, 1976), pp. 89–90. (Translation mine.)

5 "Piaccia, se lice." (Venice, 1590), Act 4, Scene 9, l. 1419. Cited after the edition of Ettore Bonora (Milan, 1977), p. 208. Further on the distinction between Guarini and Tasso can be found in Hellmuth Petriconi, "Das neue Arkadien," *Antike und Abendland* 3 (1948): 187–200.

6 Lawrence D. Steefel, Jr., discusses the symbolism of the shadow in connection with Poussin's later *Et in Arcadia ego* painting in "A Neglected Shadow in Poussin's *Et in Arcadia Ego*," *The Art Bulletin* 57 (1975): 99–101.

7 "Sie werden auf einmal, da sie nichts weniger als melankolische Gedanken hatten, von dem Anblick eines Grabmals plötzlich gerühret...aus den Gesichtern der Hirten, die eine Schäferinn von einer ausnehmend schönen Gestalt begleitet, leuchtet eine große Bestürzung und Unruhe." "Nachricht von neuen Kupferstichen aus England," *Bibliothek der schönen Wissenschaften und der freyen Künste* 10: 1 (Leipzig, 1763): 179–80.

8 Reproduced by Georges Wildenstein in *Les Graveurs de Poussin au XVIIe siècle* (Paris, 1957), p. 221. The engraving, which is a mirror image of the original, carries the title: "Le Souvenir de la mort au milieu des prosperitez de la vie." It is often attributed to Picart's son Bernard, and was probably done before the painting was acquired for the royal collection in 1685. See Doris Wild, *Nicolas Poussin*, 2 vols. (Zurich, 1980), vol. 2, p. 80.

9 See Richard Verdi, "On the Critical Fortunes – and Misfortunes – of Poussin's 'Arcadia'," *The Burlington Magazine* 121 (1979): 95–107.

10 *Critical Reflections on Poetry, Painting and Music. With An Inquiry into the Rise and Progress of the Theatrical Entertainments of the Ancients*, 2 vols. (London, 1748), vol. 1, pp. 45–6.

11 [Thomas Amory], *Memoirs: Containing the Lives of Several Ladies of Great Britain. A History of Antiquities, Productions of Nature, and Monuments of Art* (London, 1755), pp. 22–3.

12 *Leben, Bemerkungen und Meinungen Johann Bunkels nebst den Leben verschiedener merkwürdiger Frauenzimmer*, trans. Raimarus von Spieren, with additional remarks and opinions by Friedrich Nicolai and Hermann Andreas Pistorius, 4 vols. (Berlin, 1778). The publication was subjected to a lengthy, damning review by Wieland, who suspected that Nicolai himself had undertaken the translation. See Ludwig Geiger, "Wielandiana," *Im neuen Reich* 11 (1881): 426–7.

13 Angelika also included a second set of Arcadians dancing in the distance, a detail that had been added to Du Bos' description by Amory. Frances A. Gerard, *Angelica Kaufmann: A Biography* (New York, 1893), pp. 51–2.

14 *The Monument in Arcadia: A Dramatic Poem in Two Acts* (London, 1773), p. ix.

Keate's opinion would find scant support today. Petra Maisak, for instance, offers an ingenious interpretation of Poussin's Louvre version of *Et in Arcadia ego* (see Plate 2) that incorporates narrative elements. The eye reaches the striking female figure to the right, "den eigentlichen Schwerpunkt der Komposition," by a natural traversal of the painting from left to right. The three shepherds represent successive temporal stages in the process of deciphering the inscription (not-yet-read, reading, and already-read). The female figure, finally, stands in opposition to the unknowing shepherd on the far left "als Personifikation der höchsten Erkenntnisstufe, des idealen menschlichen Verhaltens, das auf virtus und tranquilitas animi gründet." *Arkadien: Genese und Typologie einer idyllischen Wunschwelt* (Frankfurt and Bern, 1981), p. 181.

15 Gottfried Schwalb der Ältere. See Gert von der Osten, *Katalog der Gemälde alter Meister in der niedersächsischen Landesgallerie Hannover* (Hannover, 1954), p. 114. The painting is reproduced in the *Reallexikon zur deutschen Kunstgeschichte*, ed. Otto Schmitt et al., vol. 6, s.v. "Et in Arcadia ego" (Munich, 1973), cols. 123–4.

16 See Joseph Longo, "Laurence Sterne und Johann Georg Jacobi," *XXXV. Jahresbericht über die niederösterreichische Landes-Oberrealschule* (Krems, 1898), pp. 18–31. The phrase appears in a story appended to *Die Winterreise*, "Das Kloster," and suggests that the motto was in common use on gravestones at the time: "Wenn ich auf schönen Fluren einen Leichenstein antreffe, mit der Ueberschrift: **Auch ich war in Arkadien**; so zeig' ich den Leichenstein meinen Freunden; wir bleiben stehen, drücken uns die Hand, und gehen weiter." *Sämtliche Werke*, 3 vols. (Frankfurt and Leipzig, 1779), vol. 2, p. 50.

17 [Julius Freiherr Soden von Saßanfart], *Lindor und Ismene* ([Ansbach, 1771]), pp. [iii]–[v].

18 In his preface to the public, Soden writes:
"Als Kind ließ ich dieses unbedeutende Ding drucken; ward auch deswegen von einigen Journalisten wie billig jämmerlich angegrinzt.
"Zufälligerweise fiel es Herrn Kapellmeister Schmittbauer zu Carlsruhe in die Hände. Seine vortrefliche Composition, nach der es auf der hannöverischen Bühne öfters aufgeführt wurde, konnte allein mich bewegen, es wieder durchzusehen.
"Ich geb' es hier verändert, so viel es bey dem Zwang der Composition und ohne Vernichtung des Ganzen, möglich war." (Leipzig, 1779), p. [3].

19 In "Die Oper an den badischen Höfen des 17. und 18. Jahrhunderts," *Sammelbände der Internationalen Musikgesellschaft* 14 (1912/13): 542–50. The manuscript score was formerly in the Musikabteilung of the Hessische Landes- und Hochschulbibliothek at Darmstadt.

20 On the journal itself, see Bettina Hurrelmann, *Jugendliteratur und Bürgerlichkeit: Soziale Erziehung in der Jugendliteratur der Aufklärung am Beispiel von Christian Felix Weisses "Kinderfreund" 1776–1782* (Paderborn, 1974). On the "Kinderoperetten" that appeared in its pages, see my study *North German Opera in the Age of Goethe* (Cambridge, 1985), pp. 209–11.

21 [Christian Felix Weisse], *Das Denkmal in Arkadien: Ein ländliches Schauspiel für die Jugend mit intermischten Gesängen in Einem Aufzuge*, in *Der Kinderfreund: Ein Wochenblatt*, pts. 321–6 (25 August–29 September 1781): 117–92. The libretto was published separately by Crusius a year later (Leipzig, 1782), and appeared as well in the series *Theatralische Sammlung*, vol. 197 (Vienna, 1797).

22 Ibid., pp. 195–6: "Möchte doch, setzte Herr Spirit hinzu, mein kleines Schauspiel

auf euch und eure Freunde eben die Wirkung thun, die dieser Kunstrichter jenem Gemälde zuschreibt."
23 Weisse edited volumes 5 to 12 of the *Bibliothek der schönen Wissenschaften und der freyen Künste* (12 vols., Leipzig, 1757–65; volumes 1 to 4 had been edited by Friedrich Nicolai and Moses Mendelssohn), and continued as editor of all 72 volumes of the *Neue Bibliothek der schönen Wissenschaften und der freyen Künste* (Leipzig, 1765–1806).

3

Dr. Burney, the bear, and the knight: E. F. Burney's *Amateurs of Tye-Wig Music*

KERRY S. GRANT

Overcome by his conundrum, Dr. Charles Burney scribbled in his notebook in a tiny, crabbed hand, "I dare not say what I have long thought. That it is our reverence for old authors and bigotry to Handel, that has prevented us from keeping pace with the rest of Europe in the cultivation of Music."[1] In penning this admission Burney acknowledged a fact that shaped much of his professional life. His dilemma was rooted in his ambition to be a music critic and historian whose work would improve the public taste and his equally fervent ambition to receive patronage from the court of King George III. Burney's musical taste was progressive, whereas the king's taste was "inveterately and intolerantly" conservative – indeed, it seemed that only the music of George Frideric Handel met with his full approval.

The way to patronage was difficult enough when every political star was in alignment. Even the most deserving candidate for favor faced intrigue and uncertainty. We have Burney's own words to remind us of the treacherous and uncertain path to patronage. When, in 1781, his son was hopeful about his own prospects for patronage, Burney recalled that similar opportunities

> in the course of my Life have made me a Castle-builder. But I still remain a drudge amid the smiles of Wealth and Power. As to Lord Fin[dla]ter's affection for you it seems like that of David for Jonathan, so wonderful as to surpass the Love of a Woman. If it is but founded on such a basis of rectitude, reason, and reflexion, as will make it durable, it may be the means of your passing through the world with honour, Comfort and happiness; but if by some false calculation, Caprice, fault or offence, on either side, it should be suddenly withdrawn it will certainly leave you more miserable, and less fit to buffet with the World, than it found you. It is not from a natural distrust, or bad opinion of Mankind that I remind you of that being Possible, and preparing you for such a Mortifying and perhaps ruinous reverse, but from long experience, and an intimate acquaintance with the vicissitudes of human affairs.[2]

The record of Burney's attempts to secure patronage reveal the importance he placed on royal preferment. He made at least seven attempts to secure royal appointments (see Table 3.1).[3] His first attempt, in 1765, was unsuccessful. In 1767 he gained an appointment to the court in the modest position of "Extra Musician" in the King's Band. His last effort, so far as we know, was an

Opera and the visual arts

Table 3.1. *A chronology of Burney's principal published works and his attempts to secure royal patronage*

Year	Publication or event
1766	*The Cunning-Man, a Musical Entertainment in Two Acts*
1767	Appointment as "Extra Musician in the King's Band"
1771	*The Present State of Music in France and Italy*
1773	*The Present State of Music in Germany, the Netherlands, and the United Provinces*
1774	Appointment as "Musician in Ordinary" to the King
1776	*A General History of Music from the Earliest Ages to the Present Period*, Volume I
1781	Failure to succeed Boyce as "Master of the King's Band"
	A General History of Music from the Earliest Ages to the Present Period, Volume II
1782	Failure to succeed Kelway as "Organist in the Queen's Band of Musick"
1783	Appointment as "Organist of Chelsea Hospital"
1783–4	Failure to obtain the post of "Composer of the State Music in Ireland"
1785	*An Account of the Musical Performance in Westminster-Abbey, and the Pantheon, In Commemoration of Handel*
1786	Failure to succeed John Stanley as "Master of the King's Band"
1789	*A General History of Music from the Earliest Ages to the Present Period*, Volumes III and IV

unsuccessful attempt in 1786 to succeed John Stanley as "Master of the King's Band." Despite numerous opportunities and the encouragement of many individuals of position and influence, all of his efforts except one failed to garner royal patronage. He succeeded only in advancing to "Musician in Ordinary to the King" in 1774. Later he received minor beneficence in a government appointment as Organist of Chelsea Hospital and, late in life, a royal pension. However, these were small compensations and lacked the public recognition attendant on such positions as "Organist in the Queen's Band of Musick," "Composer of the State Music in Ireland," or the highest musical post in the land, "Master of the King's Band." He keenly, even bitterly, resented the denial of his ambitions to hold these posts.[4]

The dates of his attempts to secure these positions, ranging from 1765 to 1786, are significant. His first great literary success, *The Present State of Music in France and Italy* was published in 1771, and the final volumes of his monumental four-volume *General History of Music* appeared in 1789. Thus, the period of his intense effort to garner royal favor coincides with that during which he published his best-known critical and historical works.[5]

Thus Burney wrote his extensive essays on Handel – contained primarily in the *History of Music* and in the *Account of the Commemoration of Handel* – while advancement at court seemed a distinct possibility, even an expectation. Because of this, the king and the wealthy and powerful men who shared his conservative tastes were an intimidating presence during the many years in which Burney wrote about the age of Handel and music in England.[6]

An important conservative voice was that of Sir John Hawkins, attorney (subsequently magistrate), musical amateur, and historian. Hawkins regarded the sixteenth century as the golden age of English music and the period of Handel, Corelli, and Geminiani as the last truly worthy age of music. In the epilogue to his *History* published in 1776, Hawkins summarized his view:

> There can be no better test of the comparative merits of the music of the present day, and that which it has taken place of, than the different effects of each. The impression of the former was deep and is lasting: the compositions of Corelli, Handel, Geminiani, yet live in our memories; and those of Purcell, though familiarized by the lapse of near a century, still retain their charms; but who now remembers, or rather does not affect to forget the music that pleased him last year.[7]

By virtue of writing a history of music at precisely the same time as Burney and from such a different critical viewpoint, Hawkins was widely regarded as a rival, and by no one more earnestly than Burney himself. Burney was repelled by the narrowness and exclusivity of the conservative position advocated by Hawkins. The proper critical stance, in his view, was an enlarged taste admiring whatever was good of its kind, of whatever age or country the composer or performer may be.[8] Hawkins represented a direct rival to Burney's efforts to achieve critical and popular success with his *History* – Burney said he had spit in his porridge – and Hawkins's voice was persuasive and authoritative. It seemed essential that he be discredited. To a significant degree Burney accomplished this by manipulating the reviews of Hawkins' work in the most important publications.[9] Burney's *History* caught the fashion of the times in any case, and, for a while at least, the critical victory was his. Despite this success, Burney never overcame his dislike for Hawkins or his contempt for his rival's *General History of the Science and Practice of Music* and the conservative taste that it espoused. Nevertheless, his dependency on the approbation of the powerful circle of men of conservative taste, including the king himself, compelled Burney to move cautiously through society. He sheltered himself from discord in society by his practice of praising what was meritorious in any work and being silent about the rest. In general he was successful with only a few harrowing, and to us amusing, incidents that threatened to undermine his effort to appear congenial with every manner of person. He did not move undetected however. Hester Lynch Thrale, for one, found that "if he has any Fault it is too much Obsequiousness."[10]

Burney's most vexing encounter with the conservatives came about in 1784 as a result of his involvement with the planners of the first great festival in commemoration of Handel. Ever eager for association with notables, he found his affiliation with the directors flattering, but he came to rue his promise to write a commemorative pamphlet for the spectacular event. He was to be edited and censored by no less than the king himself, whose deep interest in the

Plate 4 Edward F. Burney, *Amateurs of Tye-Wig Music*. Yale Center for British Art, Paul Mellon Collection.

festival and Handel led him to command that Burney's manuscript be brought to him while still in draft form. He reviewed each page and reproved Burney when he felt the historian was not sufficiently lavish in his praise of Handel. In a letter to his friend and collaborator Thomas Twining, Burney expressed the depths of his anxiety and despair:

> I will not write like Apostate. I will not deny my liberal principles. I will not abuse the lovers of the best Music of Italy and Germany and say that they are only admired through fashion and want of good taste and judgment. I will ransack the language for terms of praise in speaking of [Handel's] best works – and the Manner in which they have been lately performed; but cannot, will not say that there is no other Music fit to be heard, or as well performed.[11]

Though he struggled with his conscience and his pen, he succumbed to the wishes of the king and his cohorts. His distress at the duplicity forced upon him, vividly portrayed in letters and in essays in his notebooks, testifies to his essential integrity. The drafts of essays in which he vainly struggled to evaluate Handel's merit in a form that might deny him supremacy yet satisfy the Handelians, testify to his sincerity, but also stand now as painful evidence of the extent of his eventual capitulation. The evidence is conclusive: Burney equivocated, even prevaricated in his essays on Handel and his music.[12]

Burney's family, who routinely assisted him with the chores associated with producing his books such as copying and transcribing, knew of his predicament. His nephew, Edward Francesco Burney (1760–1848), an artist and book illustrator, was extensively involved in the production of the elaborately illustrated *Account of the Commemoration of Handel* for which he executed several of the plates. Edward, a musician of sufficient talent to play chamber music with the leading performers of his day, shared his uncle's progressive taste. Nevertheless, at his uncle's request, he placed his talents to use in celebrating and furthering Handel's reputation.

Edward later balanced the record by creating an elaborate work of art that pilloried the conservative taste and its proponents with the most delicious ridicule (see Plate 4).[13] The apparent theme of E. F. Burney's satirical watercolor *Amateurs of Tye-Wig Music* is the derogation of old music and its votaries.[14] At the time Edward created this watercolor, the tye-wig, just as the music favored by the performers in the scene, was many years out of fashion. The comic contrast between the intent, superannuated performers with limbs akimbo, performing in wholly Gothic surroundings and the young, graceful, fashionably dressed, if bemused and inattentive, auditors strikes the viewer at first glance. Closer examination reveals a myriad of allusions, and overt and subtle pictorial puns which stimulate the imagination and draw the viewer into interpretation and speculation.

Themes are clustered and worked out in direct and very subtle ways in various sections of the work. The wall on the left of the watercolor displays numerous references to Judaic and pagan antiquity which, though touched upon in other areas of the room, are collected here in the greatest profusion.

Amphion, Midas, Jubal, Vulcan, and Orpheus are in evidence, and each is associated in one way or another with sound and music.

The general theme of the wall on the right is time and fashion represented by a musical chronograph, the maestro di cappella beating time, the epigram on the crwth or crowd with its pun, "How vain the ardor of the crowd," and the amused, fashionably dressed woman whose song sheet titled "How Imperfect is Expression" makes clear her view of the proceedings. The playbill lying on the floor also refers to contemporary fashion by alluding to a benefit for "Sigr. Rossini," a reference which, if taken literally, provides a date for this piece of no earlier than 1824, the year of Rossini's great success in London.[15] The playbill also offers commentary on the scene through a reference to Rozinante, Don Quixote's horse. The name is derived from the Spanish *rocin*, a jade, and *ante*, before, implying that, once upon a time, perhaps, the creature had been a horse. Here the reading is that, once upon a time, these were fashionable men playing fashionable music, but no longer.[16]

Moving left toward the center, pastoral themes radiate from the key phrase found over the doorway: "Music hath charms to soothe the savage Breast." Representations of birds including the wise owl "who shunn'st musical noise," and the cuckoo from Vivaldi's concerto of that name are related to a subsidiary theme by another key statement on the wall: "Gently Touch the Warbling Lyre, Chloe seems inclined to rest" (a popular song by Francesco Geminiani). This quote joins the bucolic with the somnific themes represented most obviously by the boy tending the organ bellows. He sleeps with mouth agape soon to be disrupted from his slumbers by the shuttlecock (another bird?) aimed by the mischievous youth with the battledore. LULLABY (a vulgar word for the male member)[17] is marked on the front of the trousers of the sleeping boy, and so on.

The central aspect of the watercolor is the organ case with its picture of St. Cecilia, patron saint of music. It is surmounted by a bust of Handel, highlighted by a radiant coronet, proudly gazing over the scene. St. Cecilia's traditional appurtenance, the portative organ, is depicted here pointing not to heaven but crumbling and pointing earthward, illustrating her commentary on the proceedings she witnesses. A sustained series of visual puns and allusions treating the devil and things demonic, with contrasting references to angels and the angelic, occupies a portion of the central panel and figures prominently in the panel to the left. The caption of the St. Cecilia portrait and the angel decorating the Gothic frame on the portrait of Arcangelo Corelli serve to introduce the angelic theme. The key reference to the demonic is the caption on the wall: "Giuseppe Tartini playing the Devil's sonata." This is further developed by other references such as the title on the piece of music, Woelfl's *Diable à quatre*, which protrudes from the pocket of the young woman standing at the rear of the room. She holds two rods connected by a length of cord that are part of a fashionable toy, the diabolo or devil on two sticks.[18] The name Dr. Faustus and a picture of a character in conjurer's garb embellish the lamp in the center of the room. In the foreground the "violino primo" pounds his foot on a score identified as by Beethoven on the spine, but by "Beatoften" on the corner. He is "beating the Devil's tattoo"[19] by pounding his foot on the floor. The patten, secured to the shoe with a strap, serves to increase the din in the room. Normally used to protect shoes by elevating them out of muck and mire, the patten is especially comic in this context because the performer is wearing only one, suggesting that its sole purpose is to amplify the drumming of the foot on the floor so as to aid the musicians in keeping time. The density of demonic references and the overall effect of the scene suggests that it is safe to embrace the interpretation that the entire ensemble "plays the devil with the music."

There are three thematic areas in the lower portion of the work. To the left, in the area of the fireplace, modern music is deprecated. Music by the best contemporary masters is shown burning in the fireplace as mere fuel to warm the antiquated musicians. The composers of these works are ridiculed in the sketches or prints piled on the floor: Beethoven is carried off to Bedlam in the "Dog Cart Rasoumoffsky," Mozart is dismissed as "sillabub" and "Sour Kroutt," and Burney's beloved Dr. Haydn is mocked by the crowd.

The center vignette pointedly informs us of the quality of the performance of these here-silent amateurs. A child draws a rasp across a scroll of music while her companion pulls a saw across a bellows in mocking imitation of the players who, we may presume, studied their technique from the tome on which the child's foot rests – Raspe and Sawyer's *Art of Bowing*. The child's toy in the foreground is a Dutch Concert, that is, a mechanical toy representing a concert in which everyone plays or sings a different tune or simply makes noise.[20] Its presence alerts us to the incongruity of the music pictured in front of the musicians. Although they play in an ensemble, the musicians perform music by different composers from scores written in curious notations suggestive of musical styles more atavistic than those being ridiculed in the scene. Moreover, the second violin plays from a part that is upside down, although he seems unperturbed by this. He sits on Avison's *Essay on Musical Expression* as a booster seat, suggesting that he is as deficient in taste as he is inept in technique.

The lower right hand side represents and ridicules the music acceptable to the superannuated performers. The scroll labeled "stock pieces" contains the names of Handel, Corelli, Geminiani, and Vivaldi – all but one of whom (Vivaldi) Hawkins had praised in his *History* as the last great composers. The music marked "Played and approved," composed by Tye, Tallis, Birde [sic] and others, is even older than that of Handel, and its proximity to a stack of tomes with telling titles, including *Innovation the Cause of the Decline of Music*, provides Edward's commentary on these selections.

Amateurs of Tye-Wig Music is a veritable compendium of the themes of music and music-making that were widely satirized. The watercolor, though quite unusual in its sophistication, learnedness, and visual density, draws from the common images and allusions of the popular satirical prints of the day. These prints were popular effusions commenting on current social and political events, often from a very critical point of view. The arts, artists, and patrons of the arts were common subjects of the satirical print makers.[21] Sold in shops and

Opera and the visual arts

Plate 5 Anonymous print, *The Graces*. Farmington, Mass., Lewis Walpole Library.

widely circulated, the prints offer a remarkably unrestrained glimpse of events, people, and viewpoints. However, nothing in the thousands of satirical prints of the day rivals, or even suggests, the artistic merit and sophistication of Burney's watercolor. It is only in the work of William Hogarth that an artistic parallel can be found, and Edward's style has been dubbed Neo-Hogarthian by Patricia Crown, the principal scholar of his work.

The pursuit of excellence in music performance, particularly by male amateurs, was not generally endorsed in English society because it was thought to be a frivolous undertaking deflecting attention from more important concerns.[22] No one put it more plainly than Philip Dormer Standhope, Fourth Earl of Chesterfield, whose letters to his son were influential in forming social attitudes for many years after their publication in 1749. Among the many prescriptions and proscriptions in the letters is one that caught both the spirit of Georgian reserve about gentlemen musicians and the attention of a satirical print maker (Plate 5). The caption reads: "Few things would mortify me more, than to see you bearing a part in a concert with a fiddle under your chin, if you are fond of fiddling... pay fiddlers."[23] To judge from this scene, Burney's gentlemen amateurs seem to have avoided the deleterious effects of being too serious in their application to music.

As Lord Chesterfield's comment suggests (and the satiric artist has portrayed), performing music could result in ungraceful, even ridiculous postures shunned in a polite society in which grace and manners were of paramount importance. The exaggerated, awkward postures of the players in Burney's composition are reminiscent of those of the performers in many other prints, particularly those by James Gillray. Worse than the graceless postures of the performers were the indelicate circumstances and ridiculous facial expressions that could arise from the exertions of performance. In Burney's work, the flutist has been unable to contain his nasal secretions while he performs. The seated posture of cellists suggested a natural target for gout gags, a sadistic form of humor often in evidence in satirical prints. Many satirical prints suggest that the music is much too difficult for the performers, evinced not only in their intense, distorted faces but also, as here, in the distress or inattention of their audience.

The satirical prints that treat music are tasteful by the standards of the genre. The depiction of "vomiting, defecation and the like" that were frequent in prints – especially political prints from this period – are relatively uncommon.[24] Burney introduces the scatological tradition subtly, even somewhat tastefully, in a pun presented by the figure of the cellist. He sits on a copy of a treatise on the fundamental bass, an association that puns the vulgar definition of fundamental features for the posterior.[25]

The noisy distractions evident in the scene are also traditional. Dogs, cats, and other animals are ubiquitous in musical prints. Clumsy servants, inattentive guests (here located primarily in the back rooms), and noisy children are also common figures. If we allow our imaginations to make the scene audible, we are beset by a howling dog, a squealing cat, a cuckoo, a clattering tea service, a crashing lamp, and the bedlam emanating from the revels in the rooms visible in the rear of the salon.

Absorbed as they are with music-making, Edward's performers are missing more than the passing of fashion as is evident from the scenes in the two back rooms. In the room on the left, the dancers, the tambourine, the mildly erotic quotations, and the carefree atmosphere among the young women mirror a tradition that often much more pointedly portrayed music's seductive potential. The mischief of the young men, shown here frolicking and misbehaving in the room on the right unchecked by the inattentive players and auditors, is a theme often portrayed in satirical prints. These traditions reflect the belief that music and the other arts may detract from moral and proper living just as surely as excessive application to music may lessen the possibility of enjoying a prosperous, useful life.

An exceptional aspect of this work is the extensive visual punning on Handel, whose bulk and gluttony were natural targets for satirists. The well-known declaration of Alexander Pope:

> Strong in new arms, lo! giant Handel stands,
> Like Bold Briareus with an hundred hands;

which frames the bust of Handel, inspires and draws these themes together. As Patricia Crown points out, Burney represents three figures of Handelian proportions with evident similarities to the bust of Handel above the organ case, in the cellist, the maestro di cappella, and the first violin.[26] The scroll decoration of the cello, held by a performer with Handel's visage, extends the allusion to the notable composer. It is the head of a bear, "bear" being a popular cognomen for Handel. The placement of the ticket that rests beside the cellist on the chair allows Burney the visual pun: "ADMIT the BEAR[ER] to the [Concerts of] Ancient Music." This suggests a second and third level of meaning as well (although, in this as in so many instances, one is uncertain about ascribing intent). "To play the bear" was a common phrase meaning to behave in a rough and rude manner, epithets that both reflect Handel's character as popularly portrayed and, perhaps, the style of the music and the quality of the performance portrayed in this scene.[27] The plausibility of this third reading is enhanced by the allusion to this usage on the score found on the organ. The lettering of the title "thorough bass" on the music is contrived to offer the reading "tho rough" bass. The admission ticket to the "Commemoration of Jubal"[28] depicted over the mantel can only be understood as a parody of the Commemoration of Handel, the event that plunged Charles Burney into conflict between political necessity and critical veracity. Another image, that of the maestro di cappella beating time with his scroll on the right of the picture, is also a pointed reference to the Commemoration of Handel.[29]

The Handel references are abundant and quite direct. More subtle, but equally intriguing is a series of allusions to Sir John Hawkins. These are expressed in references that range from the obvious to the arcane. The portraits on the wall of eminent musicians, here provided with elaborate Gothic frames bearing visual puns of the composers' names, are based on those in Hawkins' *History*. More enigmatic is the relationship of the image in the far upper right-hand corner of the picture to Sir John's *History*. This would be perceptible only to the cognoscenti, and to few of them. It is a representation of a theoretical construct called the mundane monochord, an invention of Dr. Robert Flud.[30] Edward places this cumbrous theoretical device on the shoulders of Atlas to emphasize the dead weight of this old, quite useless and abstruse theoretical work. This unusual image is taken directly from a plate in the *History*. So, too, the crwth with its punning caption is drawn from one of Hawkins' plates.[31]

The statue of the Judgment of Midas on the mantelpiece has both an obvious and a recondite meaning. Anyone familiar with the myth would make an easy association with the artwork's obvious judgment of these amateurs and their taste in music, but the figurine would have special meaning to intimates and family members who knew Charles Burney's elaborate satirical poetic attack on Hawkins in "The Trial of Midas the Second, or the Second Congress of Musicians." The three cantos of his poem encompass one thousand lines expressing his disdain for Hawkins and his *History*, and with notable malice. Hawkins, as Midas before him, is subjected to a trial, found deficient in taste, and harshly punished. As Roger Lonsdale notes, the "labour involved in the composition of so elaborate a poem must suggest that the busy music-master genuinely detested his rival."[32] The indictment of Hawkins at the trial reads:

> That, having not before his eyes the fear
> Of the first Midas' destiny severe,
> Like Marsyas, quite unmindful of his skin,
> Against Apollo's self he dared to sin;
> For which, before this awful court he stands
> Indicted – here to answer all demands,
> By Style and Title, as the words proclaim,
> Of MIDAS, Second of that hapless name.[33]

Burney's "Trial of Midas" served as the wellspring of much of the imagery in Edward's work.[34] The thematic parallels between the works are pervasive and specific – too much so to dismiss them as the result of both men's drawing inspiration from common traditions, myths, and imagery associated with music. The inspiration is general in the deprecation of the Gothic style, but also quite specific as a close reading of the poem and a careful review of the imagery in the watercolor reveal.

The centrality of the dispute between Burney and Hawkins to Edward's conception is subtly but nowhere better in evidence than in his treatment of the portrait of Purcell that hangs on the wall to the right of the room (the wall that has as its general theme evanescent fashion and taste). The stylish, modest, contemporary frame is in notable contrast to the elaborate Gothic frames that surround most of the portraits, simultaneously adorning and ridiculing their subjects as dated and unfashionable. The exceptional portrait frame reflects an exceptional point of agreement between the two historians. They concurred that the music of Henry Purcell was worthy despite the passing of time and changing fashion in music. In the "Trial of Midas" Burney credits Hawkins for his approval of Purcell's music as one mitigating factor in his wholesale and enthusiastic condemnation of his rival's work.

> And now the Judge, though bitter is the cup,
> The Evidence entire with care sums up;
> Yet leaning gently on the Pris'ner's side,
> For he had Purcell prais'd, the Nation's pride.[35]

Notable too is the absence of Dr. William Boyce from the composers memorialized in the room. Boyce was too important a figure and much too closely associated with Hawkins to have been casually overlooked. His importance as an editor of the great edition of *Cathedral Music* added to his merit as a composer. Boyce set Hawkins' poetry to music and even helped him

Opera and the visual arts

with his *History* by transcribing pieces of early sacred music into modern notation.[36] The omission of the famed composer from Edward's watercolor is explained by his role in the poetic "Trial of Midas." Boyce is assigned the role of judge over the real-life magistrate who dared practice as a historian and judge of music:

> To judge this self-elected Judge, the choice,
> Almost unanimously, fell on Boyce:
> A Man whose probity was bias proof,
> And Music, like his manners, bold and rough:
> In both, though new refinements he withstood,
> His Heart and harmony were sound and good;
> And, rank'd like him, the chief strains divine,
> 'Twas wise 'twixt Church and stage to draw a line.
> The Pris'ner's Friend he seem'd in former days,
> Before he had disgrac'd him by his praise.[37]

Many small details point to the source of Edward's inspiration. Amid that pile of useless and outdated books Edward illustrates is found STATE OF MUSIC AMONGST THE GOTHS AND VANDALS, a reference easily associated with Burney's lines:

> "Oh! Mighty Pow'r!" they cry "Whose active rays
> Pervade our minds as well as gild our days,
> Let not this remnant of the Iron Age
> Eternal war with Taste and Feeling wage;
> Nor try, unpunish'd Doctrines to restore
> Which damp'd thy fires, and shamed us heretofore;
> Again repel us to uncultur'd ground,
> Feed us on acorns after corn is found;
> To Second Childhood make us back return,
> And all the arts of Goths and Vandals Learn!"[38]

The image of the music of contemporary composers burning in the fireplace in Edward's watercolor finds parallel in Charles's lines that accuse Hawkins of being

> Eager with fire and faggot to pursue
> Whate'er is graceful, elegant, or new — [39]

Edward's image of the "NEW INVENTED SCALES for Judging of Music: N.B. The heavier the better" – scales on which one single neume representing the "black note" tradition on one side outweighs the tower of notes representing the contemporary ornamental style on the opposing side of the scale – mirrors a rhetorical image in his uncle's doggerel:

> While on her Blindness he himself [Hawkins] avails
> And with false weights contaminates her Scales?[40]

Similarly, common themes join Charles' text and Edward's visual treatment of Beethoven. He is shown straitjacketed and being carried off to Bedlam in the "Cart Rasoumoffsky" by the artist who could find inspiration in Charles's denunciation of Hawkins' treatment of contemporary composers in the lines of testimony spoken by the personification of TASTE:

> But He, with equal pride and Inconsistence,
> My Pow'r at once disclaim'd, and my existence:
> Treating with endless rancour, spleen and spite,
> All those my inspirations most delight,
> With whom, as Lunaticks, broke loose from cages,
> Or waistcoat-strait, eternal war he wages.[41]

The title of Edward's watercolor draws our attention to Hawkins as well. The tye-wig was not only a wig much out of fashion (and thus a clever and well-understood referent to the quaintness of the scene), it was also the wig worn by barristers, fellow practitioners of the law, Sir John's much-disparaged profession. The strong secondary themes of the *Amateurs of Tye-Wig Music* – the extensive references to Handel and to the Handel Commemoration – are also linked with Hawkins in Charles' poem:

> He thought ten thousand statues would be rais'd
> To him who with such fury Handel prais'd;
> But either Britons worship other Gods,
> Or else with Midas all are so at odds,
> That those he labours most to celebrate
> Become the Objects of the public hate;
> And even Handel's altars fainter blaze
> E'er since he damp'd their fires with fulsome praise.
> Handel! the mighty Saxon Chief sublime,
> Britannia's sons subdued a second time.[42]

Edward added his own ideas to the inspiration and imagery drawn from his uncle's work and in doing so he drew from the popular imagery of the satirical print. The presence of so many common themes associated with music in the satirical prints of the period and the density of the imagery overshadow and obscure the direct and indisputable references to Burney and Hawkins as the central protagonists in this representation of the critical dispute between advocates of conservative and progressive music. Once established as an inspiration and central theme, this relationship informs the interpretation of the work and its imagery and invites further speculation.

One curious and particularly strong image in the print is the lamp shown pendulating in the center of the room. It bears the name Dr. Faustus and the image of a conjurer. Swinging because it has been struck by a projectile, the lamp is a focal point defined by its centrality, by strong diagonal lines from the lower left of the watercolor, by the gesture of the boy's upstretched arms, and by other aspects of the design. The Faust reference strengthens the emphasis given to the lamp by the composition of the piece. Edward has resorted to labeling the lamp with a name and picture, an unusually straightforward technique in a work that is, overall, crafted with greater ingenuity. Patricia

Crown interprets the lamp with its label and image as a visual pun on the Composer Frederick Lampe and a reference to the old-fashioned genre of pantomime. The juxtaposition of this image with the references to angels and devils as well as with the picture of St. Cecilia suggest to her that the whole more or less illustrates the proverb: "To light a candle before the devil and a saint."[43] This is certainly no more improbable a speculation than one is tempted to make about any one of these allusions and may indeed reflect one of the multiplicity of interpretations that Edward supports with his imagery.

However, the literal labeling of the lamp suggests an interpretation in which Faust plays a more central and explicit role. The lamp swings because the spinning top, or "devil" from the diabolo, has crashed into it. By placing the interpretative emphasis not on the lamp itself but on the top that has crashed into it, the meaning of the image becomes apparent: it illustrates a proverb in which the meanings of both images are convincingly linked. Daniel Defoe tells readers in his *Political History of the Devil* that by 1726 "as great as the Devil and Dr. Foster [Faustus]" had become a proverb, one which Edward's image convincingly illustrates. The proverb suggests a stinging criticism of Hawkins for, "whereas Faustus was no doctor and knew no more of the Devil than another body," so Sir John Hawkins was no doctor (i.e., not a professor or professional musician, in contrast to Charles Burney, who was both) and knew no more of music than another body.[44] The aptness of this reading is evident throughout Burney's attacks on Hawkins in his "Trial of Midas" and elsewhere. Of Hawkins Burney wrote:

> Around Apollo's radiant throne, a crowd
> Has late assembled, clamorous and loud;
> Complaining of a certain Scribe malign;
> Unlicenc'd by the God, or Muse divine;
> Unauthoris'd by Judgment, Talents, Taste,
> Unprincipled in present lore or past;
> Without Ear to hear, or Soul to feel,
> Without a Mask his Malice to conceal;
> Who dared traduce his Sons of high renown,
> And try to blast each well-earn'd Lawrel crown;
> Denying all the feeling world allows
> Who bind with never fading wreaths their brows.[45]

Later in the poem, when Burney introduces a debate about who is to sit as judge in the trial of Hawkins, he has a personification of Madrigal

> Cry out, with brazen voice, and vacant face,
> "Let him by *Laws of Harmony* be tried" —
> — "No, No! he's no *Musician*," one and all replied;
> "Nor yet *Historian*, every wight can tell
> Who has tried to read his Book or learn'd to spell."[46]

The presence of the illustrated proverb, The Devil and Dr. Faustus, could, perhaps, be dismissed as merely one of a number of clever allusions. However, once decoded, the meaning of the proverb to the larger intention of the design of the work must be ascribed. Edward, throughout this watercolor, uses layers of obvious meaning to cloak more obscure and specific meanings. We can echo Charles Burney's own words by declaring that there is in the whole of the print "nothing visible... which may not metaphorically [be] said to be in *perfect tune with it.*"[47]

Edward has created a remarkable watercolor that can be enjoyed without special knowledge. Visually the piece is delightful. A moment spent considering the general theme of the piece reveals the level of meaning at which the artist's good-natured contempt for conservative musical taste and its advocates is apparent. With a bit of application and sufficient knowledge, the cleverness and learning of the artist can be seen and enjoyed as individual allusions and puns are recognized and, in their turn, make evident the subsidiary themes more specific to music and aesthetics. Finally, those familiar with the life and times of the prominent patriarch of the Burney family can experience a deeper, more intimate encounter with the work by reading the watercolor in the light of that knowledge. Edward's marvelous ingenuity results in a work that serves each audience well.

Amateurs of Tye-Wig Music yields its secrets only slowly and only to the informed and diligently curious. Interpretations, even those developed after laborious investigations, carry no final authority. Edward proffers such rich associative possibilities and such dense allusions throughout this work that the invitation to engage in associations apparent and speculative is everywhere in the image. Indeed, it is difficult to know when to stop, when to gauge the limits of Edward's ingenuity and the onset of apparent associations that result merely from coincidental relationships. The elaborate and learned style of the watercolor, so exceptional despite its dependence on the visual traditions of the popular satirical print, ultimately suggests that it was intended for viewers who shared the competence, knowledge, and predilection to appreciate the references to Burney, Hawkins, and the Handelians. In this way it is very much a visual counterpart to Burney's own elaborate treatment of his rivalry with Hawkins in the "Trial of Midas the Second." That work too is learned, carefully wrought, and sufficiently personal that it could circulate only among the family and confidants, and most likely only with the author as commentator.

We are reminded by this work of the complexity of the life of Charles Burney, a life only recently shown to be that of a complicated, conflicted man quite in contrast to the unified and mythic image developed in the biography written by his daughter. Burney made it his practice to reveal of himself only that which he wished others to know, and his daughter followed his practice. Edward Burney's watercolor displays the same care in revealing something of its meaning in direct, witty, stimulating images while withholding from casual observers more profound and complex meanings that yield truth only within the range of knowledge and intimacy of the observer with its subject.

NOTES

1 Notebook in the Osborn Collection at the Beinecke Library, Yale University. Quoted in Kerry S. Grant, *Dr. Charles Burney as Critic and Historian of Music* (Ann Arbor, 1983), p. 289.
2 CB to CB Jr, 25 February 1781. Quoted in *The Letters of Dr Charles Burney*, ed. Alvaro Ribiero (Oxford, 1991), p. 318. Abbreviations are expanded and missing letters provided without comment.
3 Burney's attempts to advance in the royal court are reviewed by Percy A. Scholes in *The Great Dr. Burney*, 2 vols. (Oxford, 1948), vol. 2, pp. 321–7. See also Roger Lonsdale, *Dr. Charles Burney: A Literary Biography* (Oxford, 1965), pp. 294–5, 315, 319–22.
4 He was relieved only somewhat by the appointment granted to his daughter, Fanny, as "Second Keeper of the Robes to Her Majesty" in June of 1786, an appointment which, as Roger Lonsdale has convincingly argued, was "offered as some sort of consolation for Burney's previous disappointments." For a useful discussion of Burney's relationship to the court, see Lonsdale, pp. 292–346.
5 Only two works of little influence were written outside of this period – his biography of Metastasio and his articles on music for the *Cyclopædia* of Abraham Rees, the former scarcely read, the latter hardly known.
6 The preference for Handel's music was only one manifestation of a broad aesthetic schism in the musical audience between those favoring ancient music and those who saw progress and increasing refinement in contemporary music. Two forms of ancient music were commonly discussed. One, the music of the Greeks, Romans, and other early cultures, was largely a matter of interest to theorists, historians, and philosophers because only descriptions remained of the actual sound of this music. Burney could, and did, dismiss the proponents of this music. He was, however, required to treat this subject at considerable length and with some respect in his *History of Music* because of the strong interest of an important segment of his readership.
   The other music commonly referred to as ancient music was that embraced by the Concerts of Ancient Music, which as a rule programmed only music at least twenty years old. In practice, this could and did lead to concerts of music that was extensively or even exclusively Handel's. It was the votaries of this form of ancient music who caused Burney the greatest difficulty.
7 John Hawkins, *A General History of the Science and Practice of Music* (London, 1776; reprinted New York, 1963), vol. 2, p. 919.
8 Grant, *Dr. Burney as Critic and Historian of Music*, p. 45.
9 See Lonsdale, *Dr. Charles Burney*, pp. 209–19.
10 Ibid., p. 231.
11 Ibid., p. 302.
12 Roger Lonsdale first drew attention to the duress Burney felt when writing about Handel in his exhaustive reconstruction of Burney's biography which drew on an enormous cache of formerly unknown manuscripts and letters. The extent to which the influence of the Handelians caused Burney to prevaricate in his critical and historical essays on Handel was revealed by the study of Burney's work as a historian, in light of these same documents and the results reported in Grant, *Dr. Burney as Critic and Historian of Music*.

E. F. Burney's Amateurs of Tye-Wig Music

13 Watercolor with pen and black ink over pencil on wove paper. 19 3/16 × 28 5/16 in. The work is housed in the Yale Center for British Art, Paul Mellon Collection. Permission to reproduce the work is gratefully acknowledged as is the assistance of the staff at the Center.
14 Patricia Crown has studied this watercolor and three others with musical subjects in "Edward F. Burney: An Historical Study in English Romantic Art," Ph.D. dissertation, University of California, Los Angeles, 1977. In this work and in a valuable article, "Visual Music: E. F. Burney and a Hogarth Revival," in the *Bulletin of Research in the Humanities* 83 (1980): 435–72, she provides detailed assessments of the artistic qualities of the artworks and an instructive gloss of many of the visual puns.
15 *Il Barbiere di Siviglia* was first produced in London in 1818. However, benefits for the composer were first held in 1824 during Rossini's visit to London. See William C. Smith, *The Italian Opera and Contemporary Ballet in London, 1789–1820* (London, 1955) and Herbert Weinstock, *Rossini: A Biography* (New York, 1968), pp. 138–9.
16 *Brewer's Dictionary of Phrase and Fable*, 14th edn, ed. Ivor H. Evans (New York, 1989), p. 959.
17 John S. Farmer, *Historical Dictionary of Slang*, 2 vols. (London, 1987), vol. 2, p. 247.
18 See Emily Nevill Jackson, *Toys of Other Days* (London, 1908) and Gwen White, *Antique Toys and Their Background* (London, 1971), pp. 130–1.
19 Farmer, *Historical Dictionary of Slang*, vol. 2, p. 278.
20 Francis Grose, *Dictionary of the Vulgar Tongue* (London, 1811).
21 Several hundred prints with arts themes are housed in the extensive collections of the British Library and British Museum, the Victoria and Albert Museum, the Lewis Walpole Library, the Yale Center for British Art, the Library of Congress, the Henry E. Huntington Library, and the New York Public Library. I am grateful to the curators and librarians of those institutions for their assistance in the preparation of this study. I gratefully acknowledge research grants from the University of Nebraska at Lincoln and the State University of New York at Buffalo.
22 John Locke wrote in *Some Thoughts Concerning Education*, "Musik wastes so much of a young Man's time, to gain but a moderate Skill in it, and engages often in such odd Company, that many think it much better spared: And I have, amongst Men of Parts and Business, so seldom heard any one commended, or esteemed for having an Excellency in Musick, that amongst all those things that ever came into the List of Accomplishments, I think I may give it the last place." See Richard Leppert, *Music and Image: Domesticity, Ideology and Socio-Cultural Formation in Eighteenth-Century England* (Cambridge and New York, 1988), p. 17.
23 From *The Graces*, "Chesterfield's Principles of Politeness." Courtesy of the Print Collection, Lewis Walpole Library, Yale University.
24 Herbert M. Atherton, *Political Prints in the Age of Hogarth: A Study of the Ideographic Representation of Politics* (Oxford, 1974), p. 267.
25 Farmer, *Historical Dictionary of Slang*, vol. 1, p. 66.
26 She also finds a resemblance to Bononcini in the other performers and suggests that the resemblances are meant to reflect the famous comparison of Handel and Bononcini with Tweedledum and Tweedledee. "Visual Music," p. 458.
27 Farmer, *Historical Dictionary of Slang*, vol. 1, p. 154.
28 Jubal was the inventor of musical instruments according to Genesis 4:21.

29 Burney states that the absence of a conductor "either with a roll of paper, or a noisy baton or truncheon" was remarkable given the great size of the performing forces. The reference makes the presence of the figure, already anachronistic given the chamber setting of the performance, even more absurd. Burney notes that "*Walther, in his Musical Lexicon*, 1732, styles him [Handel] 'a very celebrated maestro di cappella,'" *Account of the Commemoration of Handel* (London, 1785), pp. 14, 55.
30 Hawkins, *A General History of Music*, vol. 2, p. 622.
31 Ibid., vol. 1, p. 266.
32 Lonsdale, *Dr. Charles Burney*, p. 205.
33 Canto II, 71–8. All quotations from the poem are taken from Sister M. Ignatia Griffin, BVM, "*The Trial of Midas the Second or Congress of Musicians* by Dr Charles Burney, 1777," Ph.D. dissertation, Fordham University, 1962.
34 Late in 1777 Burney showed his poem to Mrs. Thrale, who noted in her journal that it contained "strokes of satire well express'd with great fertility of Allusion too and his personified Characters of Science, Wit and Taste, are as happily finished as 'tis possible ... The Portrait of Science is drawn with a masterly hand a Painter might paint from it." *Thraliana: The Diary of Mrs. Hester Lynch Thrale (later Mrs. Piozzi) 1776–1809*, 2 vols. (Oxford, 1951), vol. 1, pp. 217–18.
35 Canto III, 221–4.
36 Bertram Hylton Davis, *A Proof of Eminence: The Life of Sir John Hawkins* (Bloomington, Ind., 1973), pp. 47–9.
37 Canto II, 45–54.
38 Canto I, 115–24.
39 Canto I, 95–6.
40 Canto I, 73–4.
41 Canto II, 227–32.
42 Canto II, 311–20.
43 Crown, "Visual Music," p. 459.
44 *The Oxford Dictionary of English Proverbs*, ed. J. A. Simpson (Oxford, 1970) also cites Defoe, *Review*, vol. 3, no. 81 (1706), p. 323, and Fielding, *Tom Jones*, bk. 18, ch. 8. This artwork has prompted many conversations with colleagues who have shared valuable insights and helpful critiques. I am particularly grateful to Dr. William Warner of the State University of New York at Buffalo.
45 Canto I, 15–26.
46 Canto II, 34–8.
47 *Commemoration of Handel*, p. 9.

4

New light(s) on Weber's Wolf's Glen Scene

ANTHONY NEWCOMB

> Sie werden hundertmal gehört haben, dass man nach
> Lesung eines guten Romans gewünscht hat, den
> Gegenstand auf dem Theater zu sehen, und wieviel
> schlechte Dramen sind daher entstanden! Ebenso wollen
> die Menschen jede interessante Situation gleich in Kupfer
> gestochen sehen, damit nur ja ihrer Imagination keine
> Tätigkeit übrigbleibe, so soll alles sinnlich wahr,
> vollkommen gegenwärtig, dramatisch sein und das
> Dramatische selbst soll sich dem wirklich Wahren völlig an
> die Seite stellen. Diesen eigentlich kindischen,
> barbarischen, abgeschmackten Tendenzen sollte nun der
> Künstler aus allen Kräften widerstehn.[1]
>
> Goethe to Schiller, from Weimar, 23 December 1797

The evolution of Weber's *Freischütz* according to the currently available documents has been traced with admirable thoroughness, if with now unadmired national polemics, in Georg Schünemann's introduction to the facsimile edition of the manuscript of the score.[2] The present essay concerns only one scene from the opera, albeit a famous one. It proposes that the influential Wolf's Glen Scene echoes and plays upon a group of popular entertainments rooted in the fertile terrain that Goethe was trying to put beyond the pale. These entertainments, which I shall call paratheatrical, arose out of the intersection in the entrepreneurial market of burgeoning technology, fostered by science and the Industrial Revolution, and the insatiable appetite for diversion of the growing urban middle class. As Goethe remarks above, the tastes that went with this appetite were not always the most sophisticated. The most striking instances – balloon rides, Madame Tussaud's wax gallery, the panorama, the phantasmagoria – were not considered high art.[3] Nonetheless, they were popular and commercially lucrative, they fascinated the contemporary public and press, and their descendants survive in Disneyland, Great America, and the movie industry. The last line of ancestry is particularly clear with the phantasmagoria, whose birth and growth in the late 1790s and early 1800s I propose as the source for many distinctive elements in Weber's Wolf's Glen Scene. But I should straightaway say that the phantasmagoria can be directly connected to the genesis of Weber's scene only by circumstantial evidence.

The phantasmagoria was invented by the scientist-inventor Etienne-

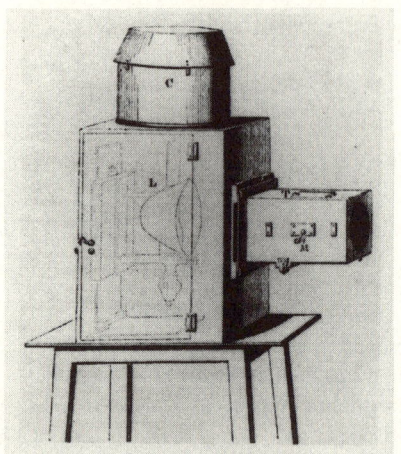 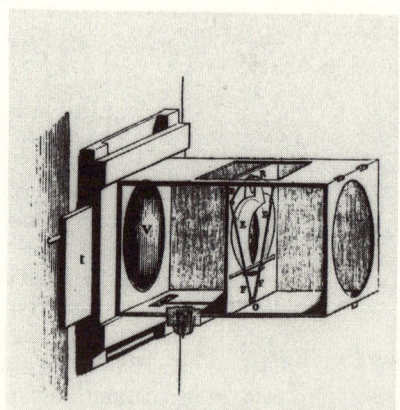

Plate 6 Fantascope invented by Etienne-Gaspard Robertson for producing projections in his phantasmagoria.

Gaspard Robertson (born E.-G. Robert in Liège in 1763) and first presented to the public in Paris in March 1798.[4] The show used a refinement of the magic lantern (the ancestor of the modern slide projector), invented by the polymath Athanasius Kircher in the mid-seventeenth century (see Plate 6). The refinement made ghosts appear, move about, and disappear in a darkened room before forty to sixty spectators. Although Robertson in his memoirs claimed that his aim was to demonstrate the scientific methods for producing these supposedly supernatural effects and tried to present his shows as a rationalistic debunking of the magical-religious hoodwinking of previous generations, Terry Castle sees Robertson's shows as an outlet for the need for mystery and the supernatural denied by enlightened secular rationality in the Napoleonic age.

In any case, the secular government of France used a political incident in the latter part of 1798 to shut down Robertson's increasingly popular shows in Paris, whence he moved his activities to Bordeaux for approximately a year. Upon his return to Paris he found that his assistant had set up shop using what Robertson describes as a shabby imitation of his methods. Robertson responded by establishing himself in a spectacularly apposite new location near Place Vendôme – an abandoned chapel in the middle of the cloister of the former Capucin convent. Its burial monuments had been violated and removed by the masters of the Revolution, adding to the potential for ghostly displeasure and return.

Robertson's shows were an immediate and clamorous success, and their fame spread rapidly. By late 1801 or early 1802, the phantasmagoria had been brought to London by the Frenchman Paul de Philipstal. It played downstairs in the Lyceum, which soon became known as the Phantascopic Theatre after Robertson's name for his projection machine. In London as in Paris, the show was an immediate hit. As Richard Altick points out, it satisfied the "popular relish for managed spectral visitations" in this age of best-selling Gothic novels. Even the newly sensational panorama playing upstairs, although it was a recent British invention of established drawing power, had now to advertise the insertion of "spectral raisings" in order to compete.[5]

The panorama and the phantasmagoria came rapidly to dominate the entertainment (as opposed to the artistic) life of the two major capitals of Europe, London, and Paris. For example, a certain F. J. L. Meyer of Hamburg reported from Paris in 1802:

> This formerly closed locus of penance and monastic devotion [the large garden and cloister of the former Capucin nuns] has been transformed into a public playground of laughter and excited curiosity. Here Robertson scares people with his spectral raisings... And in the old walkways of the cloister – in its halls, arcades, and refectories – coffee houses, restaurants, and furniture showrooms and the like are set up. In the evening, garden and cloister are illuminated and full of people. Outside in the garden the two panoramas of Paris and Toulon are to be found. These and Robertson's illusionistic games are the things here most worth seeing.[6]

This description gives an accurate idea of the kind of physical and social surroundings in which the panorama and phastasmagoria appeared. In the general journals of culture and fashion of early nineteenth-century Germany, one does not find the panorama mentioned in the sections on "Kunst," although it was a kind of illusionistic painting of the most demanding sort, nor does one find the phantasmagoria mentioned under "Theater," although the *spéctacles* of Robertson and his imitators derived from and had much in common with certain theatrical representations. Where I have found the phantasmagoria described is in accounts of social affairs, parties, and gossip in the big cities ("Fragmente aus Paris," "Berichte aus London," and so on), or in accounts of large urban seasonal fairs in Germany.

As the title of Oettermann's recent book on the panorama – *Das Panorama: Die Geschichte eines Massenmediums* – suggests, panorama and phantasmagoria belonged rather to the world of mass entertainment than of high art. Although Robertson's meticulously prepared and polished shows were attended by the highest levels of Parisian societies, the spectators did not approach with the reverence paid to the Comédie Française or the salons. Moreover, Robertson's imitators were not always so careful in their standards of production, nor were their audiences so elevated. A report on the phantasmagoria from the *Journal des Luxus und der Mode* of 1803 is typical in its tone of superiority and gentle derision:

> On the boulevards I wandered into the booths (*Buden*) of so-called experimental physics... One fellow tugged people by the sleeve into his

darkened room, where he produced by means of optical experiments a host of phantasms, which disappeared all too quickly before the eyes of a public that was as if in ecstasy.[7]

Even an enthusiastic report of what seems to be one of Robertson's shows published in the *Zeitung für die elegante Welt* of 1806 reveals the same defensiveness about the respectability of the phantasmagoria. It begins by assuring the reader that "alles ist dort auf einen sehr guten Ton eingerichtet." In the first room "the greatest variety of tools of modern physics were displayed," a comment recalling Robertson's care to maintain the connection of his "experiments" with the prestige of modern science. In fact, in the introductory rooms, he often did experiments in Galvanism, in which he was also interested, making the limbs of dead animals move.[8] After this introduction, the report continues,

> one is led into the second, darkened room, to the *Fantasmagorie*; the most beautiful for eyes and ears is the representation of a thunderstorm, in which the crossing flashes of lightning strike a villain, who then slowly fades into the distance, leaving only the rushing noise of the rain.

There follows the repeated assurance that all this is done in a "very elegant room" [*sehr elegantes Lokal*], into which choice perfumes are discreetly introduced, so that "one gladly extends one's stay with the much traveled aeronautic family" (a comment which I take to be a reference to Robertson's growing fame for balloon rides, both as a locus of scientific experiment and as a lucrative commercial attraction for a paying public).[9]

The particular scenario described by the correspondent is only one of the repertoire of favorites that can be compiled from contemporary journals and memoirs. (Richard Altick quotes another description by the famous British scientist Sir David Brewster on pp. 217–18 of *The Shows of London*.) The most complete single list (with descriptions) of scenarios that I have found is in Robertson's own *Mémoires récréatifs*, where he sometimes quotes in turn from contemporary journals. It is in reading these descriptions that the close kinship with Weber's Wolf's Glen Scene emerges most clearly.

One description, quoted by Robertson from the journal *L'Ami des lois* of 28 March 1798, tells of the successive raisings of several famous specters. The scenario for each raising is roughly the same. The master of ceremonies (as we shall call him) pours on a glowing brazier some appropriate liquids or powders (for Marat: two small glasses of blood, a bottle of vitriol, twelve drops of nitric acid, and two copies of the journal *Hommes-Libres*; for a dead loved one: sparrow feathers, a few grains of phosphorus and a dozen butterflies; and so on); he pronounces appropriate incantatory words; the various figures rise up, advance upon the audience, retreat into a point of light and reemerge in a transformed guise. Another newspaper report of November 1798 from Bordeaux specifies the subject of one scenario as the raising of the ghost of Samuel before Saul by the Witch of Endor, a model for the conjuring up of Samiel in the Wolf's Glen Scene.[10]

Saul and the Witch of Endor soon became one of the favorites in the repertoire of the phantasmagoria. Others include:

- a witches' sabbath, in which midnight bells toll; the moon decends; cats, bats, and will-o'-the-wisps flitter across the screen; a witch sits and brews beside a magic circle; others fly across the sky on brooms; and a hermit finally appears to exorcize the scene;
- a dream sequence composed of various *tableaux fantastiques* and demonic happenings;
- *La Nonne sanglante* (based on M. G. Lewis's famous Gothic novel *The Monk* of 1796);
- a temptation of Saint Anthony (a sequence of brief scenes, described by Robertson in some detail);
- a dance of death after Holbein.[11]

Not all of Robertson's subjects were horrifying: he also did a "Birth of Love" and various transfigurations and apotheoses of heroic or legendary figures. But for the general audience, as well as for our purposes concerning the Wolf's Glen Scene, the ghostly and demonic scenarios were the distinctive and memorable ones.

The important innovation is this: the phantasmagoria brought to this well-worn body of dream images, ghosts, and demons the ability rapidly to make them visually present by mysterious means in the midst of a darkened room; the ability to make them move, advance, recede, and undergo transformations; and the ability to make these scenes succeed each other in a rapid series of changing images.[12]

Robertson explained his methods in great detail in his memoirs. He brought several innovations to Kircher's magic lantern – projections of objects or transparencies with lenses and mirrors. Some of these innovations had to do with the presentation of the show itself. He projected his images usually on a semi-transparent muslin screen dropped in front of the spectators after the room had been darkened. He occasionally created the impression of phantoms floating in the room itself by projecting images on clouds of steam released into the room (hence our expression, "done with smoke and mirrors"). He removed the projector from the spectators' view, putting it behind the screen or in hidden upper recesses of the chapel (see Plate 7). He put the projector on wheels and rails, hooking the wheels up with an ingenious mechanism for changing the focus of the lens, thus enabling his images to grow and shrink (advance and recede). He worked out a two-bladed metal shutter of cat's eye-like design to diminish and increase the light evenly across the picture (thus inventing the proto-dimmer – see Plate 6). He used this together with multiple projectors to get both superimposed projections and gradual fade of one projection into another without a distracting blank zone in between. He switched scenes often. He usually projected some sort of painted slide (whose frames, like those of the panorama, should never be visible to the viewer), but he also had methods for projecting real objects.

Plate 7 Drawing of one of Robertson's presentations.

In his memoirs, Robertson touched several times on the importance of sound effects for his shows. Sometimes this involved complicated machines for counterfeiting the noise of rain (see the description of 1806 above) or wind or thunder. But oftentimes it involved musical instruments as well. Robertson's favorite was the newly invented glass harmonica.[13] In default of the glass harmonica, the *célestine* was best, after which came "wind instruments, especially horns." The other instruments that he used "with discretion" for special effects were the tamtam, or Chinese gong, and the large funeral bell.[14]

Robertson's methods, subject to imitation from the beginning, were disclosed in complete detail as part of a lawsuit involving his former assistant. This lawsuit would seem from Robertson's account to have taken place in 1806, although he does not name a precise date. After this, says Robertson with some proud hyperbole, phantasmagoria "de toutes les classes" became very common; "machines à fantômes" were sent all over Europe, and everyone had his phantasmagoria, although most, he says, could not run them properly.[15]

What has this to do with Weber's Wolf's Glen Scene? It is not my hypothesis that Weber intended to reproduce the precise methods of the phantasmagoria. For technical reasons (especially the size of the room and the strength of available lights), he could not have done so directly. My hypothesis is that he tried to reproduce its effects, and that he knew these effects well, probably even by the time he began to consider the possibility of a Freischütz opera in 1810.[16] Weber was, after all, a bright young man trying to make his way in the German world of society and entertainment, and the new high-technology, paratheatrical entertainments seem to have penetrated into this world as quickly and deeply as they did into that of France and England.

German fascination with the panorama and phantasmagoria could be predicted, if for no other reason than that German city dwellers of the early nineteenth century looked to London and Paris as the models for sophisticated living. (One of their foremost society magazines was called, simply, *London und Paris*.) In fact, the panorama arrived in Germany soon after it arrived in France. The first German panorama was installed by 1801; its rapid spread is traced in Oettermann's fascinating book.[17]

Clear traces of the phantasmagoria in Germany in the first decade of the nineteenth century can be found in the general cultural journals of the time. One visitor to the Frankfurt fair of May 1805 first reports on the business people exhibiting their wares, moves on to the *Komödie*, then to shows [*Buden*]. Among these last were "the invisible girl" – a ventriloquism act done by an Englishman whom Robertson (pp. 228ff.) claims to have discovered – circus acrobats, stone eaters, and "die Phantasmagorie des Sieur Michel de Paris." By the description this seems to have been a pretty primitive show, though perhaps the correspondent, "Pastor Walther", was not the most sympathetic audience.[18] A report of the Leipzig St. Michael's Fair of December 1805 remarks that the "ghostly appearances [*Geistererscheinungen*] announced on the first day" failed to take place because the entrepreneur, together with the evening's receipts, disappeared permanently "in front of the angry public." Indicative of the context is that an act done by a trained horse was substituted in its place on the next night.[19] At the summer fair in Munich, as part of a group of shows similar to that at the Frankfurt fair of 1805, the correspondent described a series of what he calls "transformations" that seem clearly to have been done by Robertson's methods.[20] To cite further evidence of the German connection, Robertson himself reported that the best painter of glass transparencies for his shows was a miniaturist that he encountered while in Berlin.[21] Robertson also shows up at the Leipzig Easter fair, in a report of musical events there: "But too bad! the first of these concerts was very little attended because of the promised [*verheissenen*] balloon ride of Professor Robertson, which was not realized [*erfüllten*] because of the weather."[22]

I have not found as much on the phantasmagoria in Germany as Oettermann and Buddemeier do on the panorama, and the traces that I have turned up are oblique ones by and large, rather than the direct, more extensive reports given of the panorama by them. This may be because I have not searched enough, and because no one has undertaken a history of the phantasmagoria that might guide me. But I have the impression that the phantasmagoria was present as much as the panorama, although not remarkable enough to receive mention in these journals, unless some unusual surrounding event brought it up. As the reason for this, I would propose certain contrasts between phantasmagoria and panorama – contrasts that may account for the difference of treatment in the press, and that may well have something to do with the reception of Weber's Wolf's Glen Scene.

The panorama was a monumental affair, requiring a large investment of time and capital, a specially designed, usually free-standing display space, and a huge oil painting on canvas; the phantasmagoria in its most basic form, as Robertson pointed out above, requires relatively simple equipment, a few small painted slides, and can only be viewed in a darkened room of modest size. The panorama proclaimed itself a triumph of realistic depiction of the external, physical world – a fit reflection of the nineteenth-century public ambitions; the phantasmagoria presented ephemeral illusions based in the supernatural world – equally necessary as entertainment, but less publicly applauded as cultural enterprise. Finally, the artistic standards of the panorama, if we are to believe early nineteenth-century reports, were very high. For example, the famous architect-painter-city planner-stage director Karl Friedrich Schinkel founded his reputation and his fortune in Berlin as a panorama painter in the years 1807 to 1815. The materials of the phantasmagoria, painted in tiny dimensions and blown up by the projector, were probably not as rewarding, according to the usual aesthetic criteria.

Still, the advantages were not all on the side of the panorama. The phantasmagoria alone could provide what sensitive viewers found to be a cardinal shortcoming in the panorama's attempt at realism – and that was movement, the illusion of temporality. In the case of the panorama, if one were supposed to be standing atop the dome of St. Paul's Cathedral viewing the bustling city below, how was it that the many carts or horses or people there were not moving? The objections of a correspondent from the *Zeitung für die elegante Welt* of July 1806 are typical: "The goal of a panorama is to create an illusion and to transport one into the world represented. Ah! then how disturbing are those figures – frozen as if by Oberon's horn!"[23]

I propose that the possibilities brought forward by the phantasmagoria – not only for *Geistererscheinungen* but for movement and quick transformation – suggested to Weber a novel way to stage the traditional scene from the folk tale of the bargain with occult forces – and to reinforce its visual images and rapid temporal shifts with music. It was, of course, these rapid temporal shifts and the visual immediacy that caused the phantasmagoria to return triumphantly to conquer the twentieth century, even if the panorama outlasted the phantasmagoria as a public show in the nineteenth.[24]

It is an additional irony that, although these two distinctively early nineteenth-century shows – marriages of culture, mass entertainment, and technology – seem to have made a large impression on the public of the time, virtually all actual artifacts connected with both have disappeared. Jac Remise claims to reproduce a few slides from Robertson's shows (see Plate 8 for a representative example), but he gives no authority for his claims.[25] One of the very few surviving early nineteenth-century panorama paintings, of the Versailles gardens done in America by a relative amateur, has recently been unearthed from the basements of the Metropolitan Museum in New York and installed in a special room of the new American wing.

How did Weber in fact use the effects suggested by the phantasmagoria for

New light(s) on Weber's Wolf's Glen Scene

Plate 8 Slide projection for a phantasmagoria, attributed to Etienne-Gaspard Robertson. Jac Remise, *Magie lumineuse* (n. p., 1979).

his version of the Wolf's Glen Scene? The happenings before Max arrives, though many elements from them appear in phantasmagoria scenarios recounted by Robertson, might also have occurred in an opéra comique libretto and production of 1790–1820. After this, rapid appearance and disappearance in the midst of the stage and the movement of the appearances takes us into a distinctively phantasmagoric world. The bullet casting itself brings an even faster tempo of appearance, disappearance, and change of scene, leading to the explosive conclusion: it is pure phantasmagoria.

Though previous staged versions of the Freischütz tale all have some version of the bullet-casting scene, none features the rapid succession of highly contrasting images, nor their appearance and disappearance in the midst of the

Opera and the visual arts

stage itself (as opposed to visibly moving on and off it), such as we find in the Weber–Kind version. The most recent predecessor for Weber's version for which an actual text survives (as opposed to a notice or review in a newspaper) is the Franz von Caspar "romantische Tragödie" *Der Freischütze* of 1812–13, in five acts with music by the Munich composer Carl Neuner.[26] The parallel to the Wolf's Glen Scene here is Act 4, Scenes 1–5, especially the preparation for the bullet-casting, done as a large pantomime in Scene 4 (Mayerhofer, p. 41). There is a stage machine (a snake crawls out of a hollow tree), wind machines howl, and real figures in ghostly costumes move on and off stage by the usual means (a grave opens and a figure wrapped in a shroud comes out, presumably by the common trapdoor mechanism; gremlins wrapped in gauze dance on and off the stage; the Max figure is led on by a *graue Gestalt*, who then leaves). The bullet casting itself never occurs, since the Agathe figure appears and breaks the devilish spell. And this is as "realistic" (perhaps "visually explicit" is a better phrase) as any stage depiction that one knows of until the Weber–Kind version of 1821.[27]

I say Weber–Kind. Although the libretto of the 1821 *Freischütz* is given as by Friedrich Kind, considerable evidence points to Weber as the one who conceived the design and details of the Wolf's Glen Scene. Throughout the ten-day period in which the libretto of the opera was drafted, Weber reports long conferences with Kind about it.[28] After he had sent the completed draft to Caroline Brandt and she had recommended doing away with the original opening scenes between Agathe and the Hermit, Weber wrote back to Caroline:

> I went to Kind [about 10 a.m.] and we worked on *Der Jägersbraut* [at that time the name of the opera] until 1 o'clock. Now, I hope it will look different, and it will certainly be very effective. The end as well will be somewhat different and better... Kind is now reviewing it, and then I shall do so.[29]

Small changes continued to be made in the libretto until copies were prepared in June. Even after this, Weber shortened and tightened the Caspar–Samiel dialog at the beginning of the scene with alterations in his own hand.[30] Later he was to write to his friend Hinrich Lichtenstein in Berlin:

> I can well believe that you can't make heads or tails out of many things in *Freischütz*. There are things in it that have never been presented on the stage in this way – which I had therefore to create entirely out of my own imagination, without the slightest adherence to precedent.[31]

That the ghostly appearances [*Erscheinungen*] of the Wolf's Glen Scene were among those things is suggested by Kind's public reaction to them when the opera was first presented in Dresden in January 1822. He wrote that poetry and works for the stage should represent "those mysterious [ghostly] forces in as unspecific a manner as possible," avoiding such things as "horrible images distorted to the point of repugnance."[32] Wolfgang Becker's study of Weber's stewardship of the Dresden Opera stresses that Weber took a quite opposite point of view. Partly out of a felt need to capture a broad audience for his new

German Opera Theater through striking theatrical effects, but also partly out of a genuine enthusiasm for these effects in the French opéras comiques that he had admired throughout his career, Weber insisted on the need for a maximum amount of realistic depiction of the mysterious, the spooky, and the titillating.[33] At first the official Dresden theater world resisted, according to Becker (pp. 151–2), but by 1826 the power of Weber's productions and the spine-tinglingly realistic singing and acting of Wilhemine Schröder-Devrient had converted the critics and drawn in a broad and enthusiastic public.

One of the clearest indications of Weber's personal involvement in the design of the Wolf's Glen Scene is the sheet of directions, written in his own hand, apparently as a guide to the coming Dresden premiere.[34] I have translated and commented on these directions in Appendix I; one resonance in an important theatrical encyclopedia of this entire episode is translated in Appendix II.

Clearly there is nothing "unspecific" about the manner in which these "mysterious forces" are to be presented. They are presented with the maximum visual realism attainable with the technological resources available, drawing, I believe, on the precedents and images of the phantasmagoria of the popular fairs. Technologically, one could not translate the methods of the phantasmagoria directly onto the much larger opera stages of Berlin and Dresden, first of all because there were not lamps bright enough to permit such magnification of a slide. (Recall that phantasmagoria were always done in a small darkened room, for an audience of no more than forty to sixty people.) Weber counterfeited similar effects with imaginative bits of lighting behind semi-transparent screens and with painted front-lighted figures sewn on screens and waved about from above.[35]

When Weber arrived in Berlin in early May 1821 to begin rehearsals for the premiere in June, he encountered in the set designers there a starkly different view from his own of how the Wolf's Glen Scene should be represented – a view seemingly much closer to Kind's. This led to "the most outspoken differences of opinion" between Weber and the set designer (Carl Wilhelm) Gropius (1793–1870), who was working "under the direct supervision of [Karl Friedrich] Schinkel" (*unter den Augen Schinkels*).[36] Schinkel was the chief set designer for both court theaters in Berlin; as architect, city planner, painter, and theatrical designer, he was already one of the most powerful and respected members of Berlin's artistic establishment. The struggle between Schinkel-Gropius and Weber over the production of the Wolf's Glen Scene merits a parenthesis here, for it encapsulates a basic opposition in German theater of the time. The parenthesis will lead us back via Wagner to Weber's own concern about the reception of the phantasmagoric elements in the scene.

The issue can be reduced to two differing fundamental views of the representation of actions, especially supernatural actions, on stage. One view says that content and setting should be represented as realistically as possible, such that the action on stage is not a symbolic representation of the action, but rather a presentation of the happening itself. A second says that the stage action

Opera and the visual arts

is a symbolic representation of the happening, and the stage set is a symbolic evocation of the world in which the happening is situated.[37] The first view was associated with and characteristic of popular theater, the second of theater for higher social levels (cf. the quote by Goethe at the outset of this essay). In this dilemma, Weber clearly sided with the first view, Schinkel-Gropius-Kind with the second. Max Maria von Weber (presumably using as source his father's diaries) reports as follows about the collision of the two views in May 1821:

> Here Gropius wanted to represent the horrors as derived from a battle of elemental forces and the ghostly as born out of the imaginations of Caspar and Max, and to evoke these horrors and ghosts in the souls of the spectators only through suggestion. Weber, on the other hand, was for letting loose a real, well-designed witches' sabbath... "Your intentions are too subtle for the opera", he said to Gropius. "They would be fine for *Hamlet* or *Macbeth*. But who is going to be able to match up your [proposed suggestions of] faces in the rocks and images in the clouds with the hellish spectacle of my music? Make the eyes of the owl really glow, and real bats flutter about; don't be afraid of a couple of ghosts and skeletons. Just make sure that there is an effective crescendo in the bullet-casting scene."[38]

As one can see from Weber's detailed instructions (Appendix I) he then set about to design his own phantasmagoria for the scene, "a real witches' sabbath" indeed.[39]

It may seem a strange paradox that Schinkel – the opponent of realism in the case of *Freischütz* – was an advocate and practitioner of the panorama, on whose success he built his early career and fortune.[40] The panorama, after all, was based on maximum realism and the perfection of illusion – precisely what Schinkel rejected for these stage designs. The difference, it would seem, was twofold. First, the panorama did not treat the supernatural world; second, the panorama was not theater, it was a *populäres Schaustück*. The importation of these effects into the theater was what Goethe, Schinkel, Gropius, and the like found objectionable.

In the view of modern theater historians, E. T. A. Hoffmann belonged to the Schinkel–Gropius camp as well. Both studies on Schinkel cited earlier (in note 36) invoke Hoffmann to this effect, without giving a precise source.[41] Hoffmann's "Seltsame Leiden eines Theaterdirektors" (dated Berlin, October 1818, though written earlier) certainly supports this view. When the two directors in this dialog come to the subject of stage designs (*Dekorationen*), the more authoritative ("Der Braune") complains bitterly:

> Our theaters have become panoramas and optical shows, in which one peddles dances, fights, horses, fire- and waterworks, and all kinds of fakirs' side-shows. And the masses flock to *see* all this, while one can no longer attract them through dramatic *acting*... Nothing is more ridiculous than to bring the spectator to the point where he, without needing to contribute anything from his own imagination, actually believes in the painted palaces, trees, and rocks ... First and foremost must one avoid with great care everything unseemly;

then must one rely on a deep understanding of the genuinely fantastic, which will work upon and free up the fantasy of the spectator. The stage set should not itself, as an independent striking image, attract the eye of the spectator. Rather the spectator should come to feel, as the action progresses and without being aware of it, the effect of the stage set in which the action takes place.[42]

I mention Hoffmann's place in this debate because he was a friend and near contemporary of Weber's, and because his long-supposed authorship of a famous series of reviews of the Berlin premiere of *Freischütz* has recently been questioned.[43] The reviews are critical not mainly of Weber's music, which the reviewer calls the best since Mozart and *Fidelio*, but of the current theater's fascination with demons, hellish horrors, and invocations of the devil. About the Wolf's Glen Scene he says that it is a great display piece for the scene designer and the *Maschinisten*. As a result there is too much distraction for the eye, and the ear can scarcely follow the "duster-wilden Musikstücken." He says he cannot fathom the composer's intentions in this scene: "a musical scene like this has never and nowhere been written." His reaction to the music, then, is more puzzlement than rejection; it is the style of the staging that he objects to. Whoever wrote the anonymous review, it is not in disagreement with Hoffmann's views as expressed in the "Seltsame Leiden."[44]

The importance of *Freischütz* in general and the Wolf's Glen Scene in particular for Wagner's early career especially has long been recognized.[45] Wagner, too, was caught between these two fundamental views of the representation of actions on stage. On the one hand, he wanted for the theatrical experience the kind of symbolic distance and elevated quality of the Schinkel-Hoffmann camp, and he advocated this repeatedly in his writings. On the other hand, the practical man of the theater in him wanted the kind of raw theatrical effectiveness and drawing power that the new technologies could bring. In his actual stage directions, he repeatedly had recourse to striking stage effects and a high degree of visual realism. The appearance of the phantom ship in versions of *The Flying Dutchman* antecedent to Wagner's was a well-known phantasmagoric effect in London melodramas already in the 1820s.[46] *Siegfried* especially has a number of phantasmagoric effects. And the Bayreuth production of even such an elevated symbolic drama as *Parsifal* used for the *Verwandlung* in the first act the techniques of the "pleorama" – a panoramic painting that was installed on large rollers and unrolled past the spectator, such that he or she seemed to be moving through the scenery.[47]

Detailed directions on how to stage such things are not usually to be found in scores or librettos. For Weber, as for Wagner after him, there were two principal drawbacks to writing such technically innovative stage effects into the fundamental fabric of one's operas. First, it made the operas difficult to produce for theaters of limited technical resources. Second, the techniques originated in and were associated with popular shows and the melodrama theaters of the boulevards and the lower classes.[48]

In a typical letter of 1 August 1821, Weber tries to reassure the management of the Karlsruhe theater about the first drawback.[49] Specific descriptions of the staging of the Wolf's Glen Scene in productions not under Weber's supervision are difficult to find, but those that I have seen say that the scene was considerably bowdlerized. We know that in Vienna (where the opera was done repeatedly from October 1821 on) Samiel's appearance was replaced by a backstage voice, and the entire bullet-casting scene was replaced by the finding of bolts for a crossbow in a tree stump.[50] Other theaters, even in large urban centers, felt similarly free to adapt the scene to their own capabilities.[51]

Weber's concern about the second drawback was less practically pressing but more deep-seated and lasting. Was it the Wolf's Glen Scene and its basis in the theatrical style of the *populäre Schaustücke* that had caused most of the clamorous public success of the opera? And did this popular basis cause people of taste and influence in the artistic and educated elite to look down upon the opera, thus degrading the image of German national opera – the very image that Weber had wanted to raise (in relation to the reigning Italian opera in Dresden, or Spontini's French-Italian opera in Berlin)? Zelter's report to Goethe on the Berlin premiere of *Freischütz* is famous. Although he admitted that the music had been very well received and was in fact very good, he went on to refer sarcastically to the "clouds of dust and smoke" (*vielen Kohlen- und Pulverdampf*) and concludes: "Children and women are mad for [the opera] and can't get enough of it; the devil black, virtue white, stage full of events, orchestra busy."[52] Weber himself, in reporting the phenomenal success of the opera, confided to his friend Lichtenstein:

> The devils and ghosts often make me feel a bit unsure of myself; if *respectable* men did not salute me with real approval, then I myself might think that Mr. Samiel had turned the trick single-handedly.[53]

In fact, Weber never again tried anything as closely derived from popular shows as the Wolf's Glen Scene. Although *Euryanthe* has its ghost (which Weber fiercely insisted on retaining, in the face of opposition from such influential Dresden voices as Tieck), it does not have real phantasmagoric scenes, with quick successions of ghosts and supernatural happenings appearing in the midst of the stage by trick effects of lighting. I have not tried to make a thorough survey of such scenes in later nineteenth-century opera. A moment's thought is enough to ascertain that phantasmagoric elements exist in numerous scenes. I have already mentioned those in Wagner's *Flying Dutchman* and *Siegfried*. Gounod's early opera *La Nonne sanglante* (1854) is based on a subject often used for phantasmagoric scenarios (cf. p. 65 above), and includes a specifically phantasmagoric scene (Plate 9).[54] The end of Act 2, Scene 1 of Reyer's Nibelungen opera *Sigurd* (begun in the 1860s) is an elaborate phantasmagoric scene.

The point that I would stress, however, would not be a catalog of strictly phantasmagoric scenes in opera, but rather the conceptual possibilities for staging opened up by these shows, and the connotations and resonances that these widely-enjoyed popular shows – phantasmagoria, panorama, diorama – brought to a number of works of high art for the listeners and spectators of the

New light(s) on Weber's Wolf's Glen Scene

OPÉRA. — *La Nonne sanglante.*
Séance de fantasmagorie, par M. Comte et M. Scribe.

Plate 9 Cartoon illustration of Gounod's *La Nonne sanglante* (1854). *L'Illustration* (Paris, 1855).

time. For example, Daguerre's Diorama, which opened in Paris in 1822, was at the height of its popularity there when Berlioz' *Symphonie fantastique* was written and first performed. Virtually every one of Daguerre's shows included in its two presentations one in the interior of a church and/or one of changing light effects (sunrise, sunset, thunderstorms, winter giving way to spring, and so forth) on a Swiss mountain valley – this second complete with shepherd's reed pipe playing the *ranz des vaches* behind the screen for atmosphere.[55] The resonances that parts of Berlioz' third movement and perhaps even the end of his first movement would have had for many contemporary Parisian listeners would have included some sense in which they were heard as sound tracks, so to speak, to a diorama – still vividly present in the memories of an audience for whom visual simulacra with temporal transformations were so rare. Berlioz' last movement, the Witches' Sabbath, was a favorite subject for phantasmagoric shows. His score would doubtless have been provided in the minds of many urban sophisticates with a whole series of phantasmagoric *montages*. The finale of Act 3 of Meyerbeer's *Robert le Diable* (1831) – the evocation (and ballet) of the ghosts of nuns in the graveyard of an abandoned convent – is a clear reference to Robertson's phantasmagoric shows in the abandoned Couvent des Capucines.

Theodor Adorno, in an essay of 1961 on the "image-world of *Freischütz*," remarks that "the Wolf's Glen is made up of a succession of little pictures, almost like a film, each one of which is accompanied by a ghostly appearance." It renounces, he says, the idea of the large musically continuous finale like the second act of *Figaro* or the prison scene of *Fidelio*, and relies confidently on a quick succession of images (*Flucht der Bilder*). He concludes: "Around the same year in which *Freischütz* was composed the kaleidoscope was invented. Something of the same urge that called forth that invention became music in the Wolf's Glen Scene."[56]

Clearly, I would endorse Adorno's sense that the Wolf's Glen Scene marks a distinctive intersection of burgeoning technology, instruments of popular amusement, and serious opera. He just had the invention wrong. The mistake is small but not insignificant – especially in Adorno's own social-historical terms. For to shift from the kaleidoscope to the phantasmagoria and the diorama moves us from the Biedermeier *Wohnzimmer* (the ancestor of our family room?) to the socially open, public entertainment of the urban boulevard. Paradoxically enough, this latter is the context called up by Weber's ghostly goings-on – the context of its immediate and clamorous success, and perhaps a part of its continuing success as well.

Appendix I

The eagle in the first act was stuffed in the Berlin [zoological] Museum [of which Weber's close friend Hinrich Lichtenstein was director] and prepared in such a way that one can take off and replace its wings. It hangs on a doubled string, twirled together. After the shot, one lets go of one part of this, then [the eagle] gyrates in the air and eventually plunges down when the [released] line has unraveled.

Finale of the 2nd act. Of the two thunderstorms only one can be staged, since the theater [at Dresden?] is built such that the moon itself occupies only a bit of room to the rear of the stage.

The skull is concealed.

The owl, made of wood, is anchored firmly, and moves its head and wings. Its eyes glow.

Samiel appeared in Berlin *in the rocky cliffs*. Kaspar makes his circle a bit off center-stage, in order to leave the greater part of the stage free for the ghosts [*Erscheinungen*]. On one side there is a rocky mass painted on semi-transparent cloth [*Masley*], behind which is an apparatus such that the area behind it can quickly be lit up. As long as this is *dark*, Samiel remains invisible behind the cloth, but when it is lit up, the cloth (or coarse brown gauze) becomes transparent. Behind the cloth is Samiel in a long scarlet mantle, with a transparent red skull [over his head] and a hat on top, so that he appears at this moment to be as horrifying as the prince of hell.

The skull and hunting knife [which Kaspar brings in with him and places in the circle] disappear through a trap door, back up through which comes the small brazier with glowing coals, and so on. Twigs should not be thrown on it, since they would make too much smoke. Instead, a bit of bengal powder [used in fireworks to produce an intense blue light] – or perhaps something that turns green with it – should be put on, and Kaspar should throw some more on from time to time, without the spectators noticing.

The rocky point on which Max appears will be very high but well to the front of the stage, so that his singing can project. It should be shaped as follows so that it does not obstruct view of the rear of the stage [see Plate 10] and Max clambers down offstage behind.

The ghost [*Erscheinung*] of the mother and that of Agathe were also represented as if on the rocky cliff, by children in the rear of the stage. They, too, were behind the cloth backdrop and became visible only because of the lamps next to them, which were quickly directed at them [they were otherwise turned away and covered with black boxes, a technique already described by Robertson].

Thus they could be visible and invisible as need be.

Since the hopping of *the forest birds* easily becomes ridiculous, after [Kaspar

Opera and the visual arts

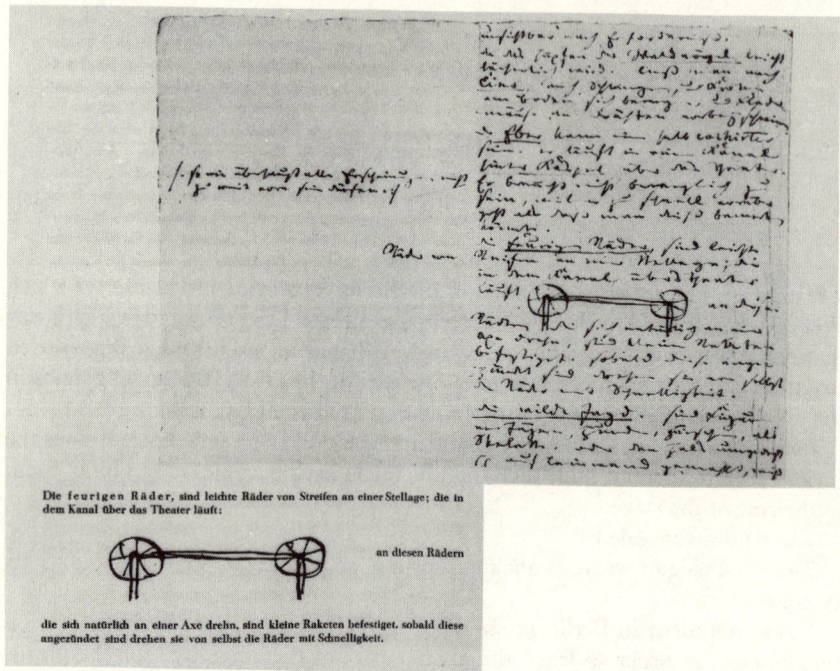

Plate 10 Weber's sheet of instructions for staging *Der Freischütz*. D-Bds, Sammlung Weberiana, Cl.II A g 2.

says] *Eins* one had serpents and toads crawl about the floor, and bats on wires whirl about.

The *boar* need only be half visible. He runs on a groove *behind Kaspar* across the stage (just as all the *Erscheinungen* should not be too far forward). He himself does [i.e., his body parts do] not need to be mobile, since he passes by too quickly for the spectator to notice.

The *fiery wheels* are thin wheels on shafts mounted on a chassis; the whole runs in a groove across the stage. On these wheels, which naturally turn on axles, little rockets are affixed. As soon as these are lit, they make the wheels rotate rapidly.

The *wild hunt* is made up of figures of hunters, dogs, stags – as skeletons, or with their heads turned backward, or some such thing – painted on linen *en grisaille* and then cut out and glued on transparent cloth [*Masley*]. They are moved back and forth in broad gestures near the top of the stage. Since one does not see the transparent cloth, the figures float freely in the air.

At the end all the rain, lightning, and thunder machines must be activated.

Both the *will o' the wisps* – little sponges on wires soaked in alcohol – and the flames coming out of the ground must be numerous. Backstage real trees were dropped from on high, which then crashed and thundered.[57]

Samiel stands behind the dead tree and holds his arm behind its trunk such that Max already has hold of him when the tree disappears.

Appendix II

From the *Allgemeines Theater-Lexicon*, ed. Blum and Herlossohn, vol. 3 (Altenburg and Leipzig, 1840), pp. 197–8.

The entry on *Erscheinungen* divides them into two types: fast and slow. "The first type [which includes people coming down on clouds or ascending through trap-doors, and so on] is inadequate when the machinery is in any way noticeable; the second when it unfolds too quickly." The author goes on to describe various ways of doing satisfactory slow *Erscheinungen*. He continues, "if surprise and quickness are the goal, however, one really must rely on lighting, or *Changements de vue*. A transparent backdrop with light that comes up suddenly, bathing in very bright light darkened parts of the stage, has come into use only recently in a few theaters, as is the case in England. These effects are best used behind scenes painted on coarse gauze. If the stage is dark and the figure behind this gauze is suddenly brightly lit, the *Erscheinung* achieves an immediacy that is scarcely achievable any other way. Very bright gas flames and a reflector (see article on *Lighting*) are especially advantageous here. When one covers the lights, then disappearance is immediate. Also the effects of the *laterna magica*, namely on columns of smoke [cf. the phantasmagoric effects of Robertson and his imitators], are still not so commonly used in this connection, as one would be tempted to believe from the convenience of the apparatus."

This particular entry in the *Lexicon* was written by Louis Schneider, *Hofschauspieler* in Berlin (ibid., vol. 1 [1839], p. xv). It seems to describe Weber's precise methods in *Freischütz*, which Schneider still links to the methods of the phantasmagoria.

The *Lexicon* as a whole prides itself on its inclusion of technical matters such as these. Its long article on lighting is indeed fascinating, as are its descriptions of the principal theaters in various cities. I wish to thank Professor Michael Tusa of the University of Texas at Austin for calling my attention to this source.

NOTES

1 "You will have heard a hundred times that, after reading a good story, one wished to see it represented on the stage. And how many bad plays have come into being thus! Similarly people want to see every interesting situation engraved in copper, so that no active role is left for their imagination. So everything should be real to the senses, completely present, dramatic – and this 'dramatic' itself should completely overshadow the really true. The artist should resist these thoroughly childish, barbaric, tasteless tendencies with all his might." (Translation mine.)

2   Carl Maria von Weber, *Der Freischütz: Nachbildung der Eigenschrift aus dem Besitz der Preussischen Staatsbibliothek*, ed. Georg Schünemann (Berlin, 1942), pp. 5–77.
3   For a wonderful compendium of these "shows", see Richard D. Altick, *The Shows of London* (Cambridge, Mass., 1978), esp. chs. 9–19 for the period that concerns us here.
4   My attention was first called to the phantasmagoria by Terry Castle's article "Phantasmagoria: Spectral Technology and the Metaphorics of Modern Reverie", *Critical Inquiry* 15 (1988–89): 26–61. Professor Castle gives ideas on the source of the word, which seems to have been invented by the prolific Robertson, on p. 27, n. 2. A principal source for details on the phantasmagoria itself is Robertson's own *Mémoires récréatifs, scientifiques et anecdotiques d'un physicien-aéronaute*, 2 vols. (Paris, 1830–4), which have recently been reprinted (Langres, 1985) with an introduction by Philippe Blon. Among the numerous inventions of Robert[son] mentioned in the article on him in the *Nouvelle Biographie générale* of J. C. F. Hoefer, vol. 46 (Paris, 1852) are a *phonorganon*, which imitates the words of the human voice, "un mégascope, un polyscope, et d'autres appareils d'optique appliqués à la fantasmagorie et à la physique amusante. Avant l'application du gaz hydrogène à l'éclairage [the so-called limelight] il inventa pour l'Opéra un ventilateur et une nouvelle lampe qui rendait la nuit et le jour avec les différents tons que présente la lumière du soleil quand cet astre se lève et se couche." Robertson died on 2 July 1837 in Batignolles, near Paris. At the end of his life he was the director of the Jardin du Tivoli in Paris, a pleasure garden combining a "cabinet de physique" with several small theaters, a shooting gallery, a dance hall, a restaurant, and a café.
5   The history of the phantasmagoria in London is traced by Altick, *Shows of London*, pp. 217–20; the passage concerning spectral visions is on p. 217. The panorama was invented (and patented) by the Englishman Robert Barker in 1787. It featured a large (some were over 100 feet in width – or circumference – and 20 feet high), continuous painting designed to be viewed by a group of spectators from a central platform in a circular room on whose walls the painting had been placed. The painting itself reproduced with detailed realism, through virtuosic use of optical-perspective effects, the view the spectator would have had if he or she stood at a certain, usually famous place, such as the top of the Dome of St. Paul's Cathedral in London. The room in which the painting was displayed was carefully designed such that the painting would be illuminated by natural light whose source was invisible to the spectator. The room was also designed such that the top and bottom boundaries of the painting would likewise be invisible to the spectator. Thus the painting had no apparent frame.

The phenomenon of the panorama spread rapidly to France and the larger urban centers of Germany. One of the second generation of French panorama painters, Daguerre, developed photography as part of his attempts to capture by means of the *camera obscura* the features seen from the purported viewpoint, so that he could take the imprint back to his studio and use it as the model for his painting. The evolution of the panorama has been traced in Stephan Oettermann, *Das Panorama: Die Geschichte eines Massenmediums* (Frankfurt am Main, 1980). The panorama and its descendants were an important influence on early nineteenth-century operatic scene painters, including Karl Friedrich Schinkel, the chief designer at Berlin when Weber's *Freischütz* was given its premiere there.

See especially Helmut Börsch-Supan, *Karl Friedrich Schinkel: Bühnenentwürfe/*

Stage Designs, 2 vols. (Berlin, 1990), vol. 1, pp. 24–33, for some details on the diorama-like Christmas displays that Schinkel designed for various clients in Berlin in 1807–15. The themes of the displays, a Christmas tradition dating back to the late eighteenth century and especially popular during the Napoleonic years, had nothing to do with Christmas. Descriptions of the displays designed by Schinkel include scenes of shepherds in Alpine valleys and interiors of famous churches. The translucent cloth on which the scenes were painted could be lit from both front and back. The spectator viewed the *trompe-l'œil* perspective paintings, which are said to have been from 6 by 10 feet to 13 by 20 feet in size, down a 30-foot long row of columns arranged so as to enhance the feeling of distance from the picture and the impression of its size. These displays were clearly very like the more elaborate dioramas staged by Daguerre in Paris in 1822 and later (see note 55 below). Schinkel, a great lover of music, had the various scenes accompanied by vocal and instrumental music (piano, solo horn, and vocal quartet are specified in the reports given by Börsch-Supan). The Berlin composer and music teacher Carl Friedrich Detroit wrote and performed music for the Christmas displays, and later (1822) took over their display as a commercial venture.

6 "Diese vormalige gesperrte Wohnung der Busse und des Mönchsglaubens, ist in einen offenen Tummelplatz des Lachens und der gereizten Neugier verwandelt. Hier spukt *Robertson* mit seinen Geistererscheinungen… In den alten Klostergängen, Hallen, Arkaden und Refektorien, sind Kaffeebuden, Speisehäuser, Meublenmagazine u. dgl. angelegt. Abends ist Garten und Kloster erleuchtet, und voll Menschen. Vorn im Garten stehen die beiden Panoramen von *Paris* und *Toulon*. Dies und Robertsons täuschende Spiele sind hier das Sehenswürdigste." F. J. L. Meyer, *Briefe aus der Hauptstadt und dem Inneren Frankreichs* (Tübingen, 1802), p. 190. Quoted in Oettermann, *Panorama*, p. 114.

7 " Auf den Boulevards gerieth ich in die Buden der sogenannten Experimentalphysik … Ein Anderer zog die Leute an dem Ärmel in seine dunkle Kammer, wo er durch optische Versuche eine Menge Gaukeleien, die dem Publikum, das wie in Ekstase stand, nur allzuschnell verschwanden, hervorbrachte." "Fragmente aus Paris," *Journal des Luxus und der Mode* 18 (1803): 242–3. I conclude that this must have been Robertson's phantasmagoria, since the "experimental physics" were not a part of other phantasmagoria.

8 Robertson, *Mémoires récréatifs*, p. 166. Robertson was a lifelong friend of Volta.

9 "Briefe über Paris," written by a certain "T. v. W.," who earlier (col. 689) had identified herself as "a German lady," *Zeitung für die elegante Welt* 6 (1806), col. 998. Hoefer's *Nouvelle Biographie générale* (vol. 46, 1852) notes a famous balloon voyage by Robertson from Hamburg on 18 July 1803 for the purpose of scientific experiments on the effects of extreme altitude – a proto-version of today's space shuttle voyages – that attained 3666 *toises*, roughly 22,000 feet. Robertson vied with another inventor of the time for the title of inventor of the parachute; he was one of its first successful manufacturers. He was by no means a flake.

10 Robertson, *Mémoires récréatifs*, pp. 130–4. See 1 Samuel 28: 7–20.

11 The last two instances reveal the closeness that some of the scenarios have to a ghostly *tableau vivant*, by which name some correspondents refer to them. Robertson, *Mémoires récréatifs*, pp. 170–4.

12 Robertson's most detailed descriptions make clear how these short scenes succeeded each other. Here is his description of a scenario he calls "Préparatifs du sabbat":

Une horloge sonne minuit: une sorcière, le nez dans un livre, lève le bras par trois fois. La lune descend, se place devant elle, et devient couleur de sang; la sorcière la frappe de sa baguette et la coupe en deux. Elle recommence à lever la main gauche; à la troisième fois, des chats, des chauve-souris, des têtes de morts voltigent avec des feux follets. Au milieu d'un cercle magique on lit ces mots: DEPART POUR LE SABBAT. Arrive une femme à califourchon sur un balai et qui monte en l'air; un démon, un incroyable sur un balai, et beaucoup de figures qui se suivent. Deux moines paraissent avec la croix, puis un ermite, pour exorciser, et tout se dissipe. (Ibid., p. 171)

13 "Quel serait l'effroi du spectateur isolé si, tout à coup conduit dans la salle des expériences fantasmagoriques, entouré des images de la mort, l'imagination frappée par la crainte des êtres invisibles, il entendait les sons plaintifs et funèbres de l'*harmonica*, et voyait paraître le spectre menaçant! Je sais bien qu'un tel spectacle serait prohibé par une police sage et vigilant..." (Ibid., p. 128). Two pages later, he attributes to the "sons trop doux and trop pénétrants de l'*harmonica* seuls" the "crise nerveuse assez violente" of a woman spectator-listener. In a letter headed "Trendy Misuses of Words" [*Modische Verwechslung der Worte*], a correspondent from Paris for the *Journal des Luxus und der Mode* is less pleased: "Ich nehme das Blatt in die Hand, das täglich alle Schauspiele ankündigt. Da finde ich angekündigt: man werde Franklins Harmonika hören, das heisst, das zarteste und lieblichste aller Instrumente. Ich gehe hin, und sehe ein wüsstes Gewirre von Gespenstererscheinungen, Schattenspielen und andern dergleichen Hocuspocus, mit einem Worte, eine *Fantasmagorie*." *Journal des Luxus und der Mode* 14 (1799): 211.

14 Robertson, *Mémoires récréatifs*, p. 203. The machines for making the noise of rain, thunder, and wind are described on pp. 204–6. The celestina is a keyboard instrument patented by Adam Walker of London in 1772. "When the keys were depressed the strings were drawn against a continuous band of silk ... driven by a weight, spring or foot treadle." *New Grove Dictionary of Music and Musicians* (London, 1980), vol. 4, p. 48.

15 Robertson, *Mémoires récréatifs*, p. 183.

16 On this possibility see Max Maria von Weber, *Carl Maria von Weber: Ein Lebensbild*, 2 vols. (Leipzig, 1864), vol. 1, pp. 202–3.

17 Oettermann, *Das Panorama*; see also Heinz Buddemeier, *Panorama, Diorama, Photographie: Entstehung und Wirkung neuer Medien im 19. Jahrhundert*, Theorie und Geschichte der Literatur und der Schönen Künste, vol. 7 (Munich, 1970). Oettermann (p. 182) refers in passing to the father of the famous panorama painter Carl Georg Enslen, a certain Johann Karl Enslen, "der um 1800 mit seinen Automaten, Phantasmagorien und aerostatischen Figuren Furore machte." I have not had access to the contemporary periodicals he cites, and in general the spread of the phantasmagoria has been less easy for me to trace, partly because I have had to search on my own, without the thorough research on the panorama of Oettermann and his predecessor Buddemeier as my guide.

18 "Pfarrer Walther's Bericht von seiner Reise zur Messe nach Frankfurt a. M. im Mai 1805," *Journal des Luxus und der Mode* 20 (1805): 412–18.

19 Ibid., p. 807.

20 *Journal des Luxus und der Mode* 25 (1810): 495.

21 Robertson, *Mémoires récréatifs*, p. 187. I would speculate that Robertson refers to the miniaturist Johann Friedrich Tielker (1763–1832), from 1793 a resident of

Berlin. Tielker's transparencies for use in simple magic lanterns or small illuminated boxes were described repeatedly with high praise in the fashion periodicals (e.g., *Zeitung für die elegante Welt* 14 [1799]: 232–4; 15 [1800]: 648). Tielker also involved himself quickly in the lucrative world of what I have called the paratheatrical entertainments of the early nineteenth century. It was he who commissioned Breysig and Katz to do the first German panorama for Berlin (*Zeitung für die elegante Welt* 15 [1800]: 648). He then trained himself to do large-scale optic-perspective painting and painted a number of panoramas himself, especially of Eastern Europe, Russia, and even China. His career and specialties offer a striking combination of the grandiose and the miniature in the nineteenth century. The combination served him well: he died wealthy and left a large collection of paintings by ancient masters (*Neuer Nekrolog der Deutschen*, vol. 10 [1832]). On his involvement with Schinkel on some projected panoramas for Berlin, see Oettermann, *Das Panorama*, pp. 157–8.
22 *Zeitung für die elegante Welt* 25 (1810): 423.
23 "Der Zweck eines Panoramas ist zu täuschen und ganz in die dargestellte Gegend zu versetzen. Ach! wie stören da jene wie durch Oberonshorn festgebannten Gestalten so widrig!" "Über Paris," *Zeitung für die elegante Welt* 6 (1806): 667.
24 See Martin Quigley, Jr. *Magic Shadows: The Story of the Origin of Motion Pictures* (Washington, D.C., 1948), esp. ch. 9, "Phantasmagoria". Robertson (*Mémoires récréatifs*, p. 182) says that by the time he wrote (early 1830s), "les expériences de fantasmagorie sont presque abandonnées." Altick (*Shows of London*, p. 219) says the association of the magic lantern show with ghosts seems to have lasted longest at the fairs, and cites an example from 1833. The lanterns themselves continued to be much used throughout the nineteenth century for home entertainment and for public educational presentations.
25 Jac [sic] Remise, *Magie lumineuse* (n. p. [Tours?], 1979), pp. 47–60.
26 See Schünemann's facsimile edition of Weber's score (cited in note 2 above), pp. 32–4. Although Schünemann did not know the author of the libretto and was working from only the Donaueschingen manuscript, Gottfried Mayerhofer located two copies of the libretto and has convincingly identified the author as the Munich poet Franz Xavier von Caspar. *Abermals vom "Freischützen": Der Münchener "Freischütze" von 1812*, Forschungsbeiträge zur Musikwissenschaft, vol. 7 (Regensburg, 1959), pp. 3–5. Curiously, Mayerhofer does not seem to know Schünemann's study, since he does not know of the music by Neuner.
27 Striking is that much of the detail of the scene is present in the source, August Apel's and Friedrich Laun's *Gespensterbuch* of 1810. Its first tale, "Der Freischütz: eine Volkssage", although it has the Wolf's Glen analog at a deserted crossroads instead (chs. 11–13), contains the owls, bats, night birds, "neblichen Gestalten" and "Dunstkörpern" that move, fiery wheels, and wild boars. Weber fleshed this out and altered it a bit. But his innovation was to have been determined to make it visually present on stage, and to have conceived a way to do so. This was where Goethe, Apel, Schinkel-Gropius, and even E. T. A. Hoffmann would disapprove.
28 See the letters to Caroline Brandt and Weber's diary entries of 20 February through 1 March 1817, as quoted in Schünemann, *Der Freischütz: Nachbildung der Eigenschrift*, p. 18. Two of the relevant letters to Caroline (those of 23 February and 3 March) are given in full in *Mein vielgeliebter Muks: Hundert Briefe Carl Maria von Webers an Caroline Brandt aus den Jahren 1814–1817*, ed. Eveline Bartlitz (Munich, 1987), pp. 343–53.

29 Letter of 21 May 1817. Weber, *Mein vielgeliebter*, p. 394.
30 Schünemann, *Der Freischütz: Nachbildung der Eigenschrift*, pp. 44–8.
31 Letter of 26 March 1821. *Briefe Carl Maria von Weber an Hinrich Lichtenstein*, ed. Ernst Rudorff (Braunschweig, 1900), p. 100.
32 "Die Dichtung und Bühnenkunst [sollte] jene unbekannten Gewalten in möglichst unbestimmten Umrissen zeigen." To be avoided are such things as the "bis zum Abscheu verzerrte Schreckbild mit glühendem, grässlich gezahnten Totenkopfe." Kind is quoted in Wolfgang Becker, *Die deutsche Oper in Dresden unter der Leitung von Carl Maria von Weber, 1817–1826*, Theater und Drama, vol. 22 (Berlin, 1962), pp. 62 and 151.
33 See Becker, *Die deutsche Oper*, pp. 58–63, 150–2. Weber makes a similar point in his supposed conversation with Johann Christian Lobe, first printed some thirty years after the fact in Lobe's *Fliegende Blätter*, vol. 1, of 1853 and most recently reprinted in *Carl Maria von Weber: Der Freischütz. Texte, Materialien, Kommentare*, ed. Attila Csampai and Dietmar Holland (Hamburg, 1981), pp. 149–69: "Ja, *Energie des Ausdrucks muss hinzukommen*; das kalt und matt und gleichgültig vor eine Kunsterscheinung tretende Publikum muss stark angegriffen, muss zur Aufmerksamkeit und Theilnahme gezwungen, muss mit Macht in den Kreis derselben hineingerissen werden, denn freiwillig erhitzt es sich nicht ... Ich will Ihnen das Wort nennen, das *mir* zur Energie des Ausdrucks hilft, es heisst – *Übertreibung*" (p. 161).
34 The sheet is preserved in the Deutsche Staatsbibliothek in Berlin. I take it to be the item described as Sammlung Weberiana Cl.II A g 2 in *Carl Maria v. Weber: Autographenverzeichnis*, ed. Eveline Bartlitz, Deutsche Staatsbibliothek Handschrifteninventare, vol. 9 (Berlin, 1986), p. 35: "Einige Bemerkungen die szenischen Anordnung des Freischützen betreffend." It is transcribed, and part of it is reproduced in Schünemann, *Der Freischütz: Nachbildung der Eigenschrift*, pp. 64–5.
35 In the summer of 1821 – that is, just after the staging of the Wolf's Glen Scene in Berlin and before that in Dresden – the stage machinery of the Dresden theater was renovated on Weber's demand, including the purchase of the most modern form of "Argand" lamps, the brightest and most smokeless form of lamp then available. See Becker, *Die deutsche Oper*, pp. 57 and 163. On the struggles with the weakness of the Argand lamp, from the 1790s through Schinkel's proposed (and unfulfilled) reforms of the 1810s, see Carl-Friedrich Baumann, *Licht im Theater*, Die Schaubühne, vol. 72 (Stuttgart, 1988), pp. 70–5. The use of gaslights to illuminate the stage seems to have been pioneered in a few London theaters in the 1816 and 1817 seasons; it spread to Paris only in 1822 (a Daguerre production) and to Germany at the end of the decade (ibid., pp. 83–5). The possibility for a real revolution in theater lighting came with the invention by the English military engineer Thomas Drummond of the oxyhydrogen lamp, or limelight, first used for lighthouses in 1826. But Baumann (ibid., pp. 132–5) finds documentation for only a slow penetration in the theater across the next decades.

Both the phantasmagoria and the diorama depended primarily on the manipulation of artificial light. (The double-effect diorama brought transformation to the painted semi-transparent screen by switching lighting from the front to the back of a screen painted slightly differently on the two sides. It was able thus to bring monks and worshippers into a church interior or bring spring foliage into a winter landscape.) Weber also, in his purported conversation with Lobe, emphasizes the control of illumination as a means of reinforcing the dramatic and musical curve of his opera:

> Do not overlook the importance for the darker elements of the plot that one-half the opera is played in darkness. Evening descends in the first act, and its second half is played in darkness. In the second act it is night during Agathe's large scene, with moonlight coming through the window, and with midnight comes the ghost scene in the Wolf's Glen. These dark images of the external world support and strengthen the dark colors of the tone pictures most effectively. Imagine *Freischütz* performed in a bright, elegant, modern room by the light of day, and something of the uncannny impression will be lost, the incursion of the dark powers will be less palpable. (p. 155 of reprint cited in note 33)

It is not clear in the above quote whether Weber refers to just stage lighting, or whether he is advocating a darkened theater as well. Both phantasmagoria and diorama require the darkened theater, of course, which had been advocated by reformers for the regular theater as well since the beginning of the century, but seems not to have been a widespread practice even when Wagner decreed it for Bayreuth in 1876 (see Baumann, *Licht im Theater*, pp. 56–60, 75–9, 128–30).

36 Max Maria von Weber, *Carl Maria von Weber*, vol. 2, p. 299. Carl Wilhelm Gropius, a pupil of Schinkel, was the son of W. F. Gropius, who produced Schinkel's Christmas shows. Carl's workshop executed sets according to Schinkel's design (*Allgemeine deutsche Biographie*, vol. 9 [1879], "Gropius"). A full sample of Schinkel's sketches for stage designs in Berlin is now available in Helmut Börsch-Supan, *Karl Friedrich Schinkel* (see note 5 above).

37 I base this section principally on Klaus Wever, "Karl Friedrich Schinkels Position und Beitrag zur Reform des Theaterraums," in *Karl Friedrich Schinkel: Werk und Wirkungen* (Berlin, 1981), pp. 183–204, and Christa Heese, "Entwurf zum Umbau des Nationaltheaters und Schinkels Theorie einer Reform des Theatergebäudes," in *Karl Friedrich Schinkel: Eine Ausstellung aus des Deutsche Demokratischen Republik* (Berlin, 1982), pp. 152–4. The opposition is most clearly laid out in Wever, pp. 185–6. A similar point about Schinkel's avoidance of realistic representation concerns the fire in his staging of *The Magic Flute* from 1815 and is made in Günter Schöne and Hellmuth Vriesen, *Das Bühnenbild im 19. Jahrhundert* (Munich, 1959), p. 13.

38 Max Maria von Weber, *Carl Maria von Weber*, vol. 2, p. 300. See also Becker, *Die deutsche Oper*, pp. 147–53 on Weber's repeated insistence on realistic representation and strong theatrical effects during his tenure there – sometimes to the displeasure of his upper-class and aristocratic patrons.

39 Weber's near contemporary Alexander Oulibicheff (Ulibishev), born in Dresden in 1794 and educated there until his removal to Russia in 1810, had no doubt about the potential of the phantasmagoria for operatic staging. In his biography of Mozart, written during the 1830s, he proposes a remedy for the usual pitiable staging of the final scene of *Don Giovanni*:

> N'avons nous pas la fantasmagorie? Hé bien, faites promener dans le vide des spectres menaçans, des larves atroces, crispées par la rage ou grimaçantes de rire sardonique; melez-y, pour le contraste, une procession de jeunes femmes pâles et blanches, que Giovanni a fait mourir d'amour; elles le regardent et elles ont l'air de pleurer sur lui.

> Ce tableau n'est-il pas de votre goût, en voici un autre...

(A. Oulibicheff, *Nouvelle Biographie de Mozart*, 3 vols. [Moscow, 1843], vol. 3, p. 200.) In a passage concerning opus 70 from his later book on Beethoven, Oulibicheff gives no doubt as to what he sees as the father of such phantasmagoric scenes:

> L'un des deux, celui en *ré* majeur, a été surnommé en Allemagne *das Geister-Trio*, le trio des Esprits, à cause de son adagio admirable, d'où l'on a prétendu que Weber avait tiré la scene fantasmagorique du *Freischütz*. C'est une erreur. La chœur des esprits de la vallée du loup et la chasse infernale ne doivent absolument rien à Beethoven. Ils appartient en entier à Weber, et personne, jusqu'à nos jours, n'a egalé ces étonnantes conceptions dans le genre démonico-fantastique.

(Oulibicheff, *Beethoven: ses critiques et ses glossateurs* [Leipzig and Paris, 1857], pp. 254–5.) I am grateful to Professor Thomas Grey of Stanford University for calling my attention to these two passages.

40 Oettermann, *Das Panorama*, pp. 158–60.
41 See Wever, "Karl Friedrich Schinkels Position," p. 197, and Heese, "Entwurf zum Umbau des Nationaltheaters," p. 152.
42 "Unsere Theater sind jetzt zu Panoramen, optischen Buden geworden, in denen mit Tanzen, Fechten, Reiten, Feuer- und Wasserkünsten allerlei Gaukelei getrieben wird, und alles das zu *schauen* rennt der Haufe, den man durch dramatisches *Spiel* nicht mehr anzuziehen vermag. Nichts ist lächerlicher als den Zuschauer dahin bringen zu wollen, daß er, ohne seinerseits etwas Phantasie zu bedürfen, an die gemalten Paläste, Bäume und Felsen... wirklich glaube... Es zuvörderst auf die sorglichste Vermeidung alles Unziemlichen, dann aber auf das tiefe Auffassen des eigentlich Phantastischen, welches herauswirkend die Phantasie des Zuschauers beflügeln soll, ankommt. Nicht als ein für sich bestehendes glänzendes Bild darf die Dekoration das Auge des Zuschauers auf sich ziehen, aber in dem Moment der Handlung soll er, ohne dessen bewusst zu sein, den Eindruck des Bildes fühlen, in dem sich die Handlung bewegt." I quote (and translate) from E. T. A. Hoffmann, *Sämtliche Werke*, ed. Rudolf Frank, vol. 10 (Munich and Leipzig, 1924), pp. 92–5.
43 The reviews are printed ibid. A recent reprint is also in Csampai and Holland, *Carl Maria von Weber: Der Freischütz*, pp. 104–14. Hoffmann's authorship is questioned in Wolfgang Kron, *Die angeblichen Freischütze-Kritiken E. T. A. Hoffmanns* (Munich, 1957). Kron's evidence seems clearly to show that Weber did not think that Hoffmann had written the reviews; that whoever wrote them wrote as if he were a frequent reviewer for the *Vossische Zeitung* at the time (which Hoffmann was not), and that the reviewer had a strangely exaggerated sensitivity to and censoriousness toward possible thematic resemblances, a stance that Hoffmann did not take. Since the evidence for Hoffmann's authorship seems to be only a suggestion made forty years after the fact by a pupil of Weber (Julius Benedict), the case for his actually having written the reviews seems slim. Still, in arguing against it using Hoffmann's aesthetic statements, Kron fails to distinguish between Hoffmann's pronouncement on what is good for novels or novellas and what is seemly on stage – a crucial issue, and Goethe's point in the passage quoted at the opening of this essay.
44 Nor is it with those outlined by Gerhard Allroggen in "Die Opern-Aesthetik E. T. A. Hoffmanns," in *Beiträge zur Geschichte der Oper*, ed. Heinz Becker, Studien zur Musikgeschichte des 19. Jahrhunderts, vol. 15 (Regensburg, 1969),

pp. 25–34, esp. p. 26. Or those of August Apel, author of the *Gespensterbuch* from which the Freischütz tale was taken. See his "Ueber musikalische Behandlung der Geister," *Leipziger allgemeine musikalische Zeitung* 8 (November 1805), cols. 119–27, 129–34. Weber's approach was the exceptional one here – at least in this realm of high art.

45 See Richard Wagner, *Mein Leben*, ed. Martin Gregor-Dellin (Munich, 1976), pp. 19, 35ff.

46 "It was under the loosely applied name of 'phantasmagoria' that the oil-lighted magic lantern was introduced into the regular theater, where it was occasionally used for special effects. In Fitzball's *The Flying Dutchman* (Adelphi, 1826), for example, it provided the phantom ship which appeared in a peal of thunder on a totally darkened stage" (Altick, *The Shows of London*, p. 219). See also James L. Smith, *Melodrama* (London, 1973), pp. 28–9.

47 For the pleorama, an invention of the 1830s, see Oettermann, *Das Panorama*, pp. 168–70. Featured were such things as Rhine journeys or trips through the Gulf of Naples. The pleorama, or moving panorama, became particularly popular in North America after the middle of the century (ibid., pp. 258ff.). Ernest Newman (*Life of Richard Wagner* [New York, 1946], vol. 4, pp. 684–5), unaware of the pleorama or its history, gives an amusing account of Bayreuth's struggle with the machinery.

48 Schinkel's friend Achim von Arnim, while acknowledging that Schinkel was "sehr fleissig," complained in 1814 that he was working "immer zuviel für Gropius [the Christmas displays] und ähnlichen Dreck." Quoted in Börsch-Supan, *Karl Friedrich Schinkel*, p. 32.

49 "Erlaube ich mir meine Oper der Freyschütz gedichtet von Fried: Kind, zum Gebrauch des Grossherzogl: Hoftheaters anzubieten. Das Personale und die Szenischen Anforderungen sind von der Art dass keine bedeutendere Bühne Schwierigkeiten finden wird sie darzustellen." Badisches Generallandesarchiv Karlsruhe 47/1105, quoted in Joachim Veit, *Der junge Carl Maria von Weber* (Mainz, 1990), p. 55, n. 14.

50 Max Maria von Weber, *Carl Maria von Weber*, vol. 2, pp. 344–7.

51 Castile-Blaze's Paris travesty is well known. Max Maria von Weber gives some details of the many fundamental changes made in the various London productions during that city's long-lasting "Freischützmanie" (ibid., vol. 2, pp. 660ff.).

52 "Die Kinder und Weiber sind toll und voll davon; Teufel schwarz, Tugend weiss, Theater belebt, Orchester in Bewegung." *Briefwechsel Goethe-Zelter*, ed. Werner Pfister (Zürich, 1987), p. 174.

53 "Der Teufelspuk macht mich selbst oft irre, und wenn nicht *ehrenwerthe* Männer mir mit Zufriedenheit die Hand drückten, so dächte ich selbst Musje [Monsieur] Samiel mache die Sache allein." *Briefe Carl Maria von Weber an Hinrich Lichtenstein*, p. 120, letter of 26 December 1822. Cf. Ludwig Spohr, *Selbstbiographie*, 2 vols. (Cassel, 1861), vol. 2, p. 149: "Closer acquaintance with the opera did not solve for me the riddle of its immense success, unless I resolved to find the explanation in Weber's gift to be able to write for the comprehension of the multitude."

54 Act 2 is made up of a drinking chorus and a subsequent phantasmagoric appearance to the protagonist Rodolphe, complete with Robertson's beloved funeral bell (*airain*). The showpiece of this scene was doubtless the *Intermède fantastique* (No. 9), with a choir in the wings singing "Hou! Hou!" and "Illou!" in head voice

offstage. Unfortunately the score that I have seen gives no stage directions for this *Intermède*, but see the cartoon taken from *L'Illustration* of 1855 (Plate 9).
55 See Oettermann, pp. 60–7 and Buddemeier, pp. 25–47, and especially the detailed newspaper report of a diorama of 1826 in Buddemeier, pp. 181–3. Schinkel's Christmas displays in Berlin, where they were still being produced in the 1820s (see note 5 above), appear to have had a direct influence on these shows, though I have not seen this suggested or documented.
56 Theodor W. Adorno, "Bilderwelt des Freischütz," in *Moments musicaux* (Frankfurt, 1964), p. 44. The kaleidoscope was "invented in 1817 by Sir David Brewster and promptly pirated. It proved a bonanza for tinmen and glass cutters... but no attempts were made to turn it into an audience show" (Altick, *Shows of London*, p. 233).

I judge that when Adorno used the word "phantasmagoria" as a chapter title in his *Versuch über Wagner*, he was using it as a word in common currency, without knowledge of the shows from which it is derived.
57 Becker, *Die deutsche Oper*, pp. 61–2, describes how various of these effects, including this one, were intensified for the Dresden premiere.

Serious opera

5

Sinfonia and drama in early eighteenth-century opera seria

REINHARD STROHM

The character, and perhaps the artistic merit, of an opera overture is often judged by the way in which it is musically integrated with the opera that follows. This integration, in turn, is predominantly sought in the overture's and the opera's thematic content – a criterion that suits Classic-Romantic instrumental music. Instrumental forms of earlier periods, such as the overture and sinfonia of the earlier eighteenth century, are often less dependent for their form and character on specific individual themes: circular reasoning thus leads to the conclusion that they were *not* usually integrated with their respective operas.

It is indeed widely believed that musical correspondence, or integration, of overture and opera was not practiced before the so-called Gluckian reform. Gluck's famous admonition, in his preface to *Alceste* (1769), that the overture "ought to prepare the spectators for the dramatic subject that is to be performed, and ought to be, so to speak, its *argomento*,"[1] has been interpreted as a watershed between the abstract Baroque sinfonia or overture, consisting of little more than festive noise, and the Classic-Romantic overture that is thematically integrated with the opera (which implies its being thematically constructed).

In this contribution, evidence will be adduced to suggest that the task of "tying the overture to the opera in mood and theme"[2] was more widely accepted by opera composers in the early part of that century than is often believed. At first, however, a possible misunderstanding of Gluck must be ruled out. He did not mean to recommend that the overture-*argomento* be identifiable with specific musical themes or motifs; it would be hard to prove this to be the case even in *Alceste*. Furthermore, Gluck's and Calzabigi's recommendations to opera composers published in this famous preface are derived (as already observed by Alfred Einstein) from a long tradition of thinking about operatic reform. The mentor of both men, Francesco Algarotti, had similarly lamented the monotonous noise of current opera sinfonias, and their musical separation from the following drama. Such an abstract independent sinfonia, he says, is as inadequate as a preface (*esordio*) of a poetic work that presents nothing but clichés suitable for any kind of *orazione*.[3] It appears that Gluck's recommendation differs little from Algarotti's, except by replacing *esordio* with *argomento*. Both these terms, to be sure, belong to the traditional vocabulary of literary rhetorics and poetics.

Serious opera

A well-known article by Daniel Heartz likens the function of the overture of Mozart's *La clemenza di Tito* to that of a dramatic argument in Gluck's sense, i.e., to a summary of antecedents and main elements of the drama such as a poet would offer to introduce a dramatic work.[4] One of the characteristics of Mozart's overtures highlighted in Heartz's study is the emphasis on tonal, not only thematic, relationships with the opera. Another, equally significant for the following discussion, is "Mozart's practice of tying the overture together with the end of the opera, a not unnatural consequence of their having been written within a short time of each other."[5]

Heartz does not have to make explicit that those elements of the *Titus* drama which in his hearing had a generative influence on the overture are by no means simply "the plot." There is both more and less to the integration of overture-opera in this case than, for example, in Weber's or Wagner's overtures.[6] There is less of a tangible identity of themes, and therefore less reference to identifiable situations in the drama – but more multiple cross-referencing with motivic patterns or harmonic progressions that appear to represent the morals and passions of the leading characters (Sesto and Vitellia). There is also, surely, the generic unity provided by musical clichés denoting the Holy Roman-Roman Imperial setting: trumpets and drums, fanfares, C major, unisono slide figures in the strings, dotted rhythms. Most of these devices would fit any symphonic or operatic work alluding to grandeur and rulership, of course. But how this array of semantically stereotyped elements prevails, in both the overture and the finale of *La clemenza di Tito*, over the passions of hatred, anguish, and guilt as represented by the rival flat keys and minor modes, results from a process of individualization. It is as predictable dramaturgically as it is musically individual and powerful. In this opera seria, the harmonic-thematic resolution of the overture predicts, like a symphonic oracle, the denouement of the drama.

If we can describe the relationship between a Classical overture and its opera in terms borrowed from the literary poetics (*argomento*) or rhetoric (*esordio*) of the previous (Baroque) era, then poetics and rhetoric might also contribute to a better understanding of the opera introductions of that era itself. Can the Baroque opera sinfonia in general have been expected to function as an *argomento*?

The "argument" was, in the seventeenth and eighteenth centuries, familiar to theatergoers as a printed introduction to the subject matter of a drama or opera libretto.[7] It was not a preface, nor necessarily a synopsis of the plot; more often the author concentrated on the pre-history of the action in order to prepare the spectator for basic conflicts and constellations between the characters. Rarely did an *argomento* give away the turning points of the dramatic intrigue. Sometimes it mentioned them, but only in a roundabout way. When listening to the music, the opera audience could experience a marvelous analogy between overture and "argument," brought about by the semantic ambiguity of instrumental music itself: even where the overture appeared to tell the outcome of the drama, the feeling of suspense did not collapse because the orchestral statements remained enigmatic.

Just as Algarotti's *esordio* was a fixed part of a literary work according to the tradition of rhetoric, so the practice of the *argomento* was rooted in the classicist (Aristotelian) poetics of drama, which through the French Classical theater so strongly influenced Italian opera of the early eighteenth century. The classicist poetics was well known to dramatists and is reflected in such commentaries as Pierre Corneille's *Trois Discours sur le poème dramatique* (1660) or Metastasio's *Estratto dell'arte poetica d'Aristotile e considerazioni su la medesima* (1773).[8] One of the most fundamental rules established by Aristotle – although less debated in the eighteenth century than the notorious three unities – was the division of a tragedy into six ingredients or "inherent parts" (Corneille: *parties integrantes*, Metastasio: *parti di qualità*). They were, in descending order of importance:

sujet (*soggetto* or *azione*, also *azione principale*),
mœurs (*costumi*),
sentiments (*sentenza*),
diction (*discorso*),
musique (*musica*),
décoration (*decorazione*).

(The last two elements were often quoted in reverse order.) Now it is in the *argomento* of a drama that a playwright or librettist should explain the major issue, i.e., the *soggetto* or the *azione principale* – although he will rarely give a detailed account of the whole "plot," which is not the same thing in any case. He may, furthermore, summarize the characters' *mœurs*, or *ethos* (Aristotle's term), and he may even hint at some of the passions they are going to experience and express – *sentiments*, *sentenza*,[9] *pathos* – but without giving a full account of these fleeting conditions.

This usage alone might shed new light on the role of the sinfonia in opera seria. If, in considering eighteenth-century drammi per musica, we cannot find that any of the thematic material of the arias is announced in the opening sinfonia, this may simply mean that none of it is deemed fundamental or general enough for such a cardinal position in the musico-dramatic discourse. What we are tempted to hear as perfunctory, cheerful noise[10] could have been intended by the composer as relating to subject or morals rather than to affections or plot. The sinfonia that seems to refer only to itself may rather refer to the drama all wrapped up in one single concept. With respect to the subject matter of the average opera seria, stereotypes loom so large in any case that orchestral pieces illustrating them can hardly be expected to have much individuality.

It was probably welcome to classicist critics that the orchestral introduction, by sounding celebrative and conventional, could reflect the contemporary setting in which operas were performed. To the Aristotelian, tragedy is a ceremonial reenactment or celebration of heroic deeds and fortunes of the past. It is something people *do with the past*. The orchestral music that announces such a theatrical reenactment, i.e. an opera, is already part of the celebratory act itself. The frequent allusions to dance in Baroque sinfonias and overtures are often the announcement of the royal (and real) dances at the ends of acts or of the whole opera; dance and ceremony are ritual actions naturally associated with Classical and classicist drama.

Let us also consider the state of the instrumental language of that period. Parameters such as key, mode, instrumentation, meter, characteristic rhythms, dance patterns, large-scale form, and temporal disposition were used by composers to individualize truly "abstract" genres such as the sonata. They could just as well become vehicles for dramatic meaning and integration in sinfonias – in preference to thematic-motivic material. It should of course be kept in mind that the three-movement form of the sinfonia, which was still around in the 1770s, calls for strategies of interpretation different from those demanded by the more concentrated one-movement form.

We have now cast our net so wide that we should be able to catch some dramatic meaning in the following random examples of early eighteenth-century sinfonias. We shall discover more that is dramatically relevant or individual than we may have bargained for: there will even be thematic integration and pre-announcements of specific motifs. The Gluckian watershed should not worry us. All that is needed to understand these earlier compositions might be to give up nineteenth-century aesthetic prejudices.

Giovanni Battista Pergolesi's sinfonia to *Adriano in Siria* (1734) can hardly escape the verdict of conventionality: no dramatic content, no connection with the opera, just stereotyped instrumental formulae seem to characterize this orchestral piece. Were we to find a connection with Metastasio's drama even in such a work, uncomfortable questions about the uses of musical convention might arise. Here is a suggestion.

According to Metastasio's *argomento*, the drama effects a development – that of Hadrian from an emperor freshly elevated by the troops to an emperor worthy of his glory. His virtue, which had "fallen asleep," is awakened: he becomes a victor over himself.[11] This event in Hadrian's personal development is surely the "principal action" of the work. It was a suitable *sujet* – from the poet's point of view – to honor the emperor who had commissioned the libretto. The other elements of the drama which the *argomento* quotes are significant because they help this main event to come about. They are partly ethical characteristics – Osroa's ferocity, Farnaspe's innocence, Sabina's tolerance – and partly fleeting passions such as Hadrian's own "amorous doubts" and Emirena's anxieties. What should we expect the composer to do with this menu of *parties integrantes*?

The first scene actually presents the Roman troops acclaiming Hadrian as emperor in a chorus, which constitutes the first step in the main action. After Hadrian's reply, the first stanza of the chorus is sung da capo. Pergolesi's score[12] uses an abridged version of the libretto: the chorus is not notated but rather the sinfonia is to be repeated, surely because it provided suitable music to illustrate the ceremonial acclamation and the main *sujet*. Now, Pergolesi's sinfonia as a whole has in common with the *end* of the opera at least its key, D major, and most probably also a connection with the emperorship of Hadrian, because the finale (with horns instead of trumpets) is another chorus of soldiers in D major, "May Augustus' name be heard up to the ether." Even without the support of motivic-thematic connections, it must be legitimate to relate the sinfonia to the *sujet*, especially the first Allegro movement. I suggest that its excited runs in eighth notes through all the stringed instruments, succeeding each other in quasi-fugal imitation, are a simile of the approaching troops, who hasten to greet the new emperor. The key, the trumpets, and the general heroic tone of the movement confirm the stereotype of rulership. The Allegro would thus present, in order to announce the subject matter, Hadrian's elevation, which is the immediate pre-history of the opening scene. In the Andante, a G major melody expectedly introduces soft, charming, and sentimental traits appropriate to the passive and loving character of Emirena (but not to her plight and passion); the sextuplets correspond to the triplets of her first, presentational aria, "Prigioniera abbandonata."[13] The final movement is predictably a minuet, with trumpets again and in D major. The minuet represents, as it so often does, a combination of festal celebration and high-ranking etiquette. Interestingly, in Pergolesi's abridged version of the first scene the repeat of the sinfonia overlaps with the appearance of the Parthian heroes Farnaspe and Osroa, who approach with their train across a bridge.[14] This dramaturgical cut may not be entirely fortuitous, but planned to give the minuet the function of linking, like a bridge, the Roman imperial company with the equally dignified and heroic Parthian princes. In operas of the time, dance movements including minuets quite consistently allude to exotic or pastoral characters or themes. In a contemporary performance, the Parthians would be immediately recognizable by their exotic costume; the scenery would depict the Eastern metropolis of Antiochia, a "setting" which is here so important to the subject that it is part of Metastasio's title. To illustrate the "setting" of a drama was another purpose for which dance movements were often used allusively. If these guesses are correct, then Pergolesi's sinfonia not only announces the main *sujet* centering on Hadrian and his deserved emperorship, but also refers to the ethos and dignity of other main characters and even to the "setting." It does not replace the *argomento*, but shadows it. We could perceive the three-movement discourse as saying, with a telling amplification of Metastasio's title, "Adriano – ed Emirena – in Siria."

Some years ago I offered a brief characterization of Johann Adolf Hasse's sinfonia for his *Siroe, Rè di Persia* (Bologna, 1733).[15] The relationship between sinfonia and opera appears, in this case, as a network of a few selected musical parameters that appear in varied combinations. For example, the sinfonia's main key, G major, also ends the opera and is its most frequently employed key. The tempo and meter of the first movement, fast and common time, recur at strategic points in arias, sometimes connected with G major, sometimes not. The last movement is a fast minuet or passepied (3/8), resembling the final G major coro ("I suoi nemici affetti"). But the first aria of the opera, King Cosroe's blustering reprimand of his son, "Se il mio paterno amore," is a fast minuet (3/8) in B♭ major, and his even more threatening aria in the second act,

"Tu di pietà mi spogli," is in a fast 3/8 meter and in G major again. Are we invited to perceive a connection between Cosroe's doomed kingdom and fast 3/8? The middle movement of the sinfonia deviates in tempo and meter (Lento, 3/4), but not in key, although it starts ambiguously, more as if in D major. The sarabande type of slow triple meter (Lento, 3/8) occurs in the opera only once – for the first aria sung by a female character, "Ancor io penai d'amore." Emira's nostalgic aria, in D major, has an alternating section (G major, fast duple meter) to illustrate her aggressions, too. It is possible to hear this section as corresponding to the first movement of the sinfonia, and therefore the whole self-presentational aria of the prima donna as an inversion and exaggeration of the first two movements of the sinfonia. The subject of the drama is, in fact, the deadly revenge planned by Emira against the guilty but not villainous Cosroe, which is finally overcome by her love for Siroe, who becomes king in place of his father.

Some more expressive items to be found along the path of the drama, such as the traitor Medarse's simile aria and Cosroe's ombra aria, are not reflected in the sinfonia. Nor are most of the numbers given to the title role, the immaculate Siroe, whose states of mind and lamentable fate appealed to many composers. This may be seen as a solution typical for Hasse, whose stylistic decisions tend to keep to the middle road, and whose selection of musical parameters within an opera can be very economical. But by denying the more extreme elements of the action a place in the musical *argomento*, and by referring to the main subject as it unfolds between the only two characters of mixed *ethos*, Hasse also decided in favor of a classicist dramaturgy. He combined the stereotypical building materials of his work in a carefully balanced unity, in which the one rare or "individual" element of the score, the sarabande type, is allowed to form a semantic link between the sinfonia and the opera.

To consider here the sinfonia of Leonardo Vinci's *Didone abbandonata* (Rome, January 1726)[16] means exposing my case to the most serious objection – that of the alleged interchangeability of opera sinfonias in this period. The problem is closely related, of course, to that of aria transfers and text parodies. The *Didone* sinfonia served *in toto* as the introduction to Vinci's opera *Astianatte* (Naples, autumn 1725); its last movement also concluded the sinfonia for his *Siroe, Rè di Persia* (Venice, February 1726). Vinci cannot have "integrated" his sinfonia equally well with all three operas, even assuming that this was his intention. Significantly, he also made double use of some of the arias heard in these three operas, each time employing parody texts; undeniably some of these texts fit the music better than others.

We should question the traditional view that operatic music has to be totally stereotyped and abstract to be suitable for such transfers. Could it not be that in at least one of these transfers the individualized character of the original work was successfully transplanted, even gaining a new meaning from its new artistic context? So much of the meaning of music is contextual in any case. It could be, furthermore, that some combinations of sinfonia and opera were more cogent than others, just as some aria texts fitted the music better than others – a variation that can have arisen quite naturally from fluctuations of circumstance, artistic intention, and capability.

In circumstances investigated elsewhere,[17] it is likely that Leonardo Vinci, when composing the score of *Didone* for the Carneval of 1726 in Rome, decided to use some of the music already in *Astianatte*, given in Naples in the autumn season of 1725. Since *Siroe* was scheduled for the Carneval of 1726, too, but in Venice, he was able to divert some pieces to that performance as well, significantly reducing his total work load. The sources of the operas seem reliable enough to assure us that these transfers were the composer's own intentions. As a result (and in addition to a few musical borrowings from even earlier operas), *Didone* shares four arias with *Astianatte* and two with *Siroe*, and the latter two works also share two arias. Details of the text setting strongly suggest that three of these six arias in *Didone* were originally composed for this opera, all on words by Metastasio: "Fra lo splendor del trono" (sung by Jarba in Act 1), "Ardi per me fedele," and "L'augelletto in lacci stretto" (both sung by Selene in Act 2). These three settings fit their dramatic circumstances perfectly: they were composed for *Didone* and then transferred and fitted with new texts. In the other three cases, the original contexts are in the other operas.

To give caution its due, we cannot be certain that transfers of sinfonias or parts thereof were made for the same reasons and with the same results as those affecting arias. Nevertheless, it is important that Vinci's dramaturgy did allocate a specific "home" to the aria music, rather than providing *passepartout* compositions.

The sinfonias of all three operas are in F major, but none of the operas gives particular preference to that key or ends in it. A feature of the first and third sinfonia movements is the use of *trombini* (so styled in most sources) in F; the score of *Siroe*, in the concordant third movement, calls the same parts *corni*. The first movement is characterized by an attack of fanfares in the strings in dotted rhythms, followed by very energetic violin figurations, and repercussions of pedal-point harmonies. In a later episode, the two violins have complementary sixteenth-note figurations. I suggest that these, and the dotted rhythms, link up with solos sung by Enea, communicating both his royal status and his agitated mind, for example in his opening accompagnato-arioso "Dovrei...ma no..." This piece begins in F major and ends in B♭ – just as does the first act, and indeed the whole opera, if the sinfonia is considered part of it. Of Enea's other arias, all but one have either poignant dotted rhythms or energetic violin figuration or both, comparable to the first movement of the sinfonia:

"Quando saprai chi sono" (G major, Act 1, Scene 10, a ciacona; the subject of the words is Enea's royal status),
"Se resto sul lido" (ending the first act, in B♭),
"Vedi nel mio perdono" (F major, Act 2, Scene 8), and

Serious opera

"A trionfar mi chiama" (F major, Act 3, Scene 8, referring to Enea's mission).

Of these, the last-named has no dotted rhythms but features two *corni di caccia* in F, and a texture most closely related to a stereotypical first movement of a sinfonia. Very similar violin figurations also occur in Jarba's "Chiamami pur così" (F major, Act 2, Scene 17): Jarba asserts his power against Didone, who has just called him a barbarian. All these arias are in duple meter (fast and slow). The only other aria for Enea, "Vivi superbo e regna" (C major, Act 3, Scene 1), seems to speak of Enea's royal attitude (*ethos*) of *superbia*, but in fact refers, contemptuously, to that of Jarba. Although it has a few traits recalling the other numbers, it is Enea's only aria in triple meter (fast 3/8).

An open-scene sinfonia occurs near the beginning of the third act, just before the traitor Jarba tries to attack Enea with his soldiers. The dotted rhythms and fanfares in D major, shared between strings and two *trombe* in D, refer to Enea, not to Jarba.

In *Astianatte*, there are only two arias that resemble the first movement either by key or meter or by typical figurations and texture. The closer match is found in Pirro's remonstrating "Ti calpesto o crudo fato" (Act 1, Scene 11), in F major with two *corni da caccia*. Pirro is in this drama the half-barbarous king who threatens the honor of Andromaca and the life of her son Astianatte. Parallels between the *Didone* and *Andromaca* dramas have been drawn.[18]

The second movement of the sinfonia is somewhat unusual for Vinci with its totally serious tone; it begins with a Corellian string of suspensions and adds diminished-seventh chords and a pathos-laden fermata. It is in D minor, Largo, and in a sarabande-like 3/4 meter. The only corresponding piece in the opera is the very last number, Didone's cavatina "Va crescendo il mio tormento" in D minor, Largo, and 3/8.[19] The Corellian suspensions are the second idea of the ritornello.

The slow movement of the *Siroe* sinfonia is – quite comparably – in D minor, Adagio, and 3/4, making more use of repetitive violin figuration. No aria in that opera corresponds to it, however, except perhaps Emira's "Ancor io penai d'amore" (G minor, slow, 3/8), which seems no surprise given the significance of that aria also in Hasse's setting of the libretto (see above). In Vinci's *Astianatte*, it is again the prima donna who matches the tone of the slow sinfonia movement with a single aria, the first act's cavatina "Un tuo vezzo amato figlio" (D minor, Largo, 3/8), where she starts to pour out her grief but is interrupted.

In *Didone abbandonata* the second movement ends or is interrupted on a dominant fermata (as is Didone's cavatina "Va crescendo"). It leads into a fast dance movement in 6/8 – a gigue-forlana – with a few dotted rhythms. It is easy to relate this piece to Selene's "L'augelletto in lacci stretto" (Andante, 6/8), particularly its tied-over notes and scalic motifs, which are relevant to the imagery of the words. Slightly looser connections seem to exist with Didone's more assertive first aria, "Son regina e sono amante" (fast 3/8, Act 1,

Scene 13) which is, by comparison, too agitated. Its figurations would even resemble the first movement of the sinfonia if turned into duple meter. These three arias are all in C major.

Selene's aria has been secondarily employed in *Astianatte* as "Io non vi credo, pupille belle" of Oreste (Act 2, Scene 10). No aria in *Siroe* matches this type of music (Medarse's "Deggio a te del giorno i rai," Act 2, Scene 6, is too slow), demonstrating that the movement did not originate for that opera.

It is probably transparent that the three composers Pergolesi, Hasse, and Vinci had similar conceptions of an opera sinfonia. What they all want to express is a generalized image of the most important subject matter and characters of the drama, hierarchically differentiated. The first movement presents the royal and male subject, the second a suffering female or a conflict with her or within her, and the third catches a glimpse of further characters and their backgrounds (pastoral, or otherwise diversified from the main subject). If the functions of the three movements were to be identified with dramaturgical terms, the first would be dedicated to the *soggetto* and the *ethos* of the leading character(s), the second to the *pathos* and probably also the *ethos* of the prima donna, and the third would mix *soggetto* and perhaps aspects of setting, or *decorazione*, and might have a physical connection with the beginning of the drama itself. The first and last arias of certain characters, the beginnings and ends of acts as well as of the opera, will be consciously placed to respond to the sinfonia. Quasi-correspondences with similar vocabulary in other parts of the drama may attempt to mislead us; but Vinci's Jarba is shown by the structure of the whole opera to be a false king. Pergolesi's first movement illustrates an event – a tableau – not actually seen but implied in the poet's *argomento*. Hasse demonstrates his interpretation of the *soggetto* by alluding to the real dramatic conflict of guilt and royalty, rather than the pathetic title hero; he also highlights the conflicts *within* his leading characters Cosroe and Emira. All three composers make use of the structures of the operas themselves to balance and explicate the instrumental introductions. All three sinfonias, stereotyped as they may be, somehow reflect their composers' interpretations of the dramas in terms of traditional dramatic theory.

At this point it might be argued that our three "Neapolitan" composers, who presumably learned from each other,[20] were developing a pre-Classical approach to writing opera sinfonias which was really more characteristic of a later age. The true Baroque sinfonia and overture would not yet show such reformist traits. As for the overture (the use of the French form was widespread for Italian opera introductions, especially in centers outside Italy), I hope to illustrate the problem at some other time. As for the writing of sinfonias, let us consider an example by the antipode of the Neapolitans in matters of contemporary opera, Antonio Vivaldi.

Vivaldi's *Giustino*, performed at Rome in Carneval of 1724, is a work that stands outside the Neapolitan and Metastasian sphere of influence, not exactly in terms of time and place but quite decidedly in terms of music and dramaturgy. It is almost a fairy-tale opera, overlong, anti-rational, with all the

Ex. 4 Vivaldi, *Giustino* (Rome, 1724)
a. Sinfonia I, bars 58–61
b. Anastasio, "Un vostro sguardo," bars 31–4

trimmings of the Venetian Seicento.[21] Nevertheless, the *argomento* of the libretto, arranged by an unknown hand (A. M. Lucchini?) from Beregan and Pariati, stresses the conventional *soggetto* of honor and glory at imperial courts:

> At the time when the Empress Arianna, widow of Zenone, elevated Anastasio to the empire, Vitaliano the Younger moved from Asia Minor with a powerful army, and having triumphantly crossed the Bosphorus, laid siege to Constantinople. At the same time, Giustino, having left behind his plough, got up to fight for the Greek emperor, and having captured Vitaliano, merited coronation with the imperial laurels. On these given facts is the present drama constructed.

Already the verbal shape of this *argomento* implies that not so much the well-known tale of a peasant made emperor as the double success of an imperial couple triumphing over adversity and of virtue rewarded with laurels form the *azione principale* of this libretto.

The sinfonia of the opera, written for strings only, has the three movements: C major, fast, common time; C minor, Andante e piano, 3/8; C major, Allegro, 3/8. Several actual motifs of the sinfonia recur in the opera, sometimes literally. The noisy and assertive first movement presents two repetitive motivic groups (labeled "a" and "4" respectively in my analysis)[22] which also appear in two arias of the emperor Anastasio. A striking unisono motif (not, by the way, a melodic stereotype of opera seria) links the sinfonia with Anastasio's first aria, "Un vostro sguardo" (Act 1, Scene 2), which expresses love as well as military prowess. Anastasio says that the lovely glances of his wife Arianna will help him protect her from the enemy Vitaliano, who intends to capture her. The motif underscores the words "più forza avrà" (see Ex. 4). Of the emperor's other, more indirectly related arias, his most imperial is "Verdi lauri, cingetemi il crine." It introduces a scene of triumph exactly in the

Ex. 5 Vivaldi, *Giustino*
a. Sinfonia II, bars 26–9
b. Sinfonia II, bars 41–3
c. Arianna, "La cervetta timidetta," bars 19–25
d. Arianna, "La cervetta timidetta," bars 37–9

Serious opera

Ex. 6 Vivaldi, *Giustino*
a. Sinfonia III, bars 1–4
b. Leocasta, "Nacque al bosco," bars 13–16

middle of the opera (C major, Act 2, Scene 9). Anastasio has the role of the primo uomo, although the opera's title names the "actual" dramatic hero Giustino.

The second movement of the sinfonia takes much of its music from the prima donna Arianna's last aria, "La cervetta timidetta" (Act 3, Scene 7), which is in B♭ but displays a strange leaning towards C minor. It expresses Arianna's anxiety and longing for her husband, Anastasio (Ex. 5). (Also, in Act 1 Arianna has a significant love aria in C minor.)

The last movement is an energetic passepied whose bouncy, rustic triplet figures seem reflected in Leocasta's first aria of the opera, "Nacque al bosco e nacque al prato" (Act 1, Scene 6; see Ex. 6).

But here, the seconda donna Leocasta really speaks of Giustino: having just been rescued by him from a wild monster, she imagines the young peasant as a wildflower blossoming in the courtly life to which she is going to introduce him (like *My Fair Lady* in reverse). Thus her aria uses the minuet characteristics also to describe *him* – and to refer to courtly etiquette. The composer's decision to let this aria respond to the minuet-like last movement of the sinfonia links courtly dance, pastoral imagery, and the portrayal of the two secondary (but still very important) characters whose love will be crowned in the end. Nevertheless, the two have to share the third movement of the sinfonia, whereas Anastasio and Arianna each have one full movement to themselves.

The minuet-like ending of the sinfonia leads into a magnificent opening tableau where Arianna is seen crowning Anastasio to the sound of celebratory soli and chorus in minuet patterns (A major, 3/8). The end of the opera witnesses the second coronation – of Giustino as co-emperor and of his newly-acquired bride, Leocasta. The final coro, "Doppo i nembi e le procelle," is a complex minuet-chaconne in 3/4 and C major, with a contrasting middle section in C minor sung by Arianna and Giustino. The tonal layout thus matches that of the sinfonia, corroborating the association of the imperial couple with C major and C minor, respectively. And the solo-chorus structure of the opening coronation minuet is also mirrored here.

Source studies show that Vivaldi wrote the sinfonia originally for this opera, although borrowings from a wide variety of previous works form the backbone of the rest of the score. (They include the opening theme of *La primavera* – also employed here with dramatic significance – and, in fact, the finale or some version of it.)[23] It is also certain that he composed "La cervetta timidetta" as an afterthought when the opera was almost completed – to replace a different, borrowed aria – and that he only *afterwards* wrote the sinfonia. It is as if the sinfonia had been intended to impress the final mark of unity on the whole opera. Vivaldi does not shun direct thematic references, but he also relies on structural connections – by analogy and symmetry, for example. Like any other opera composer of the period, he works with stereotypical musical ideas such as triplets, unisonos, major-minor contrasts; but he achieves semantic relevance with exactly this musical vocabulary. And finally, his sinfonia represents a dramaturgical choice as do those of the Neapolitan composers, especially Hasse's. In Vivaldi's interpretation, not the ascent of the peasant Giustino as such – the dramatic "plot" and its hero – are chosen for emphasis through the sinfonia, but the notion of imperial glory, doubly preserved through bravery and love. Thus the sinfonia sides with the emphasis of the *argomento* and, in a sense, against that of the opera's title. In any case, such a musical introduction has to be viewed against the title and *argomento* of the drama to reveal its true function – and against the structural counterparts in the music of the opera itself.

NOTES

1 My translation, from the Italian given in Giorgio Pestelli, *L'età di Mozart e Beethoven* (Turin, 1979), p. 289.
2 Nicholas Temperley, article "Overture," in *The New Grove Dictionary of Music and Musicians* (London, 1980), vol. 14, p. 34.
3 "Saggio sopra l'opera in musica," in *Scritti*, ed. Giovanni da Pozzo (Bari, 1963), p. 159.
4 "Mozart's Overture to *Titus* as Dramatic Argument," *Musical Quarterly* 64 (1978): 29–49.
5 Ibid., p. 30.
6 Thematic integration in works of that period came increasingly into conflict with symphonic forms. See Reinhard Strohm, "Gedanken zu Wagners Opernouvertüren," in *Wagnerliteratur – Wagnerforschung*, ed. Carl Dahlhaus and Egon Voss (Mainz, 1985), pp. 69–84.
7 Much of what follows could be confirmed by the brilliant *argomenti* of the leading eighteenth-century librettist, so seldom read today, Metastasio.

Serious opera

8 Pietro Metastasio, *Tutte le opere*, ed. Bruno Brunelli, 2nd edn (Milan, 1965), vol. 2, pp. 957–1117.
9 Strange as it may sound, the Italian word for "passion" here is *sentenza*, not *sentimento*, as explained by Metastasio in the *Estratto*, p. 1029.
10 Much – although not all – of the sinfonia of Gluck's *Orfeo* might fall under this verdict.
11 "Era in Antiochia Adriano, e già vincitore de' Parti, quando fu sollevato all'Impero." There follows a description of the events, historical and otherwise. The author concludes: "Le dubbiezze di Cesare fra l'amore per la principessa de' Parti e la violenza dell'obbligo che lo richiama a Sabina, la virtuosa tolleranza di questa, le insidie del feroce Osroa, delle quali cade la colpa sull'innocente Farnaspe, e le smanie d'Emirena ne' pericoli or del padre, or dell'amante ed or di se medesima, sono i moti fra' quali a poco a poco si riscuote l'addormentata virtù d'Adriano, che, vincitore alfine della propria passione, rende il regno al nemico, la consorte al rivale, il cuore a Sabina e la sua gloria a se stesso." Metastasio, *Tutte le opere*, vol. 1, p. 529. The *argomento* of Pergolesi's libretto is identical to the quoted passage.
12 Giovanni Battista Pergolesi, *Adriano in Siria*, ed. Dale Monson, vol. 3 of *Complete Works*, ed. Barry S. Brook, Francesco Degrada, and Helmut Hucke (New York and Milan, 1986).
13 I say more on this aria and on the relationship between aria conventions and dramaturgy in "Auf der Suche nach dem Drama im dramma per musica: Die Bedeutung der französischen Tragödie," in *De musica et cantu: Studien zur Geschichte der Kirchenmusik und der Oper*, ed. Peter Cahn and Ann-Katrin Heimer (Hildesheim, 1993).
14 "Replicandosi la sinfonia, passano il ponte Farnaspe ed Osroa col seguito…" Pergolesi, *Adriano in Siria*, Act 1, Scene 1. It seems acceptable to repeat, as a recent recording does, the minuet from the sinfonia alone, or even to perform it as a chorus of soldiers and courtiers with the words given by Metastasio.
15 *Die italienische Oper im 18. Jahrhundert* (Heinrichshofen, 1979), p. 204. The score is published in facsimile as vol. 33 of *Italian Opera 1640–1770*, ed. Howard Mayer Brown (New York, 1977).
16 The score discussed here is reproduced in vol. 29 of Brown (ed.), *Italian Opera* (1977).
17 Strohm, *Die italienische Oper*, pp. 172–81. An English version appears in Reinhard Strohm, *Essays on Handel and Italian Opera* (Cambridge, 1985), pp. 213–19.
18 Ettore Paratore, "L'*Andromaque* del Racine e la *Didone abbandonata* del Metastasio," in *Scritti in onore di Luigi Ronga* (Milan, 1973), pp. 515–47. Additional results might have been obtained by considering Antonio Salvi's libretto version of *Astianatte*, which is also the one set by Vinci.
19 The fact of the tempo equivalence of quarter- and eighth-note in these particular instances must be demonstrated elsewhere. For more on the music of the cavatina, see my essay mentioned in note 17.
20 Hasse and Vinci both lived at Naples from 1724 to 1729, and Pergolesi may even have studied there with Vinci around 1729.
21 Antonio Vivaldi, *Giustino*, ed. Reinhard Strohm (Milan, 1991).
22 See my introduction to Vivaldi, *Giustino*, p. 24, n. 21.
23 For details on these cross-relations, which also involve instrumental concertos, see ibid., pp. 24–8. A full account of the compilation of the autograph is found on pp. 73–83.

6

The dramatic role of the chorus in French opera: evidence for the use of gesture, 1670–1770

MARY CYR

> cette partie de la tragédie pompeuse,
> élévée, étendue & imposante
> (Bernard de la Cépède, *La Poétique de la musique*
> [Paris, 1785], v. 2, p. 254)

By the beginning of the eighteenth century, the chorus had virtually disappeared from Italian opera seria, but it still retained a prominent role in French tragédie en musique and opéra ballet.[1] An ensemble of several singers per part, the *chœur* usually remained on stage throughout each act, commenting upon or even announcing events as they unfolded. That the expressions of the chorus were actually a mirror of the audience's own emotional response may help to explain why the chorus retained such an important role during the eighteenth century. Even toward the end of Rameau's career in the 1760s, when criticism was brought against the chorus for raising the cost of productions, it was still defended by some critics as one of the enduring attractions of the Académie Royale de Musique.[2]

At least by the beginning of the eighteenth century, and probably earlier as well, the chorus was divided into two rows, called the *premier rang* and *second rang*, on either side of the stage. The orchestra could also be divided on the two sides, a position which must have presented some ensemble difficulties, although it had the virtue of allowing the king an unobstructed view. A well-known engraving by Jean Le Pautre (1618–82) shows a performance of Lully's *Alceste* on 4 July 1674 in the marble court at Versailles, with an "infinité de lumières" on the roof and windows and around the balconies. Twenty musicians occupy each box, and continuo instruments (theorbos and bowed strings) are visible on both sides. In this case, the chorus members appear to have stood within the boxes, since two rows of dancers occupied the sides of the stage.[3]

Division of the chorus into two groups remained the norm for eighteenth-century performances as well, although spatial division of the orchestra was rarely employed. An exceptional use of divided choral and instrumental forces can be found in Michel Pignolet de Montéclair's *Jepthé* (1732), the score of which preserves numerous directions for antiphonal effects. In the third act, an eight-part chorus ("Pour le vainqueur signalons nôtre zèle") is divided into

Serious opera

two four-part groups, and some phrases in the ensuing chaconne are sung by divided sopranos.[4] The choral group on each side is accompanied by a continuo group from the same side ("basses et bassons du côté droit," then "basses du côté gauche"). The libretto lists thirty-four singers in all, seventeen on each side; as we shall see, this number was larger than usual (by about four singers) for the 1730s,[5] presumably to enhance the antiphonal effects.[6]

After 1714 the two groups of singers in the chorus were identified in printed librettos according to the placement of the royal boxes, with the *côté de la reine* on the left side facing the stage, and the *côté du roi* on the right side. Riccoboni describes how these names originated at the Paris Opéra:

> La première Loge à droite, en regardant le Théâtre, est appellée La Loge du Roi; & toutes les autres, qui suivent jusqu'au fond de la Salle, le côté du Roi. La première Loge à gauche, en regardant le Théâtre, est appellée La Loge de la Reine, & toutes les autres qui suivent, le côté de la Reine: & en effet ces Loges sont destinées au Roi & à la Reine, lorsque Leurs Majestés veulent honorer le Spectacle de leur présence; ce qui arrive presque jamais, parce qu'à la Cour il y a un Théâtre, où les Comédiens vont représenter toutes les fois qu'ils en reçoivent l'ordre.[7]

At the Théâtre Italien and Comédie Française, spectators were seated on the stage, but a royal ordinance already in place in the late seventeenth century forbade their presence on stage at the Opéra because of the space required for the decoration, machines, and chorus.[8]

Although visual evidence for the precise placement of Rameau's chorus at the Paris Opéra is lacking, a plan for the Théâtre du Château de Choisy provides a close approximation of how the chorus might have looked. Similar in design to the Paris Opéra, the Théâtre du Château de Choisy was begun in 1750, but the decoration was not completed until 1763. The stage had room for a chorus of thirty-two, a figure very close to the size of Rameau's chorus in the 1730s. In a plan for the stage dating from 1773 (Figure 6.1), the position of each singer is shown – twelve women and twenty men – with the *dessus* at the front on each side, and the *basses*, *tailles*, and *hautes-contres* in a line toward the back and curving toward the center of the stage.[9] A watercolor from the same year for the theater at Versailles shows that the same formation was used for a larger chorus of forty-eight singers, with two lines curving around the sides toward the center at the back of the stage.[10]

When the chorus increased in size during the late 1740s and the 1750s to about forty singers,[11] it must have strained the already cramped space for dancers and scenery virtually to its limits. Louis de Cahusac was one of several critics who found the sight of the chorus pleasing, however incongruous their immobility seemed:

> Ils sont placés en haie sur les deux ailes du théâtre; les hautes-contres & les tailles forment une espèce de demi-cercle dans le fond. Les *chœurs* remplissent le théâtre, & forment ainsi un fort agréable coup d'œil; mais on les laisse immobiles à leur place: on les entend dire quelquefois que *le terre s'écroule*

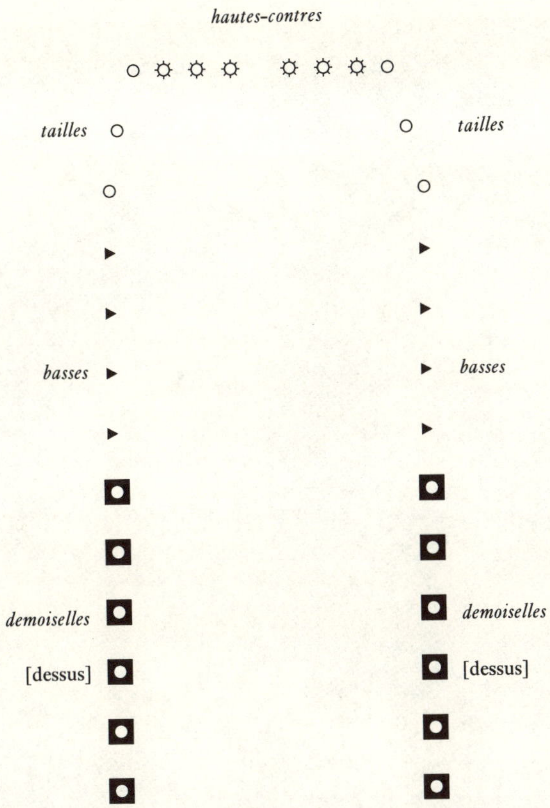

Figure 6.1 Plan for the stage of the Théâtre du Château de Choisy in 1773, showing the placement of members of the chorus. F-V, Ms. F. 87. f°9 r°. (See the original engraving reproduced in *Rameau Colloque*, figure 76.)

> *sous leurs pas, qu'ils périssent*, &c. & pendant ce tems ils demeurent tranquilles au même lieu, sans faire le moindre mouvement.[12]

The habitual presence of the chorus on stage throughout an act also drew criticism, and the chorus seemed particularly conspicuous during a long scene in which they were not required to sing. The anonymous author of a pamphlet entitled *Lettres à madame la Marquise de P... sur l'opéra* (Paris, 1741) criticizes a tender scene at the end of the second act of Lully's *Alceste* which is sung in simple recitative culminating in a duet phrase sung by Alceste and her lover Admète, who has been fatally wounded in battle.[13]

> Au milieu de tout ce que la passion exprime de vif & de tendre dans les adieux d'Alceste & d'Admète, n'est-il pas bien amusant de voir un Chœur qui prend froidement la parole pour se rendre garant des sentimens d'Admète, ou pour lui faire des complimens?[14]

The immobility of the chorus may have been dictated by a lack of space as well as custom, but the observation that the chorus did not act bears further

Serious opera

Plate 11 Design for the final act of Lully's *Amadis* (1684), drawing by Jean Bérain. F-Pn.

consideration, for the evidence is far from conclusive. A few visual documents provide us with further evidence in this regard.

By comparison with the large number of portraits and costume designs that survive, there are only a few drawings or engravings that depict the chorus. Although we cannot be sure that any of these is an accurate representation of a particular performance, the chorus appears in its usual place on stage, and it is reasonable to suppose that the members of the chorus would have looked

The chorus in French opera, 1670–1770

Plate 12 Collasse's *Thétis et Pélée* (1689), engraving by J. Dolivart after Bérain. F-Po, Réserve 926(3), p. 38.

somewhat similar. A drawing by Bérain, for example, illustrates the decor for the final act of Lully's *Amadis*, performed in Paris on 18 January 1684 (Plate 11). In the background, the façade of Apollidon's palace can be seen, "ornée de petites flèches, dont la profusion et les formes évoquent le gothique flamboyant."[15] Quinault's libretto for *Amadis* marked a return to glorification

Serious opera

Plate 13 Costume for a male chorus member in Lully's *Armide*, by Boquet. F-Po, D. 216 V A. 2 folio 99.

of the king's military exploits, reflected in the valor of Amadis.[16] The chorus is depicted by Bérain in sixteenth-century attire appropriate for this tale of chivalry.[17] In addition to a chorus of about fifteen, divided on the two sides of the stage, five principals are visible. We can observe that each of the five soloists appears to strike a different pose, incorporating a gesture with one or both arms. Individuals in the chorus, too, use different gestures of the arms.

Another design by Bérain engraved by J. Dolivart (Plate 12) illustrates the final scenes in Collasse's *Thétis et Pélée*, first performed in 1689. The scene is prepared for the marriage of Thétis and Pélée, in which "les Dieux Célestes sont placés de tous cotés sur des Nuages, et les Dieux Terrestres sont en bas." With Pan at the left, attended by "les Faunes et les Sylvains," and Flore, Palès, and Bacchus in the foreground, the moment of the final chorus of all the divinities appears ready. Although it is difficult to discern either the number of chorus members or their gestures, the chorus seems to be slightly larger – twenty or thereabouts – than in the two earlier depictions of Lully's works, and some singers have at least one hand raised. Several of the men are also holding staffs with their left hands.

Three additional drawings of costumes for performances during the 1760s also suggest that chorus members may have used simple dramatic gestures, in which one arm might be raised waist high but remains close to the body. Boquet's drawing of a male chorus member for a performance of *Armide*

The chorus in French opera, 1670–1770

Plate 14 Costume for a female chorus member "à la Romaine" (1768), Boquet. F-Po.

(Plate 13) was probably executed for one of the revivals in the 1760s.[18] Another drawing in exceptionally fine detail by Boquet shows a chorus member dressed in "Roman style" for a performance in 1768 (Plate 14), and the hand gesture appears to be an indicative one with the head slightly turned. Although I have been unable to identify the specific performance in 1768 for which Boquet's design was executed, we may assume that the chorus of Romans in Rameau's *Le Temple de la Gloire* (1745) would have been similarly attired. Another costume for a male chorus member in the 1769 performance at Fontainebleau of Rameau's *La Princesse de Navarre* (Plate 15) shows an aged Arabian astronomer, simply dressed in pantalons, holding the tool of his profession, a telescope, in his right hand. All of the visual evidence suggests, therefore, that the chorus members incorporated gestures of the hands and at least some movement of the arms. Whether they also used expressive gestures of the face, such as grief or fear, is not known, although these might be appropriate along with gestures of the hands and arms.[19]

Historical evidence, on the contrary, suggests that the chorus's physical movement was severely restricted, a situation that drew criticism from several writers. The anonymous author of the *Sentiment d'un harmoniphile* (1756), for example, complains that the chorus in Act 3 of Rameau's *Castor et Pollux* ("Brisons tous nos fers"), sung by a three-part male chorus of demons of the underworld as they restrain Pollux from entering,[20] loses coherence without

111

Serious opera

Plate 15 Costume for a male chorus member in the 1769 revival of Rameau's *La Princesse de Navarre*. F-Po, D. 216 VIII.

action or motion by the chorus. Not only did their stationary posture seem incongruous, but also, according to this writer, the dramatic sense of the scene was lost because the chorus stood with arms "crossed" (for more on this point, see below):

> ... ce concours de gens qui ne prennent aucun intérêt à ce qui se passe refroidit l'action; ... ce défaut d'action dans les chœurs ... est sensible dans l'acte des enfers, pendant le chœur "Brisons tous nos fers" ... Il faudrait que le chœur formâ des flots presque continuels de gens qui se poussent et qui sont repoussés, et que leur attitude fût celle d'une troupe qui s'oppose de toute sa force à l'entreprise d'un héros qu'elle ne peut intimider; et non pas offrir pour défendre l'entrée des enfers un tas de gens inanimés qui viennent les deux bras croisés former un contraste choquant avec la pétulance de Pollux.[21]

Another document that provides some evidence about the action on stage during the same scene from Rameau's *Castor et Pollux* is a printed libretto with manuscript annotations by a certain Monsieur de Laval.[22] The libretto cannot have been earlier than 1757, since it lacks the prologue, which was omitted that year and in subsequent revivals in the 1760s. Michel Jean de Laval (1725–77) entered the Académie Royale as *figurant surnuméraire* in 1746 and took part in many performances of Rameau's works; after 1769, he devoted himself to choreography.[23] If he is the M. Laval in question, we can assign the annotated libretto of *Castor et Pollux* to a performance in the 1760s, or possibly even later.

At the beginning of Act 4,[24] with the chorus on stage, a manuscript notation indicates that dancers are to be sent to a position beneath the stage in preparation for their appearance ("envoyer aux trapes sous le théâtre les Démons de la Danse," p. 37). As an earlier drawing by Bérain shows, a mechanism was employed to lift the demons instantaneously from a trap below the stage, concealed from the front by painted flames (Plate 16). A notation in the libretto provides the direction "Ouvrir les trapes des Demons" at the beginning of Scene 3, indicating the entrance of the demons to join Pollux, Phébé, and Mercure, and the chorus follows during the demons' pantomime. The action generated by the chorus, "Brisons tous nos fers," therefore has its realization in the dancers' pantomime at precisely the moment the chorus sings. The chorus's immobility was compensated for to some extent by the dancers, whose motions and gestures became the visual expression of the words sung by the chorus. At the end of the chorus, a manuscript notation indicates an exit for everyone during the *divertissement* in which Pollux and Mercure victoriously overcome the demons.[25] After a change of scene to the Elysian Fields and Castor's monolog ("Séjour de l'éternelle paix"), another manuscript notation in the libretto cues the entry of the dancers before the chorus sings ("Sur les derniers mesures du chant du monologue, la Danse entre sur la simphonie qui précède le chœur," p. 44). Although neither the libretto nor the annotations indicates exactly where the chorus enters, they must already have been on stage during Castor's monolog.

The puzzling description by the author of the *Sentiment d'un harmoniphile* in which chorus members were observed with arms "crossed" (*croisés*) is found in at least two other sources as well. In the article "Poésie" for the *Encyclopédie*, Baron von Grimm attempts to relate the chorus to that of spoken tragedy, but finds them a poor comparison. Their performance, he observed, was often too loud, and they were always stationary when singing "ces froids & bruyans couplets qui débitent les choristes de l'Opéra française sans actions, les bras croisés, & avec un effort de poumons à étourdir l'oreille la plus aguerrie!"[26] Much later (in 1811), the librettist Pierre Laujon recalled performances during his youth, presumably in the 1760s, in which the men sang "with their arms crossed and the women holding fans, which meant that they could not make a single gesture."[27] No visual document that I am aware of supports the claim that men in the chorus stood with their arms crossed; on the contrary, visual evidence supports the use of individual poses with one or both arms raised to the side or holding an object. One possible explanation for the term *croisé* might be a type of gesture itself, as for example, one of repose.[28]

A soloist singing with the chorus might also portray the emotions of the entire group through his or her gestures. An anonymous author (possibly Voltaire or Baron d'Holbach) cites such a passage in Mondonville's *Titon et l'Aurore* (Act 2, Scene 4), in which the soloist Eole joins a chorus of the winds.

Serious opera

Plate 16 Machinery for the appearance of demons, drawing by Bérain. F-Pn.

In the 1753 performance, according to this writer, the scene did not succeed because the heavy scepter Eole held prevented him from making the vivid, emphatic gestures that ought to have accompanied his words: "Conseillons à Eole de poser sa masse de Bedeau pendant l'exécution de Chœur des Vents, afin d'avoir les bras libres, le tout pour le plus grand effet de ce Chœur fameux qui n'en a fait aucun jusqu'à ce jour."[29] Mentioning the same scene as an example, M. de Bethizy also describes the importance of the soloist's gestures, which seem to animate the chorus and make up for their immobility, since the soloist is usually downstage in front:

> Les Acteurs qui chantent ces morceaux que les chœurs accompagnent, paroissent sur le devant du théâtre, ils expriment par leurs gestes ce qu'ils disent, ils sont animées & ils semblent animer les autres, parce que le Spectateur occupé de l'action des principaux personnages, ne fait point d'attention à l'immobilité de ceux qui chantent avec eux. M. Rameau a fait un grand nombre de chœurs admirables en ce genre, auxquels on peut joindre le chœur des vents dans l'opéra de *Titon & l'Aurore*.[30]

An example of a musical passage in which gestures might be appropriate is the chorus, "Brillant soleil," from the *acte des Incas* in Rameau's *Les Indes galantes*. Bâton le Jeune cites this passage in his *Examen de la lettre de M. Rousseau sur la musique françoise* (2nd edn, 1754) as an example of the close relationship between compositional technique and the expression of

> un concours de peuple poussé par un même tems, ni de la même manière, quoique l'acclamation paroisse générale...Nous avons un exemple bien frappant sur un double dessein, dans le chœur *brillant Soleil*, de l'Acte des *Incas*. On y entend chaque partie passer successivement & distinctement du dessein qu'elle quitte à celui qu'elle reçoit d'une autre qui prend le sien. Cet enchaînement est éclairci par la *tenue* du mot *Soleil*, qui passe alternativement dans toutes les parties; & les intervalles de ces passages sont remplis par une harmonie noble, mâle, & qui caractérise l'élévation du sujet.[31]

Bâton le Jeune does not go so far as to say that the chorus members' gestures accompany each musical phrase they sing, however this interpretation would certainly enhance the visual realization of Rameau's highly contrapuntal musical texture.[32]

Although much remains to be discovered concerning the appropriate movements of the chorus and how gestures of the eyes, face, arms, and hands may have been incorporated, visual evidence supports the use of at least some gestures with one or both arms, even if other physical movement is restricted.[33] Because of the contrapuntal complexity of Rameau's choral writing, his music seems particularly well suited to the use of slightly different gestures by soloists and members of the chorus, according to the demands of their individual parts.

NOTES

1 See Donald Jay Grout, "The Chorus in Early Opera," in *Festschrift Friedrich Blume*, ed. Anna Amalie Abert and Wilhelm Pfannkuch (Basel, 1963), pp. 151–61, and Paul-Marie Masson, *L'Opéra de Rameau* (Paris, 1930; reprinted New York, 1972), pp. 287–312. Both authors quote testimony from French and Italian observers that the French excelled in the use of the chorus. Tommaso Traetta's

choral dialogue in the second act of *Ippolito ed Aricia*, modeled on Rameau's chorus in *Hippolyte et Aricie*, was viewed as unique by the Italian audience at the time of its performance in Parma in May 1759. See Daniel Heartz, "Operatic Reform at Parma: *Ippolito ed Aricia*," in *Atti del convegno sul settecento parmense nel 2° centenario della morte di C. I. Frugoni* (Parma, 1968), pp. 271–300.

2 The anonymous author of *Lettres sur l'état présent des nos spectacles avec des vues nouvelles sur chacun d'eux, particulièrement sur la Comédie Française & l'Opéra* (Amsterdam, 1765) remarks that some critics even suggested abolishing the chorus at the Opéra: "ils les regardent comme une dépense superflue... que notre Opéra conserve ses chœurs, ils font un de ses principaux ornemens" (p. 63).

3 Neal Zaslaw has studied the Le Pautre engraving carefully for the exact size and distribution of the chorus and orchestra. He observes seven singers in the left box and five in the right one. See his article, "Lully's Orchestra" (in which the engraving is also reproduced), in *Jean-Baptiste Lully: actes du colloque Saint-Germain-en-Laye Heidelberg, 1987*, ed. Jérôme de la Gorce (Laaber, 1990), pp. 543–5. On the size and disposition of Lully's orchestra, see also Jérôme de la Gorce, "L'Académie Royale de Musique en 1704, d'après des documents inédits conservés dans les archives notariales," *Revue de musicologie* 65 (1979): 174f.

4 F-Pn, Vm^{2}299 (Act 3, Scene 6); the score is marked "tous les dessus du côté droit" and "dessus du côté gauches," pp. 138–47.

5 According to the lists of singers in published librettos from the early 1730s, the usual size of the chorus was about thirty. See Lois Rosow, "Lully's *Armide* at the Paris Opéra: A Performance History, 1686–1766," 2 vols., Ph.D. dissertation, Brandeis University, 1981, vol. 1, p. 233; Antonia Louise Banducci, "*Tancrède* by Antoine Danchet and André Campra: Performance History and Reception (1702–1764)," Ph.D. dissertation, Washington University, 1990, p. 334; and my article, "Changes in the Size and Distribution of Parts Within the Chorus of the Paris Opéra During Rameau's Career" (forthcoming in *Music & Letters*).

6 Libretto in F-Pn, shelf number Th^{B}1723A, p. xvi.

7 Riccoboni, *Réflexions historiques et critiques sur les différens théâtres de l'Europe* (Amsterdam, 1740), p. 107.

8 Henri Lagrave, *Le Théâtre et le public à Paris de 1715 à 1750* (Paris, 1972), pp. 109–10, and Riccoboni, *Réflexions historiques*, p. 140. Lagrave gives the dimensions of the stage at the Salle de l'Opéra (Palais-Royal): stage depth 16.95 meters, and stage width at the front 9.40 meters. A drawing by George Wille the younger of the Théâtre Italien in 1767 (Paris, Cabinet des Estampes) shows no spectators on the stage, however the front boxes extend onto the stage area; see Daniel Heartz, "Opéra-Comique and the Théâtre Italien from Watteau to Fragonard," in *Music in the Classic Period: Essays in Honor of Barry S. Brook* (New York, 1985), pp. 69–84.

9 Thierry-G. Boucher, "Rameau et les théâtres de la cour (1745–1764)," in *Jean-Philippe Rameau: colloque international organisé par la Société Rameau, Dijon, 21–24 septembre 1983*, ed. Jérôme de la Gorce (Paris and Geneva, 1987), p. 576.

10 The "plan de la Musique du Roy au grand théâtre de Versailles" (F-V Ms 131) is reproduced by Lois Rosow, "Performing a Choral Dialogue by Lully," *Early Music* 15 (1987): 329. I am indebted to Antonia Banducci for the shelf number of the watercolor.

11 For a fuller discussion, see my article, "Changes in the Size."

12 Louis de Cahusac, "Chœur," in *Encyclopédie ou dictionnaire raisonné des sciences, des arts et des métiers* (Paris, 1751; reprinted New York, 1969), vol. 1, p. 573.
13 A facsimile of this scene (Act 2, Scene 8) from the 1778 libretto is included in Buford Norman, "Ancients and Moderns, Tragedy and Opera: The Quarrel over *Alceste*," in *French Musical Thought, 1600–1800*, ed. Georgia Cowart (Ann Arbor, 1989), pp. 177–96.
14 Anonymous, *Lettres à Madame la Marquise de P... sur l'opéra* (Paris, 1741), p. 104. The author's criticism seems to place blame upon the composer as much as the singers for the lack of involvement of the chorus: "Je sçais bien que souvent les Chœurs de nos Opéras ne sont aussi qu'une foule de gens désœuvrés qui ne viennent sur le Théâtre que parce que leur Maître le leur commande, ou que le Poëte les y envoye; mais enfin, il n'ont point de tems fixé & déterminé pour parler, & ils n'embarrassent point continuellement la Scene de leur présence" (p. 103f).
15 Quoted from the 1684 libretto, in Jérôme de la Gorce, *Bérain, dessinateur du Roi Soleil* (Paris, 1986), p. 85.
16 See Robert M. Isherwood, *Music in the Service of the King* (Ithaca, 1973), pp. 229–35.
17 Bérain also designed the costumes for a performance at Versailles in 1685.
18 Performances of Lully's *Armide* took place in 1761–2, 1764–5, and 1766 (the last performance). See Lois Rosow, "Lully's *Armide* at the Paris Opéra," vol. 1, pp. 235–7, and her essay, "How Eighteenth-Century Parisians Heard Lully's Operas: The Case of *Armide*'s Fourth Act," in *Jean-Baptiste Lully and the Music of the French Baroque: Essays in Honor of James R. Anthony*, ed. John Hajdu Heyer (Cambridge, 1989), p. 228.
19 Dene Barnett, *The Art of Gesture: The Practices and Principles of 18th Century Acting* (Heidelberg, 1987), pp. 36f.
20 Rameau, *Œuvres Complètes*, vol. 8, *Castor et Pollux* (1737 version), Act 3, Scene 4, pp. 199–212.
21 Anonymous, *Sentiment d'un harmoniphile* (1756), pp. 35–6. The passage is also quoted by Masson, *L'Opéra de Rameau*, p. 293, who attributes its authorship to Morambert.
22 F-Po, A. I. D. 3117.
23 Marie-Françoise Christout, "Laval," in *Enciclopedia dello spettacolo* (Rome, 1959), vol. 6, pp. 1286–7.
24 Act and scene numbers in the following discussion refer to the revised version of 1754.
25 According to the 1754 libretto (*Œuvres Completes*, vol. 8, p. 413), "Les démons continuent leur danse, les Furies sortent des enfers et paraissent, armées de flambeaux et de serpents. Pollux combat les démons. Mercure les frappe de son caducée et s'abîme avec Pollux dans la caverne."
26 Grimm, "Poésie," in the *Encyclopédie*, vol. 2, p. 1448.
27 Rosow, "Performing a Choral Dialogue," p. 329.
28 See, for example, the engraving by Bonnart (late seventeenth century) of a gentleman standing with hands crossed, in Wendy Hilton's *Dances of Court and Theater: The French Noble Style, 1690–1725* (Princeton, 1981), p. 66.
29 [Voltaire? or Baron d'Holbach?], *Arrêt rendu à l'amphithéâtre de l'Opéra, sur la Plainte du Milieu de Parterre intervenant dans la querelle des deux COINS* (Paris, 1753), reprinted in Denise Launay, *La Querelle des bouffons* (Geneva, 1973), vol. 1, p. 285.

30 Launay, *Querelle*, vol. 1, p. 299.
31 Ibid., vol. 1, pp. 926ff.
32 For further discussion of pantomime and gesture linked to dramatic action, see Daniel Heartz, "From Garrick to Gluck: The Reform of Theatre and Opera in the Mid-Eighteenth Century," *Proceedings of the Royal Musical Association* 94 (1968): 111–27.
33 For additional evidence about the chorus's entrance from the rear of the stage, see Antonia Banducci, "Staging a *tragédie-lyrique*: A 1748 Promptbook of Campra's *Tancrède*," *Early Music* 21 (1993): 180–90.

7

Transforming opera seria: Verazi's innovations and their impact on opera in Italy

MARITA PETZOLDT McCLYMONDS

Mattia Verazi, court poet at Mannheim and Stuttgart, stands as a significant figure within the trend towards a Franco-Italian synthesis in mid-eighteenth-century opera. In many ways, Verazi's work exemplifies Gluck's professed goals as set forth in the Dedication to the published score of his *Alceste* (1769): that the overture ought to apprise the spectators of the nature of the action that is to be represented and to form, so to speak, its argument; that the concerted instruments should be introduced in proportion to the interest and the intensity of the words, and not leave a sharp contrast between the aria and the recitative in the dialog; that the poet devise a new dramatic scheme, replacing florid descriptions, unnatural paragons, and sententious, cold morality with heartfelt language, strong passions, interesting situations, and an endlessly varied spectacle.[1]

Like Gluck, who undertook to divest *Alceste* "entirely of all those abuses, introduced into it [Italian opera] either by the mistaken vanity of singers or by the too great complaisance of composers," Verazi, in the prefaces to *Europa riconosciuta* and *Troja distrutta* for Milan in 1778, claims a similar desire "to reform those abuses introduced of a licentious execution that are often tolerated as custom," and to add "variety, verisimilitude, and action" to his *dramma in azione*, while at the same time following the Metastasian example in "shunning crude, unseemly language and striving for purity, elegance, and sweetness."[2] Metastasio himself commented in reference to Verazi's most radical work, *Europa riconosciuta*, "I find my friend, Signor Verazi, always equal to himself: flowing, happy, clear, and rich in that enviable fertility of fancy which constitutes the principal merit of dramatic poetry, and which communicates itself to all the inferior arts employed in its support."[3] In practice, Verazi's primary goals appear to have been to devise ever more powerful means of seizing his spectators and strongly moving them to awe, terror, or tears. His late works summarize thirty years of gradual modifications in Italian practice skillfully blended with spectacular elements, such as chorus, ballet, pantomime, and stage effects, all assembled for maximum dramatic impact.[4]

The first libretto attributed to Verazi is Jommelli's *Ifigenia in Aulide* (Rome, 1751). Shortly thereafter, in 1755, Verazi followed his collaborator to Stuttgart, where he wrote Jommelli's two French-inspired operas of that year, *Enea nel Lazio* and *Pelope*. A year later, he became court poet for the Palatinate at

Mannheim, where, by 1762, he was also functioning as Italian Private Secretary to Elector Karl Theodor. Having retired from service when the court moved to Munich in 1778, Verazi wrote his last large-scale operatic works for the opening of La Scala in Milan, 1778–9.

Several aspects of Verazi's first opera, *Ifigenia in Aulide*, suggest Jommelli's influence. Many of the aria texts exceed the normal double quatrain by as many as six lines, better serving the extraordinarily long arias in vogue at mid-century. Furthermore, Verazi provided Jommelli with passionate aria texts to be amplified with expressive music, and strong dramatic scenes to be realized in obbligato recitative.[5]

Here Verazi shows an early inclination to depart from contemporary practice for the sake of greater dramatic impact. He planned each act so as to maintain action throughout and to drive toward a climax at the end. We can also notice already a tendency to amplify the horrifying aspects of the plot and to relate the aria more closely to the action than was customary. Though vestiges of both Racine's play and Zeno's libretto still remain, the endings of the first two acts depart from both models.[6] In earlier versions all of the characters learn of Ifigenia's fate at the same time. In Verazi's version the horror of the situation sustains and builds as each learns of it and reacts individually.

In the last act, both Zeno and Verazi adopt Racine's means of saving Ifigenia from death, but Verazi's audience is not spared the horror of the sacrificial scene, which earlier audiences learned of as Agamemnon related the sequence of events to the grieving Clytemnestra. In Verazi's version, the sacrificial scene brings the opera to a spectacular and dramatic close. A lugubrious sinfonia and the processions of royal guards and sacred ministers impart a dreadful solemnity to the occasion. Ifigenia, clad in sacrificial white and festooned with flowers, is led to the altar and pyre. A willing victim, she bids farewell to her grieving father and her distraught beloved in a long obbligato recitative and aria. Suddenly news arrives that another Ifigenia, heretofore known as Erifile, is the true sacrifice the gods are demanding. Erifile then sings an impassioned recitative and arioso and flings herself into the sea. In a mixture of horror and relief the remaining characters join in an ensemble, alternating solos and tutti refrain as they beg for the heavens to bestow peace upon all. A major aria without subsequent exit, the tragic, staged suicide, and the extensive final ensemble all represent significant departures from established practice.

Verazi's first two operas for Stuttgart of 1755, *Pelope* and *Enea nel Lazio*, are both French-inspired pieces on mythological subjects in which deities descend from above to participate in the plot and contribute to the spectacle. The librettos are still constructed in the Italian manner with a succession of recitatives and arias, but they are infused with spectacular stage effects, choruses, pantomime, and very likely dancing, although the last is never specifically mentioned in the librettos. A spectacular event occurs in the first half of each act, and chorus alone or in combination with aria or ensemble replace some of the usual concluding arias to Acts 1 or 2.[7]

The spectacular scenes constitute the most notable departure from mainstream Italian operatic practice. Jommelli depicts some of the action in sinfonias, but much of it is described in programmatic obbligato recitative. In Act 2, for example, Neptune describes the tumultuous sea stirred up by his appearance with an obbligato recitative in which undulating strings and accent-punctuated repeated notes build to a climax of string figuration. Both the sea and the music calm as Neptune lands.

Two other operatic ingredients first appearing here in *Enea* will claim Verazi's creative attention in future operas: the large ensemble and the strong opening scene. To strengthen the opening of *Enea*, Verazi created a solemn temple scene made ominous and terrifying with intense choruses, obbligato recitative, and a dramatic closing aria, and he placed his first great quintet near the end of Act 3.

Verazi wrote no significant librettos for Mannheim until Traetta was invited to compose an opera for the court in 1762. In writing *Sofonisba* for Traetta, Verazi was again working with a composer who knew how to handle both drama and spectacle. Still Verazi's idiosyncratic kind of Franco-Italian synthesis was to prove a great deal more radical than the traditional French pieces Traetta had composed for Parma.[8]

Pierre Corneille's dramatization of Sofonisba's story had its origins in Roman history. Francesco Silvani, in his operatic version for Antonio Caldara in 1708, had simply ignored the tragic ending.[9] Not so Verazi. The mounting horror of impending tragedy extends over several scenes as Sofonisba prepares to quaff the fatal cup. First she muses over her strange situation in obbligato recitative and arioso, punctuated with a poignant refrain "che fier destin, che strano caso è il mio" (what savage fate, what strange destiny is mine). After a tender duet with her little son, she sends him away in order to carry out her irreversible deed. The scene does not end in an aria. Too late, Siface and Massinissa arrive to report that all has been resolved. They can do nothing but watch Sofonisba die and join with the rest of the cast in a final mournful quintet. Such an extended death scene and tragic ending would have been a shock to an audience used to the final, breathtaking succession of events that always produced the happy ending in Metastasian drama.

Sofonisba was undoubtedly the first opera in which Verazi combined the sinfonia with the opening scenes of the opera, although the libretto does not specifically link the two, as in later operas. An elaborate pantomine preceding the first scene depicts a city wall under siege. As the walls give way, the aggressors enter victoriously. In the manuscript score at the Staatsbibliothek Preussischer Kulturbesitz, Berlin, the first of two final Allegro movements in the sinfonia bears the words, "Musica per l'aspro ed ostinato combattimento è che de le servirà per l'ultimo Allegro della sinfonia." (Music for the harsh and relentless fighting and for the final Allegro of the sinfonia.)

For the first time in *Sofonisba*, footnotes contain extensive directions for actions to be executed during the normally static aria. In Sofonisba's aria "Crudeli, aimè! Che fate?" Traetta dispenses with the introductory ritornello and moves immediately from obbligato recitative into a fragmented, declamatory aria in G minor over string tremolos marked Allegro descretto. In several places the aria is interrupted with a French scream and a few measures of obbligato recitative. The first two lines of the second stanza are marked Maestoso with a fermata over "chi." The rest of the aria is marked Allegro agitato. Traetta noted at various points in the aria where the actions specified in Verazi's footnotes should be carried out.

Also for Traetta, Verazi wrote his first ensemble of diminishing forces – parallel in effect to the final scenes of a Metastasian Act 1 or 2. The trio at the end of Act 2 Verazi rendered as an action ensemble undoubtedly intended to be through composed. Siface is in such a fit of despair that he threatens to stab his beloved Sofonisba. Impressed with the force of their passion, Massinissa relents and orders them to flee. They sing together and then move to leave with their child. Massinissa reacts first to stop them and then to let them go. He then closes the ensemble alone on stage. Unfortunately Traetta followed the usual procedure of setting the words twice, which must have greatly diminished the effect.

Two years later, in 1764, De Majo, maestro di cappella at Naples, came to Mannheim to set Verazi's *Ifigenia in Tauride*. De Majo had just come from Vienna, where he had composed Marco Coltellini's libretto, *Alcide negli orti Esperidi*, his first experience with an opera representing a Franco-Italian synthesis.[10]

The libretto for *Ifigenia* leaves no doubt that the sinfonia was intended to accompany the stage action. A storm and shipwreck occur during the first Allegro. The central Andante represents the calming of the storm and the landing of the survivors. A battle takes place during the second Allegro, and the survivors are captured and taken away. Nicholas Guillard later adopted this opening for Gluck's *Iphigénie en Tauride* for Paris in 1779.[11]

Verazi may not have been called upon to provide excuses for the appearances of deities in machines in Mannheim, but there was no lack of natural or man-made spectacle. In the middle of Act 1, Verazi suspends the exit aria convention in order to create an enormous scene complex that extends very nearly to the end of the act. Into an arena containing caged wild animals, the warrior Merodate enters, riding in a chariot drawn by tamed beasts and accompanied by military music. Slaves follow the chariot leading chained animals as nuptial gifts for the Princess Tomiri. Merodate does not leave after his obbligato recitative, his cavatina, or after a chorus of his warriors. Nor does he leave after a subsequent aria. Rather, the amphitheater fills for musically accompanied gladiatorial games. The scene finally ends with battle music. Verazi concludes Act 1 with yet another first. Duets were never written for any other than the principal couple, yet here, two men, Oreste and his faithful friend Pilade, bring the act to a close.

For *Ifigenia* Verazi once again rejected the usual ending in which Ifigenia, having learned the true identity of Oreste, turns on the tyrant Toante and kills him. Verazi planned a far greater spectacle that unmistakably parallels the ending to Metastasio's *Didone abbandonata*. With the city under attack and the temple in flames, Toante refuses several attempts to save himself and remains behind to close the opera in a final programmatic recitative with arioso before perishing as the temple collapses.

At a time when operas never had more than one or at the most two ensembles, and choruses were generally cut from Metastasian librettos, Verazi's *Ifigenia* had one quartet of diminishing forces, two duets, one of which is briefly interrupted midway by an interjection from a third party (*pertichino*), three trios (all through composed), and four scenes with chorus.

With the completion of a new theater especially suited to spectacle in the French style at the palace of Ludwigsburg near Stuttgart, Verazi was once again called upon to write new operas for Jommelli. In his *Fetonte* of 1768, Verazi provided Jommelli with the most radical opera he would ever set to music.[12] *Fetonte* represents Verazi's most extensive use of spectacle, ballet, and chorus to this point, breaking up the inevitable succession of recitatives and exit arias through the use of cavatinas and ensembles with diminishing forces.

In the first scene of Act 2, Orcane sings a cavatina without exit. Then two characters leave together following a duet, which takes the place of two arias. Phaeton concludes this scene-group with a solo scene and aria. The rest of Act 2 is made up of two large diminishing ensembles, each introduced with an aria. The procedure works this way (Figure 1). Normally, scenes five through seven would have been made up of a succession of exit arias. Instead, Climene sings and exits. Without any further recitative, the remaining four characters sing a quartet; two leave, and a duet concludes the ensemble. In the sequence at the end of Act 2, Phaeton sings an aria but does not leave. Instead, he goes directly into a trio with Libia, who has just arrived, and Climene, who was already in the scene. Phaeton leaves, and two women, Libia and Climene, conclude the ensemble and the act with a duet.

In Act 3, only two arias and a duet precede the two final scenes, which employ continuous orchestral accompaniment. In the penultimate scene, Climene and Orcane describe Phaeton's fateful ride in programmatic obbligato recitative. Near the end of the scene, a chorus of humanity begs for the intervention of heaven as the earth begins to tremble and catch fire. Jove appears and strikes Phaeton from the skies, from whence he falls into the sea. The last scene is an action ensemble finale of a type heretofore only found in comic opera. Seeing that Phaeton has perished, Climene rejects her two suitors and throws herself into the sea. The opera ends with a final chorus of terrified people attempting to escape the smoke, flames, and destruction.

Dwindling resources were soon to put an end to the days of spectacular opera and ballet at Ludwigsburg. Verazi did only one more opera there, *Calliroe* in 1770.[13] Antonio Sacchini came from Venice to compose it, since Jommelli had gone back to Italy in 1769, never to return. In *Calliroe*, Verazi continued with the techniques he had pioneered in earlier operas. Lope de Vega's Juliet story provided the idea for a nonpoisonous potion that allowed a happy ending this time. Again, as in *Fetonte*, internal sections of the opera are consolidated into ensembles, and the opera closes with an action ensemble that expands, finale

Leggi sdegno, non soffro consigli:
Non pavento minacce, perigli.
Oltraggiata, sol bramo, sol voglio
Tant' orgoglio, ₌ superbi, punir. a)

SCENA VI.

EPAFO, ORCANE, LIBIA, e FETONTE.

Ep. a Lib.   *Orc. a Fet.*
Tu più saggia   Meno audace

Ep. a Lib.   *Orc. a Fet.*
Cangia   Frena

Ep. ed Orc.
Il fasto, e l'ire.

Ep.   *Orc.*
Un sorride! b)   L'altra tace! c)

Ep. a Lib.   A 4.   *Orc. a Fet.*
Quel silenzio contu-   Quel fallace ₌ tuo
mace   contegno
  Ep.

a) *Parte.*
b) *Guardando Lib.*   c) *Guardando Fet.*

Ep. ed Orc.
Il mio sdegno ₌ irriterà.
Lib. e Fet.
Men s'ostenta, più l'ardire
Divisar talor si fà. a)

Orc. a Fet.   *Fet. ad Orc.*
Ascolta. b)   O tutto inteso. c)

Ep. a Lib.   *Lib. ad Ep.*
Spiegati. d)   O detto assai. e)

Orc. a Fet.   *Fet. ad Orc.*
Geloso ardor...   Giamai f)
  L'alma non t' in-
  fiammò.

Lib. ad Ep.   *Ep. a Lib.*
Ma che più vuoi? g)   Compreso
  Il tuo pensier non ò.

Lib. ad Ep.   *Fet. ad Orc.*
Se il favellar sì   Debito omaggio, il
poco   sai, h)
Di due pupille   È di beltade
intendi,   amore.
  Ciò

a) *In atto di partire.*   b) *Ritenendolo.*
  c) *Tornando indietro.*
d) *Richiamandola.*   e) *Arrestandosi; ma*
  sprezzante.
g) *Con intolleranza.*   f) *Con derisione.*
  h) *Con ironia amara*
  & insultante.

Ciò, che saper   Nè può vietarsi a
pretendi, a)   un core

Tutto è palese   Sol perche piace
a lui.   altrui,

Già da quest'oc-   Di tributare a lei ₌
chj miei ₌

Tradita io fui.   Gli affetti sui.

Lib.   *Fet.*
Del suo destino in-   De' dritti altrui dub-
certo b)   bioso c)

  A 2.
Chi al fuoco tormentoso
Di gelosia s'accende,
Degrada i merti suoi, ₌
Se stesso offende. d)

SCE-

a) *Accennando Orc. con*   c) *Come sopra fino*
ironia insultante.   *al fine.*
b) *Come sopra fino*   d) *Partono insieme.*
al fine.

SCENA VII.

ORCANE, ed EPAFO.

Ep.   *Orc.*
Sol di gioco, e   Vil cagion di reo
scherno oggetto   diletto
  A 2.
Divenuto io quì sarò!

Ep.   *Orc.*
Che sospendo? a)   Che mi arresto? b)
Ep.   *Orc.*
Già mi scuoto.   Già mi desto.
Ep.   *Orc.*
Ah paventi   Si sgomenti
  A 2.
Provocar chi me tentò.

Ep.   *Orc.*
Sordo ai pianti, alle   Implacabil, e cru-
querele, c)   dele, d)
Al mio piede ₌ in-   Stragi, morti, affan-
van mercede   ni, e lutto
Domandar l'ascol-   Da per tutto ₌
terò. e)   spargerò. f)

SCE

a) *Pensoso.*   b) *Turbato.*
c) *Agitato.*   d) *Furioso.*
e) *Parte.*   f) *Parte.*

Figure 1. Verazi and Jommelli, *Fetonte* (Ludwigsburg, 1768), Act II, Sc. 5–7. Libretto in US-Wcm, Schatz 8460.

style, from a quintet to an octet, rather than diminishing as the internal ones do. *Calliroe* has twelve arias, four duets, two diminishing trios, one big internal, diminishing ensemble involving a battle that goes from five singers to three, to one, and an ensemble finale.

Verazi was to write his most radical operas not for Germany but for Milan, where he was engaged for the fall and Carneval seasons 1778–9 to combine spectacle, chorus, dancing, and decoration in magnificent operas for the grand opening of the new opera house, La Scala.[14] When Gluck declined to come because of heavy commitments in Paris, his disciple Salieri was engaged to compose the first opera, *Europa riconosciuta*.[15] Into this opera and its ballets Verazi poured all of his most successful spectacular effects. A storm-and-shipwreck sinfonia moves directly into a scene complex of obbligato recitative, cavatina, action ensemble, battle, and chorus that could be appropriately labeled "Introduzione." Verazi wrote great detail into the footnotes of his libretto. Besides line-by-line instructions for the actions to accompany the singing, Verazi also noted musical details, specifying such things as the instruments to be scored, the style of composition desired, and the formal construction to be followed.

Most startling of all, he wrote roles for five principal characters; there are no secondary roles. The first act has no true arias, and only two of the five arias in the second act conclude with an exit. There is no third act. The first duet is an angry exchange between Semele and the tenor Egisto, and the second a proper love duet, but by the end of Act 1 the audience had yet to hear the prima donna Balducci in either an aria or a duet. The second act has a duet for yet another unusual combination – one member each from the principal couples – former lovers now reunited under impossible circumstances. If this were not enough, Egisto is slain on stage in full view of a very shocked audience. No wonder the Milanese formed the opinion that Verazi was a "bad poet."[16]

Bowing to public displeasure, Verazi cast his second opera, *Troja distrutta*, along somewhat more conservative lines.[17] There are fewer ensembles and more arias, which he was obliged to leave free of interruptions and actions. Nevertheless, casting was even more unorthodox than in *Europa*. He called for only one primo uomo and a tenor along with the same two prime donne, but billed in reverse order, and a seconda donna. The spectacle also remained. The last three movements of the sinfonia accompany a chorus terrified by the trembling earth and lightning emanating from a dark cavern. No introduzione follows, but the first act concludes with a true multisectional action-filled ensemble finale with chorus covering four scenes and expanding in forces.

In Act 2 Verazi indulged the audience with a fairly conservative succession of arias. The same cannot be said for Act 3. The first three scenes involve an elaborate, dramatic pantomime as the horse is wheeled into the city, and the Greeks emerge, spreading terror, fire, destruction, and death as they overcome the vulnerable Trojans. The remaining four scenes of the opera are almost entirely orchestrally accompanied, moving freely among the textural options of recitative, ensemble, arioso, cavatina, and chorus. Paride and Elena throw themselves into the flames together, and Cassandra and Deifebo remain behind with the Trojan women to conclude the opera in ensemble and chorus with their Greek captors.

Verazi's last two operas for La Scala, *Calliroe* and *Cleopatra*, demonstrate exactly which among his innovations the Italian public was willing to tolerate.[18] All spectacle, ballet, and chorus has disappeared, but Verazi's many ensembles including those with fluctuating personnel and with action remain. *Calliroe* had always had a happy ending, but in *Cleopatra*, the story was allowed to proceed to its tragic close as both Anthony and Cleopatra die on stage in the finale.

In attempting to identify those of Verazi's ideas that might have been adopted by others during the last half of the century, one must eliminate the French elements that he shared with those working around Gluck in Vienna and with Frugoni's translations of French opera, which Traetta set for Parma. Spectacle involving machines, mythological subjects, gods involved in the affairs of men, chorus alone and in combination with soloists, the ballet, the dramatic fluidity that the aria without exit allowed, and death and tragedy played out on the stage are all elements from seventeenth-century opera still present in eighteenth-century French opera, but purged from Italian opera in the Arcadian reform early in the century.

Verazi's particular contribution lay in the infusion of Italian dramaturgy with French spectacular elements, such as natural or man-made spectacle, pantomime, and chorus, while at the same time loosening the dramaturgical convention of the exit aria through constructions designed to achieve a heightened dramatic effect. In the more traditional of such constructions he, like Gluck, freely combined the already established textural options of chorus, recitative, arioso, and ensemble into scene complexes. His second, more radical approach challenged the hierarchy of singers by greatly increasing the number of ensembles in each act and thereby reducing drastically the number of arias and the amount of simple recitative. Further, Verazi's ensembles were no longer formal, static expressions of collective emotion but might expand or contract in the number of persons, extend over several scenes, involve action, and even include chorus. The aria itself was charged with passion and might be interrupted with recitative, with action, or with interjections from other characters or chorus (*pertichini*). Finally Verazi restored the strong medicine of terror, horror, and tragedy to create intense moving drama free from the often contrived, compulsory happy ending.

The crosscurrents of experimentation with French elements in opera occurring between Parma, Mannheim, Stuttgart, and Vienna in the 1750s and 60s had very little effect on Italian theaters. Most of them simply lacked the special facilities, the dancers, and the chorus required. Nor did Italian audiences and patrons feel the need to alter greatly a form that had developed to suit their cultural and social customs. Still, a greater interest in spectacle does seem to have developed in the 1770s, not as a direct result of Verazi's work, but indirectly through the modification of Verazi's radical techniques in

Turin, where the librettist Vittorio Amadeo Cigna-Santi worked from 1755 to 1775.

The Turinese court theater had done Frugoni's *Medo* set by Girolamo Abos in 1753, and Cigna's first libretto, *Andromeda*, dealt with Perseus' encounter with the Minotaur. He reworked his first Verazian libretto, *Enea nel Lazio*, for Traetta in 1760, two years before Traetta went to Mannheim to set Verazi's *Sofonisba*. Cigna wrote his own frequently set tragedy, *Motezuma*, the year after Turin produced Traetta's *Sofonisba* in 1764. Still Cigna's tragedy is less shocking, because Motezuma has the good taste to die offstage. Verazi's *Ifigenia in Tauride* must have inspired the ending, in which the villain, Cortes, is left alone on stage, with the treasure and the city in flames around him.[19]

Spectacle opera suited to the Turinese taste also proved attractive to other Italian theaters, and Cigna's operas soon began appearing in all the major houses. The formula entailed lavish, spectacular stage effects added to a traditional libretto with a happy ending, and minimal demands for ballet and chorus. Even tragedy could be tolerated, but no staged death. It was Cigna's *Mitridate, Rè di Ponto* that Mozart composed for Milan in 1770. Further, Jacopo Durandi, Cigna's replacement in Turin for the 1769–71 seasons, was responsible for one of the two *Armida* librettos that, as a composite, were revised and set during the last half of the century by many composers, including Haydn.[20]

Verazi's operas for La Scala were to have a much more direct and far-reaching impact on Italian operatic theater than the negative reception accorded them in Milan might lead one to expect. From 1779 on, features he pioneered begin to appear in other librettos. The Florentine Theater in particular began to produce operas with tragic endings, going so far as to depict death and even murder on stage. These operas were in turn passed on to Venice and Milan, so that by 1790 "morte" operas had become fashionable: *La morte di Cesare, La morte di Cleopatra, La morte di Semiramide*.[21]

A number of young Venetian librettists who began working in the 1780s and 90s cautiously incorporated one or more of Verazi's innovations into their operas. The first of these is Gaetano Sertor, who began his career in 1779 and had his first opportunity to experiment in collaboration with Francesco Bianchi in Naples. Their two operas of 1781, *Arbace* and *Zemira*, have multiple ensembles and cavatinas, an ensemble of expanding personnel, and a modest introductory ensemble. Near the end of *Arbace*, we learn of the death of the tyrant in the flames of the city. When the operas were done in Venice the following year, the ensemble of expanding personnel disappeared, but *Zemira*, composed by Pasquale Anfossi, who set Verazi's *Cleopatra* in Milan, acquired a short duet without subsequent exit, and a final coro expanded with solo sections. Sertor's *Osmane*, which Giuseppe Giordani set for Venice in 1784, has an ensemble that begins with dramatic short soli rather than following the traditional format in which each character has a long solo alone at the beginning of an ensemble. Arias are both interrupted and concluded with recitative.[22]

Sertor returned to Naples in 1785 to write a spectacle opera for Pietro

Guglielmi. *Enea e Lavinia* has two terrifying scenes, both borrowed from Verazi's *Enea nel Lazio*. One is a scene complex in which Juno appears in a cloud, delivers a vendetta, and leaves everything in ruins. In the second, the ominous ghost of Dido interrupts Lavinia's *sonno* aria.[23] Later the same year, Sertor went to Munich to write an *Armida* for Alessio Prati. Like Mozart's *Idomeneo* four years earlier, *Armida* has the lavish spectacle typical of Verazi's operas, the choruses, ballets, and pantomimes, as well as the requisite quartet, but otherwise the format is much more conservative than Verazi's. Only the multiple cavatinas, some sung by more than one person, the occasional aria without exit, and the solo with chorus in the French style can be singled out as formally non-traditional.[24]

Mozart's *Idomeneo* was unusual for the erstwhile Mannheim, now Munich, court in its close adherence to a French model, and much of its spectacle springs from Danchet's libretto. Still, we know from Mozart's letters that it was Lorenzo Quaglio, the court theatrical architect who had worked with Verazi from the beginning, and Claude Legrand, the choreographer whom Verazi had taken with him to Milan, who together refined the terrifying finale of Act 2, in which all flee the wrath of Neptune, leaving Idomeneo on stage alone.[25] Nor were storms at sea, festivals of celebrating survivors, or the voices of oracles new to these veterans. The many ensembles, the arias without exit, and the ample opportunities for dramatic obbligato recitative also follow in the Verazi tradition.

While Sertor was in Germany, Giovanni de Gamerra, who had no librettos to his credit after Salieri's *Daliso e Delmita* for Vienna ten years earlier, was called to Naples to write what would prove to be a highly successful opera for Giovanni Paisiello. The composer had just returned from St. Petersburg, where he had been working with another Viennese product, Marco Coltellini. In his *Pirro* for Naples in 1787, Gamerra, who had unsuccessfully advocated more freely constructed librettos for opera in Milan in the early 1770s, took the step that Sertor had been either unwilling or unable to make, and, following Verazi's lead, appended an extensive introduzione at the beginning of the opera and action ensemble finales at the end of both Acts 1 and 2. This opera was done in Venice later the same year.[26]

The first works of another young Venetian librettist, Giuseppe Foppa, marked the beginning of a new era in Venetian opera. His *Alonso e Cora* (1786) and *Calto* (1788), both set by Bianchi, employ ballet and chorus along with multiple ensembles including a duet for two men and extensive scene complexes, one of which comprises all of the very short Act 3 in *Alonso*.[27] Hereafter chorus, ballet, scene complexes, and multiple ensembles and cavatinas became regular ingredients in Venetian opera, while the number of exit arias shrank to as little as one for each principal. As ballets increased within the opera itself those between acts disappeared. Foppa's work also marks a trend towards an increasing number of plots based on subjects taken from other than classical sources. Ferdinando Moretti, court poet in Milan, was not far behind. His libretto for Angelo Tarchi's *Il conte di Saldagna* of 1787 has multiple choruses and ballets, an aria interrupted by two other characters (*pertichini*), which was to become a regular occurrence in arias of the 1790s, and the death of the poisoned hero during the final coro.[28]

Sertor returned to Venice in 1788 to write the first Venetian "morte" opera, *La morte di Cesare*, with music by Bianchi. Here Caesar is killed behind closed doors, though his corpse lies on stage for the final scenes.[29] The Florentine shabby shocker of the 1780s, *La vendetta di Nino ossia La morte di Semiramide*, in which Arsace murders his own mother on stage in order to appease the ghost of his father, was not done in Venice until 1791, when the deed occurs accidentally.[30]

Finally Antonio Sografi, the youngest of the innovative Venetian librettists, in his first opera, *Gli Argonauti in Colco, ossia La conquista del vello d'oro* of 1790, achieved a fluidity of construction that went even beyond Verazi. The number of exit arias was cut drastically and replaced with cavatinas, ensembles, and choruses, some of them long, involved, and full of action, others so short as to be no more than lyrical expressions hardly interrupting the action.[31]

Along with a trend towards more modern, realistic subject matter went a reverse trend towards more productions of spectacle opera on mythical subjects in the French style, but these, like the incorporation of ballet, chorus, and scene complexes into Italian opera, could just as well have been an outgrowth of Gluck's operas, which were widely though infrequently performed in Italy, often with very little modification.

While a clear linking of Verazi with all of the operatic innovations made in Florence, Naples, and Venice in the 1780s and 90s may be impossible to make with absolute certainty, there can be no doubt that he more than any other librettist of his time was the harbinger of things to come. It remained for a new generation of librettists gradually to break free of the traditional methods and ultimately bring to fruition his goals as well as Gluck's.

NOTES

This chapter is a revised version of a paper read at the national meeting of the American Musicological Society, Vancouver, 1985.

1. Ranieri de' Calzabigi and Christoph Willibald Gluck, *Alceste* (Vienna, 1769). Dedication translated in Oliver Strunk, *Source Readings in Music History from Classical Antiquity through the Romantic Era* (New York, 1950), pp. 673–5.
2. Mattia Verazi and Antonio Salieri, *Europa riconosciuta* (Milan, 1778), p. 7; Verazi and Michele Mortellari, *Troja distrutta* (Milan, 1778), p. 8. Both librettos in US-Wcm.
3. Letter to Verazi from Metastasio, 3 September 1778, translated in Charles Burney, *Memoirs of the Life and Writings of the Abate Metastasio*, 3 vols. (London, 1796), vol. 3, p. 219.
4. These early pages, dealing with Verazi's career and works and provided here as background to an assessment of Verazi's position in eighteenth-century opera, are a reworking and condensation of an earlier, more detailed piece, "Mattia Verazi and the Opera at Mannheim, Stuttgart, and Ludwigsburg," which I prepared for a

symposium, "Crosscurrents and the Mainstream of Italian Serious Opera, 1730–1790," sponsored by the Department of Music History, the University of Western Ontario, 11–13 February 1982, and published in *Studies in Music from the University of Western Ontario* 7 (1982): 99–136.

5 [Verazi] and Jommelli, *Ifigenia in Aulide* (Rome, 1751), libretto in B-Bc VV 20.565 along with the autograph of Act 3, complete manuscript scores in F-Pn, I-Nc and Mc, and P-La. In his correspondence of the late 1760s and early 1770s, Jommelli complains about the inadequacy of the customary double quatrain of poetry for aria texts and the difficulty of composing expressive music when the words do not justify it. See Jommelli-Verazi correspondence in Marita McClymonds, *Niccolò Jommelli: The Last Years, 1769–1774* (Ann Arbor, 1980), pp. 95–6, 751–3.

6 Apostolo Zeno and Antonio Caldara, *Ifigenia in Aulide* (Venice, 1718), libretto in US-Wcm, Schatz 1484. First performed in Vienna the same year.

7 Verazi and Jommelli, *Pelope* and *Enea nel Lazio* (both Stuttgart, 1755), librettos in D-Sl, fr.d.4 192, manuscript score for *Pelope* in I-Nc, music for *Enea nel Lazio* lost.

8 Verazi and Tommaso Traetta, *Sofonisba* (Mannheim, 1762), libretto in D-MH, music manuscript in US-Wcm.

9 Francesco Silvani and Caldara, *Sofonisba* (Venice, 1708), libretto in US-Wcm, Schatz 1500.

10 Verazi and Gianfrancesco de Majo, *Ifigenia in Tauride* (Mannheim, 1764), libretto in I-Bc, 2785, manuscript score in D-B.

11 Nicholas Guillard and Gluck, *Iphigénie en Tauride* (Paris, 1779), libretto in US-Wcm, Schatz 3903.

12 Verazi and Jommelli, *Fetonte* (Stuttgart, 1768), libretto in US-Wcm, Schatz 4860, manuscript score in D-Sl, published score in *Denkmäler deutscher Tonkunst*, rev. edn, ed. Hans Joachim Moser from the 1907 edn of Hermann Abert (Wiesbaden, 1957), vols. 32–3.

13 Verazi and Antonio Sacchini, *Calliroe* (Stuttgart, 1770), libretto in US-Wcm, Schatz 9210.

14 For a detailed chronicle and in depth analysis of Verazi's operas for Milan, see Marita McClymonds, "Verazi's Controversial *drammi in azione* As Realized in the Music of Salieri, Anfossi, Alessandri and Mortellari for the Opening of La Scala, 1778–1779," in *Melange: Omaggio al Prof. Claudio Sartori*, ed. François Lesure (Rome, in press).

15 See note 3. Manuscript score in F-Pn, X.147 A&B, and A-Wn, 17836.

16 "... e sempre in via di satira, e con dileggiamento, consicchè Verazi significa quasi per nome [illegible] sia Poeta Cattivo," from *Gazzettino Guarnieri: Gazzetta di Milano per il secondo semestre del 1778 sino al 1780* (12–19 August 1778): 30; quoted and translated in Kathleen Kuzmick Hansell, "Opera and Ballet at the Regio Ducal Teatro of Milan, 1771–1776: A Musical and Social History," Ph. D. Dissertation, University of California at Berkeley, 1980, p. 269. For further literature on the outcry against Verazi in Milan, see ibid., pp. 268–70; and Carlo Antonio Vianello, *Teatri spettacoli musiche a Milano nei secoli scorsi*, Raccolta di memorie storiche ed artistiche milanesi, vol. 2 (Milan, 1941), pp. 119–25.

17 See note 3. Manuscript score in F-Pn D. 8308 (1–3).

18 Verazi and Pasquale Anfossi, *Cleopatra* (Milan, 1779), libretto in US-Wcm, Schatz 278, manuscript score in F-Pn, D.122–14. Verazi and Felice Alessandri, *Calliroe* (Milan, 1779), libretto in US-Wcm, Schatz 142, manuscript score in F-Pn, Ab.o.158$^{1-3}$.

19 [Carlo Frugoni] and Girolamo Abos, *Medo* (Turin, 1753), libretto in US-Wcm, Schatz 10. [Vittorio Cigna-Santi] and Gioacchino Cocchi, *Andromeda* (Turin, 1755), libretto in US-Wcm, Schatz 2051. Cigna-Santi and Traetta, *Enea nel Lazio* (Turin, 1760), libretto in US-Wcm, Schatz 10391. Cigna-Santi and De Majo, *Motezuma* (Turin, 1765), libretto in US-Wcm, Schatz 5858.

20 [Jacopo Durandi] and Anfossi, *Armida* (Turin, 1770), libretto in US-Wcm, Schatz 226. For the history of the *Armida* librettos related to the one Haydn used, see Marita McClymonds, "Haydn and His Italian Contemporaries: *Armida abbandonata*," in *Joseph Haydn: Proceedings of the International Joseph Haydn Congress, Vienna, 1982*, ed. Eva Badura-Skoda (Munich, 1986), pp. 325–32.

21 Pietro Giovannini, Antonio Sografi, Alessio Prati and Sebastiano Nasolini, *La morte di Semiramide* (Padua, 1790), libretto in I-Pci and Vcg; [Gaetano Sertor] and Gaetano Andreozzi, *La morte di Giulio Cesare* (Rome, 1790), libretto in I-PAc, Rsc, Vgc; [Sertor] and Francesco Bianchi, *La morte di Giulio Cesare* (Venice, 1790), libretto in I-Vcg: [Sertor] and Niccolo Zingarelli, *La morte di Cleopatra* (Vicenza, 1791), libretto in I-Rsc, Vcg, Vgc, Vnm. See Sartori, *Catalogo unico* for other titles and productions.

22 Sertor and Bianchi, *Arbace* (Naples, 1781), libretto in I-Nc, Rari 15.11(5); Sertor and Bianchi, *Zemira* (Naples, 1781), libretto in I-Nc, Rari 10.10.21(10). Sertor and Giovanni Borghi, *Arbace* (Venice, 1782), libretto in US-Wcm, Schatz 1239; Sertor and Anfossi, *Zemira* (Venice, 1782), libretto in US-Wcm, Schatz 272, Sertor and Giuseppe Giordani, *Osmane* (Venice, 1784), libretto in US-Wcm, Schatz 3848.

23 [Sertor] and Pietro Guglielmi, *Enea e Lavinia* (Naples, 1785), libretto in US-Wcm, Schatz 4285.

24 Sertor and Prati, *Armida abbandonata* (Munich, 1785), libretto in US-Wcm, Schatz 8450.

25 Mozart's letters to his father, 13 and 15 November 1780, transcribed in *Mozart Briefe und Aufzeichnungen*, ed. Wilhelm Bauer and Otto Erich Deutsch, 7 vols. (Kassel, Basel, Paris, London, New York, 1960), vol. 3, pp. 16–21; translated in Emily Anderson, *The Letters of Mozart and his Family*, 3 vols. (London, 1938), vol. 2, pp. 981–6.

26 Giovanni de Gamerra and [Salieri], *Daliso e Delmita* (Vienna, 1776), libretto in US-Wcm, ML 48.A5 v.45. Gamerra and Giovanni Paisiello, *Pirro* (Naples, 1787), libretto in I-Bc, 3868 (Venice, 1787), libretto in I-Bc, 3869.

27 [Giuseppe Foppa] and Bianchi, *Alonso e Cora* (Venice, 1786), libretto in US-Wcm, Schatz 994; Foppa and Bianchi, *Calto* (Venice, 1788), libretto in US-Wcm, Schatz 996.

28 Ferdinando Moretti and Angelo Tarchi, *Il conte di Saldagna* (Milan, 1787), libretto in US-Wcm, Schatz 10216.

29 Sertor and Bianchi, *La morte di Cesare* (Venice, 1788), libretto in US-Wcm, Schatz 1005.

30 [Giovannini] and Prati, *La vendetta di Nino* (Florence, 1786), libretto in US-Wcm, Schatz 8452; *La morte di Semiramide* (Venice, 1791). This libretto has long been mistakenly attributed to Moretti, but in a letter dated 12 November 1987, Robert Weaver writes, "The *Gazzetta universale*, p. 224, and *Gazzetta toscana*, p. 53, have notices that correct the *Indice dei spettacoli*, which assigns the text to Ferdinando Moretti, by stating that the true author of the poetry is Abate Pietro Giovannini." Heretofore, Giovannini's only claim to fame has been his enormously successful libretto for Giuseppe Sarti's *Giulio Sabino* (Venice, 1781), libretto in US-Wcm,

Schatz 9438. For further discussion of Giovannini's libretto and its successors as well as of *morte* operas in general, see Marita McClymonds, "The Venetian Role in the Transformation of Italian opera seria During the 1790s," in *I vicini di Mozart: Il teatro musicale tra sette e ottocento*, Studi di Musica Veneta, vol. 15, ed. Maria Teresa Muraro (Florence, 1989), pp. 221–40, and "*La morte di Semiramide ossia La vendetta di Nino* and the Restoration of Death and Tragedy to the Italian Operatic Stage in the 1780s and 90s," in *Atti del XIV Congresso della Società internazionale di musicologia*, 3 vols. (Turin, 1990), vol. 3, pp. 285–92.

31 Antonio Sografi and Giuseppe Gazzaniga, *Gli Argonauti in Colco, ossia La conquista del vello d'oro* (Venice, 1790), libretto in US-Wcm, Schatz 3657.

Handel and Gluck

8

Handel's *Serse*

WINTON DEAN

Handel's *Serse* is unique among his London operas for containing a buffo part, and for that reason has been called (not quite accurately) his only comic opera. Several earlier works, notably *Agrippina* and *Partenope*, had guyed the conventions and characters of contemporary opera, and these are nothing if not polished comedies. Certainly the flavor of *Serse* differs considerably from that of most Handel operas, and in some degree from all of them. It was a total failure at its first production (the flavor was clearly not to the taste of London audiences in 1738), yet with the exception of *Giulio Cesare* it has proved by far the most popular of Handel's operas in the present century. No doubt the obvious charm and tunefulness of the music is largely responsible for this; perhaps also the brevity of most of the arias. But there has been little unanimity among recent productions about what sort of opera it is. Like another comedy of ambivalent character, *Così fan tutte*, it has been subjected to a wide variety of eccentric interpretations, many of them remote from anything its authors could have intended. There is of course no obligation on modern producers to replicate the performing conditions of Baroque opera, but it would seem advisable to understand what they were, and to grasp the kind of artistic effect at which Handel was aiming. All too often a subtle drama of character, rich in irony, has emerged as a farcical romp.

There is another reason why *Serse* repays scrutiny, though it cannot be fully explored here. The same subject, indeed virtually the same libretto, had been treated by two earlier composers, Francesco Cavalli in 1654 and Giovanni Bononcini in 1694, and neither of their operas is negligible. The re-use and refurbishing of old librettos was commonplace throughout the Baroque period, but this threefold setting by three distinguished composers at intervals of more than a generation is particularly revealing. The fact that the main plot remained essentially unaltered facilitates assessment of the changing nature of the art as reflected in the taste of audiences and the development of conventions. Moreover, as is now well known, the relationship of Handel's opera to Bononcini's is not confined to sharing a libretto.

Since our main concern is with Handel's opera, it is necessary to summarize the action as he treated it. The characters are two brothers, Serse (King of Persia) and Arsamene; two sisters, Romilda and Atalanta, daughters of Serse's general Ariodate; Amastre, a princess betrothed to Serse; and Elviro, Arsamene's servant. Arsamene and Romilda are in love; Atalanta also loves Arsamene; Serse has shown no interest in Amastre. The italicized stage directions are taken from Handel's autograph and the 1738 printed libretto.

Act I. The curtain rises on *a summer house on one side of a garden, in the middle of which is a plane tree, and Xerxes* [Serse] *under it*. He craves a blessing on the tree, which he *stands and admires* with rapture. Arsamene enters in search of Romilda, accompanied by Elviro, *who looks drowzy*. *A short symphony* is *heard*, and presently Romilda's voice *in the summer house*; she mocks the king's love for the tree, which can give him no more tangible return than the murmur of its leaves. Serse, captivated by the voice and hearing his name mentioned, at once has designs on the singer and cross-questions Arsamene about her identity. Arsamene prevaricates, pointing out that it is unlawful for a king to marry anyone but a queen. Serse, after vainly ordering his brother to plead his cause, goes off to do it himself. Arsamene, confident of Romilda's love, warns her of Serse's intention, thereby giving secret hope to Atalanta. Serse invites Romilda to share his throne, overheard by Arsamene, who comes forward to protest and is forthwith banished. Romilda remains *pensive and motionless*; Serse pleads his love, but she will never betray hers for Arsamene. The set changes to *a Courtyard*, where we encounter Amastre, *sole Heiress of the Kingdom of Tagor, design'd Consort to Xerxes*, disguised *in a man's habit, followed by a page*. She too is sworn to fidelity. She steps aside as Ariodate enters *followed by soldiers, with prisoners, and colours, taken from the enemy*. Serse congratulates him on his victory and promises that Romilda shall marry a prince "equal to Xerxes, and of Xerxes' line." Ariodate departs joyfully with his followers; Serse sees the victory as a good omen for his own love. Amastre at first thinks he is referring to her, and is mightily indignant when she finds he is not. She nearly betrays herself, but Serse dismisses her with the remark that this soldier seems a little odd in the head. Arsamene gives Elviro a letter to Romilda asking for a meeting. Elviro complains that his master's conduct has landed him too in trouble and banishment. *He thinks awhile, and then, as having fallen on an expedient*, goes off to deliver the letter. Amastre, disgusted at Serse's treachery, plans vengeance. Atalanta advises Romilda to accept Serse, since Arsamene loves someone else. If so, Romilda replies, she will indeed turn her affections towards the king. Atalanta congratulates her on her prudence and says she herself will ask for Arsamene – not that she loves him, but she might bring herself to do so. Romilda sees through this and tells her not to deceive herself. Atalanta resolves to gain her ends by exploiting her charms.

Act II. A square of the city. Amastre, *and after her* Elviro, *who cries flowers, and speaks in a broken dialect* (*la lingua franca* in the Italian text; the English translation gives him the sort of language Burney attributed to Handel). In this ironical scene, with both characters disguised, Amastre learns of the love triangle between Serse, Arsamene, and Romilda. Elviro is terrified that he has revealed too much, and Amastre goes off with a heavy heart. Atalanta enters *at a distance*. She begins to express the pangs of love, but is interrupted by Elviro calling his wares. When she buys some flowers he reveals himself and gives her Arsamene's letter to Romilda, which she promises to deliver. She tells him that Romilda has abandoned Arsamene for Serse; he boils with rage but takes to his heels at the approach of Serse. The king finds Atalanta reading Arsamene's letter, which she claims is addressed to her: Arsamene is pretending to love Romilda in order to hide his affair with Atalanta. But, she warns Serse, Arsamene will deny it. Serse is amazed, then delighted, and willingly agrees to Atalanta's marrying Arsamene. Serse now shows the letter to Romilda. Believing it to be addressed to Atalanta, she is overwhelmed; but she must love Arsamene, even if he has betrayed her. Alone, she gives way to bitter resentment and jealousy. Elviro comes on Amastre *going to kill herself*. He stops her; when she calls on her faithless lover to take her life, he thinks her mad. He tells Arsamene, inquiring about the delivery of his letter, that Romilda now loves Serse. Arsamene bewails the loss of all he held dear. The next set is dominated by *a bridge built over the sea, uniting the two shores. A chorus of mariners* sings Serse's praise. He orders Ariodate to marshal his forces; before the third day's dawn he will cross the Hellespont into Europe. Meeting the dejected Arsamene, he tells him he can have his girl. Arsamene takes this as a bitter jest, especially when he is offered Atalanta. He stoutly demands Romilda. It is now Serse's turn to disappoint Atalanta; she must forget Arsamene, who does not love her. But she cannot forget him; and the king reflects on the uncertainties, hopes, and fears of love. Elviro, looking for his master, contemplates the bridge with alarm; a storm is rising and he prefers wine to water. He sings a drinking song as the bridge collapses. In *a place of retirement contiguous to the town* Serse *on one side* and Amastre *on the other* complain of the pangs of jealousy. In a scene full of ironical cross purposes she claims to be a soldier wounded in Serse's cause, he asks her to serve again, and she agrees to consider the matter. *She withdraws to one side.* Serse now demands an answer from Romilda. She puts love above wealth and fortune, and when he presses her Amastre rushes forward, warns her not to trust him and *puts herself in a posture of defence*. Serse departs *in anger. The guard attack Amastre, who defends herself.* Romilda sends them away in Serse's name and advises Amastre to follow in case he discovers her. Alone, she declares that her love will never swerve.

Act III. A gallery. Arsamene and Romilda demand an explanation from Atalanta, who is full of excuses: it was to help them that she misled the king. When they fall into each other's arms, she trots off to seek a new lover. At the approach of Serse Arsamene *hides*. Serse renews his siege of Romilda, asks why she released that soldier, and at last gains her consent to marry him if her father approves. He goes off contented; when Arsamene bitterly reproaches Romilda *she falls into the arms of her women*. She says farewell to Arsamene: she loves him too much and can only die. *Her women lead her off, supporting her.* Arsamene is heart-broken. In *a Grove* Serse tells Ariodate that if he agrees Romilda shall have a royal consort. "A person whom thou'lt own Equal to us, and of our royal stem" will visit his apartment, and she is to accept him. Ariodate assumes this refers to Arsamene and is delighted. *Romilda in anger, who meets with Xerxes.* She rejects his offered diadem: she was once loved by Arsamene – with kisses. Serse accuses her of inventing this to prevent their marriage, but decides to make sure and orders his guards to kill Arsamene. She shall be "widdow of that kiss" and then marry him. *Exit in rage.* Romilda meets Amastre *with a letter in her hand* and asks "him" to warn Arsamene of the sentence. In return Amastre gives Romilda the letter for the king, whom she still loves, though his faithlessness torments her.

Arsamene taxes Romilda with sending the warning to get rid of him; after a duet of mutual reproach they go out *on different parts of the stage.* The final set is *a large temple, with the image of the sun. An altar lighted. A chorus of priests round the statue.* Ariodate enters *at the farther end of the stage* with Romilda and Arsamene still quarreling, and astonishes them by announcing that they are to be married on Serse's orders. They quickly consent; after joining their hands he hurries off to inform the king while the chorus of priests acclaim the happy event. Serse decides it is time to inform Ariodate that he himself is the bridegroom, and is thunderstruck on learning that Romilda is already married to his brother. *A page brings a letter to Xerxes, and speaks softly to him.* Assuming it is from Romilda, he gives it disgustedly to Ariodate to read aloud. It is a dejected declaration of love and reproach. When Ariodate reads the signature – Amastre – Serse *takes the letter in a passion and examines the subscription ... Ariodate withdraws to one side of the stage.* This is the last straw: Serse invokes the Furies to shake their poison over him. *In going off, he is met by* all the other characters. They try to appease him, but he draws his sword and orders Arsamene to kill Romilda. Amastre asks if she may "pierce th'ungrateful heart Which has with treachery repaid true love." When Serse consents, *she snatches the sword out of his hand, and claps it to his breast,* announcing her identity. Serse is shamed into repentance, embraces her, and asks all to forgive his anger.

Much opprobrium has been heaped on this libretto. Burney called it "one of the worst that Handel ever set to Music: for besides feeble writing, there is a mixture of tragi-comedy and buffoonery in it, which Apostolo Zeno and Metastasio had banished from the serious opera" – though he had the honesty to add that "it gave Handel an opportunity of indulging his native love and genius for humour."[1] Burney's vision was blinded by the taste of his age, which rejected most pre-Augustan art as primitive and childish; but his criticism as usual enshrines a truth. Several of Handel's operas are based on old seventeenth-century librettos, but they are generally purged of their comic and secondary scenes, modernized in layout with new aria texts to accord with later taste.[2] This is only in part the case with *Serse*. Burney could not see that the "tragi-comedy and buffoonery" was retained deliberately, and that the character and strength of the opera depend on it.

The antecedents of the libretto have been examined in two scholarly articles by Harold S. Powers;[3] but there is perhaps a little more to be said. The source is Nicolò Minato's *Xerse*, set by Cavalli for Venice in 1654, and forty years later remodeled by Silvio Stampiglia for Giovanni Bononcini's first opera (Rome, 1694). Minato took a scrap of ancient history and embroidered it with the trappings and intricacies of post-Renaissance drama. His Argument acknowledges Book VII of Herodotus' *History* as the original of the plane-tree incident and the destruction of the Hellespont bridge (chapters 31, 33, and 34), but not the derivation of further details from Book IX (chapters 108 ff.), where Xerxes falls in love with his brother's wife. The intrigue however takes a more savage course than in the opera, and Amestris (Amastre) plays a far from edifying part.

Needless to say, Minato makes no attempt to evoke ancient Persia or the majesty of the great king who "sate on the rocky brow" and met his Trafalgar at Salamis. The tone of his libretto is colloquial, even flippant. As can be seen from all the operas of this period, Venetian audiences liked complicated plots with several interrelated strands, a multiplicity of characters from high and low life (all of whom could be held up to ridicule), and a kaleidoscopic alternation between intensely emotional situations on the one hand and farce and sharp satire on the other, with a touch of the supernatural thrown in. In addition to the seven characters of Handel's opera Minato has seven more. Xerse, Romilda, and Amastre each have attendants with whom they can share their thoughts: Eumene, the king's favorite eunuch; Clito, Romilda's skittish page; and Aristone, Amastre's uncle and elderly guardian. The other four are Periarco, ambassador from Amastre's father the King of Susa; Sesostre and Scitalce, two magi to whom Xerse entrusts the protection of the plane tree; and the captain of the royal guard. These peripheral figures add a few extra twists to the intrigue, but contribute nothing to the central plot.

Stampiglia's adaptation for Bononcini eliminates Periarco, the two magi, and the captain of the guard, and reduces the prominence of Eumene, Clito, and Aristone. Bononcini's opera was first performed in 1694 by an all-male cast, since Papal ordinance required female parts on the Roman stage to be taken by castrati. His high male parts are Xerse and Clito (soprano), Arsamene and Eumene (alto). Elviro and Aristone are tenors. Stampiglia strengthens the plot by cutting the scene in which Xerse entrusts the plane tree to the magi, which in Minato breaks the thread of the action between the king's apostrophe to the tree and Romilda's ridiculing him for it. Stampiglia omitted the last seven scenes in Act 2, which are largely concerned with Periarco's embassy to arrange the marriage of Amastre and Xerse and conclude with a military tattoo, substituting a solo scene for Arsamene lamenting his fate. He also abridged the verbosity of the closing stages of Act 3 after the action has finished. He retained a good deal of the original text, especially in the recitative, but only eight of Minato's thirty-four arias. While the plot and the actions of the characters remain constant, the plan is less haphazard and more responsive to specifically musical demands. There is also a gain in dramatic coherence: Xerse does not end with a lament (as in Cavalli's opera) but with an outburst of baffled rage, "Crude furie degl'orridi abissi."

Handel's libretto is a shortened version of Stampiglia's. He and his unknown collaborator (if indeed he had one; he could have done the job himself) further tightened the structure, abolishing Eumene (though he was included in the original scheme), Clito, and Aristone and making substantial cuts on Act 3. Romilda, Arsamene, and Atalanta each lose three arias, Amastre and Ariodate two, and Serse and Elviro one. Five of Stampiglia's eight duets, several of them very short, also disappear. The words of thirty-nine out of forty-one solo vocal movements, all three surviving duets, and both accompanied recitatives were taken over from Stampiglia, in a few cases slightly modified. The only new texts were Elviro's "Signor, lasciate" and "Del mio caro baco" and three of the four choruses. The words of the Act 1 chorus "Già la tromba" had been an aria for Ariodate. Bononcini has no choruses or even a final ensemble; he ends with an aria, "Cara voi siete," addressed by Xerse to Amastre. Handel may have transferred this to Romilda to compensate her for the loss of three arias earlier in the act, but the switch is a dramatic gain. Although most of the changes were improvements – especially in the sluggish Act 3, where Handel omitted three duets and no fewer than eleven arias (eight in succession at one point) – they did give rise to certain obscurities. The later scenes of Act 2 are bedeviled by the suppression of Eumene, who in Stampiglia rescues Amastre from the guards, and Romilda's vacillation in Act 3 seems merely capricious instead of a maneuver to save Arsamene's life.

Neither the libretto nor the music of Handel's opera is typical of its date (1738), by which time the full-blown Metastasian opera seria was firmly established on the Continent. Fewer than half of the solo vocal movements (twenty out of forty-one) have a da capo or dal segno, and three of these, including one of the biggest ("Crude furie"), are not followed by an exit. On the other hand the twenty-one ariettas or ariosos, which vary between an interrupted snatch of song and a complete cavatina (an aria without B section or da capo) include eight followed by an exit, one of which, "Nè men con l'ombre," precedes a change of set. The proportion of exit pieces (twenty-five out of forty-one) is lower than in Bononcini's opera. The design differs markedly from that of all Handel's other operas, and even more from the Metastasian pattern. Only the immature *Almira*, the one other opera to contain a buffo part, has a greater number of solo movements, and in none is the da capo so devalued.

Serse is thus in part a throwback to the seventeenth century, even towards the earlier Venetian form. It is difficult to determine to what extent this was the result of a conscious attempt to revive an obsolete form, to the fact that Handel's score was partly dependent on Bononcini's, or to a desire to revive his operatic fortunes by offering the public something more flexible than the usual opera seria of which it might be beginning to tire. Perhaps his motives were a mixture of all three. He had previously shown a leaning towards Venetian opera, which had brought him his first public triumph in *Agrippina*, and several of his recent operas, notably *Giustino* (based on a Venetian libretto of 1683), had been marked by a growing flexibility of form. Whatever the reasons, *Serse*, reproducing not a little of the ironic compound of farce, satire, and passionate emotion characteristic of Cavalli's opera, which Handel probably never knew, and combining it with aspects of his mature style, stands alone, apart from its period. There is even something of a Janus in its posture. Rudolf Steglich, in his preface to the Halle score, claims that it represents an important stage in the development of Baroque opera seria towards the dramma giocoso of Mozart under the influence of the Enlightenment. But the movements he cites in support – "A piangere ogn'ora," "Ah tigre infedele," and "L'amerete?" – are among those most indebted both to Minato's 1654 libretto and to

Bononcini's music. They represent a link not with Mozart but with the succession to Monteverdi.

Nevertheless the mention of Mozart is apposite, both to the libretto and the music. The libretto, if not faultless, is neither trivial nor absurd. Like Da Ponte's texts for Mozart it is a sophisticated comedy with passionate undertones that, magnified by Handel's genius, touch the springs of tragedy. Indeed the light bantering tone of the dialog, a sort of chatty stichomythia, is not so very remote from Da Ponte. Granted the highly artificial convention, in which the plot is spun by tergiversation and intrigue (a convention more proper to comedy than tragedy), the treatment of character and incident carries conviction. And it passes the supreme test: in alliance with Handel's music it springs to palpitating life in the theater.

Of all the great opera composers Handel comes nearest to Mozart in his ability to explore the hair-line between comedy and tragedy, and to cross it at will without curdling the one or debasing the other. Each combines lyrical euphony with a finely tempered irony, and moves with absolute surefootedness between the sinister and the farcical, the flippant and the tragic. The resemblance is strongest in the sphere of character. Both composers possess something of Keats' negative capability, the power to enter other states of being and interpret them from within; in painting the foibles and frailties of human nature, they reveal the complex truths and turbulent passions beneath, so that while we laugh at the characters' antics we also feel with them. Nowhere is this kinship more evident than in *Serse*.

The clearest parallel, between Elviro and Leporello, each at the start of the opera grumbling sleepily at being forced to attend his master's love assignations, is not the most significant. Dent[4] saw in Handel's two sisters a foretaste of Fiordiligi and Dorabella; but the climate of *The Marriage of Figaro* is closer. Serse is as dangerous as the Count, and as comprehensively duped. Romilda has something of the Countess' noble forbearance, and Atalanta a dash of Susanna's devilry. There is even a faint anticipation in Amastre's "Or che siete" of two arias in Mozart's first act, "Non so più" and "Non più andrai." Where the comparison breaks down, of course, is in the absence of anything corresponding to Mozart's great ensembles. But for all the differences in idiom *Serse* ranks not far below Mozart's three Da Ponte operas in the hierarchy of operatic comedy.

The extent of Handel's indebtedness to Bononcini's *Xerse* can be measured with the aid of Powers' second article, which quotes most of the more striking parallels, and the reproduction of Bononcini's complete score in volume 8 of *Handel Sources*, edited by John H. Roberts.[5] Handel seems to have passed Bononcini's score through his imagination and transfigured it, an ironical footnote to their rivalry in the 1720s. Many of his finest arias owe a hint, and sometimes more, to his predecessor. The fact that he had mined the same source in all seven of his preceding operas from *Ariodante* to *Faramondo*, as well as in *Alexander's Feast* and the 1737 *Il trionfo del tempo*,[6] besides confirming that this was his regular habit, proves his acquaintance with Bononcini's *Xerse* several years before his own setting, and suggests that the libretto may have been his personal choice.

The following pieces in *Serse* owe a principal part of their thematic material to Bononcini's setting of the same words: "Ombra mai fù," "O voi che penate" (together with the previous sinfonia), "Meglio io voi," "Un cenno leggiadretto" (B section), "Ah! chi voler fiora" (6/8 setting), "Ah! tigre infedele," "L'amerete?," "Quella che tutta fè," "Sì, la voglio," and "Crude furie." Other movements are clearly indebted for models, outlines, or suggestions, among them "Và godendo," "Soggetto al mio volere," "Più che penso," "Or che siete," "Se bramate" (Adagio sections), "Gran pena è gelosia," "Cagion son io," and "Caro voi siete." In this connection tangential resemblances may be significant. The first four notes of "Sì, sì, mio ben" and the first three of "A piangere ogn'ora" are the same in both operas, though the continuations are quite different; it is likely that a glance at Bononcini set Handel on his course. He also seems to have followed Bononcini's track in the recitatives of the first four scenes of Act I. Nor is this all. The two scenes in Handel's opera that strike us as most remarkable for flexibility of design, those that begin the first two acts, are based with some precision on Bononcini in layout, scoring, and thematic material. They are also close to Minato (apart from the omission of the magi episode); indeed these scenes are very similar in all three operas. The unusual sequence of keys (E minor, A major, G minor) in the confrontation between Serse and Romilda in Act 2, Scenes 4–5 is Bononcini's. Handel saw that it was good and kept it.

Several things are notable about these borrowings. All but one ("Cagion son io," which takes one of its subsidiary phrases from Bononcini's aria "Perde il senno") occur in settings of the same text. This is rare with Handel but not unique; there are examples in *Tamerlano* and *Faramondo* of material taken from Gasparini's settings. Most of the *Serse* borrowings cover only a few bars, and not consecutive ones. Handel has assimilated them and mixed them with material of his own. In nearly every case the matter for astonishment is not what he took but what he wrought with it; he raises it to a higher degree. Some of the most memorable instances are quoted below.[7] Perhaps the most extraordinary is "Sì, la voglio," the aria in which Arsamene reacts to Serse's suggestion that he is not interested in Romilda. Roberts has subjected this to detailed examination,[8] and has shown that Handel quotes directly from Bononcini's setting and two different arias in Alessandro Scarlatti's *Attilio Regolo* and indirectly from Keiser's *Claudius* and two versions of an aria in his own *Il trionfo del tempo*, as well as from an earlier setting in the *Serse* autograph. Yet the result not only sounds entirely spontaneous; it is one of the most brilliant dramatic strokes in the opera. This is surely not the product of conscious patchwork, but of Handel's subconscious mind working on a medley of ideas floating in his memory. It is not theft but a strange form of re-creation. Exactly why Handel needed to compose in this way is a puzzle that musical psychology has not yet solved.

It is not easy to be fair to Bononcini's score when placing it beside Handel's;

Handel's Serse

Ex. 7 a. Giovanni Bononcini, *Xerse* (Rome, 1694), Xerse, "Io le dirò che l'amo"
   b. Handel, *Serse* (London, 1738), Serse, "Io le dirò che l'amo"

even allowing for the fact that in the intervening forty-four years the art had developed firmer outlines and a richer vocabulary, the contrast between a mediocre and a superabundant talent is too marked, whether or not Handel is using the same material. Nearly all Bononcini's melodic ideas are short-breathed, narrow in compass, and – above all – rhythmically impoverished. Where Handel will extend or develop an idea, Bononcini merely repeats it, often unvaried even in pitch. To take one example, his setting of Serse's "Io le dirò che l'amo" early in Act 1 runs to twenty-three bars but contains only two short and flavorless phrases. The voice sings the first four times unvaried (worked in simple canon with the bass), three times a third higher in the relative major, then three times at the original pitch. The second phrase occurs nine times, sometimes with a brief flourish at the end. The lame result is in stark contrast with Handel's flexible setting of the same words (see Ex. 7a–b). This is by no means a unique example: an aria not in Handel's opera, "Sento che l'alma mia," sung by Romilda in Act 3, exists in two versions. Both have a rather otiose obbligato for solo violin, and in both the voice begins by repeating the same one-bar phrase five times in identical rhythm, and brings it back many times later. Bononcini doodles with formulae; he seems unable to build a flexible musical paragraph.

Nevertheless his opera has flashes of inspiration. One of them is the unexpectedly spacious Largo, "Speranze mie fermate," with which Amastre launches Act 2 (sixty-five bars against Handel's nine), another, a strange chromatic piece for Romilda in Act 3, "Che barbara pietà," headed "siciliana" but in common time and moving with the gait of a recitative. It is scarcely a surprise that Handel had raided both before setting *Serse*, the first for a cavatina in *Berenice*, "Se non ho l'idol mio," the second for Alcina's great accompanied recitative "Ah! Ruggiero crudel." He also took hints from Bononcini's expressive setting of the duet "Gran pena è gelosia" and his "Sì, la voglio," one of the liveliest and most dramatic arias in *Xerse*, which begins without recitative cadence or ritornello and has admirable string parts. This is exceptional; most of Bononcini's arias are stereotyped, seldom omitting or misplacing an initial ritornello or exploiting the opportunities for contrast in the B section. Two-thirds of them have continuo support only, but half of these end with a four-part ritornello after the da capo, a scheme common at the turn of the century. Bononcini manages this well, often urging the melody to a new climax, so that the ritornello is the most interesting part of the aria. A few arias are more fully scored, with an obbligato for violin or cello; Xerse's "Il core spera" boasts a lengthy and fully written out part for archlute. But when Bononcini does expand, it is seldom at the dictation of the plot. His musical climaxes scarcely ever coincide with dramatic climaxes (he has no accompanied recitatives), and he concludes the opera with a continuo aria lacking even a final ritornello. The first two acts each end with a perfunctory dance movement, for "struzzi" (ostriches?) and comedians in Act 1, sailors in Act 2.

Bononcini is at his happiest with the lighter characters, Ariodate and Adelanta. Ariodate has four arias (two more than in Handel), and they display a fair ration of bass vigor. Handel found useful material in the first of them, "Già la tromba," for "Revenge, Timotheus cries" in *Alexander's Feast*. Dance rhythms are used appropriately for Adelanta, including a gigue ("Non sempre la costanza" in Act 1) not unlike several Handel movements of this type, for example "Ne gigli" in the cantata *Clori mia bella Clori*. The settings of "Un cenno leggiadretto" and "Nò, nò, se tu mi sprezzi" have similar bouncy rhythms, though still fettered by two- and four-bar phrases. But despite occasional felicities Bononcini's score shows little sign of that overall balance that distinguishes Handel's style from very early in his career. Perhaps that was not to be expected in 1694. In Act 3 he holds back the long awaited resolution with a string of superfluous arias, several of them to make up the complement of a subsidiary singer. Where Handel cuts idle arias and distributes the rest according to the character's importance in the plot, Bononcini thinks first of the singer. Moreover he misses obvious dramatic points: when Stampiglia brings back the words of the duet "Troppo oltraggi" in Act 3, Bononcini does not clinch the reminiscence by quoting the music.

Burney, unaware of the Bononcini borrowings,[9] was disconcerted by the mixture of styles in Handel's opera. While pointing to the many reflections of the "modern" manner of Hasse and Vinci he declared that "there are more old-fashioned and worn-out passages in some of the songs, than in any other of [Handel's] works of this period," and ranked the opera "by no means ... with Handel's best dramatic productions."[10] This stylistic discrepancy is unlikely to worry modern listeners, even supposing they are able to detect it. Perhaps our ears are not fully attuned to the niceties of eighteenth-century idiom. Apart from a few instances, for example in *Israel in Egypt*, the vast majority of Handel's borrowings would probably never have been suspected had someone not unearthed the evidence. Whatever Handel touches is apt to sound like Handel.

The seven characters in Handel's opera are viewed symmetrically, three from a serious and three from a predominantly satirical angle, with the earthy humanity of Elviro holding the two groups in balance. The self-willed tyranny of the autocrat (Serse), the stupidity of the successful soldier (Ariodate), and the mischief-making of the coquette (Atalanta) are held up to exposure and ridicule. But the range of emotion is very wide, more so than in *Agrippina* and *Partenope*; the light structure of the music is deceptive here. Arsamene, Romilda, and Amastre suffer the pangs of frustrated or unrequited love, and as a consequence inherit the incomparable width of Handel's sympathies. But so from time to time do Serse and Atalanta. It is the quicksilver play of these emotional shadows and cross-currents, and the abrupt juxtaposition of the grotesque and the heartrending, especially in Act 2, that give the opera its perpetual fascination.

Serse himself is presented as pompous, touchy, and capricious, a royal ass. This is explicit in the printed libretto's note to the reader, which speaks of "some imbicilities [sic], and the temerity of Xerxes (such as his being deeply enamour'd with a plane tree, and the building a bridge over the Hellespont to unite Asia to Europe)," and Romilda's mockery in the first scene as well as in the fatuous ambiguity of his plans for the wedding. Such a man invites ridicule when the consequences of his vanity and incompetence are finally visited on him. But the picture is modified in two important respects. Serse is a formidable figure: he commands absolute power, and can condemn his brother first to exile and later to death. Like the grimmer tyrants of Handel's earlier operas, he is not to be trifled with. Something of this can be read in the prancing swagger of "Più che penso." Secondly, if he is the slave of unworthy desires, he does feel them, the more so as the opera proceeds. Handel could not withhold all sympathy from brutal and uncouth figures, provided they were capable of passion. Much of Serse's music is extraordinarily beautiful, and this goes some way to mitigate the harshness of his conduct.

The quality of "Ombra mai fù" requires little emphasis – "in a clear and majestic style, out of the reach of time and fashion," as Burney prophetically put it.[11] But four things need saying. Handel found the melodic germ in Bononcini's version, which he characteristically expanded from twenty-eight bars to fifty-two; his setting of the words "di vegetabile cara ed amabile soave più" at their second appearance (bars 29–34) is almost identical with

Handel and Gluck

Ex. 8 a. Bononcini, *Xerse*, Xerse, "Più che penso"
    b. Handel, *Serse*, Serse, "Più che penso"

Bononcini's at their first (bars 7–12),[12] but makes a far stronger impact in the new context. The tempo is Larghetto, not Largo, and should not be dragged. The music depends on the sonority of low-pitched strings in conjunction with a mezzo soprano voice; its magic evaporates if the voice part is sung in a lower octave. As the first formal movement after the overture it has the important function of setting the tone for what follows; its ironical confrontation of a ridiculous situation with an exquisite melody fulfills this perfectly, though the very familiarity of the piece may obscure the deftness of Handel's art.

At first Serse is toying with Romilda, as with a new plaything. "Io le dirò," another immortal tune, is light as a feather, and his first plea of love, "Di tacere," though couched in G minor with a feint to B♭ minor, does not engage him deeply. "Più che penso" with its coiled elastic string figures, carried into the bass but not the upper parts of the B section, thereby reinforcing the impact of the da capo, is a splendid realization of the words. The more he thinks of Romilda, the more his passions are roused; the three unaccompanied *ad libitum* bars at the approach to the main cadences, first in the dominant and later in the tonic, suggest his fancy beginning to roam. Handel infuses Bononcini's bland antiphonal opening with a breadth and rhythmic energy that is positively convulsive (Ex. 8a–b).

By Act 2 Serse is in the toils, as the haunting little F minor arioso "È tormento troppo fiero,"[13] taking its color from the opening words, makes clear. This is one of several such pieces in the opera: short, simple, lightly accompanied (sometimes, as here, by bass alone), but of piercing beauty. If Handel is repaying his debt to the Venetians, he gives compound interest. In the tiny duet "L'amerete?" he actually simplifies Bononcini, whose bass moves in quarter notes throughout. Handel's entire accompaniment consists of twenty-one notes, and he waves a magic wand over Bononcini's vocal lines (Ex. 9a–b). Romilda's cadence in E minor is followed at once by the A major ritornello of Serse's first full-scale aria since "Più che penso," "Se bramate d'amar." This has a grandeur and range of emotion scarcely to be expected from the tree-worshipper of Act 1. The virile main theme, strongly projected by all the oboes and two-thirds of the violins, finds issue now in admirably expressive coloratura, now in Adagio episodes ("ma come, non sò" [Ex. 10], "quest' alma non può") that interrupt both parts with a poignant enrichment of harmonic detail, different on each occasion. Most notable is the Neapolitan touch late in the A section. This man is indeed in love. Burney draws attention to "a base in iterated quavers, very much in the style of Hasse and Vinci; indeed, no Music fifty years old can have a younger appearance."[14] Yet the Adagios borrow their plan, if not its execution, from Bononcini.

In "Il core spera e teme" Serse reflects on the vicissitudes of love; the serene E♭ melody with its linked cadences and sumptuous string writing suggests a certain self-indulgence, but the sheer beauty of the music, especially the sequences towards the end of the A section, defies criticism.[15] The duet with Amastre, very effectively placed after Elviro's drinking song (G minor following

Ex. 9 a. Bononcini, *Xerse*, duet, "L'amerete?"

E minor, a typical shift for a change of set), reverts to something near tragedy. It is brief, unorthodox, and ironical. Both complain of the pains and betrayals of love, but whereas Serse has Romilda in mind, the disguised Amastre is thinking of Serse, who of course has no idea of her proximity. Almost half the piece consists of ritornello; the voice parts are simple and unadorned, and only for two and a half bars at the end are they heard together. At this point, after the bleak octaves of the ritornello and the simple harmonic layout that follows, the Neapolitan sixth chord on "pena" strikes with redoubled force.

Serse's love song in Act 3, "Per rendermi beato," reverts to a lighter tone – appropriately, for he thinks he has won and is happy to play the moth to Romilda's flame. His final outburst, "Crude furie degl'orridi abissi," with its leaping arpeggios and octaves and strings buzzing like an angry swarm of bees, is a brilliant send-up of all operatic invocations to the Furies. There is no

b.

b. Handel, *Serse*, duet, "L'amerete?"

mistaking the note of parody, underlined by the major tonality and the swooping downward scales, not to mention the hyperbole of the words. These frantic expostulations, at once indignant and hilarious, strike the exact chord of impotent outrage. Once more Handel found his material in Bononcini, including the main theme and the idea for the violin arpeggios, but completely transformed it; the scales and the iterated eighth and sixteenth notes (Vinci again!) are new, and the formal and tonal structure greatly strengthened, as Powers has shown in a detailed analysis.[16] "Curious, spirited, and original" is Burney's apt verdict.

In contrast to his brother, Arsamene is a potentially tragic figure. So deeply felt is his music that although he has no long arias and (except in "Sì, la voglio") no coloratura to speak of, he is in some respects the most memorable

Handel and Gluck

Ex. 10 Handel, *Serse*, duet, "L'amerete?"

figure in the opera. This absence of vocal display, which perhaps had its origin in Marchesini's limited powers, becomes a central feature of the characterization, nicely set off by Serse's longer and showier excursions. Five of Arsamene's six solos are in triple or compound time, and apart from the linked pair in Act 2, Scene 9 all are in minor keys. This is excluding his first utterance, "Tu le dirai che l'ami," in which he repeats Serse's music with new words applicable to what he believes to be his own situation – a mordant touch of double irony, as we soon discover.[17] Both his subsequent arias in Act I are slow pieces in triple time with violin and bass support, devoid of all frills. "Meglio in voi" is his resigned acceptance of banishment, "Non sò se sia la speme" a haunting lament for the loss of his beloved, the strong Neapolitan inflections creating a mood of desolate sadness. For "Meglio in voi" Bononcini provided the main theme and the eighth-note accompaniment figure. The difference between his stiff working and the expressive flexibility of Handel can be sampled in the opening bars (Ex. 11a–b).

Bononcini receives a still more striking composition lesson in "Quella che tutta fè" (Act 3, Scene 7). This little siciliano – it is only thirty-one bars long including the da capo – is one of the gems of Handel's score, expressing Arsamene's agonized sense of betrayed faith when Elviro tells him that Romilda loves Serse. Nothing could sound more spontaneous. Yet Bononcini's rhythmically monotonous setting contains the seeds of almost everything: the rough contour of the main theme, narrower in span and in common time, the functional interval of a fourth in the bass, and the general plan of the aria. Powers[18] analyzes the "extraordinary motivic integration" by which Handel not only combines Bononcini's two ideas but makes one generate the other. The repetitive tread of the main theme he transforms into a characteristic swaying melody by varying the intervals, rhythm, and harmony, adding such enrichments as the Neapolitan turn in bar 6 and the grand paragraph of the B section. The exquisite drop from F minor to E♭ in bar 4 is foreshadowed in Bononcini, who however devalues it by repeating the same melodic pattern for

Ex. 11 a. Bononcini, *Xerse*, Arsamene, "Meglio in voi"
b. Handel, *Serse*, Arsamene, "Meglio in voi"

the third time, whereas Handel's rising interval on the second beat of the bar is different on each occasion (Ex. 12a–b).

The evolution of this aria is fascinating, quite apart from its Bononcinian ancestry. The first version in Handel's autograph had a six-bar ritornello (the inner parts not filled in), starting with the one bar he retained but with a

Ex. 12 a. Bononcini, *Xerse*, Arsamene, "Meglio in voi"

striking chromatic extension, and a contrasted Allegro B section in common time with a bass in reiterated eighth notes (Ex. 13a–b). Handel kept the melodic and harmonic outline of the B section in a very different rhythm and tempo, and brought it to a climax by using in the bass the rising chromatic scale figure of his rejected ritornello. Moreover bars 3 and 4 of the eventual A section replaced a single bar (x) that lacked the magic shift to E♭. Handel hit on this (picking up Bononcini's hint) *after* he had written the Neapolitan G♭ bar that crowns it so beautifully. The first version ran to thirty-six bars (without da capo), compared with twenty for the final aria.

The scene in which Serse offers his brother the wrong girl shows Arsamene in a new light. He enters dejected with another spare Larghetto in triple time, "Per dar fine" (G major after the repeat of the sailors' chorus in F, as the plot takes a new turn); Burney thought it "very much in the style of a French *air tendre* of the last age."[19] The pathetic arioso droops to the tonic minor, almost like a Schubert song, and is too dispirited to return. Serse briskly assures Arsamene that all is well: he can have Atalanta, since he does not want Romilda. This fires Arsamene to "Sì, la voglio," his sole aria in common time, fast tempo, and a major key (apart from "Per dar fine," which cannot sustain it) and his one burst of coloratura. It is an electrifying stroke, musically and

Ex. 12 b. Handel, *Serse*, Arsamene, "Meglio in voi"

dramatically, thanks to the care with which the context has been prepared. The sudden Allegro, opening without ritornello, the upper strings emphasizing the off-beats, not only galvanizes a character in danger of lapsing into a congenital underdog, but completes a satisfying cavatina-cabaletta pattern with a return to the G major of "Per dar fine."[20] The coloratura expresses his resolution with admirable energy, reinforced by the clattering repeated chords of the B section as he invokes the denizens of the underworld. The remarkable synthesis in this aria has already been mentioned. The first version in the autograph is again longer and more leisurely, and much corrected, though Handel did not complete the skeleton draft. It runs to thirty-five bars without reaching the end

Handel and Gluck

Ex. 13 a. Handel, *Serse*, Arsamene, "Meglio in voi," first version, Largo
b. Handel, *Serse*, Arsamene, "Meglio in voi," first version, Allegro

of the A section, which totals thirty bars in final form; Handel probably scrapped it to give greater snap to Arsamene's reaction. The final version also threatened to get out of hand and was cut by seventeen bars. Again Burney's sensitive nose detected a cross-bred rat: "an old melody, with a very modern accompaniment."[21]

Arsamene's aria in Act 3, "Amor, tiranno amor," is another amorous plaint, very like "Non sò se sia" except that the Neapolitan color is absent and the accompaniment is in four parts. It adds nothing to the character; the early part of this act is the one slack stretch of the score. The quarrel duet with Romilda is a powerfully dramatic movement in truncated da capo form; after a long B section the A major first part slips unobtrusively back, not in its leisurely exposition but with the swift cut and thrust initiated at bar 19. As in many Handel ensembles of opposition, the upper parts (two violins) are independent and screw up the tension by cutting pungently across the voices. The ironical two-bar reference to this duet in the recitative just before Ariodate tells the lovers they are to be married at Serse's command is a happy touch.

The two sisters, like the two brothers, act as foils to one another. While Romilda's portrait is primarily serious and Atalanta's light and satirical, neither is restricted to a single range of emotion. Romilda indeed is that rare phenomenon, an ill-treated heroine with a sense of humor. Her first appearance is unusual. After Serse's apostrophe to the tree and Elviro's grumbles to Arsamene we hear a twelve-bar sinfonia, exquisitely scored for two recorders, muted upper strings, and pizzicato basses doubled *piano* by the bassoon. Master and servant listen entranced, as well they might, to the sensuous murmur of the double thirds. The sinfonia pauses on the dominant, then begins again, and after hesitating at the same point is extended and developed in a shapely binary design. We first hear Romilda offstage,[22] like a Puccini heroine, in an arioso mocking the barrenness of the king's infatuation for a vegetable that can offer him only the rustle of its leaves. The music, after two false starts, turns out to be a further extension of the sinfonia, and the melody in thirds identifies itself as the voice of the tree. Both sinfonia and arioso are interrupted by snatches of recitative from the watchers, first the eager Arsamene and sleepy Elviro, then – when Romilda mentions his name – the king himself, who is instantly enraptured. As he asks the embarrassed Arsamene who it is, she sings another arioso or arietta, accompanied this time by the recorders in unison and the strings without mutes (violins only till the final ritornello). The teasing melody, in 6/8 time with cross-rhythms in the second half of the bar and sly echoes between voice, recorders, and later violins, inflames Serse beyond the point of no return. The whole scene, including "Ombra mai fù" with its accompanied recitative and the tiny double aria "Io le dirò," sung by the two brothers in turn, is a miracle of musico-dramatic art. Like most of Handel's openings, besides setting the temper of the score, it launches the plot and establishes the leading characters (no fewer than four of them); but the extreme fluidity of design, unencumbered by rigid forms, da capos or exits, with the heroine concealed, is unique in his operas.

There is no sinfonia in Cavalli's manuscript (one may have been inserted in performance); he sets the interruptions in the same meter as the aria, not as a contrasting simple recitative. The Stampiglia-Bononcini version has the same layout as Handel's and was clearly its model in general plan and many details, notably the sinfonia ("Concerto di Flauti," scored for two recorders in thirds and continuo) and the threefold opening of Romilda's "O voi che penate"; but, whereas Handel preserved Bononcini's first two intervals (a rising fourth and sixth), he changed the last, another sixth, into an octave. The resemblance extends to the repetition of the first part of the sinfonia – though Handel's is longer as well as much richer, $12+22$ bars instead of $6+8$ – and the scoring and plan of "Và godendo" (a minuet in 3/8 with the voice leading, imitated by the recorders in unison, and a fully scored final ritornello. Both composers used the recorders in the same three movements of this scene and nowhere else in the opera. There is no mention of mutes, pizzicato, or bassoons in Bononcini. Handel further sharpened the contrast between the full accompaniment of sinfonia and arioso and whispered comments of the watchers by leaving most of the latter without continuo support.[23]

Exceptionally, Romilda concludes the first set not with a full aria but with a cavatina, which would be unthinkable at this date in a heroic opera. But if "Nè men con l'ombre" is short in span, it is superb in quality, with a noble melody from the same stable as the *Berenice* minuet and a violin accompaniment in slurred sixteenth notes marked "Larghetto e pianissimo." Only in the final ritornello, where Handel adds the full body of strings and gives the tune for the first time to the orchestra,[24] is there a *forte* mark. We are left in no doubt of Romilda's love for Arsamene. "Se l'idol mio," addressed to Atalanta, is less striking, though it expresses well enough Romilda's mingled resolution and apprehension, the smooth violin thirds of the second part setting off the angularities and unisons of the first, and contrasts nicely with Atalanta's "Un cenno leggiadretto" at the end of the act.

It is in Act 2 that Romilda rises to her full stature. When Serse reveals Arsamene's apparent betrayal, her first reaction is the touching declaration of faith in the duet "L'amerete?". But no sooner has Serse gone than she gives vent to her bitterness, jealousy, and despair in an accompanied recitative and aria that would grace any heroic opera. The recitative is packed with those searching progressions that Handel reserved for outbursts of intense passion. The aria begins without ritornello or accompaniment as if Romilda cannot wait for the instruments;[25] the contrasts of loud and soft, unisons and full harmony, jagged rhythms and torrential scale figures, are typical of the jealousy affect (compare "Gelosia, spietata Aletto" in *Admeto* in the same key and "È gelosia" in *Alcina*). The restless tonality of the short B section spurns the relative major. The key, G minor, stands at the furthest extreme from Serse's in "Se bramate," and the whole scene, from before the duet, has no simple recitative at all.

The act ends with two consecutive arias for Romilda, in A minor and A major. This is not quite a cavatina-cabaletta structure: both arias are in da capo form, and the intermediate action with Amastre and the guards disturbs the dramatic unity, which however Handel may have sought to restore through the tonality. "Val più contento core" is not specially distinguished. His original idea, canceled in the autograph, was to divide the continuo into two antiphonal groups, each with its own harpsichord. "Chi cede al furore" on the other hand is enough to immortalize Romilda as an operatic character. The words are pallid; it is the dramatic situation – the heroine resolved never to betray her faith – that inspired Handel to create this irresistible paean of a melody, twenty bars long, soaring over the entire soprano compass of a twelfth from D to A. When in the middle of the A section he resumes it from the beginning in the tonic, its second strain expands and proliferates in a huge paragraph with the crowning eighth-note figure divided between the voice and unison violins. The piece is pure melody; though 127 bars long, the A section never ventures beyond the dominant, and even the B section is reluctant to leave the home coverts.

In Act 3 Romilda does momentarily swerve; we might have expected an anguished aria of farewell at her exit in Scene 4. But there are enough pieces of this kind in the opera, including one for Arsamene in the same scene, and Handel was wise not to risk blurring the impression he created at the end of Act 2, and which he confirms in the last aria, "Caro voi siete." Here Romilda is back in the warmth of A major (the key of three of her arias, as well as the duet with Arsamene), blessed with another delightful melody, which like "Và godendo" plays with a prettily syncopated variant of 6/8 rhythm.[26] It serves appropriately for the coro as well, with new material in the vocal parts but the same instrumental figures binding the two pieces together in a satisfying and gracious finale.

Atalanta is one of opera's immortal flirts. She believes in living by her charms and is not above stealing her sister's lover; but she is capable of genuine emotion, as Handel shows by a touch here and there. She is more lightly drawn than Romilda; of her six solos, only two have a da capo, and one of these is so short that it ranks as an arietta rather than an aria. Her first utterance, "Sì, sì mio ben," has an equivocal flavor. Ostensibly describing to Arsamene Romilda's love for him, she in fact gives expression to her own. Handel writes a plaintive F♯ minor siciliano, full of Neapolitan inflections and without ritornello. It is touchingly beautiful; but by interposing a couple of bars of simple recitative towards the end, emphasizing Atalanta's vicarious posture, Handel prevents it becoming too serious and establishing the character on the wrong lines. "Un cenno leggiadretto" at the end of the act shows her in her true colors, sharpening her little claws and shamelessly proclaiming the means by which she stoops to conquer. The delicious ritornello with its pussyfoot repeated and staccato eighth notes, followed by the leaping violin figures for the coy glances designed to ensnare her victims, tells the whole story before the voice comes in (Ex. 14). Trills and a saucy upward scale figure are presently called in to decorate the approach to cadences. Handel may have derived a hint or two from Bononcini's first part; he lifted the initial two bars of his B section

Handel and Gluck

Ex. 14 Handel, *Serse*, Atalanta, "Un cenno leggiadretto"

and continued them with an improved line and rhythm. Neither the triplet nor the leap of a fifth, a minor sixth, and an octave are in Bononcini, whose widest step is a minor third (Ex. 15a–b). As a character study the aria makes a perfect foil to Romilda's at the end of Act 2. Both have a very short B section without upper instruments, and the purpose is the same: to offer the minimum of necessary contrast before the da capo, for each enshrines the mood that gives the key to the character.

In Act 2 we see Atalanta from more than one angle. The tiny "A piangere ogn'ora" on a ground bass (the structural principle of this scene) promises beautiful things, but is cut off almost at once for the same reason that recitative is interpolated into "Sì, sì, mio ben." In "Dirà che amor" the kittenish side returns to the fore, again associated with a seductive tune, which subsumes the first part in a single paragraph without modulation or accidental. As in so many of Handel's melodies, the top note (A – the only time it occurs in Atalanta's music) is consummately placed. The aria is Atalanta's warning to Serse that though Arsamene really loves her he will deny it; and a repetition of the entire aria a moment later with more emphatic words emphasizes the brazenness of the lie. (This also occurs in Bononcini's opera.) When presently Serse exposes her bluff, she reacts with the most deeply felt music in the part (all the chief characters except Amastre have their profoundest music in the second half of this act). For all her butterfly habits she cannot at once forget Arsamene, and the long cavatina "Voi mi dite che non l'ami" tells us that behind her scheming there is a heart. The characteristic tune, differently treated (in common instead of triple time) in the almost contemporary Concerto Grosso in B♭ (opus 6, no. 7), makes a moving impression here, and is most beautifully extended in the eleven-bar final ritornello. Atalanta's one contribution to Act 3, the arioso "Nò, nò, se tu mi sprezzi," returns her conclusively to her spiritual tonic as she flounces off in search of a new lover.[27]

Handel's Serse

Ex. 15 a. Bononcini, *Xerse*, Adelanta, "Un cenno leggiadretto"
b. Handel, *Serse*, Atalanta, "Un cenno leggiadretto"

Amastre, as befits her courage and assumed sex, is given resolute, rather stern music. She is a little slow to come to life, but the stiff D minor octaves of "Se cangio spoglia" project her situation (inward and outward) firmly enough, and "Saprà delle mie offese" is a vengeance aria charged with rhythmic energy. The bare texture of the first part, based on arpeggio and scale figures with more octave stamping, contrasts well with the full accompaniment and repeated chords of the second, against which the voice develops melodic and rhythmic ideas heard earlier, giving a strong sense of unity in variety. Amastre initiates the more emotional climate of Act 2 with one of those vivid fragments in which the opera is so rich, a nine-bar arioso in pure C major. The depth of her love for Serse shines through "Or che siete speranze tradite," an aria of touching sadness tinged with passion. The rhythmically reiterated two-bar phrases paint the numbness of her heart, and are cleverly prevented from becoming mechanical by the more flexibly articulated bass. We next see her on the point of suicide; but Elviro turns her rage once more on Serse, whom she denounces in a powerful F♯ minor cavatina, "Anima infida." The material is singularly varied, angular strides and leaps alternating with rapid repeated notes and chords over a running eighth-note bass; Burney signalized it as "a fine mixture of old and new passages and effects, with a Corelli bass, and a modern accompaniment."[28] Amastre is too angry for a ritornello at the start, but her accumulated emotion overflows in a splendid instrumental coda that develops all the principal ideas, including the first phrase of the voice (hitherto its exclusive property), in a new and powerful synthesis. Amastre's finest solo however is the last, "Cagion son io," in which she recognizes that she is the cause of her own grief, for she cannot help loving her betrayer. This is another cavatina of disarming simplicity, with the upper strings doubling the voice almost throughout and only the barest harmony. Everything hangs on the perfection of the melodic line, whose irregular phrase lengths and syncopations (hemiola) suggest a catch in the throat of the singer. Towards the end Handel slipped in a borrowing from his youth: the distinctive phrase with rising sevenths over a pedal (bars 25–35) occurs in a different meter but the same key at bars 17–22 of Narciso's aria "Volo pronto" in *Agrippina*.

Ariodate's two arias depict the bluff, not over-intelligent soldier in Handel's usual bass manner (compare Ercole in *Admeto*, who likewise operates in flat minor keys). The complacent downward scales in "Soggetto al mio volere" recall "O ruddier than the cherry," but they are more directly anticipated in Bononcini's setting. Elviro is an unusual figure in Handel, though he has many parallels in the tradition of intermezzo and opera buffa. While his status and conduct are very close to Leporello's, his music springs from a more vernacular and less sophisticated origin. His songs are all short and easy; the da capo is not for him, and his voice for the most part either hugs the instrumental bass or, when he plays the flower-seller, enunciates the most rudimentary phrases above it. Handel may have picked up the gawky 3/4 tune of "Ah! chi voler fiora" from the streets of London. He told Lady Luxborough that hints for some of his best songs came from this source,[29] and one such cry, taken down from a match-seller "near a brandy shop St Giles's in Tyburn Road," survives in his autograph in the Fitzwilliam Museum (Ex. 16a–b).[30] There is an oddity here. A little later we find Elviro singing the same words to a new melodic fragment in 6/8 over a descending scale in eighth notes that threatens to behave like that favorite academic gambit, a ground. This idea, taken over from Bononcini, recurs several times during the scene, which it helps to bind together musically and dramatically. It behaves irregularly, as we might expect, never reappearing in quite the same form and annexing several different keys, major and minor. Its final occurrence, after Atalanta has cut off Elviro's explosive outburst "Ah! tigre infedele" on the dominant and sent him packing at the approach of Serse, makes a witty exit line. Since Elviro a little earlier has broken up an arioso of Atalanta's, it also rounds off a dramatic tit for tat.

Handel's Serse

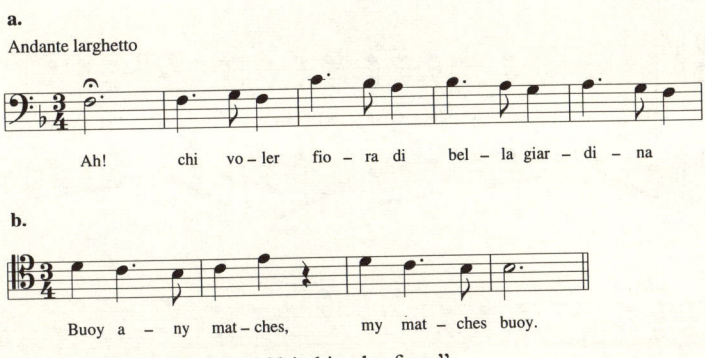

Ex. 16 a. Handel *Serse*, Elviro, "Ah! chi voler fiora"
b. Match-seller's cry, from Handel's autograph

Why did Handel not bring back the 3/4 melody? Because he had not yet thought of it; it is a later insertion. His first idea was in 3/8 (soon altered to 6/8), and was at the same time the source of the 6/8 echoes and a derivative of Bononcini's setting. Handel improved the latter, adding a pert little ritornello that breaks in at irregular intervals, then scrapped this in favor of the 3/4 version; he left the echoes of an arioso that no longer occurs in the score (Ex. 17a–b). The whole episode, inherited from Minato (who makes even more of it), is as fluid in construction as the opening of Act 1. Of the first six solos in the act (excluding Elviro's 6/8 fragments) only one runs its full course as a da capo aria, and the seventh ("Dirà che amor") runs it twice. Several are either interrupted or very brief. At least two, "A piangere ogn'ora" and "Ah! tigre infedele," are modeled on Bononcini's settings, and the layout with Elviro's repeated calling of his wares is likewise Bononcini's. Yet Handel gives it a personal and more unified stamp, partly by altering the proportions (Bononcini's "Speranze mie fermate" is very much longer, and his music for "Ah! tigre infedele" comes back a second time) and partly by hinting at a ground bass structure in several of the solos.

After his big scene Elviro fades out of the plot, apart from his pithy reactions to the storm on the Hellespont (his drinking song "Del mio caro baco" amusingly sprouts a new tune with "Waltzing Mathilda" proclivities in the ritornellos after each of its binary sections); but he has left his mark. He has a comic scene with Clito in the last act of Bononcini's opera. In Cavalli he tries to steal the gold decorations on Xerse's plane tree and is frustrated by the magi.

The three choruses – soldiers in Act 1, sailors in Act 2, priests in Act 3 – are musically slight, as usual in the operas (there were probably not more than two or three singers to a part); but their impact is not negligible. This is due to the contrast in color (orchestral as well as vocal; a single trumpet plays in two of them, a pair of horns in the third), and still more to their placing. Each is repeated so as to frame one of the three public scenes, the return of Ariodate's victorious army, the bridging of the Hellespont, and the marriage, supplying the personal plot with a background in relief. The instrumental movements are

Ex. 17 a. Bononcini, *Xerse*, Elviro, "Ah! chi voler fiora"
b. Handel *Serse*, Elviro, "Ah! chi voler fiora," first setting

of higher quality. The overture is suitably light-fingered, with a neat catch in the rhythm of the Allegro and a genial 6/8 gigue. The Act 1 sinfonia, apart from its magical scoring and an open-air flavor characteristic of Handel's garden scenes, is dramatically important. That which opens Act 3 is a beautiful example of the ample sonority Handel could draw from three-part strings; Dent found "a quite unusual melodiousness and charm ... with suggestions of both Scarlatti and Purcell."[31]

Frequent reference has been made to the flexibility of design – mingling of forms, junction, and interruption of movements, the decline of the da capo, use of recurring motives both to unify the action (opening sets of Acts 1 and 2) and for dramatic irony (Act 3, Scene 10), the unorthodox structure of all three duets (as in *Orlando* there are none of the honeyed congruences of the Royal Academy operas)[32] – and to its source in the seventeenth century. This is not the whole explanation. There is a link with the more organic methods Handel was beginning to employ in the oratorios of the 1730s, notably *Athalia* and *Saul*, and on another level with the limited capacities of his 1738 company, more suited to slighter, less taxing pronouncements than the big virtuoso aria. Only Caffarelli and to a lesser degree Francesina had any claims to be singers of the front rank. Montagnana's powers were in steep decline; Merighi too had seen better days; the technique of the others was very modest. This is obvious from an inspection of the score; yet it operates not as a limiting factor but as a source of strength, especially in characterization. Handel possessed that rare faculty of genius not only for discovering the most suitable material, but for doing so at the right time.

An inspired economy likewise distinguishes the scoring, based in the solo music almost exclusively on strings and continuo. Handel adds a little brass in the ceremonial choruses, and oboes in the overture, choruses, and two arias in Act 2, where they strengthen the top line in unison. Otherwise the only picturesque touch is the use of recorders in the garden scene. Yet he is able to achieve striking effects by expanding the string layout, whether in the B section of an aria ("Saprà delle mie offese," "Se l'idol mio") or in the final ritornello ("Nè men con l'ombre," "Val più contento core"). The minor mode, apt for unrequited passion, is prominent in the first two acts. Although their sustained opening scenes are confined to flat keys, all three acts end emphatically on the sharp side. There is a special appropriateness in the establishment of A major, the key of Romilda's great declaration of faith, as an ultimate tonic.

Appendix

SOURCES AND EDITIONS

Burney wrote of the autograph: "Appearances remain in his foul score of a mind disturbed, if not diseased. There are more passages, and even whole pages, cancelled in this score, than in any one of all his former operas."[33] This is a libel. Several other autographs, for example *Giulio Cesare*, *Riccardo Primo*, and *Saul*, are much more disordered. There is no evidence of mental disturbance, only of a severe artistic conscience. The foliation is scrupulous, and half a dozen extra leaves cued in with more than usual care.

Some of the cancellations are the result of changes in the libretto during composition, some of second thoughts, others of a conflict between the musical urge to expand (whether from Bononcini's material or Handel's own) and the dramatic requirements of brevity and a swiftly moving action. It is fascinating to watch this struggle, and to observe how again and again Handel's eye for the proportions of a scene conquers the impulse to give the music its head. In the flower-selling episode the brief settings of "Speranze mie fermate" (nine bars), "A piangere ogn'ora" (four bars), and "Ah! tigre infedele" (sixteen bars) were all the product of rigorous contraction. "A piangere ogn'ora" was first set to the music of "È tormento"; but Handel must have changed his mind quickly, for the latter is in its place on the verso of the next leaf. As already noted, "Ah! chi voler fiora" received a new setting, and three important arias in Act 2, "È gelosia," "Quella che tutta fè," and "Sì, la voglio," were extensively rewritten in the same keys and using some of the same material, and much reduced in length. Otherwise the pieces most ruthlessly cut were "O voi che penate" (nineteen bars), "Io le dirò" (thirteen bars from a total of thirty-two), "Meglio in voi" (fifty-six bars from a total of 111), "Più che penso" (fifteen bars),[34] and "Speranze mie fermate" (six bars from a total of fifteen). "Non sò se sia" and "Saprà delle mie offese" each had its opening ritornello shortened by eight bars. "Un cenno leggiadretto" shows interesting improvements in detail and a reduced B section. "Chi cede al furore" lost sixteen bars towards the end of the A section, but the little echo in bars 35 and 36 is an insertion. While a constant striving for terseness is the outstanding feature of the autograph, two arias in Act 3, "Per rendermi beato" and "Del ciel d'amore," were expanded from cavatinas at a late stage by the addition of a B section and da capo.

The changes to the libretto chiefly concern Eumene, who was retained in the original plan. Many recitatives were prepared for him (words and tenor clef) in the first two acts, but Handel set none of them, and he disappeared before the skeleton of Act 3 was written. The consequent modifications were extensive and sometimes damaging (for example in Act 2, Scene 13). Ariodate received some of Eumene's lines, but much was cut and rearranged. There is a good deal more of Stampiglia in Handel's autograph than in the 1738 printed libretto. Barclay Squire's statement that Amastre was originally called Eumene is incorrect.[35]

There are sketches in the Fitzwilliam Museum for the voice part of "Io le dirò," two shots at the melody afterwards used for "Và godendo," which may have been conceived as an instrumental movement, perhaps a minuet in the overture, and a complete treble-and-bass sketch for the gigue in the overture. Characteristically the final form of this is shorter than the sketch.

Having completed *Faramondo* on 24 December 1737, Handel began *Serse* on Monday the 26th, resting only over Christmas Day (he wrote Sunday the 25th on the first page of the autograph, but crossed it out). He finished Act 1 on 9 January 1738, Act 2 on 25 January, Act 3 on 6 February, and the fully realized score ("geendiget auszufüllen") on 14 February – a slow rate of striking by his standards. The first performance took place at the King's Theatre on 15 April, with the following cast: Serse – Gaetano Majorano, known as Caffarelli; Arsamene – Maria Antonia Marchesini; Ariodate – Antonio Montagnana; Elviro – Antonio Lottini; Romilda – Elisabeth Duparc (la Francesina); Atalanta – Margherita Chimenti; Amastre – Antonia Merighi. After a total of five performances, the last on 2 May, *Serse* slept for 186 years. The absence of contemporary comment is remarkable.

The libretto, "printed by J. Chrichley, near Charing-Cross," mentions no author or adapter but names the composer as "Frederick Handel," one of the rare indications that Handel, like Bach, was known by his second Christian name. Walsh published an unusually complete score, lacking only the simple recitatives, on 30 May 1738 and the overture in parts on 21 October that year.

As with other late and unsuccessful operas, manuscript copies are scarce, and they show no major variants. Contemporary copies are in the Bodleian Library, Oxford (S1 and S2, with gaps supplied by a later hand, no recitatives), the Fitzwilliam Museum, Cambridge (Barrett Lennard Collection, S5), and Manchester Central Library (Aylesford Collection, S2). The Aylesford Collection has a set of instrumental parts (S2). They are very incomplete, omitting twenty movements, among them the overture, fourteen arias, and three choruses, and were not copied from the Aylesford score; S2 supplied four movements with oboe parts that are almost certainly wrong. The Gerald Coke Collection has a set of parts for the overture, and British Library RM 19 a 1 an arrangement of it for harpsichord (S2).

There are two performing scores in the Staats- und Universitätsbibliothek, Hamburg, a full score (written by Smith) and a cembalo score (Acts 1 and 3 S1, Act 2 Smith). The latter is the more interesting: it contains (in pencil) some additional bass figuring in the recitatives, dynamics, and fermatas. Most of them seem to have been written by the continuo player as reminders, but they throw a little light on Handel's performance practice; the fermatas are not all as shown in the printed scores, and the octave leaps in the bass of "Quella che tutta fè" are marked *forte* in bars 6, 12, and 13 even though they occur outside the ritornellos while the voice is singing. Handel himself made one interesting change, though whether before the first performance or during the run it is impossible to determine: by altering "Chi cede al furore" from a dal segno to a da capo aria he gave maximum exposure to the glorious opening ritornello.

Chrysander's score (1884) omits a number of stage directions in the autograph. The most explicit is *Parte con Elviro, che và collando la testa* after Arsamene's "Meglio in voi" (Act 1, Scene 5). The Halle score, edited by Rudolf Steglich (1958), differs little from Chrysander. The preface mentions Minato's libretto and a German translation of it by Christian Postel (*Der mächtige Monarch der Perser Xerxes in Abydus*, set by Förtsch for Hamburg in 1689), but not Bononcini's opera. In his realization the editor has seen fit to modify many of Handel's recitative cadences, thereby stultifying the entire tonal articulation of the opera.

The only vocal score (Peters, 1924), arranged by Oskar Hagen for the first modern revival at a time when Handel's operas were thought to need a face-lift before they were fit for the stage, is a grinning parody. Arias are switched capriciously between characters and scenes, undercutting both the musical and the dramatic design. The numerous cuts include many of the finest arias, among them "È tormento," "È gelosia," "Per dar fine," "Sì, la voglio," "Il core spera," "Chi cede al furore," and "Cagion son io." Those that survive are subjected to extraordinary butchery. All the longer pieces and several of the shorter are mutilated. "Io le dirò" becomes a duet for tenor and baritone. "Anima infida" is given a bogus ritornello and parked at the end of Act 2. "Voi mi dite" is transferred to Romilda in place of "È gelosia," and the second part of "Quella che tutta fè" to Atalanta. Ariodate and especially Elviro are pushed into the foreground. The recitatives are almost entirely recomposed.

Serse was the fifth Handel opera to reach the stage in modern times, in Hagen's version at Göttingen on 5 July 1924. This enjoyed immediate and wide success in Germany, receiving at least ninety performances in fifteen cities before the end of 1926. *Serse* has been heard in twenty-four different countries in more than 130 productions, ninety-seven of them in German-speaking countries. The great majority, including all those based on the Hagen version (still on view at the Munich Opera as late as 1965) and the popular Joachim Herz production (Leipzig, 1972, performed all over Europe), seriously distorted the opera, often almost beyond recognition. Not until very recently has the pitch of Handel's voice parts been retained, though the Westminster recording under Brian Priestman (1966) was a model here. The revival by the English National Opera in 1985 treated the score with respect and gave the opera complete, demonstrating (not for the first time) that cuts in Handel's operas are both damaging and unnecessary; but the temptation to debase this ironical comedy by "improving" the plot and introducing coarse buffoonery and tasteless irrelevance seems irresistible. *Serse* has still to come fully into its own.

NOTES

1 Charles Burney, *A General History of Music from the Earliest Ages to the Present Period (1789)*, 2 vols., ed. Frank Mercer (London, 1935; reprint New York, 1957), vol. 2, p. 822.
2 *Giulio Cesare* and *Admeto* are prominent examples.
3 "*Il Serse trasformato,*" *Musical Quarterly* 47 (1961): 481–92 and 48 (1962): 73–92.
4 Edward J. Dent, "The Operas," in *Handel: A Symposium*, ed. Gerald Abraham (London, 1954), p. 57.
5 Issued by Garland Press (New York and London, 1986).

6 Roberts's preface, ibid., provides an astonishingly long list of borrowings.
7 See also Powers' second article.
8 "Handel and Charles Jennens's Italian Opera Manuscripts," in *Music and Theatre: Essays in Honour of Winton Dean* (Cambridge, 1987), pp. 181–8, 202.
9 Chrysander seems to have known of them, to judge from an enigmatic sentence in his preface to the Händel Gesellschaft edition, but he was not letting on.
10 *A General History of Music*, vol. 2, p. 823.
11 Ibid., p. 821.
12 Both are quoted by Powers in "*Il Serse trasformato*," pt. 2, p. 87.
13 In Bononcini this is a full da capo aria with a reinforced final ritornello. Handel's timing, at the start of a scene, is a clear improvement.
14 *A General History of Music*, vol. 2, p. 822.
15 There is a hint here of "Fell rage and black despair" in *Saul*. Several other movements in *Serse*, notably in Arsamene's music and the "Goliath" octaves of "Gran pena è gelosia," look forward to the oratorio composed later the same year.
16 "*Il Serse trasformato*," pt. 2, pp. 82–6.
17 The repeat is in Bononcini, but a fifth lower owing to the different pitch of the voices.
18 "*Il Serse trasformato*," pt. 2, pp. 88–90.
19 *A General History of Music*, vol. 2, p. 822.
20 Bononcini established no link between the two arias. His setting of "Per dar fine," a brilliant F major Vivace in 3/8 with a patter of sixteenth notes, seems oddly unsuitable. His "Sì, la voglio" is in D major.
21 *A General History of Music*, vol. 2, p. 822.
22 She may be visible to the audience in her summerhouse, but not to the other characters.
23 For a full comparative analysis of the three settings, see Powers, "*Il Serse trasformato*," pt. 2, pp. 74–7.
24 This was a second thought; he began by copying the opening ritornello.
25 Bononcini also set the aria as a G minor Andante without ritornello, but there is no common material. This was another aria that gave Handel trouble.
26 Bononcini's aria, in 3/8, was the model in a number of rhythmic and melodic details, as well as in key.
27 Both Cavalli and Bononcini give her a later aria, but it adds nothing and indeed confuses the picture.
28 *A General History of Music*, vol. 2, p. 822.
29 See her letter of 16 October 1748 to William Shenstone in *Handel: A Documentary Biography*, ed. Otto Erich Deutsch (London, 1955), p. 653.
30 J. A. Fuller-Maitland and A. H. Mann, *Catalogue of the Music in the Fitzwilliam Museum, Cambridge* (London, 1893), p. 217.
31 *Handel: A Symposium*, p. 57
32 Also to be noted is the frequency with which one character's aria follows the recitative of another, whether as answer or comment. This always tends to quicken the dramatic pace.
33 *A General History of Music*, vol. 2, p. 823.
34 This aria is partly canceled in pencil, but there is no indication in the performing scores that it was further shortened or omitted.
35 *Catalogue of the King's Music Library, Part I: The Handel Manuscripts* (London, 1927), p. 79.

9

The "sweet song" in *Demofoonte*: a Gluck borrowing from Handel

JOHN H. ROBERTS

"There is a sweet Song in Demofoonte called Ogni Amante sung by Riccarelli," wrote William Mason to the poet Thomas Gray on 25 December 1755. "Pray look at it."[1] He was referring to a pasticcio version of Metastasio's *Demofoonte* that had opened at the King's Theatre in the Haymarket on 9 December and scored a resounding success, thanks in large measure to the talents of the prima donna Regina Mingotti, who since her arrival in England the previous year had done much to revive the flagging fortunes of Italian opera on the London stage. Mason's interest in this aria of the primo uomo Giuseppe Ricciarelli was prompted not simply by its inherent charms but by its resemblance to a famous piece, the overture minuet from Handel's opera *Arianna* of 1734. "Tis almost $\frac{\text{Notatim}}{\text{verbatim}}$ the Air in Ariadne," he declared, "but I think better. I am told tis a very old one of Scarlattis wch if true Handel is almost a musical Lauder" – a comparison more topical than exact as William Lauder, whose attempt to convict Milton of plagiarism with fabricated evidence had been exposed in 1751, was a literary forger, not a plagiarist.

This letter has been cited as one indication that Handel's habit of borrowing from other composers was well known to his contemporaries, though its tone of amused surprise would seem to suggest quite the opposite. Another contemporary observer, Charles Burney, noticed the same relationship but construed it very differently. To him "Ogni amante" appeared to be "an imitation of Handel's minuet in Ariadne, not very well done: the air itself is much better. These cookeries," he continues, "are generally intended to flatter Handel's admirers; but they never succeed: every note that is added, changed, or omitted, disappoints the ear, and offends reminiscence."[2]

No complete score of this *Demofoonte* pasticcio has survived, but nine of the twenty vocal numbers in the 1755 libretto are preserved in two printed editions issued shortly after the first performance. John Walsh published five arias as *The Favourite Songs in the Opera Call'd Il Demofoonte*, advertised on 24 December,[3] and *Four Songs in the Opera Call'd Il Demofoonte Sung by Sigr[a]. Mingotti* were brought out separately and sold by Felice Giardini, leader of the Haymarket orchestra, and others. Burney explains that "at this time Mingotti and Giardini not allowing the opera-copyist to dispose of the favourite songs to Walsh upon the usual easy terms, had them printed elsewhere."[4] Among the

A Gluck borrowing from Handel

Table 9.1. *Extant arias from* Demofoonte *(London, 1755)*

Aria	Source
Favourite Songs	
"Ogni amante"	Gluck, *Issipile* (Prague, 1752)
"Tu sai chi son"	?*Demofoonte*
"La destra ti chiedo"	Gluck, *Demofoonte* (Milan, 1742)
"Padre, sposa"	Jommelli, *Cajo Mario* (Rome, 1746)
"No, non chiedo, amate stelle"	Jommelli, *Demofoonte* (Milan, 1753)
Four Songs	
"Padre, perdona"	Hasse, *Demofoonte* (Dresden, 1748)
"In te spero, o sposo amato"	?*Demofoonte*
"Se tutti i mali miei"	?*Demofoonte*
"Or che salvo è l'idol mio"	Hasse, *Arminio* (Dresden, 1745)

Walsh songs is "Ogni amante," which like everything else in these two collections bears no indication of its composer.

The 1755 libretto credits the music of *Demofoonte* to Jommelli, but only two of the surviving arias seem to be his, Cherinto's "No, non chiedo" from his second setting of Metastasio's libretto (Milan, 1753) and Timante's "Padre, sposa" from *Cajo Mario* (Rome, 1746).[5] Another aria for Cherinto, "Solo effetto," must likewise have come from Jommelli's 1753 *Demofoonte*, where the text, which derives from Metastasio's *Ipermestra*, can be found in the same scene as in the London pasticcio, and he may well have been the composer of some of the eight lost arias that took their texts from the original Metastasian libretto. Two of the published arias for Dircea (Mingotti) are from Dresden operas by Hasse, "Or che salvo" from his second *Arminio* (1745)[6] and "Padre, perdona" from his first *Demofoonte* (1748), in which Mingotti had created the role of Creusa. Gluck's *Demofoonte* (Milan, 1742) is the source of the duet "La destra ti chiedo," but I have been unable to trace the three other arias in the prints – all on *Demofoonte* texts – including "Se tutti i mali miei," which Burney wrongly identifies as being from Hasse's 1748 setting.[7] Possibly they belong to Galuppi's 1749 setting for Madrid, which Mingotti might have known from her engagement there from 1751 to 1753. Apparently no score of Galuppi's opera is preserved.[8]

"Ogni amante" turns out to be neither an old aria of Scarlatti (which would hardly have passed muster at the Haymarket in 1755) nor a local "cookery," but something much more interesting – an aria from one of Gluck's lost operas. The music is largely identical with "Se all'impero" in *La clemenza di Tito* (Naples, 1752), the text comes from Metastasio's *Issipile*, which Gluck had set for Prague earlier in 1752. Only four numbers from *Issipile* survive in manuscript, but the "Ogni amante" text is found in the Prague libretto,[9] and the numerous discrepancies between the *Clemenza* version and the London print make it plain that this is no arranger's retexting of an existing aria but an alternative version by the composer conceived for other words.[10] Ricciarelli,

Handel and Gluck

Ex. 18 continues opposite

who sang "Ogni amante" in London, had taken part in the Prague production of *Issipile*, though he did not sing this aria, and it must have been he who brought it to England and requested its insertion in *Demofoonte*.

Handel had composed his *Arianna in Creta* for his first season of mortal combat with the company formed expressly to destroy him, the so-called Opera of the Nobility. Opening at the King's Theatre in January 1734, it proved more than a match for the rival opera, Porpora's *Arianna in Nasso*, and was briefly revived at the end of the year. Long after both operas had vanished from the stage, however, the minuet in Handel's overture remained one of his most popular compositions. Not only was it frequently performed instrumentally, it also became a popular song – no mean tribute in view of its two-octave melodic span. Many an uncomfortable lover must have intoned its harrowing line to the somewhat incongruous words

A Gluck borrowing from Handel

Ex. 18 continues on next page

Handel and Gluck

Ex. 18 continues opposite

How is it possible, how can I forbear!
So many charms all around you wear,
Thy ev'ry part hath such power to move,
Who sees admires, and who knows you doth love.[11]

Its continuing popularity later in the century is attested by two classics of English dramatic literature. In Goldsmith's *She Stoops To Conquer* (1773) a

A Gluck borrowing from Handel

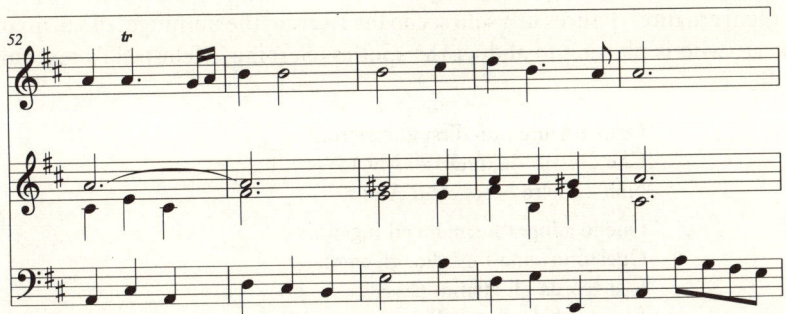

Ex. 18 Handel, *Arianna* (London, 1734), Overture, Minuet, bars 1–56

"shabby fellow" who fancies himself a gentleman declares that his dancing bear will perform only to "the very genteelest of tunes. 'Water parted,' or the minuet in *Ariadne*," and in Sheridan's *The Critic* (1779) "soft musick" ushers in the mock-tragic heroine and her confidante as Puff exclaims, "Here they are – inconsolable to the minuet in Ariadne."[12]

Musically, the minuet is the last movement of the overture to *Arianna*, following a typical slow introduction and quick fugue – the latter based on a canzona by Johann Kaspar Kerll.[13] Dramatically, it is part of the opera proper. As the autograph shows, the curtain rises at the beginning of the minuet, which accompanies an opening pantomime depicting the arrival of the annual tribute exacted from Athens by Minos, King of Thebes – seven youths and seven maidens who will be thrown to the dread Minotaur unless a champion can be found to save them. According to the stage directions, we should see a "seashore with ships and galleys, from which the prisoners emerge, on one side a royal throne, on the other a great stone tablet, upon which are carved the terms of the tribute of Athens. The seven Athenian youths, led by Teseo, disembark, as do the seven maidens."[14] Handel had done something very similar in *Giulio Cesare* in 1725, where the overture minuet (likewise with horns) turns into a chorus acclaiming the victorious Caesar.

The form of the *Arianna* minuet may be described as AABA, the second and third statements of A differing from the first in having two horns in addition to the basic complement of strings and oboes. Handel also dispenses with horns in the B section (Ex. 18). What is most unusual about this minuet from a musical point of view is the fourth and fifth phrases of A (bars 13–20). At the beginning of the fourth phrase there is a sudden hush, and the line itself, thanks in part to the hemiola in bars 14–15, takes on new breadth and nobility. The fifth phrase, softer still, has the effect of an elongated echo of the fourth. In the second A, the dynamic shift is even more striking as the horns fall silent at bar 33. They then reenter *forte* in bar 37, reversing the previous echo effect. One cannot help wondering whether Handel meant by these hushed moments to hint at the sad fate that presumably awaits the Athenian visitors, whose ship, in one version of the story, was equipped with black sails.

Issipile was Gluck's second opera for Prague, two years after *Ezio* in 1750.

"Ogni amante" figures in a solo scene for Learco, the unmitigated villain of the piece, who is plotting to abduct the spotless heroine. Metastasio's text runs as follows:

> Ogni amante può dirsi guerriero,
> Che diversa da quella di Marte
> Non è molto la scuola d'Amor.
>
> Quello adopra lusinghe ed inganni:
> Questo inventa l'insidie, gli agguati;
> E si scorda gli affanni passati
> L'uno e l'altro quand'è vincitor.

> Every lover may call himself a warrior,
> For the school of Love is not very different
> From that of Mars.
>
> The one makes use of charms and deceits:
> The other invents snares, ambushes;
> And each forgets past anxieties
> When he is the victor.

Although the text is in da capo form, Gluck set it as a more ample rondo with three statements of the first stanza separated by two statements of the second. The three A sections are largely the same, the two B sections more broadly related. A ritornello, which is simply an instrumental version of the initial A, opens and closes the aria.

The first two vocal sections of the aria are shown in Ex. 19. Gluck based his A section on Handel's A, with horns. Beginning with an adaptation of Handel's opening four-bar phrase (a) – the relationship is most apparent with the instrumental version of the melody – he then passed directly to the original third phrase. Of this he adopted only the first two bars (b), replacing Handel's ensuing rapid fall with a quasi-sequential two-bar continuation of his own. He then proceeded to Handel's fourth phrase, or rather to a combination of the fourth and fifth (c and d): the downward octave leap of the flute in bar 30 clearly emanates from the one, the harmony and long notes in the voice in bars 30-1 from the other. As in Handel, there is a sudden hush at this point, coinciding with the textual reference to "the school of love," and the horns drop out. To conclude the section Gluck added a new four-bar phrase, which he then repeated as a closing ritornello. Although the material is new, the reentry of the horns and the dynamic shift to *mezzo forte*, then *forte molto* on the restatement, are evidently modeled on the conclusion of the second A in the *Arianna* minuet.

In the B section (bars 43–64) Gluck followed his model much more closely. At the outset, two two-bar phrases are expanded to four-bar units (e and f), but from bar 51 onward (g) there is a one-to-one correspondence between aria and minuet, except that Gluck stretches the last pair of phrases from four bars into five. His expansion of the opening phrases allowed him to link the turn to the minor to "past anxieties" and the return to the major to the concept of victory.

A Gluck borrowing from Handel

Ex. 19 continues over page

The debt to Handel is obvious, yet so is the extent and complexity of the transformation. Particularly in its vocal form the melody, now confined to a ninth, has gained in smoothness while losing much of its former sweep and energy. The phrase structure is radically different. Where Handel had laid out his tune entirely in four-bar phrases except for one pair of two-bar units and had given a clear binary shape to both A and B, Gluck includes three five-bar

Ex. 19 continues opposite

phrases and avoids any sense of binary structure. The stylistic gap between the two composers is also evident in the decreased amount of motivic evolution in Gluck's melodic line, especially in the B section: whereas each of Handel's five phrases begins with some form of the same motif, Gluck's melody has no such unifying thread.

As one would expect, Gluck's bass line is much less contrapuntally conceived than Handel's, and his harmony moves somewhat more slowly. The contrast can be seen especially clearly in the opening phrase. Handel's bass line runs

A Gluck borrowing from Handel

Ex. 19 Gluck, *Issipile* (Prague, 1752), "Ogni amante," bars 22–64

mostly in contrary motion with the treble, and its adherence to the tonic note in bars 1–2 only lends force to its bold movement in bar 3 against a repetition of the melodic pattern from bar 2. Gluck's bass on the other hand is entirely in similar motion with the treble for the first three bars, joined in bar 3 by all the other moving parts, articulating one basic harmony. Gluck does introduce some snatches of imitation between the two upper voices, at the beginning of his second and fourth phrases (bars 26–7 and 34–6). But it is noteworthy that when he repeats the fourth phrase, he cheerfully obscures this contrapuntal nicety by adding a bass line in parallel thirds with the violin entry and shifting part of the flute's answer into the violin line (bars 38–40).

Gluck evidently took great care over the instrumental accompaniment. In place of Handel's oboe he added a flute (an instrument he used sparingly at this time), which was probably doubled by the first violin, leaving the "viol." line in the print to the second violin.[15] The horns, employed in both ritornellos as well as in all three A sections, have less active parts than in Handel without by any means being reduced to just providing harmonic background. A particularly lively viola part looks forward to Gluck's later operas. It is of course possible that the version published in London does not accurately represent what was performed in Prague. Two of the arias in the *Demofoonte* editions are found with somewhat fuller scoring in manuscript scores of the operas from which they come: Hasse's "Or che salvo" appears to have been robbed of a pair of flutes, Jommelli's "Padre, sposa" of two oboes and two horns.[16] Given the comparatively rich instrumentation of "Ogni amante" as published, though, it seems unlikely that it suffered such depredation.

Gluck had presumably encountered the *Arianna* minuet during his stay in England in 1745–46, when he served for a season as house composer of the Haymarket Theatre. The idea of converting it into an Italian aria may have been suggested to him by an anonymous arrangement found in the Viennese pasticcio *Andromeda*, performed at the Imperial Theater in 1750, the same year Gluck finally settled in Vienna.[17] Along with numbers by Abos, Bernasconi, Hasse, Galuppi, Jommelli, Leo, and Wagenseil (the apparent compiler), the score contains the *Arianna* minuet arranged as an aria for the contralto Vittoria Tesi, "Se dal ciel voi balenate." The musical text adheres closely to the original, the voice simply doubling the instrumental melody line. But, as in "Ogni amante," the structure is expanded, in this case by the addition of an opening ritornello, consisting of the first eight bars of A with horns, and a full reprise of bars 1–31 after the B section. Especially since Handel's music was otherwise little known in mid-century Vienna – this is the first public performance of any of his works on record – this adaptation may well have led directly to the one Gluck made for Prague two years later. Alternatively, it could be that Gluck himself brought the minuet from England to Vienna, perhaps recommending it to La Tesi, who created the title role in his *Semiramide riconosciuta* in 1748.

When he transformed "Ogni amante" into "Se all'impero" for his next opera *La clemenza di Tito*, Gluck was obliged to make a number of changes in

Ex. 20 a. Gluck, "Ogni amante," bars 22-5
b. Gluck, *La clemenza di Tito* (Naples, 1752), "Se all'impero," bars 22-5

the aria. Transferred from an alto to a tenor, it had to be transposed from D major to G major, and the different textual form caused him to give the third phrase a feminine ending and extend the A section by three bars. He further enriched the scoring by providing largely independent parts for the flute and first violin and having the viola play throughout the B section rather than entering halfway through. In several places, Gluck also improved his own counterpoint. In the opening phrase, the bass was rewritten entirely (Ex. 20a-b), though the version in the first bar had been adumbrated by the second and third statements of A in *Issipile*. And in the B section the vocal line was altered to disguise, thinly enough, two sets of parallel octaves (Ex. 21a-b). Though surely unaware of Handel's famous remark about his ignorance of counterpoint, Gluck was obviously anxious to remedy his shortcomings.

This is not the only instance of Gluckian borrowing. Gluck was of course an inveterate self-borrower, as Klaus Hortschansky has copiously demonstrated,[18] and four examples of his drawing on other composers have long been known. He reworked an aria from Ferdinando Bertoni's *Tancredi* (Turin, 1766) for *Le feste d'Apollo* (Parma, 1769) and later inserted his version into the Paris *Orphée* (1774) as "L'espoir renaît dans mon âme." As it happened, Bertoni's aria was already known in Paris, and a heated controversy erupted in 1779 over which composer had copied the other.[19] An aria in Gluck's *Antigono* (Rome, 1756), which was subsequently transplanted to *Telemaco* (Vienna, 1765) and finally became "Je t'implore et je tremble" in *Iphigénie en Tauride* (Paris, 1779), is based on the first eleven bars of the Gigue from the B♭ Partita of J. S. Bach, a relationship noted by Jahn as early as 1859,[20] and Saint-Foix discovered that Gluck used two movements from symphonies by his putative teacher Sammartini in the overture to *Le nozze d'Ercole e d'Ebe* (Pillnitz, 1747) and the introduction to the second part of *La contesa de' numi* (Copenhagen, 1749).[21]

Ex. 21 a. Gluck, "Ogni amante," bars 43–50
b. Gluck, "Se all'impero," bars 46–53

I have also found another Gluck borrowing from Handel. In Gluck's first opéra comique, *La Fausse Esclave* (Vienna, 1758), the *ariette* "Tendre Agathe" is an adaptation of the aria "Il cor mio" from *Alessandro*, first performed in London in 1726. Gluck undoubtedly became acquainted with this piece during his English sojourn. Not only was *Alessandro* revived in London in 1743–4 (without Handel's direct participation), but "Il cor mio" and another aria from that opera were sung in a concert on 25 March 1746 "For the Benefit and Increase of a Fund establish'd for the Support of Decay'd Musicians, or their Families" (later the Royal Society of Musicians).[22] Since all the singers came from Gluck's Haymarket company, and the program included five excerpts from his opera *La caduta de' giganti*, he presumably directed the performance.

Handel's aria is sung by Alexander the Great to his future wife Roxana before leaving for battle. Still apprehensive that he might desert her for her

A Gluck borrowing from Handel

Ex. 22 continues over page

Handel and Gluck

Ex. 22 continues opposite

A Gluck borrowing from Handel

Ex. 22 Handel, *Alessandro* (London, 1726), "Il cor mio," bars 1–57

rival Lisaura, she sends him off with a gentle warning, "Vittorioso torna, ma più fedel, ma più amoroso" (Return victorious, but more faithful and more loving). He responds:

> Il cor mio ch'è già per te
> Tutto amore e tutto fè,
> Con più gloria tornerà,
> Ma non già
> Più amoroso e più fedel.

> My heart that has already given you
> All love and all faith,
> With greater glory will return,
> But not in fact
> More amorous and more faithful.

Handel set these words with a smooth and unadorned melody which, in the opinion of Burney, "is, and ever must be, pleasing to lovers of elegant simplicity."[23] But by emphasizing the momentary ambiguity of the fourth line, he also gave this love song a teasing quality: moving directly from "con più gloria tornerà" to "ma non già" and then pausing, Alexander seems to be saying that he will not return – until he goes on to reveal his true meaning in line five (Ex. 22). After playing this game twice, Handel varies it by reversing the elements of the third line, so that it is "con più gloria" (separated by a pause from "tornerà") that is juxtaposed with the deceptive "ma non già."

Gluck's air is in G major, a third higher than the E♭ major of "Il mio cor," though he may have known Handel's aria in A major (the key in most printed editions of *Alessandro* other than Cluer's 1726 score) or E major (in which Monticelli sang it in 1743 and presumably in the 1746 benefit).[24] The opening and closing ritornellos are new, if largely based on Handel, but the vocal portion – some fifty-six bars of 3/8 time – corresponds more or less exactly to the vocal portion of Handel's A section, except for the conversion of the one brief flush of coloratura into an internal ritornello in bars 51–2 (Ex. 23). Since Gluck's opera survives only in keyboard arrangements, we cannot judge how his scoring may have compared with Handel's. It seems likely (as suggested to

Handel and Gluck

A Gluck borrowing from Handel

Ex. 23 Gluck, *La Fausse Esclave* (Vienna, 1758), "Tendre Agathe," bars 1–65

me by Bruce Alan Brown) that the omission of the orchestral interjections after the first three phrases was a copyist's oversight, since similar passages later in the aria were retained.

The text of "Tendre Agathe" was adapted from the Paris libretto on which Gluck's is based, *La Fausse Aventurière* (1757), where it had been sung to an unidentified setting of "Prigioniera abbandonata" from Metastasio's *Adriano in Siria*.[25] In sharp contrast with *Alessandro*, it expresses sentiments of disappointed love, though the audience knows Agathe is merely shamming as part of a plot to trick her prospective father-in-law into consenting to her marriage. The dramatic logic of Handel's peculiar interplay of phrases is inevitably lost, but Gluck manages to turn his orchestral interjections to account as sobs and sighs illustrating "va pleurer," "va gemir," and "va soupirer."

It could be argued that the case of "Tendre Agathe" is somewhat different from Gluck's other known borrowings. *La Fausse Esclave* after all contained, along with his own music, a great many *vaudevilles*, some with tunes by Mondonville, Rameau, and Rousseau. Yet a clear distinction existed between the simple *vaudevilles* and the more elaborate *ariettes*, and the printed libretto specifically states that all the "airs nouveaux" (which include "Tendre Agathe") were composed by Gluck.[26]

The motives that led Gluck to borrow from other composers varied widely. A simple desire to spare himself some trouble sufficiently explains his more or less wholesale appropriation of instrumental movements by Sammartini. The impetus for the Bertoni adaptation on the other hand probably came not from the composer but from the soprano Antonia Maria Girelli, who sang Bertoni's aria in 1766 and Gluck's reworking in 1769. Under the circumstances what is chiefly remarkable is that Gluck recomposed the aria as extensively as he did. Practical considerations may also have played a part in his borrowings from Handel, but on a more fundamental level we may surmise that he turned to this distinctly old-fashioned music because he had a particular admiration for its composer.

Michael Kelly, the Irish tenor and memoirist, was personally acquainted with Gluck, who coached him for a Viennese production of *Iphigénie en Tauride* in 1783. He tells how one morning Gluck said to him:

> "Follow me up stairs, Sir, and I will introduce you to one, whom, all my life, I have made my study, and endeavoured to imitate." I followed him into his bed-room, and, opposite to the head of the bed, saw a full-length picture of Handel, in a rich frame. "There, Sir," said he, "is the portrait of the inspired master of our art; when I open my eyes in the morning, I look upon him with reverential awe, and acknowledge him as such; and the highest praise is due to your country for having distinguished and cherished his gigantic genius."[27]

The newly discovered borrowings give additional weight to Kelly's testimony and urge us to look more closely into the question of what specifically Gluck learned from Handel.

On 24 March 1757 two numbers from the pasticcio *Demofoonte* were performed at the annual benefit for the Royal Society of Musicians, the same event in which Gluck had apparently participated eleven years earlier.[28] Ricciarelli sang "Ogni amante" and was later joined by Mingotti in the duet "La destra ti chiedo" from Gluck's *Demofoonte*. The program printed in the *Public Advertiser* identifies the composer of "Ogni amante" as "Scarlatti," suggesting that the gossip reported by Mason the previous year had come to be accepted as fact. What makes this concert particularly noteworthy is that the audience almost certainly included Handel. He had played an active role in the society ever since he had organized the first of its concerts in 1739. According to Burney "he seldom was absent" from the yearly benefit.[29] In 1757 Handel was seventy-two years old and totally blind, but that year his health reportedly improved considerably, and it seems unlikely he would have missed this important occasion. One can only wonder what his reaction must have been when he heard performed an anonymous transformation of his celebrated minuet and learned that the piece was attributed to a composer who had died eight years before *Arianna* was written. Was he annoyed at the implication, surely not lost on many cognoscenti, that he was "almost a musical Lauder"? Or did he perhaps laugh inwardly (as Mattheson says he liked to do) at the thought that after all he had borrowed from other composers without detection he should finally be accused of purloining what another composer had taken from him?

NOTES

1 *Correspondence of Thomas Gray*, ed. P. Toynbee and L. Whibley (Oxford, 1935), vol. 1, p. 451. An earlier version of this essay was read at the annual meeting of the American Musicological Society in New Orleans in October 1987, and a preliminary report of its findings was included by Bernd Baselt in a paper delivered at the Gluck congress in Vienna in November of that year. See B. Baselt, "Zum Thema Händel und Gluck," in *Kongressbericht Gluck in Wien*, ed. G. Croll and M. Woitas (Kassel, 1989), pp. 141–5.
2 Charles Burney, *A General History of Music From the Earliest Ages to the Present Period (1789)*, 2 vols., ed. Frank Mercer (London, 1935; reprint New York, 1957), vol. 2, p. 854.
3 W. C. Smith and C. Humphries, *A Bibliography of the Musical Works Published by the Firm of John Walsh during the Years 1721–1766* (London, 1969), p. 126.
4 Burney, *A General History of Music*, vol. 2, p. 854, n. (b).
5 I am grateful to Paul Cauthen, Marita P. McClymonds, and Frederick L. Milner for assistance in identifying the published arias.
6 J. A. Hasse, *Arminio*, ed. R. Gerber, Das Erbe deutscher Musik, vols. 27–8 (Mainz, 1957–66), vol. 28, pp. 347–53.
7 Burney, *A General History of Music*, vol. 2, p. 854.
8 Galuppi's setting was performed in Madrid as late as 1755. On his success in Spain, see *B. Galuppi detto "Il Buranello" (1706–1785): Note e documenti* (Siena, 1948), pp. 42–5.
9 A. Wotquenne, *Thematisches Verzeichnis der Werke von Chr. W. v. Gluck (1714–1787)* (Leipzig, 1904), pp. 45–7, 195–6; J. Liebeskind, *Ergänzungen und Nachträge zu dem Thematisches Verzeichnis der Werke von Chr. W. von Gluck von Alfred Wotquenne* (Leipzig, 1911), p. 14.
10 In "A Comparative Study of Five Musical Settings of *La clemenza di Tito*," Ph.D. dissertation, University of Michigan, 1956, vol. 1, p. 272, William Weichlein cited a manuscript copy of this aria in his possession which contained both the *Issipile* and *Tito* texts. I have been unable to trace this manuscript, and without further information it is impossible to know what it may have represented.

11 *The British Musical Miscellany*, vol. 2 (London, 1734), p. 121. For a list of contemporary editions, see William C. Smith, *Handel: A Descriptive Catalogue of the Early Editions*, 2nd edn (London, 1970), pp. 18–19.
12 *The Collected Works of Oliver Goldsmith* (Oxford, 1966), vol. 5, p. 118; R. B. Sheridan, *Plays*, ed. C. Price (Oxford, 1975), p. 367. "Water parted from the sea" is an air in Arne's *Artaxerxes*.
13 J. K. Kerll, *Ausgewählte Werke*, vol. 1, ed. A. Sandberger, *Denkmäler der Tonkunst in Bayern*, ser. 3, vol. 2: 2 (Leipzig, 1901), p. 29.
14 G. F. Handel, *Werke*, ed. F. Chrysander (Leipzig, 1858–94), vol. 83, p. 6. In the autograph, British Library, R. M. 20.a.6, the stage directions are on fol. 3^v.
15 I owe this observation to Bruce Alan Brown.
16 I am informed by Paul Cauthen that the horns are lacking in some scores of *Cajo Mario*.
17 Further on this pasticcio, see T. Antonicek, *Zur Pflege Händelscher Musik in der 2. Hälfte des 18. Jahrhunderts*, Veröffentlichungen der Kommission für Musikforschung, vol. 4 (Vienna, 1966), pp. 40–1.
18 Klaus Hortschansky, *Parodie und Entlehnung im Schaffen Christoph Willibald Glucks*, Analecta musicologica, vol. 13 (Cologne, 1973).
19 See Christoph Willibald Gluck, *Orphée et Euridice*, ed. Ludwig Finscher, *Sämtliche Werke*, ser. 1, vol. 6 (Kassel, 1967), pp. xxiii–xxiv, and ed. C. Saint-Saëns and J. Tiersot (Paris, 1898), pp. l–lxxix, which includes a vocal score of Bertoni's aria. Gluck was often accused of plagiarism by his Parisian enemies. In 1777 one Piccinnist pamphlet asserted he had borrowed from Pergolesi, Vinci, Leo, Pulli, Jommelli, Galuppi, Piccinni, Sacchini, and Traetta; see *Querelle des Gluckistes et des Piccinnistes*, ed. F. Lesure (Geneva, 1984), vol. 2, p. 254.
20 The literature on this relationship is summarized in George J. Buelow, "A Bach Borrowing by Gluck: Another Frontier," *Bach* 12 (1981): 44.
21 Georges de Saint-Foix, "Les Débuts milanais de Gluck," *Gluck-Jahrbuch* 1 (1913): 43–5. See also Bathia Churgin, "Alterations in Gluck's Borrowings from Sammartini," *Studi musicali* 9 (1980): 117–34.
22 Otto Erich Deutsch, *Handel: A Documentary Biography* (London, 1955), p. 631.
23 Burney, *A General History of Music*, vol. 2, p. 740.
24 A penciled note in the main conducting score of *Alessandro*, Hamburg, Staats- und Universitätsbibliothek, MA/999, fol. 108v, indicates that at one stage it was planned to transpose "Il cor mio" into G major for the 1743 revival. I am indebted to Richard King for information on the tonal odyssey of this aria.
25 L. Anseaume and P. A. L. de Marcouville, *La Fausse Aventurière: opéra-comique en deux actes, mêlé d'ariettes* (Paris, 1757), p. 42. To make the text fit Handel's music Gluck omitted two lines and brought back the words "Tendre Agathe" in the later part of the aria.
26 For another account of this borrowing, see Bruce Alan Brown, *Gluck and the French Theatre in Vienna* (Oxford, 1991), pp. 213–14.
27 *The Reminiscences of Michael Kelly of the King's Theatre and Theatre Royal Drury Lane*, 2nd edn (London, 1826; reprint New York, 1968), vol. 1, p. 252.
28 *The London Stage, 1660–1800: A Calendar of Plays, Entertainments & Afterpieces together with Casts, Box-Receipts and Contemporary Comment*, vol. 4: 2, ed. G. W. Stone, Jr. (Carbondale, Ill., 1962), p. 588.
29 Charles Burney, *An Account of the Musical Performances in Westminster-Abbey* (London, 1785; reprint New York, 1979), p. 34.

10

Zéphire et Flore: a "galant" early ballet by Angiolini and Gluck

BRUCE ALAN BROWN

Gasparo Angiolini's 1765 manifesto of ballet reform, the *Dissertation sur les ballets pantomimes des anciens pour servir de programme au ballet pantomime tragique de Sémiramis*, almost certainly written with the aid of Ranieri de' Calzabigi,[1] derived much of its authority from its model, a similarly titled essay by Voltaire which had likewise prefaced a tragedy about the Babylonian queen.[2] A principal concern in both the Parisian and Viennese Semiramis dissertations was to restrain the more decorative, "galant" features of modern dramatic compositions, of whatever sort, which the writers found to be alarmingly prevalent. Voltaire decried the "maximes de galanterie" which defaced the tragédies lyriques of Quinault and Lully, and called for "[d]es termes mâles et énergiques" in their stead.[3] Angiolini and Calzabigi proudly laid claim to the tragic genre in dance, criticizing the frivolity of most earlier ballets, as well as the "êtres fantastiques personifiés" which in French operas and opéra ballets alike provided spectators with relief from the intensity of the drama.[4] Ably seconded by the composer Christoph Gluck, Angiolini put his theories into practice in three major ballets, each accompanied by a printed program or essay: *Don Juan, ou le Festin de pierre* of 1761, *Citera assediata* of 1762, and *Sémiramis* of 1765. The severity of the latter work so alienated the Viennese public that Angiolini and Gluck saw fit to make a tactical retreat, and provide happy endings for their last two major ballets.[5] In view of this trajectory of reform and retrenchment, it is interesting to find in their ballet *Zéphire et Flore* of 1759 – a work not previously mentioned in the literature on Gluck – an early point of reference that is specifically designated as "galant" by two contemporary critics. By virtue of its very subject matter – the loves of the gods – *Zéphire et Flore* belongs to a category of art that critics have generally labeled "galant."[6] The ballet thus affords a rare opportunity to gauge the aesthetic distance traveled by Angiolini during the first of his two terms as choreographer for Vienna's French theater (Burgtheater) – a period spanning precisely the years 1759 to 1765 – and to determine the degree to which Gluck's music for *Zéphire et Flore* anticipates the innovatory features found in his better-known scores for *Don Juan* and *Sémiramis*.

We are informed of the premiere of *Zéphire et Flore* by the courtier and diarist

Johann Joseph Khevenhüller-Metsch, who noted the following in his journal entry for 12–13 August 1759:

> Den 12. hatten wir den sonntägigen Gottesdienst zu Schönbrunn, Nachmittag aber weder Cercle noch Comédie, welches beiden auf morgen als den 13. gesparhet wurde, um den doppelten Gala-Tag wegen der beiden Ertzherzoginnen Elisabethae und Charlotte Geburts-festen zu feieren, wegen welchen aber sonsten nichts publiques ware. Das Spectacle bestunde in einer ersten Repraesentation der Fille d'Aristide [recte: *La Fille arbitre*, by Affichard and Romagnesi], und einen neuen Ballet, les amours de Flore et Zéphire benahmset.[7]

Khevenhüller names neither choreographer nor composer – possibly their identities were common knowledge. But court payment records show that Angiolini and Gluck had recently taken over these functions in connection with the French theater's ballet company, including its performances at Laxenburg and Schönbrunn palaces, from their predecessors Franz Hilverding and Joseph Starzer. Angiolini's Parisian-trained mentor, whom he invariably called "Monsieur Hilverding" in his later writings, had been enticed to the Russian court at St. Petersburg in November of 1758, with Starzer following him there a few months later.[8] From Khevenhüller's wording one may surmise that *Zéphire et Flore* was commissioned specifically for the birthday celebration at Schönbrunn. Gluck's works were in fact frequently in demand for imperial celebrations throughout the later 1750s and early 1760s. His opéra comique *L'Arbre enchanté*, for instance, was performed for the nameday of Emperor Francis Stephen in October of 1759, and in 1765 both of the above-named Archduchesses Elisabeth and Charlotte (Maria Carolina)[9] sang along with two of their sisters in Gluck and Metastasio's serenata teatrale *Il Parnaso confuso*, as part of the festivities for the wedding of their brother Joseph with Princess Josepha of Bavaria.

Zéphire et Flore is mentioned specifically in the context of Angiolini's succession to his teacher's post in a long, anonymous article on Vienna in the *Journal encyclopédique* for 15 December 1759.[10] After descriptions of three ballets by Hilverding, it is stated that

> Le Sr. Angiolino son éléve, éclairé par les mêmes conseils que son Maître, a donné des Ballets qui font très bien auguer de ses talens. On a gouté entr'autres *Les Nôces de Persée* & *d'Androméde, les Miquelets, le Naufrage, les Corsaires*. Son Ballet *de Flore* qui a déjà paru trois fois à la Cour, & dont je vous réserve la description, ne le céde point aux plus galants du Sr. Hilverding.[11]

No description of *Zéphire et Flore* follows, in this or any subsequent issue. A spectator's description of the work is provided, however, in the May 1760 issue of the *Journal étranger*. Turning from Vienna's mores and intellectual life to its theaters, the (again anonymous) author comes to

> la partie des Spectacles, que je regarde comme supérieure à Vienne; c'est celle des Ballets. J'en ai vûe ici de la plus grande magnificence. Ceux qui m'ont le

plus frappé, sont le *port de Marseille*, & la *Boutique du Perruquier*, donnés au Théâtre Allemand, *Flore & Zéphir* & le *Berger Magicien*, à la Comédie Française.[12]

(Noble theater-goers in Vienna could easily compare the various spectacles offered them, since ballets, plays, and operas were all intermingled during a single evening's performance, and many of these spectators rented boxes in both the French and German theaters.) The writer treats each ballet in turn; in discussing *Zéphire et Flore*, he at first echoes the views of the author of the letter in the *Journal encyclopédique*.

> Le Ballet de Flore étoit aussi galant qu'on puisse en imaginer. On y voyoit une entrée des Aquilons à la suite de Borée, qui, dans les transports de sa jalousie, venoit ravager les jardins de Zéphir, & renverser les fleurs écloses sous les pas de son Amante. La Décoration de ce Spectacle tenoit de l'enchantement. Les Aquilons sortoient du sein des nuages qui troubloient les airs. Une harmonie terrible & frémissante accompagnoit une Danse furieuse. Zéphir s'envoloit de frayeur; Flore éperdue tomboit sur un siége de gazon. Il faudroit avoir vû Madame *Angiolini*, pour se figurer tout ce que l'attitude de sa tête ajoûtoit de touchant à la langueur de son expression. On peut avoir plus de finesse dans les pas, ou plus de précision dans les mouvemens, un balancement plus méthodique dans les bras, ou plus de légereté dans la taille; mais on n'a point un ensemble mieux composé par la Nature & par l'Art que Mad[a]me Angiolini. C'est la Danseuse des Amateurs voluptueux. Ils ne la verront plus sur le Théâtre; elle l'a quitté à la fin du Carnaval: mais elle y laisse son mari, joli Danseur, & bon Compositeur de Ballets, & même de Musique.[13]

The description of the action, though more fragmentary than Angiolini's own scenarios for *Don Juan* and *Sémiramis*, is nonetheless valuable, as it allows us to identify one of the Viennese stage designs in the so-called "Durazzo Collection" (named after the former theater director, Count Giacomo Durazzo) as a representation of this very work (see Plate 17).[14] The drawing corresponds in every detail to the scene described in the *Journal étranger* report: stiff-limbed *aquilons* spewing forth from a cloud; the menacing Boreas in the foreground – recognizable, as are his followers, by their wings;[15] Flora falling onto a turf bench, or *siège de gazon*, at stage left; and the timid Zephyr, fleeing off stage. (The goddess can be distinguished from her attendants by her more prominent position, and by the more elaborate garlands of her skirt, compared to those on the other women's identical costumes.)[16] The actions of Boreas and his troupe are anything but *galant*; rather, it was probably the "magical" stage décors, and above all the delectable anguish of Flora that, in the mind of the *Journal étranger* critic, made the ballet seem *galant* in the extreme. In this context the rapturous praise of Angiolini's wife Maria Teresa, *née* Fogliazzi, in the role of Flora is significant, constituting as it does the most complete description of her talents to have survived.[17]

The remark at the close of the above account of *Zéphire et Flore* concerning Gasparo Angiolini's composition of ballets "and even of music" might suggest

Plate 17 *Zéphire et Flore*, No. 5; unattributed drawing from the largely dispersed "Durazzo Collection." University of Salzburg, Institut für Tanzforschung.

that he had written the music for this work. Indeed, he is known to have composed the music to at least one of his Viennese ballets, *Le muse protette dal genio d'Austria* (1764), and to a great many of his later ballets for Russia and Italy. But in the case of *Zéphire et Flore* the evidence points decisively to Gluck.

The music to *Zéphire et Flore* survives in a set of unattributed manuscript partbooks (Violino Primo, Violino 2do, Viola, Basso [/Violoncello/Fagotto]; Sign. K. II 63) in the castle archive in Český Krumlov, the southern Bohemian estate of the Schwarzenberg family. The more than 180 ballets in this collection, of which many are unique sources, constitute a substantial portion of the Viennese ballet repertory between the 1750s and the 1790s.[18] The collection was assembled in large part by Prince Joseph Adam von Schwarzenberg (1722–82), who ordered scores or partbooks from Viennese court copyists of his favorite operas and ballets, performances of which he had likely witnessed during his frequent periods of residence in the capital.[19] The orchestral parts for *Zéphire et Flore*, like those to a great many other ballets and opéras comiques at Český Krumlov, are in the hand of Bonifacius Carl Champée, chief copyist for the French theater during the 1750s and early 1760s. Exceptionally, there is even a signed receipt from Champée for these materials (Sign. III B 3b/11, No. 1308), showing that the ballet was copied for Schwarzenberg some two months after its premiere:[20]

Zéphire et Flore *by Angiolini and Gluck*

Ex. 24 continues over page.

Handel and Gluck

11. Minore

Ex. 24 continues opposite.

Zéphire et Flore *by Angiolini and Gluck*

Ex. 24 Gluck, *Zéphire et Flore* (Schönbrunn Palace, 1759), Nos. 10–11

Den 1 Xb 1759
N 1308. Für Ihro Hochfürstl. Drl: von Schwartzen
berg *Cop*irt im *Monnath 8bre*

Den [*sic*] *Ballet* von *Zephire* und *Flora*

à 4 fl. 12 xr

[sign.] *Champée*

Exemp[lum] Ma[nus]

Quittire hiemit den
Empfang *à* 4 fl. 12 x:
[sign.] *Champée*

[verso]

*Approb*antur zur Ausgaab 4. fl. 12x^r.
Wien den 23ten *Jan.* 1760.
[sign.] Jph Schwarzenberg mp

4. fl. 12. xr *Cop*iirung eines *ballets*.

Although the partbooks for *Zéphire et Flore* bear no composer's name (as is the case with the vast majority of ballet manuscripts at Český Krumlov), the work's date of August 1759 falls within the period during which Gluck was responsible for composing music for the French theater's ballet troupe. Confirmation of his authorship is provided by No. 3 of the ballet, which Gluck reworked as an air with chorus, "Cet asile aimable et tranquille," in the

Parisian version of *Orphée et Eurydice* (1774), and by Nos. 10 and 11, a pair which Gluck reused three times: as vocal numbers, in the opera seria *Il trionfo di Clelia* (1763) and the opéra comique *La Rencontre imprévue* (1764); and again as dance movements, in the "tragédie-opéra" *Iphigénie en Aulide* (1774); see Ex. 24. In the libretto of *La Rencontre imprévue* the single piece produced by the (re)texting of this pair of dances is labeled "AIR parodié"; this would seem to refer back to the ballet, performed less than four years earlier, before essentially the same audience, rather than to the parody in *Il trionfo di Clelia* ("Ah! ritorna, età dell'oro"), a work written for Bologna.

Minuets similar to these two from *Zéphire et Flore* can be found in several other works from this period of Gluck's career. The constant eighth-note motion of the "Majore" (No. 10) is seen, for instance, in "Un air fin," a "Menuet" sung by the Marquis in *Le Diable à quatre*, from the same year 1759, and in Fatime's air "C'est ainsi" from *Le Cadi dupé* of 1761. The ballet's "Minore" (No. 11) is a close relative of the danced Trio of the triple-meter air "Avec quelle ardeur" in Gluck's opéra comique *Cythère assiégée*, another work from 1759; both movements are in G minor, with voluptuous melodies and a staccato arpeggiated accompaniment in the middle voices. In reworking the two dances in *La Rencontre imprévue*, Gluck expanded the "Majore" with ritornellos and cadential repetitions, and smoothed out some rough spots in the part-writing (such as the leaps by seventh in the bass line in bars 5–8).[21] In the "Minore" he provided the voice with a more sustained version of the violin line (which could suggest sighing but which was too fragmentary to support a text); he then suppressed the soaring bassoon line in the tenor register, to avoid clotting the texture. The original versions of both dances have charms of their own, and Gluck's changes are not necessarily to be considered improvements.

The mid-eighteenth-century theatrical reform was marked not only by a renunciation of unnecessary ornament, but also by more direct and serious-minded uses of antiquity in both subject matter and dramaturgy. Judged according to what is known of its plot, Gluck and Angiolini's *Zéphire et Flore* would seem to fall short of this new, higher standard. The ballet is not a direct retelling in dance of a story handed down by the Greek and Roman poets (as was the case with the "Entrée de Borée" in an earlier ballet by Quinault and Lully), but a *galant* elaboration based only loosely on mythology. Its plot probably owed more to dictionaries of fable and to previous dramatic treatments of this subject than to a confrontation with original sources, of the sort Angiolini tells us lay behind his *Sémiramis* ballet.[22] One of the era's most widely used guides to mythology, Pierre Chompré's *Dictionnaire abrégé de la fable* (1727 and subsequent editions), positively discourages first-hand investigation of ancient writings on mythology, and closely circumscribes the uses of fable for modern readers:

> ON sait que la Mythologie est un tissu d'imaginations bizarres, un amas confus de faits, quelquefois vrais dans le fond, mais sans chronologie, sans ordre, ... qu'enfin c'est un assemblage de contes misérables, la plupart

> destitués de vraisemblance, & dignes de mépris. Mais on sait aussi que la connoissance de ces chimeres poétiques & païennes est absolument nécessaire pour entendre les Auteurs. Dans cette vue l'on a ici rassemblé par ordre alphabétique, ce qu'il y a d'essentiel à savoir sur cette matiere, afin d'épargner aux jeunes gens la peine d'aller puiser dans des sources souvent empoisonnées.[23]

Chompré goes on to stress the attention given in his dictionary to the iconography of mythology – to the attributes used by modern-day painters and sculptors (and, one might add, choreographers) in portraying fabulous personages.

Not only for Angiolini's *Zéphire et Flore*, but also for many other "ballets de fables,"[24] mythology provided little more than the basic premise. Such is the case, for instance, in Hilverding's very free treatment of the story of Cupid and Psyche (1752), the action of which ranges from Cupid's palace to the "deserts" of Lapland. (In a later revival of this ballet the role of Psyche was taken by Mme Fogliazzi Angiolini; see Plate 18.)[25] The principal source for the legend of Flora and Zephyr is Book V of Ovid's *Fasti*, the poet's unfinished explication of the Roman calendar, with all its associated feasts, historical events, and myths. There Ovid has Flora herself relate the events of her abduction by the god of the west wind, within a discussion of her yearly feast, the Floralia (28 April to 3 May):

> 'Twas spring, and I was roaming; Zephyr caught sight of me; I retired; he pursued and I fled; but he was the stronger, and Boreas had given his brother full right of rape by daring to carry off the prize [Oreithyia] from the house of Erechtheus. However, he made amends for his violence by giving me the name of bride, and in my marriage-bed I have naught to complain of...[26]

Around the turn of the eighteenth century the subject of Flora and Zephyr was turned to frequently for decorative schemes (often as an allegory of spring), and also for plots for operas and ballets.[27] One of the better-known French dramatizations was the 1688 opera *Zéphire et Flore* by Michel Du Boullay, with music by Louis and Jean-Louis Lully (first and third sons, respectively, of Jean-Baptiste).[28] In Du Boullay's plot, as later in Angiolini's, Flora is loved not only by Zephyr but also by Boreas. The librettist provided a fig leaf of authenticity by having Boreas justify the work's plot, in his opening monolog in Act I, with reference to his own prior rape of the Athenian princess Oreithyia – the same episode cited by Ovid as a precedent for Zephyr's actions:

> INfortuné Borée, hélas! quelle est ta peine,
> D'aimer toujours quelque Inhumaine!
> Que m'a servy le genereux effort
> De m'affranchir des fers de l'ingrate Orithie?
> A Flore de nouveau mon ame assujettie,
> N'en attend pas un plus doux sort...

Du Boullay fleshed out the opera's plot with the usual secondary intrigues and characters – the latter including, confusingly, a confidante of Flora named

Plate 18 Teresa Fogliazzi Angiolini in the role of Psyche, in Hilverding and Starzer's *Psyché et l'Amour* Dance Collection, The New York Public Library for the Performing Arts, Astor, Lenox and Tilden Foundations.

Cloris: essentially the same name (Chloris) by which Flora had been known before her elevation to the rank of a goddess by Zephyr. Probably for reasons of *bienséance*, Boreas' abduction of Flora occurs off stage, and is only related indirectly, after the fact.

Closer in time to Angiolini and Gluck's ballet there was another vogue for Zephyr and Flora pieces, started by a work in which the myth was only alluded to: Rebel and Francœur's *Zélindor, Roi des Sylphes*, on a libretto by Moncrif. The opera was given at Versailles and later in Paris in 1745, and restaged several times. Here, too, a god falls in love with a mortal maiden, but before marrying her he must first overcome his doubts as to her fidelity, since:

> Comme un Zéphir qui caresse
> Une fleur sans s'arrêter,
> Une volage maitresse,
> S'empresse de nous quitter.

In *Zéphire et Fleurette*, a parody of this opera by Favart, Panard, and Laujon (written in 1745, but not performed until 1754), the comparison is brought to the foreground, and the premise reversed: the wind-god himself (taking the place of Zélindor) becomes an incarnation of flightiness in love. This is the case also in the opéra comique *Zéphire et Flore* by Denis Ballière de Laisement, likewise from 1754. Though the relevant lines from Ovid's *Fasti* are cited ostentatiously on the title page of the libretto, the opera's plot strays far from classical sources. As in the earlier work by Du Boullay and the Lullys, this opera opens with Boreas' protestations of love for Flora. His language parodies not Ovid, but rather a favorite vaudeville: "Votre cœur, aimable Aurore," from Mondonville's recent "pastorale héroïque" *Titon et l'Aurore*. Flora, who loves Zephyr but worries about his wandering eye, explains her predicament using a well-known air from Rousseau's *Le Devin du village*:

> Air: *Non, non, Colette n'est point trompeuse.*
>
> Non, non, le Zéphir n'est qu'un volage,
> Inconstant dans ses plaisirs...

Late in the work, Flora confers her choice on Zephyr, which leads to a scene very much like that depicted in the drawing of Angiolini's *Zéphire et Flore*. But in the opera Boreas's threat of vengeance on Flora's beloved flowers is simply laughed off.

By the 1750s, then, there was a well-established tradition on the French stage of Zephyr and Flora pieces which, with their emphasis on rape and infidelity (and despite an occasional bow to Ovid), had become markedly *galant*, even *risqué* in tone.[29] But even if Angiolini had been unaware of any of the pieces mentioned above, there was one other balletic treatment of the theme that can hardly have escaped his notice. This was the "Ballet des Fleurs," from the entrée "Les Fleurs, Fête Persane" in Fuzelier and Rameau's *Les Indes galantes* of 1735. This *divertissement*, choreographed by the innovative and famously expressive dancer Marie Sallé, amounted to a veritable *ballet en action* – one of the few such pieces cited as precedents by Angiolini's rival Jean-Georges Noverre in his *Lettres sur la dance* of 1760.[30] Hilverding probably witnessed performances of *Les Indes galantes* in person, during his studies in Paris in the 1730s with the dancer Michel Blondy. The action in Angiolini and Gluck's ballet is essentially the same as in Sallé and Rameau's, if one merely substitutes Flora for the Rose, the Queen of the Flowers, and flowers for Flora's attendants:

> Ce ballet représente pittoresquement le sort des Fleurs dans un jardin. On les a personnifiées ainsi que Borée, les Aquilons et Zéphire, pour donner de l'âme à cette peinture galante, exécutée par d'aimables esclaves de l'un et l'autre sexe. D'abord les Fleurs choisies qui peuvent briller davantage au théâtre dansent ensemble et forment un parterre qui varie à chaque instant. La Rose, leur reine, danse seule. La fête est interrompue par un orage qu'amène Borée; les Fleurs en éprouvent de la colère; la Rose résiste plus longtemps à l'ennemi qui la persécute; les pas de Borée expriment son impétuosité et sa fureur; les attitudes de la Rose peignent sa douceur et ses craintes. Zéphire arrive avec la clarté renaissante; il ranime et relève les Fleurs abattues par la tempête, et termine leur triomphe et le sien par les hommages que sa tendresse rend à la Rose.

As we shall see, Rameau's and Gluck's responses to these very similar programs were parallel in several respects – unavoidably so, given the standardization of musical gestures available for depicting breezes and storms. In any case, Angiolini's imitation of this "peinture galante" in *Zéphire et Flore* can be understood as a gesture in homage to Mme. Sallé, just as his master Hilverding's ballet *Le Turc généreux* of the previous season can be seen as a reinterpretation of the entrée by that name in the same opéra ballet by Rameau.

The story of Zephyr and Flora continued for some years to attract choreographers. Jean Favier, who had worked in Vienna briefly during the early 1750s, created a *Zefiro, e Flora* in 1771 for Verona,[31] for instance, and in 1796 in London Charles Didelot made the story a vehicle for important innovations in ballet technique.[32] Angiolini's 1759 ballet seems itself to have spawned progeny. A three-act version of the story, by Hilverding and Starzer, called *La Victoire de Flore sur Borée*, was performed for the Russian court in St. Petersburg on 29 April 1760 (Old Style). In Vienna there was another treatment by Angiolini and Gluck, called *La Fête de Flore, ou le Retour du printemps*, given in the Burgtheater on 3 May (the final day of the Floralia) 1761; its "Musique tendre" (Count Zinzendorf's characterization) is apparently lost. On 23 June 1763 *L'Empire de Flore* had its premiere; the Viennese theater chronicler Philipp Gumpenhuber names no choreographer, and there is no description, but the (anonymous) music survives at Český Krumlov. Finally, there was another *Retour du printemps* on 5 May 1765 (for which there are likewise extant partbooks in the Schwarzenberg archive), this one with choreography by Hilverding (then newly returned from Russia).

Angiolini and Gluck's *Zéphire et Flore* of 1759 displays the typically small dimensions of works presented to the Habsburg court during its yearly retreats to Laxenburg or Schönbrunn palaces, during which a full schedule of balls, *cercles*, meals (often with *Tafelmusik*), hunting, and other diversions limited the amount of time available for the theater. The relative paucity of titles, tempo indications, and dynamic or expressive markings in the manuscript partbooks may be a sign that the work was composed in some haste – though the manuscripts of many other Viennese ballets at Český Krumlov are similar in

Table 10.1. *Angiolini/Gluck*, Zéphire et Flore

No.	Title/Tempo	Key[a]	Meter	Bars	Instrumentation
	Sinfonia	G–V/G	2/4	61	Vn. 1–2, Va., B.c.
1.		G	C	28	Vn. 1–2, Va., B.c.
2.	Adagio	G	3/4	20	Vn. 1–2, Va., B.c.
3.		G	6/8	46	Vn. 1–2, Va., B.c., Bn.
4.		g–V/B♭	6/8	24	Vn. 1–2, Va., B.c., Bn.
5.		V⁶/g–D	C	83	Vn. 1–2, Va., B.c.
6.		d/D–V/D	C	41	Vn. 1–2, Va., B.c.
7.		D	12/8	8	Vn. 1–2, Va., B.c.
8.		b	12/8	8	Vn. 1–2, Va., B.c., Bn.
9. [= 7.]		D	12/8	16	Vn. 1–2, Va., B.c.
10.		G	3/4	24	Vn. 1–2, Va., B.c.
11.	Minore	g	3/4	28	Vn. 1–2, Va., B.c., Bn.
12.	Finale	G	2/4	30	Vn. 1–2, Va., B.c.

| = linked to previous or following movement.
[a] Lower-case letters denote minor mode.

this respect. The ballet's reduced orchestration (strings, plus obbligato bassoon in four movements) may also point to a commission close to the date of the premiere, or perhaps to limitations on the numbers of musicians available for service at Schönbrunn. In its movement plan and succession of keys, *Zéphire et Flore* follows precedents established by Starzer over the previous decade, from which Gluck would deviate but little in the coming years (see Table 10.1).

As often in Viennese ballets, the opening Sinfonia is linked to the first movement by a half-close on the dominant; two further pairs of movements (Nos. 4–5, 6–7) are similarly joined, providing continuity at the point of greatest dramatic interest in the work. This group of numbers is expanded further in either direction by the pairing of *maggiore* and *minore* movements (Nos. 3–4, 7–9, 10–11). The joyous Finale is of a type routinely described in Gumpenhuber's scenarios as "des plus brillants."

Those portions of *Zéphire et Flore* where binary dances prevail give the impression of a decorative, episodic ballet – the norm on European stages before Hilverding and Angiolini's reforms. The drones heard throughout No. 3 create a pastoral tone which may have corresponded to the choreography of much of the work. But with the arrival of Boreas and his troupe in No. 5 – a violent, through-composed movement eighty-three bars in length – we are thrust into a different aesthetic altogether. Gluck cleverly manipulates the listener's expectations of binary form in order to achieve the maximum possible surprise at this moment. Although No. 3 is a rondo structure, with a minor-mode episode of its own, No. 4 in the tonic minor is perceived as a large-scale Trio, after which one expects No. 3 to return. Gluck begins a repeat of the second part of No. 4, but upon reaching V of III (B♭) he abruptly begins the next number with a hushed deceptive cadence to V⁶/i (see Ex. 25). The

Handel and Gluck

Ex. 25 continues opposite

Zéphire et Flore *by Angiolini and Gluck*

Ex. 25 Gluck, *Zéphire et Flore*, No. 4 (2nd half), No. 5 (bars 1–12)

tremolo, rushing scales, and diminished-seventh chords are common enough in pieces of this type, but other features are more specifically suggestive of Gluck: the violins' ominous, irregularly resolved dissonance in bar 2, for instance, and the resolute dotted figure against tremolo in bars 37–41, a texture heard at the crux of the action in the later ballet *Achille in Sciro*, as well as *Armide* of 1777 (see Ex. 26).

The movement that follows (No. 6) must surely have been a solo for Mme. Angiolini, so thoroughly is its music in accord with the *Journal étranger* critic's description of her distress. Plaintive appoggiaturas, in the inner voices as well as in the melody, make for a high level of dissonance, while a Gluckian turn towards the minor dominant lends poignancy to the harmony (see Ex. 27).[33]

Ex. 26 continues opposite.

Ex. 26 Gluck, *Zéphire et Flore*, No. 5 (bars 29–49)

After a *petite reprise*, the music moves to the major tonic, and seems to depict Flora's recovery from her swoon, encouraged by Zephyr's gentle breezes.[34] Again there is a momentary turn to the minor, as if the awakening Flora recalls the horror of a few moments before (see Ex. 28).

Though the description in the *Journal étranger* is concerned mainly with the ballet's central action, passing references by the writer, and the nature of the music itself, allow one to speculate about some earlier portions of the plot. The alternation in the Sinfonia of paired eighth notes (sometimes with the second of them shortened by a rest) and impetuous sixteenth notes suggests the coming rivalry between the brothers Zephyr and Boreas. In all likelihood the curtain rose to reveal Zephyr's gardens (later trampled by Boreas, according to the account); wafting triplet figures intertwine with and echo each other, suggesting a *pas de deux* by the wind god and his bride Flora (see Ex. 29). Voice exchanges are used to similar effect in several movements – notably the final Chaconne – of Gluck and Angiolini's *Les Amours d'Alexandre et de Roxane* of 1764. No. 2 of *Zéphire et Flore*, an Adagio, was likely a solo for Mme Fogliazzi Angiolini. In texture and style it resembles pieces labeled "Aria" in ballets by Hilverding and Starzer, such as a solo that Mme Fogliazzi had danced in the 1754 ballet *L'Espagnol, ou la Sérénade*. It is tempting to think that the delicate figures in Lombard rhythm in this piece accompanied the sprouting of flowers under Flora's footsteps, as described in the *Journal étranger* account (see Ex. 30).

However attractive or distinctive the music of *Zéphire et Flore* may be, and however advanced the choreography of the episode shown in the drawing from the Durazzo Collection, it remains a fact that neither Gluck nor Angiolini chose to acknowledge openly this child of their collaboration. Gluck wrote not at all of his efforts in the area of pantomime ballet – though he did plunder his ballet scores in writing his later operas. Angiolini, more outspoken on the history and theory of his art, nevertheless did not seek to perpetuate the fame of any but the most important of his Viennese ballets, particularly those with printed programs. In recounting (in his *Lettere ... a Monsieur Noverre*) the process of study, self-scrutiny, and imagination that had led him to create true dramas in dance, Angiolini wrote with a mixture of pride and disdain of his early efforts as a choreographer for the Burgtheater:

> In the first three years [the seasons 1758/9 through 1760/1] I was not able to offer any novelties besides some national ballets which, put together in my

Handel and Gluck

Ex. 27 continues opposite.

Ex. 27 Gluck, *Zéphire et Flore*, No. 6 (bars 1–20)

own manner, and exact in the usages, the customs, and I daresay even the spirit of the various countries, produced an effect that surpassed my hopes. As I had not been able to clothe the other historical and fabulous ballets with any novelty, they owed the greater part of their effect to the ability – which was great in those times – of the dancers who performed them.[35]

Not until 1761, he noted, did his ideas begin to cohere somewhat and to "germinate," resulting in the breakthrough of *Don Juan*. Though Calzabigi is nowhere mentioned in this account, one is tempted to infer that the poet's arrival in the Austrian capital in that year supplied the critical mass necessary for the realization of his plan (if it was his plan) to revive the ancient idea of pantomime ballet.[36] In any case, Angiolini's statement concerning the

Ex. 28 Gluck, *Zéphire et Flore*, No. 6 (bars 21–32)

importance of the performers to the success of his early ballets is borne out in the *Journal étranger* description of *Zéphire et Flore*. The rhetoric is awash in sensuality, with respect to the performance of Mme. Angiolini ("la Danseuse des Amateurs voluptueux"), but there is also a good deal of technical language, as the critic describes her less-than-perfect, but superbly balanced collection of skills.

In attempting to determine whether *Zéphire et Flore* came closer to being a courtly *divertissement*, or a powerful, forward-looking danced action, it would be useful to know whether Angiolini himself danced the role of Boreas, or that of the timorous Zephyr, alongside his wife as Flora. No cast list survives, but

Zéphire et Flore *by Angiolini and Gluck*

Ex. 29 continues on next page

Ex. 29 Gluck, *Zéphire et Flore*, No. 1 (first half)

a report in the *Journal encyclopédique* on the pair's performances as husband and wife in Hilverding and Starzer's *L'Enlèvement de Proserpine*, from the 1756/7 season, offers additional evidence on which to base speculation:

> Toute l'Italie a rendu justice aux graces de Mlle. Fogliazzi, & à la justesse de l'expression qu'elle met dans tout ce qu'elle represente. Elle s'est acquittée parfaitement du role de Proserpine. Le Sieur Angiolino, son Epoux, auroit été mieux dans celui de Pluton; mais il a preferé sa legereté ordinaire à un genre de danse & d'habit plus analogues au sujet, & au Personnage grave dont il étoit chargé.[37]

There was something of a tradition in Vienna at this time of husband-and-wife roles on stage being taken by partners in real life. Other examples include Vincent Hédoux, playing opposite his wife in Gluck's opéra comique *Le Cadi dupé*, and a whole series of German plays in 1758 and 1759 on the subject of Joseph Kurz-Bernardon's second marriage, to the dancer Teresa Morelli. The *Journal encyclopédique* correspondent's criticism of Angiolini for having brought "sa legereté ordinaire" to a role requiring different qualities suggests that in *Zéphire et Flore*, the part of Zephyr would have suited his talents better than would that of Boreas. But looking again at the stage design for No. 5, it is hard to imagine Angiolini yielding to another dancer a role as impressive as that of Boreas. With limbs akimbo, hair unkempt, and spewing vapor from his bulging cheeks, the god of the north wind overwhelms his rival, who is seen tumbling awkwardly out of third position. As choreographer and *premier danseur*, Angiolini had the right to take the most prominent male role in a ballet (though at the discretion of the theater director). But without access to the complete choreography of *Zéphire et Flore*, it is impossible for us to say that Zephyr's part would not have made up elsewhere for the obvious dominance of Boreas' role in the central scene.[38]

As we have seen, Angiolini did not entirely give up composing ballets in the "galant" manner after embarking on the series of overtly reformist works with Gluck. Indeed, the second of the three ballets for which he or Calzabigi provided programs, *Citera assediata* of 1762 (based on Gluck's earlier setting of an opéra comique text by Favart), was so conspicuously an exercise in *féerie* that Angiolini felt compelled to address the issue directly:

Zéphire et Flore *by Angiolini and Gluck*

Ex. 30 Gluck, *Zéphire et Flore*, No. 2 (first half)

> The drama that I am putting into ballet is more poetic than theatrical; the catastrophe is mediocre, and the passions are weak and without contrast; yet there is a certain chiaroscuro in it which has always pleased me, and which has induced me to translate it into dance.[39]

In his 1773 *Lettere...a Monsieur Noverre*, Angiolini compared this work favorably to his earlier efforts in "historical and fabulous ballets, which for me had remained colder than the others," and whose design contained all sorts of "common errors."[40] *Zéphire et Flore* was most probably among the works he was thinking of in this connection. Even with the recovery of Gluck's often ravishing music for this ballet, it would make little sense to make extravagant claims regarding the work's importance. At a time when *galant* or rococo art is enjoying a broad rehabilitation, we can relish the delicate nuances and pastoral simplicity of *Zéphire et Flore* without demanding a great deal of the work in terms of theoretical rigor. Yet in one respect, with this ballet Angiolini and Gluck were already setting off on a path that would lead to important results. As we have seen, they returned to the same subject two years later, staging a *Fête de Flore* during the Floralia itself – a festival that had traditionally included theatrical performances. Gluck's music for this work is lost, but we do have that which accompanied Angiolini's recreation of ancient funerary rites – with Vergil as his guide – in *Orfeo ed Euridice* of 1762. (Angiolini cites his Classical sources proudly in the libretto of the opera.) The pure *galant* idiom of the E♭-major dance around Euridice's tomb in this revived ancient rite in no way detracts from the work's seriousness of purpose. In *Sémiramis*, from three years later, ceremony constitutes the preponderance of the action, and *galant* style is used mainly as a sign of the protagonist's moral corruption. The recovery of Angiolini and Gluck's *Zéphire et Flore* allows us to see that the tensions between *galant* and reformist tendencies are present from the beginning of their collaboration.

NOTES

1 The unpaginated pamphlet was originally published in Vienna by Johann Thomas von Trattner; a facsimile edition with a preface by Walter Toscanini was published by Dalle Nogare e Armetti of Milan in 1956.
2 Voltaire, *Dissertation sur la tragédie ancienne et moderne* (1748), in Voltaire, *Œuvres complètes*, 70 vols. (Kehl, 1785–9), vol. 3, pp. 323–49.
3 Ibid., p. 330.
4 The stage was but one of many sites of the anti-*galant* reaction around mid-century, which continued well into the next century. For a discussion of the debates over French painting, see Mary Sheriff, *Fragonard: Art and Eroticism* (Chicago and London, 1990), Introduction.
5 See the *Lettere di Gasparo Angiolini a Monsieur Noverre sopra i balli pantomimi* (Milan, 1773), p. 20. The ballets in question were *Iphigénie en Aulide* (now lost), and the unperformed *Achille in Sciro*, both of 1765.
6 Colin Bailey, Senior Curator of the Kimbell Art Museum, has sought to correct this notion to some extent, in his paper "Ingenious Art or *Mythologie Galante*? Towards

a Reading of Eighteenth-Century Mythological Painting," delivered at the conference on "Themes and Oppositions in the Rococo" at the William Andrews Clark Memorial Library of the University of California, Los Angeles, January–February 1992.

7 Rudolf Graf Khevenhüller-Metsch, and Dr. Hanns Schlitter, eds., *Aus der Zeit Maria Theresias: Tagebuch des Fürsten Johann Joseph Khevenhüller-Metsch, kaiserlichen Obersthofmeisters 1742–1776*, 7 vols. (Vienna, Leipzig, and Berlin, 1907–25).

8 The succession is documented in the "Hofzahlamtsbücher" for the quarter-years (according to the theatrical season) 1758/9–IV and 1759/60–II (Vienna, Hofkammerarchiv, Sign. 353 and 354; the book for the quarter 1759/60–I is missing), and also in the 1758 volume of Philipp Gumpenhuber's "Repertoire de Tous les Spectacles, qui ont été donné au Theatre pres de la Cour [/de la Ville]..." (Harvard Theater Collection, MS Thr. 248); see Bruce Alan Brown, *Gluck and the French Theatre in Vienna* (Oxford, 1991), pp. 283–4.

9 The sisters were born on 13 August in 1743 and 1752, respectively.

10 Several earlier reports on the Viennese theaters had appeared in this international literary periodical, published at various times in Liège, Brussels, and Bouillon. See Gustave Charlier, *Le Journal encyclopédique, 1756–1793: Notes, documents et extraits* (Paris, 1952).

11 "LETTRE DE VIENNE Ecrite aux Auteurs de ce Journal, sur l'état des Sçiences & des Spectacles," *Journal encyclopédique* (15 December 1759), pp. 127–38 (135–6).

12 "LETTRE écrite de Vienne," *Journal étranger* (May 1760), pp. 86–111 (106). It would seem from this statement that *Zéphire et Flore* was given in the Burgtheater following its performances at Schönbrunn.

13 Ibid., pp. 109–10.

14 On the recent history of this collection, now sadly dispersed, see Marian Hannah Winter, *The Pre-Romantic Ballet* (London, 1974), p. 100.

15 Pierre Chompré (*Dictionnaire abrégé de la fable pour l'intelligence des poëtes, des tableaux & des statues, dont les sujets sont tirés de l'histoire poétique* [Lyon, 1782], p. 79), notes that Boreas was typically represented as wearing "des brodequins aux pieds, & des ailes aux épaules, pour exprimer sa légéreté." The winged *aquilons* in the *Zéphire et Flore* picture lack buskins, as also the capes that Chompré says such beings were sometimes given by artists and sculptors.

16 Chompré (*Dictionnaire*, p. 178) notes that "On représentoit cette déesse ornée de guirlandes, & auprès d'elle des corbeilles pleines de fleurs."

17 According to Casanova, who in 1754 attempted without success to win her away from her dancing partner Angiolini, Fogliazzi "avait de l'esprit, un ton excellent, de la littérature, et, qui plus est, était fort jolie" (Casanova, *Mémoires*, ed. Robert Abirached and Elio Zorzi, 3 vols. [Paris, 1958–60], vol. 1, p. 722). In the years following her retirement at the close of the 1759/60 season she bore her husband five children; see Robert Haas, "Die Wiener Ballett-Pantomime im 18. Jahrhundert und Glucks Don Juan," *Studien zur Musikwissenschaft* 10 (1923): 6–36 (8).

18 For an overview of this repertory through 1765 see Appendix I of Brown, *Gluck and the French Theatre in Vienna*.

19 Much the same was done by Prince Paul Anton Esterházy; *Zéphire et Flore* was among the Viennese ballets he ordered – though the copy does not survive. See János Harich, "Inventare der Esterházy-Hofmusikkapelle in Eisenstadt," *Haydn-Jahrbuch* 9 (1975): 5–125 (73). On Prince Schwarzenberg's patronage of music and

theater see Jiří Záloha, "The First Opera Repertoire of the Castle Theater in Český Krumlov," *Current Musicology* 15 (1973): 64–72, and "Die Schwarzenberger und ihr Interesse für das Theater und die Musik," *Opera historica* (České Budějovice, 1992), pp. 73–5.

20 Champée and his colleagues, as also later Viennese copyists such as Sukowaty, regularly sold commercial copies of both scores and parts, which differ hardly at all from the materials they prepared for the court musicians themselves. These copies sometimes carry prices, and one Champée-copied keyboard score of Gluck's *L'Arbre enchanté* of 1759 (D-Mbs, Mus. mss. 3686) includes a "Catalogue / de / tous les Operas Com[m]iques" available from the French theater's copying workshop. Despite his French surname, Champée seems not to have been a native speaker of French: he gives the title of Gluck's ballet in a mixture of French, German, and Italian, and the German portions of his receipt are in a fluent *Kurrentschrift*.

21 See Gluck, *Sämtliche Werke*, ser. 4, vol. 7, ed. Harald Heckmann (Kassel, 1964), No. 25.

22 As Jean Starobinski points out ("Le Mythe au XVIIIe siècle," *Critique* 30: 366 [Nov. 1977]: 975–97 [979]), in European culture at large there was a split between normalizing, codifying uses of "fable" in the arts and literature, and the more erudite pursuit of "mythology" as a means of access to the more remote aspects of ancient civilization and religion. In Angiolini's œuvre this latter tendency is evident in his ostentatious citation of Greek or Roman plot sources (as in the ballets for *Orfeo*), and his reliance on ancient writings in order to reestablish choreography as a self-standing form of dramatic expression.

23 Chompré, *Dictionnaire*, p. iii. Chompré's dictionary was recommended in Louis de Jaucourt's article on "Fable" in the *Encyclopédie*; see Starobinski, "Le Mythe au XVIIIe siècle," p. 978.

24 So called in two of the sets of partbooks for three dozen Viennese ballets by Hilverding, later assembled for Count Durazzo, and now in the Biblioteca Nazionale, Turin (Collezioni Foà 108–10 and Giordano 101–3).

25 For a contemporary synopsis of this work derived from the *Golden Ass* [*Metamorphoses*] of Apuleius, see Brown, *Gluck and the French Theatre*, pp. 176–82.

26 Publius Ovidius Naso, *Fasti*, transl. James George Frazer; 2nd edn, revised by G. P. Goold (Cambridge, Mass. and London, 1989), pp. 274–5 (V:201–6):

> ver erat, errabam: Zephyrus conspexit, abibam.
>   insequitur, fugio: fortior ille fuit,
> et dederat fratri Boreas ius omne rapinae
>   ausus Erecthea praemia ferre domo.
> vim tamen emendat dando mihi nomina nuptae,
>   inque meo non est ulla querella toro.

27 See Colin Bailey and Carrie A. Hamilton, eds., *The Loves of the Gods: Mythological Painting from Watteau to David* (New York, 1992), p. 222.

28 Earlier French stage works treating the loves of these deities included the *Ballet Royal de Flore* (1669) by Lully and Isaac de Benserade, the seventeenth-century popularizer of Ovid; and the above-mentioned ballet *Le Triomphe de l'Amour* by Quinault and Lully (1681), of which the seventh *entrée* was called *Borée*, and the nineteenth *Les Zéphirs*. The reign of the Sun King also saw productions of the ballet *Le Palais de Flore* (1689; author and composer unknown); the opéra ballet *Les*

Zéphire et Flore *by Angiolini and Gluck*

Saisons by Abbé Picque (1695; compiled by Collasse from music by Jean-Baptiste Lully), of which the first act was entitled *Le Printems, ou Zéphire & Flore*; and another *Zéphire & Flore* (1706; text by the Abbé Genest, music by Marchand [probably not Louis]), the last of three *intermèdes* in the fifth of the "Grands Nuits de Sceaux." The list continues with a *divertissement* with music by Cappus, *Le Retour de Zéphire* (1728); see below for further works on this theme.

29 In 1747 there was also an opéra ballet by Pierre-Charles Roy and Charles-Louis Myon, *L'Année galante*, which contained an *acte* entitled *Le Printems, ou Zephire & Flore*.

30 (Lyon, 1760; reprinted New York, 1967), p. 126; cited in Wendy Thomson, "Marie Sallé," *The New Grove Dictionary of Opera*, 4 vols. (London, 1992), vol. 4, cols. 144–5 (145). The year 1770 also saw the performance of a pastorale héroïque called *La Fête de Flore*, by Jean-Claude Trial (on a text by J. P. A. Razins de Saint-Marc), on 13 November at Fontainebleau.

31 Given with the *Armida* of Giacomo Duranti (text) and Vincenzo Manfredini (music), during the 1771 carnival season of the theater of the Accademia filarmonica. There is no description of the ballet's action in the libretto of the opera.

32 See Wendy Thomson, "Dance, §V, 1," in *The New Grove Dictionary of Music and Musicians* (London, 1980), vol. 5, pp. 195–201 (200–1).

33 There are similar harmonic turns in the E♭ *ballo* near the beginning of Gluck's *Orfeo ed Euridice*, and in No. 1 of his and Angiolini's ballet *Achille in Sciro* (see Brown, *Gluck and the French Theater*, Ex. 8.13, p. 344).

34 The moment recalls Milton's verses in *Paradise Lost*, as Adam contemplates the sleeping Eve:

> ...then with voice,
> Mild as when Zephyrus on Flora breathes,
> Her hand soft touching, whispered thus: "Awake!"

35 Angiolini, *Lettere*, p. 16: "Ne' primi tre anni altra novità non seppi dare, che de' balli nazionali, i quali combinati alla mia maniera, altronde esatti negli usi, e ne' costumi, ed oso dire nello spirito stesso delle nazioni, mi produssero un effetto, che sorpassò le mie speranze. Gli altri balli storici, e favolosi, non avendo io saputo rivestirli d' alcuna novità, dovevano la più gran parte del loro effetto all' abilità, che era grande in que' tempi, de' ballerini esecutori."

36 One complication is the difficulty of knowing the degree to which theater director Durazzo helped in the creation of ballets. He was accustomed to choosing the subject to be treated, both before and after the departure of Hilverding; see Durazzo's letter of 20 December 1759 to Charles-Simon Favart, in Favart, *Mémoires et correspondances littéraires, dramatiques et anecdotiques*, ed. A.-P.-C. Favart (Paris, 1808), vol. 1, p. 3. In one of the two reports (cited above) in which *Zéphire et Flore* is described, we read that for Hilverding and Starzer's *Pygmalion*, *Les Misantropes amoureux*, and *L'Inconstant ramené* (all from 1758), "M. le Comte de Durazzo en avoit fourni le sujet & le dessein." Angiolini is then said to have been "éclairé par les mêmes conseils que son Maître." But his contribution is likely to have varied from work to work.

37 *Journal encyclopédique* (15 September 1757) pp. 125–34 (130).

38 Boreas had made an earlier appearance on the stage of the Burgtheater, as Psyche's tormentor in Hilverding and Starzer's ballet *Psyché et l'Amour*. At the time of the 1755 revival, in which Fogliazzi took the role of Psyche, she and Angiolini were the

first couple in the theater's dance troupe, at 2268 fl., 45 xr., and 2730 fl. per annum, respectively (followed by Pierre and Louise Bodin at a combined salary of 4743 fl., 45 xr.). Thus Angiolini probably had first claim to the role of Boreas; the part of Cupid was likely played by a youth.

39 Angiolini, program to *Citera assediata* (Vienna, 1762 [unpaginated]): "Il Dramma ch'Io metto in Ballo è più Poetico, che Teatrale; La catastrofe è mediocre, e le passioni sono deboli, e senza contrasto: pure nel medesimo si ritrova un certo chiaroscuro che mi è sempre piaciuto, e che mi à indotto a trasportarlo in Ballo per preferenza."

40 Angiolini, *Lettere*, pp. 17–18: "... i balli storici, e favolosi, che più freddi degli altri m'erano restati..."

11

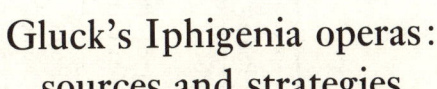

Gluck's Iphigenia operas: sources and strategies

JULIE E. CUMMING

Gluck was an idealist. He had a vision of a new kind of opera – a neoclassical vision shared by many other European intellectuals. It was neoclassical in that it took Greek drama as its model; it was also neoclassical in its ethics and aesthetics. It had a high moral tone, and was concerned with political virtues such as resistance to tyranny, as well as personal loyalty to friends and family. Its aesthetic was that of classical sculpture, as described by Winckelmann: "noble simplicity and calm grandeur," an aesthetic of balance, proportion, and rejection of excess, that could still move the heart and spirit.[1]

But Gluck was also a pragmatist. He accepted and enjoyed many different varieties of musical theater, and chose his subjects and style after careful consideration of his audience and his patrons. Even among his "reform operas" for Vienna and his tragédies lyriques for Paris there is a broad range of subjects and approaches. It was this very willingness to set his hand to a variety of styles, and to take music and dramatic ideas from a variety of sources, that enabled Gluck to envision and create his new operatic genre.

In Gluck's Iphigenia operas the idealist and the pragmatist come together with different results: *Iphigénie en Aulide* (Paris, 1774) is flawed, while *Iphigénie en Tauride* (Paris, 1779) is commonly agreed to be Gluck's best opera. Paradoxically, Iphigenia in Aulis, not Tauris, was the libretto subject advocated by the operatic reformers of the 1750s. Aulis did not, however, become a popular subject for reform opera, while Tauris did. We will examine the tangled fortunes of these two dramas in order to understand the context for Gluck's greatest success.

Euripides' twin tragedies, *Iphigenia in Aulis* and *Iphigenia in Tauris*,[2] were common subjects for opera librettos throughout the eighteenth century (see Table 11.1). In *Iphigenia in Aulis*, the Greeks are becalmed at Aulis where they have gathered to sail for Troy. An oracle demands that Agamemnon sacrifice his daughter Iphigenia in order for the winds to blow. Agamemnon is torn, and vacillates, but finally agrees; Iphigenia goes willingly to the altar. At the last minute the goddess Diana carries her off, leaving a hind in her place.

In *Iphigenia in Tauris*, Iphigenia is a priestess at the temple of Diana in the barbarian kingdom of Tauris. Her brother Orestes, a small child when she was sacrificed, lands in Tauris with his faithful friend Pylades. He is being pursued

Table 11.1. *Aulis and Tauris before Gluck*

Iphigenia in Aulis			Iphigenia in Tauris		
Text	Music	Date: Place	Text	Music	Date: Place
Euripides		c. 410 BC	Euripides		c. 414 BC
Racine		1674: Paris			
			Duché & Danchet	Desmarets & Campra [rev. Berton]	1696–1704: Paris 1762: Paris
Riva & Aureli	Coletti	1707: Venice			
Capece	D. Scarlatti	1713: Rome	Capece	D. Scarlatti	1713: Rome
Zeno	Caldara	1718: Vienna	Pasqualigo	Orlandini	1719: Venice
	Orlandini	1732: Florence		Vinci	1725: Venice
	Porpora	1735: London			
	Porta	1738: Munich			
	Abos	1745: Naples		Mazzoni	1756: Treviso
	Sarti	1777: Rome		Monza	1784: Milan
	Giordani	1786: Rome		Tarchi	1785: Venice
			Barlocci	Micheli	1722: Rome
			Pasquini	Reutter & Caldara	1728: Vienna

Librettist	Composer	Date: Place
Villati	Graun	1748: Berlin
Verazi	Jommelli	1751: Rome
Algarotti (scenario)		*1755*
De la Touche		*1757: Paris*
Cigna Santi	Bertoni	1762: Turin
	Franchi	1766: Rome
Coltellini	*Traetta*	*1763: Vienna*
	Galuppi	*1768: St. Petersburg*
Verazi	*De Majo*	*1764: Mannheim*
	Monza	*1766: Turin*
	Jommelli	*1771: Naples*
Landi	*Agricola*	*1772: Berlin*
Du Roullet	*Gluck*	*1774: Paris*
Guillard	*Gluck*	*1779: Paris*

Italics indicate a reform opera.

I list here only first performances, not revivals (except for the revival of the Demarets-Campra *Tauris*). This does not claim to be a complete list, just extensive.

Sources: Sartori, *Libretti italiani a stampa fine al 1800* (Milan, 1976); Sonneck, *Library of Congress Catalogue of Opera Librettos Printed before 1800* (Washington, D.C., 1914); Stieger, *Opernlexicon* (Tutzing, 1975).

by the Furies for having killed his mother Clytemnestra, and must do penance by finding the statue of Diana in Tauris and returning it to Greece. Orestes and Pylades are captured, and the tyrant, Thoas, demands that they be sacrificed. Iphigenia does not recognize them, but feels a strange affinity to Orestes; there is a recognition scene, an attempt to escape, and a final *deus ex machina*.

Iphigenia plays a very different role in the two stories. In Aulis she is the helpless victim, willing to sacrifice her life for the sake of Greece; in Tauris, like Agamemnon in Aulis, she is the unwilling executrix of a barbaric law, while the victim is Orestes. Effective moments in Aulis include love scenes between Iphigenia and Achilles, the rage of Clytemnestra, and the vacillations of Agamemnon. Tauris' dramatic high points include the suspense around the recognition; the conflict between the barbaric tyrant, Thoas, and the pure Greek virgin, Iphigenia; and the noble friendship of Orestes and Pylades. The dramas share the willing victim (Iphigenia in Aulis, Orestes in Tauris), the threat of the sacrificial knife, and the moral dilemma symbolized by human sacrifice.

The Iphigenia best known in the eighteenth century was the creation of Racine, not Euripides. Although Racine's *Iphigénie* is based on Euripides' *Iphigenia in Aulis*, everyone else came to Euripides through Racine. The chief eighteenth-century translation of the Greek dramas, Le Père Brumoy's *Théâtre des Grecs*, was first published in Paris in 1730, with numerous later editions well into the nineteenth century.[3] Brumoy was a real lover of the Greeks, and felt strongly that they should be read and appreciated for what they were, but even he could not escape from Racine. Parallel passages from Racine's *Iphigénie* are found as footnotes at the bottom of almost every page of his translation of Euripides' *Iphigenia in Aulis*, and in his "Réflexions" he concludes that "il m'a parû qu'on ne pouvait mieux sentir les beautés d'Euripide qu'en les rapprochant de celles de Racine."[4]

In *Iphigénie* Racine takes many liberties with the Greek drama. He rejects both of the well-known Classical versions of the story, in which Iphigenia dies (according to Aeschylus, Sophocles, Lucretius, and Horace), or is saved by Diana (according to Euripides and Ovid). Racine could not accept the killing of "une personne aussi vertueuse et aussi aimable" as Iphigenia, nor could he accept divine intervention, "qui serait trop absurde et trop incroyable parmi nous." He comes up with a third ending in which another woman named Iphigenia, but known as Ériphile, is sacrificed in Iphigenia's place. Ériphile betrays Iphigenia because of her own love for Achilles; thus, as Racine says, "le dénoûment de la pièce est tiré du fond même de la pièce."[5]

Racine's procedure in *Iphigénie* was typical of the Metastasian librettists as well: a plot from a Classical source is adapted by the addition of new love interests and by the exclusion of divine intervention. *Iphigénie*, therefore, was an ideal source for opera seria librettos, and composers and librettists were quick to realize this. Zeno's *Ifigenia* (first set by Caldara, 1718) became very popular; it was set by many different composers and revived again and again (see Table 11.1).⁶ Tauris was not as popular as a subject for opera seria, probably because it did not easily adapt to the Metastasian pattern.

Midcentury saw the development of an operatic reform movement and a new, purist, idealist neoclassicism in all the arts. Greek dramatic subjects for opera gained a new relevance. Aulis, never forgotten thanks to Racine and Zeno, became a focus for discussion and debate. Much of this discussion seems to have originated in Berlin, at the Court of Frederick II, but it echoed all over Europe. Frederick commissioned Villati to write a new Aulis libretto, probably on the basis of his own scenario; the music was by Graun, and the opera was first performed in 1748.⁷ (See Table 11.1.) Frederick advocated various reforms of Italian opera, and indeed the opera has unusual numbers of accompanied recitatives and ensembles, as well as integrated choruses and ballets. One scene in the opera would recur in most of the later Aulis operas: at the final sacrifice, Iphigenia enters in white as part of a procession accompanied by a "lugubre sinfonia."⁸ This is just the kind of scene to appeal to neoclassical sensibilities: the innocent virgin on her way to the sacrifice, in a procession that suggests a Classical frieze. Homage is paid to Racine in the *argomento*, but Ériphile is omitted, and Diana saves Iphigenia at the end, so the libretto is actually closer to Euripides.

In 1755 Francesco Algarotti published his *Saggio sopra l'opera in musica*, the principal handbook of the operatic reform movement.⁹ Algarotti had worked as an operatic advisor at the courts of Berlin and Dresden, and recommended a return to Greek tragedy, with integrated chorus and dance in the French style. In the conclusion he recommends as librettos his own sample dramas, included as appendices: a brief outline of an *Enea in Troia*, after Vergil, and a full-length libretto of an *Ifigenia in Aulide* in French prose. A footnote refers to a successful *Ifigenia in Aulide* done in Berlin, which can only be Graun's and Villati's of 1748.¹⁰ The plot, like Villati's, is closer to Euripides than to Racine, and there are choral scenes, integrated dance, ensembles, and accompanied recitative.

Also in 1755 Frederick commissioned a painting, to be entitled *Le Sacrifice d'Iphigénie*, from the Parisian artist Carle van Loo.¹¹ The subject is treated as it had been in the Berlin opera, with Diana hovering above the sacrifice, about to substitute a hind in Iphigenia's place. In the fall of 1757 the painting was exhibited in the Paris Salon, and caused a small pamphlet war among the literati concerning the appropriate behavior of Agamemnon and Clytemnestra in relation to earlier literary and pictorial sources, including Euripides and Racine. In February of 1757 Diderot had recommended Racine's *Iphigénie* as the ideal libretto for a new kind of opera. He quotes two of Clytemnestra's impassioned evocations of her daughter's impending sacrifice, and describes the appropriate musical effects, including Italianate obbligato recitative and aria.¹²

But in spite of all this propaganda in favor of Aulis on the part of Frederick, Algarotti, and Diderot, Aulis did not become a subject for radical attempts at reform opera. There are a variety of possible explanations. It was not ideally suited to the neoclassical aesthetic – the plot is too complex, Agamemnon too morally ambiguous. Racine's version of the story, with its love triangles and contrived dénouement, is even more problematic in this regard. At the same time, Racine's authority was so great that every libretto on the subject had to come to terms with his version. Real reform could not be accomplished with a subject that had already become a modern classic in its own right.

Instead it was Tauris that became the preferred subject for reform opera. It is one of the simplest of the Greek dramas, with only four characters. The emotional force of the plot comes in part from the impending sacrifice, as in Aulis, but also from the suspense about the recognition of the siblings. There are no morally ambiguous characters, and the heroic friendship of Orestes and Pylades was very appealing to proponents of neoclassicism. Brumoy comments on the force of the story, especially in contrast to modern French tragedy, at the end of his "Réflexions" on *Iphigenia in Tauris*.

> Il est même impossible de ne pas remarquer dans tout le cours de cette Pièce un air de vérité particulier au goût Grec, ... chose qu'on ne sçauroit certainement dire de la plûpart de nos Tragédies Françoises, que nous laissent d'ordinaire beaucoup plus d'admiration pour l'art du Poëte quand elles réussissent, que d'impression de vérité à l'égard de l'action représentée.[13]

Tauris was also brought to the attention of reformers by the 1757 Paris production of Guimond de la Touche's spoken tragedy.[14] The play was well received both by the proponents of neoclassicism and by the general public. In the *Correspondance littéraire* Grimm reported on the astonishing success of the play, and praised De la Touche for having had the courage to "supprimer un amour épisodique, dont Racine, selon sa coutume, avait défiguré son plan." He continues:

> C'est un grand mérite d'avoir suivi en cela le grand goût des anciens, et il faut beaucoup de talent pour intéresser, intriguer, et faire de fortes impressions, avec trois personnages. Toute la tragédie se passe, comme dans Euripide, entre Iphigénie, Oreste, et Pylade.[15]

The first performance of De la Touche's tragedy was on 4 June 1757; by July, Favart had produced a parody at the Comédie Italienne.[16] It mocks many elements of the drama. Iphigenia's opening dream is called a veritable "Dictionnaire à l'usage des songes," including, among other fearful images:

> Abime, accens plaintifs, poignards, lambeaux sanglans,
> Ombre, crime, remords, effroi, genoux tramblans.[17]

When Orestes has his vision of the Furies Favart compares him to a mad dog, and Pylades is afraid to come too close for fear of being bitten. Iphigenia and Orestes break into song at the recognition scene, with the comment "c'est l'opéra tout pur."[18] But Iphigenia retains her last line from De la Touche's tragedy, a sentiment dear to the Enlightenment: "La loi de la nature et donc la loi des cieux," and goes on to praise De la Touche with the following appreciative comment:

> Messieurs, loin de vouloir, dans cette Parodie,
> Lancer des traits méchans contre la Tragédie,
> Nous respectons l'Auteur dont le brillant pinceau
> A placé l'amitié dans un cadre si beau.[19]

In 1761 De la Touche's tragedy was revived in Vienna; as of 25 April it had already been performed twenty-seven times in the Burgtheater.[20] Interest in Tauris was increasing, but decreasing for Aulis (see Table 11.1). In 1763, the year after Gluck's *Orfeo*, Vienna saw the first reform opera on the subject: *Ifigenia in Tauride*. The librettist was Coltellini, a follower of Calzabigi, and the composer was Traetta.[21] Gluck knew the opera well. He was in Vienna for its first performance, and conducted the Florence revival in 1767.[22] Mannheim saw the production of another *Ifigenia in Tauride* by Verazi and De Majo in 1764.[23] All three were to influence Gluck's treatment of the subject fifteen years later.

After Traetta, Gluck could not write an opera on the subject of Tauris for Vienna. But the plot of his pantomime ballet of 1765, *Sémiramis*, has many similarities to Tauris. It is based on Voltaire's tragedy of 1748.[24] Both stories revolve around the recognition of long-lost family members. Like Orestes in Tauris, Semiramis has killed a close relation, is tormented with remorse, and has visions of her victim. Like Iphigenia, Semiramis' son Ninias must sacrifice a family member. *Sémiramis* was to be an important musical source for *Iphigénie en Tauride*: here Gluck grappled with the dramatic issues of the Tauris material, and developed a musical language to express them which he could draw on later. (See Table 11.2 below.) In May of 1765 Gluck wrote a pantomime ballet called *Iphigénie* with Angiolini. The score and scenario are lost, but we can assume with some confidence, given the identity of the title with Racine's *Iphigénie*, that the subject was Aulis, not Tauris.[25]

It was shortly after the failure of *Paride ed Elena* (Vienna, 1770) that Bailli du Roullet approached Gluck with the idea of collaborating on a French opera. With the departure of Durazzo in 1764, and the poor response to his latest work, Gluck must have been delighted with the opportunity to write for a new audience, in a different tradition; he also anticipated difficulties.[26] Both Gluck and Du Roullet set out to court the French public in letters to the *Mercure de France*.[27] They wanted to please both the intellectuals such as Rousseau, Grimm, and Diderot, and the conservative lovers of French culture. Gluck's letter to the *Mercure de France* makes much of his consultations with Rousseau. The subject, Iphigenia in Aulis, realized the proposals of Algarotti and Diderot, and Euripides' drama provided it with an impeccable classical pedigree. At the same time Gluck and Du Roullet signaled their respect for French culture by touting the libretto more as an adaptation of Racine, the greatest of the French dramatists, than as a revival of Euripides. As Du Roullet said, "l'Auteur, en suivant Racine, ... s'est assuré de l'effet de son ouvrage." The libretto only rarely quotes Racine, but Clytemnestra's monolog reproduces the passages from *Iphigénie* recommended by Diderot almost word for word.[28] Thus the hommage à Racine was skillfully arranged so as to please both the French conservatives and intellectuals. All this was good politics, and *Iphigénie en Aulide* was a success. But the reworking of Racine had some unfortunate artistic consequences, for which the opera was criticized. Particularly problematic are the second act *divertissement* and the dénouement.

Du Roullet omits Ériphile, thus simplifying the plot and making it closer to Euripides; but he fails to remove the vestiges of her subplot. The conquest of Lesbos has no place in the plot without Ériphile, but Gluck and Du Roullet make Achilles' triumphant display of booty from Lesbos into the required *divertissement* of Act 2. The pointlessness of this episode ends up destroying the pacing and the dramatic tension. In the words of an early critic, "et au rebours des autres Opéra du même genre, ce sont les danses et les divertissemens qui en deviennent le partie fatiguante, parce qu'ils sont très-négligés, qu'ils n'ont aucun caractére relatif á l'action, et qu'ils n'expriment rien."[29]

In the first (1774) version of the opera Gluck and Du Roullet tried to follow Racine and avoid divine intervention at the dénouement.[30] Calchas, the priest, suddenly reports a divine inspiration, telling him to spare Iphigenia, while the altar is destroyed in a burst of flame and the winds begin to blow. An unhappy compromise, with all the dramatic weakness of divine intervention, but none of the thrill and magic of machines. This ending was perceived as weak by the critics. Some wanted a traditional operatic *deus ex machina*;[31] others read the ending as sudden comic cowardice on the part of Calchas: "Le sévère Sacrificateur, qui est, au fond, le meilleur homme du monde quand il a peur, change d'avis en voyant, d'un côté, le vengeur de la victime, et de l'autre, la foudre."[32] Gluck and Du Roullet revised the ending for the revival in 1775, so that Diana herself appeared and allowed Iphigenia to go free and marry Achilles. While this ending works better, it still does not follow Euripides (in which Iphigenia is spirited away), nor (like Racine) does it allow for the subsequent history of the characters (especially Iphigenia in Tauris).

The many compromises – between spoken drama and opera, Racine and Euripides, progressive and conservative elements – were made in an attempt to please everybody. Unfortunately, Gluck and Du Roullet ended up by compromising the quality of the opera. Gluck's valiant attempt to appease the quarrelsome French audience also resulted in similar problems in some of the later operas. With *Armide* Gluck paid his homage to Lully and Quinault, while setting Armide's famous soliloquy, "Enfin, il est en ma puissance," in a style designed to satisfy Rousseau. But his excessive respect for the integrity of Quinault's libretto required him to keep *Armide*'s unnecessary fourth act. *Echo et Narcisse* is the unfortunate result of the attempt to please the French with a new example of one of their national genres, the pastoral. It was only with *Iphigénie en Tauride* that Gluck, uniting knowledge of his audience and dramatic experience, succeeded both in pleasing his public and in creating an effective drama.

Neither version of *Iphigénie en Aulide* allows for a sequel in Tauris, because in both Iphigenia lives to marry Achilles. It is not clear when Gluck resolved to write an opera on Tauris, and various stories and imbroglios surround its creation.[33] We can, however, establish some of the history of the libretto and its composition. In 1776 Du Roullet published a "Lettre sur les drames-opéra," in which he justifies the divine intervention of Diana at the end of *Iphigénie en Aulide*, but goes on to say that the goddess carries Iphigenia off to Tauris, which, of course, she doesn't in the Gluck opera.[34] Du Roullet may have been preparing the audience for the opera to come. Gluck began work on the opera sometime early in 1778.[35] He corresponded with the primary librettist, the young Nicolas-François Guillard, but Du Roullet played a large role in the libretto's creation.[36] It is clear from the letters and the revisions in the manuscript copies of the opera that Gluck had a major role in its creation as well – in small details of wording and in larger matters of dramatic structure. The opera was first performed 18 May 1779.

The libretto was based on the spoken tragedy of Guimond de la Touche.[37] The parodist Favart had already recognized the operatic quality of this spoken drama in 1757 with his comment "c'est l'opéra tout pur." Grimm's praise of De la Touche's neoclassical simplicity was echoed by the critics of Gluck's opera, twenty-two years later:

> Nous croyons devoir le [l'Auteur] louer de n'avoir introduit dans son sujet aucun épisode étranger. L'intérêt roule uniquement sur l'état malheureux où se trouvent *Oreste* et *Pilade*, sur l'amitié connue de ces deux Héros, sur le contraste du caractère noble et tendre d'Iphigénie avec le cruel ministère dont elle est chargée, et enfin sur la manière dont est ménagée la reconnoissance du frère et de la sœur...
>
> Nous ne croyons pas inutile de remarquer que le mot *Amour* n'est pas prononcé dans le cours entier des quatre Actes qui composent cette Pièce, et c'est sans doute le premier exemple de ce genre donné au Théâtre de l'Opéra.[38]

The changes made by Gluck and Guillard in De la Touche's scenario served to simplify the action further and to point up the dramatic tension of the plot, by concentrating the drama on the relationship of Orestes and Iphigenia. Most of those changes were inspired by Gluck's experience of earlier operatic treatments of the story. It is interesting to note that while Gluck borrowed dramatic or musico-dramatic plot devices from operas of other composers, his musical borrowings are from his own earlier works, especially the pantomime ballet *Sémiramis*, and that musical and dramatic borrowings often occur at the same moment in the opera (see Table 11.2). We will consider three central episodes in the opera where Gluck and Guillard varied the De la Touche scenario: the Introduction, Orestes' vision of the Furies (Act 2, Scenes 3–4), and the recognition scene (Act 4, Scene 2).

One of the most famous and effective moments in *Iphigénie en Tauride* is the Introduction, an orchestral tempest. There was no way of representing such a

Handel and Gluck

Table 11.2. *Gluck's borrowings in* Iphigénie en Tauride

	Musical[a]	Dramatic
Act 1		
Introduction	*Île de Merlin*: Overture	De Majo: Sinfonia
Storm	(See Table 11.3)	
Act 2		
Introduction to scene 1	*Sémiramis*: No. 10 (Ghost appears)	
O[b]: Air, "Dieux, qui me poursuivez"	*Telemaco*: "Non dirmi, ch'io"	
	Feste: "Quell'alma agitata"	
Scenes 3–4	*Sémiramis*: Sinfonia, Nos. 8 and 1 (See Table 11.4)	Act 2, Scene 4
O and Furies; I's entrance		
I: Air, "O malheureuse Iphigénie"	*Clemenza*: "Se mai senti"	
Chorus, "Contemplez ces tristes apprêts"	*Clemenza*: "Se mai senti," B section: "Al mio spirto"	
Act 4		
I: Air, "Je t'implore"	*Antigono*: "Perchè, se tanti"	
	Telemaco: "Se a estinguer"	
Hymne, "Chaste fille"	*Sémiramis*: No. 11 (Ritual approach to tomb)	
	Feste: Coro, "Lodi eterne"	
Lento and recit.	*Sémiramis*: No. 14 (See Table 11.5)	Traetta, Act 3, Scene 5
I takes knife; recognition		De Majo, Act 3, Scene 3
Air, Greek woman: "Tremblez"	*Sémiramis*: No. 2 (S's consternation about ghost)	
D: Obbligato recit: "Je prends soin"	*Sémiramis*: No. 5 (People swear to accept S's choice of spouse)	Euripides
Chorus, "Les dieux"	*Paride*: Coro, "Vieni al mar"	

[a] Adapted from Klaus Hortschansky, *Parodie und Entlehnung im Schaffen Christoph Willibald Glucks* (Cologne, 1973), Table 54, pp. 322–4.
[b] O = Orestes; I = Iphigenia; D = Diana; S = Sémiramis.

storm in a spoken drama, and De la Touche began, as had Euripides, with Iphigenia's dream. But the tempest plays a key role in the opera: it both wrecks the boat of Orestes and Pylades, and represents Iphigenia's internal torment. As such it follows the precepts of Algarotti and Gluck, as expressed in Gluck's preface to *Alceste*: "la Sinfonia debba prevenir gli Spettatori dell'azione, che ha da rappresentarsi, e formarne, per dir così l'argomento."[39] De Majo's *Ifigenia in Tauride* (Mannheim, 1764) begins with a storm overture, and Gluck probably got the idea there. The music is borrowed from Gluck's own overture to *L'Île de Merlin* of 1758. But in spite of the fact that both the idea and the music are borrowed, Gluck's treatment of the scene is original.

Both of the earlier overtures begin with the storm and proceed to calm – *L'Île de Merlin* in two movements, De Majo's *Ifigenia* in the traditional three. (See Table 11.3.) *L'Île de Merlin* begins with a conventional descriptive symphony. In De Majo's *Ifigenia* the overture is a scene unto itself. During the Allegro con brio a ship is wrecked on the rocks; during the Cantabile the survivors struggle to shore; and during the final Allegro bellicoso the Scythians fight and capture the survivors. Only then does Iphigenia enter.

Gluck reverses the order of the movements of his earlier overture; he begins with "Le calme," and then proceeds to the tempest.[40] Iphigenia and her priestesses enter when the tempest is at its peak and cry for mercy over the furor of the wind and waves. Thus it is not an overture in the traditional sense at all: it is not separable from the opera, but begins the action. As a contemporary critic commented, "La Pièce commence, pour ainsi dire, avec le premier coup d'archet, et n'a pas de Symphonie qu'on appelle proprement Ouverture."[41] The effect is to make us identify with Iphigenia and her priestesses, as we experience the sudden onset and increasing fury of the tempest. The human drama is born out of the storm, the visible sign of the wrath of the gods. When it ceases we are prepared for the storm that remains in Iphigenia's heart. The opening does not merely "apprise the spectators of the nature of the action that is to be represented," as Gluck recommended; it *is* that action.

All of the versions of the story include a scene in which Orestes has a vision of the Furies and of the ghost of his mother. In De la Touche we learn of his vision from his own lips while it is going on; we must imagine it. But in opera Orestes' vision could be represented on stage, and such scenes had many precedents in French opera. Ballets of Furies were also a popular feature of reform opera. In the section of the *Saggio sopra l'opera* on dance, Algarotti comments that ballet should be imitative of nature and and of the affections, and comments especially on the "tragicissimi effetti che operò in Atene il ballo delle Eumenidi."[42] The choreographer Angiolini, intimately involved in all the early reform operas in Vienna, claimed to recreate ancient dance, and seems to have found the role of Furies especially appealing: Gluck's *Don Juan* (1761) and *Orfeo* (1762), and Traetta's *Armida* (1761) and *Ifigenia in Tauride* (1763) all used them. On the occasion of Traetta's *Ifigenia in Tauride* the Viennese diarist Zinzendorf described Orestes' dream of his mother, and went on "et cela amène les furies,

Handel and Gluck

Table 11.3. *Sources for Gluck's introduction to* Iphigénie en Tauride

A: *L'Île de Merlin* (1758) *Iphigénie en Tauride* (1779)
   Ouverture
   (1) Allegro – D, 4/4   reworked as Tempête (2)
   (2) Allegretto – D, 3/8   reworked as Le calme (1)

B: De Majo: *Ifigenia in Tauride* (1764)
   Sinfonia
   (1) Allegro con brio – E♭, 4/4
       Ship wrecked on the rocks
   (2) Cantabile – G (with flute solo)
       Storm ends; survivors struggle to shore
   (3) Allegro bellicoso – E♭, 2/4 with triplets
       Scythians fight and capture survivors.
   Scene i: Iphigenia enters, speaks with one of the survivors, Pylades.

C: *Iphigénie en Tauride* (1779)
   Act 1, Scene 1
   (1) Le calme (Gracieux un peu lent) – D, 3/8
   (2) Tempête (Allegro) – D, 4/4
       Tempête de loin, doucement; Tempête un peu plus en avant; Tempête très
           fort; La pluie et la grêle; La tempête cesse →
       Iph.: stanza 1, "Grands dieux! soyez nous secourables"
           Tempête; La tempête cesse →
       Chorus of priestesses: refrain (= stanza 1, "Grands dieux!...")
           Tempête; La tempête cesse →
       Iph.: stanza 2, "Si ces bords cruels et sinistres"
           Tempête; La tempête cesse
       Chorus of priestesses: refrain
           Tempête; La pluie et la grêle; La tempête cesse →
       Iph.: stanza 3, "Que nos mains, saintement barbares"
           Tempête; La tempête cesse tout a fait →
       Chorus of priestesses: refrain
           Toujours en diminuant
       Iph.: Ces Dieux, que notre voix implore,
           apaisent enfin leur rigeur:
           le calme reparaît.
       Récitatif:
           Le calme reparaît,
           mais, au fond de mon cœur, hélas!
           l'orage habite encore.

qui depuis le ballet de Don Juan sont fort arrivés au Théâtre français de Vienne."[43] The opportunity for a dance of the Furies must have been one of the appealing features of Tauris in the first place.

Gluck, now working with Angiolini's competitor, Noverre, improved on the scene as presented in Euripides and De la Touche, by introducing Iphigenia during Orestes' vision, at which point Orestes mistakes her for Clytemnestra.

Gluck's Iphigenia operas: sources and strategies

The improvement was not in Guillard's original libretto, as we know from the letter from Gluck to Guillard of 17 June 1778. Gluck objects to ending the second act after Orestes' mad scene:

> cela detruit l'Ideé qu'il croit voir sa mere en voyant Iphigenie, il doit encore etre occupè de son songe, en disant ces paroles: *ma mere! Ciel!* Autrement ils seroint [*sic*] sans aucun effet. L'acte serà un peu plus long, mais n'importe; tout est y plus chaude.[44]

Versions of the mistaken identity scene occur in both Traetta and De Majo. Of the two, Traetta's scene seems to have been the model for Gluck. In De Majo's scenario the order of events is reversed: Orestes mistakes Ifigenia for Clytemnestra, and then has a visionary seizure during which he sees the Furies and his mother's ghost. Traetta and Gluck, on the other hand, both follow the same basic order of events. (See Table 11.4.) But Traetta's treatment seems lame and inept in comparison to Gluck's: Orestes' closed, periodic cavatina, "Per pietà, placatevi," seems out of place in a mad scene, Iphigenia's arrival comes too far after Orestes' awakening, and Traetta takes no musical advantage of the mistaken identity episode, which is entirely in simple recitative.

Gluck took the music for this scene from his own earlier work once again, here the pantomime ballet *Sémiramis*. (See Table 11.4, right column; the quotations are from the scenario of the ballet). We can imagine Gluck figuring out how to improve on Traetta's scenario, telling Guillard what to write, and realizing that he had already written appropriate music. The result is a scene of exceptional emotional force. We see Orestes' troubled state of mind before he goes to sleep, and watch his unconscious struggle as he falls asleep, during "Le calme rentre dans mon cœur"; we sense the accumulation of tension as his cries of torment alternate with the obsessive chorus; and we recognize the confused state between sleep and waking that causes him to confuse Iphigenia with his mother at the climactic end of the number, in which Orestes shrieks "Ciel" on a high F over a diminished-seventh chord. Gluck was thus able to use his knowledge of Traetta's opera and his own previous music to create a new scene that is more gripping than either of his models.

Gluck's and Guillard's final dramatic inspiration was the decision to delay the moment of recognition until the moment of sacrifice, providing a single resolution for both of the principal sources of dramatic tension in the opera. In Euripides and De la Touche, Iphigenia and Orestes recognize each other in the middle of the drama, and then spend much of the rest of the time planning to escape. Traetta combines the recognition and sacrifice scenes, but Iphigenia learns of Orestes' identity indirectly, as Pylades announces to Thoas that the Greeks will revenge the death of the son of Agamemnon, Orestes. De Majo and Verazi provide the closest precedent for Gluck: they have Iphigenia recognize Orestes while binding his temples with the sacred band, in preparation for the sacrifice. Gluck and Guillard improved on all their predecessors.

Gluck's continuing role in the creation of this scene is revealed in a variety

Table 11.4. Comparison of Orestes' vision of the Furies

Traetta, *Ifigenia in Tauride*	Gluck, *Iphigénie en Tauride*	Gluck, *Sémiramis*
	II.iii. Orestes, alone.	Sinfonia: "The Queen is seated and asleep, leaning on a table covered with books and papers. Her sleep is extremely agitated; it seems that she is having frightful dreams."
	1a. Intro: 4/4, G, Lentement	
	1b. Obbligato recitative "...tonnez! écrasez moi." He falls.	No. 8 (mm. 21–6): "All at once the sky darkens, thunder roars, lightning strikes."
	Accompanied recitative "Ou suis-je?...tranquillité succède."	No. 8 (Presto, mm. 27ff): "Terror seizes everyone, and the temple is empty in an instant."
	2. Air (of sorts): 2/4, A, Andante "Le calme rentre dans mon cœur." He falls asleep.	
II.iv. Orestes, who sleeps; Chorus of Furies, who surround him, showing him the ghost of his mother.	iv. Orestes unconscious, the Eumenides appear and surround him.	Sinfonia, continued.
1. Coro: 3/8, E♭ – C minor "Dormi Oreste..." Or: "Crude larve...che volete?" "Vendetta, vendetta..."	1. Introduction 4/4, D	No. 1: "The ghost of Ninus appears; Semiramis believes she sees it in a dream, and her trouble increases. The ghost, after threatening her with a dagger which it holds in its hand, shakes her, wakes her,
2. Orestes: Cavatina, 2/2, B♭ "Per pietà, placatevi"	2. Chorus: 4/4, D minor, Animé "Vengeons et la nature et les Dieux...il a tué sa mère." Interspersed with frequent cries from Orestes.	

3. Coro: 3/8, D (& Ballo?)
"Nere figlie dell' Erebo"
Or.: "Ah perdono, crudel Genitrice."
"L'infelice non l'ebbe da te."
Furies disappear, with the ghost.
Orestes wakes.

Recitative (17 lines)
Or.: "Che fiero caso è mio"
Priestesses enter.
Ifigenia enters.

4. Coro: 2/4, B♭ (Priestesses)
"In queste amare lagrime"
Recitative (O and I)
Or (3 ll.): "Or, che più vi trattiene?"
Ifigenia: "Giovanetto infelice!"
Or.: "Ohimè! Che veggio!..."
(Thinks Ifigenia is Clytemnestra, for 15 lines)
Ifigenia: "Infelice! Delira."
(Orestes comes to his senses, and Ifigenia questions him.)

The ghost of Clytemnestra appears briefly, then disappears.

Iphigenia enters:
Or.: "Ma mère! Ciel!"
Furies disappear.

v: The door to the room opens, the priestesses appear; the Furies disappear imperceptibly.
Accompanied recitative
Iph: "Je vois toute l'horreur que ma présence vous inspire…"
(Orestes comes to his senses, and Iphigenia questions him.)

and disappears."

Handel and Gluck

Table 11.5. *Borrowings from* Sémiramis *for the recognition/sacrifice scene*

Gluck, *Sémiramis*, No. 14, ed. Richard Engländer. Scenario, XVII; music, 111–12.

Adagio, 2/2
Alors Alors Sémiramis paroît, pâle, échevelée, la mort peinte sur son visage, & se traînant à peine.
Semiramis appears, pale, disheveled, with death painted on her face, and dragging herself with difficulty.

Allegro, 4/4
Des femmes accourent & la soutiennent.
Some women run to her and hold her up.

Tempo primo, 2/2
Ninias s'appercevant qu'il a tué sa mère, court se jeter à ses piés; il y déplore son erreur & sa malheureuse destinée. Il lui présente le poignard teint encore de son sang, la supliant de lui donner la mort. Le fer échape de la main de Sémiramis. Elle reconnoît son fils, l'embrasse, lui pardonne, tombe, & meurt.
Ninias, realizing that he has killed his mother, runs to throw himself at her feet; there he deplores his error and his unhappy destiny. He presents Semiramis with the dagger still colored with her blood, begging her to give him death. The dagger falls from the hand of Semiramis. She recognizes her son, embraces and pardons him, falls, and dies.

Gluck *Iphigénie en Tauride*, Act 4, scene 2, ed. Gerhard Croll, pp. 264–5, 316

Text	Music
(se traînant avec peine à l'autel)	Accompanied recitative
I. Barbares, arrêtez, respectez ma faiblesse.	
(Elle frémit en fixant Oreste.	Lento, a minor, 4/4
Une Prêtresse lui présente le couteau sacré.)	(= *Sémiramis* No. 14, Adagio)
I. Dieux!	
(Prenant le couteau)	(harmony = *Sémiramis* No. 14, Allegro)
I. tout mon sang se glace dans mon cœur. Je tremble, et mon bras plus timide...	
Pr. Frappez, Frappez!	
O. Iphigénie, aimable sœur! C'est ainsi qu'autre-fois tu péris en Aulide.	Lent (= *Sémiramis* No. 14, Tempo primo)
I. Mon frère! je me meurs...	
Pr. Oreste! notre Roi.	Vite (newly composed music)

(From "Frappez, Frappez!" this is the first version of this scene; see Table 11.6.)
I. = Iphigénie; O. = Oreste; Pr. = Prêtresses.

of sources. In the letter of June 1778 to Guillard it is clear that Gluck already has a good sense of the pacing and action in the final act:

> Je voudrois encore, que Thoas arrive à la 4 Scene furieux, avec une Aire d'invective, et que tous les vers soint [soient] faits propres paor [pour] etre chantez jusqu'à la catastrophe sans recitatif, cela donneroit une chaleur au denouement, et à tous les Acteurs, et chœurs un mouvement d'un grand effet.[45]

The first manuscript score of the opera (P1), the first libretto, and the first printed edition (O) also reveal three different versions of the text and music of the recognition scene, which Gerhard Croll has sorted out and published in the new edition. Gluck was the controlling force.

Gluck began by borrowing from his pantomime ballet, *Sémiramis*, this time for the tension-filled moments before and during the recognition. He turned to No. 14, during which Semiramis emerges from the tomb and Ninias, her son, realizes that he has mortally wounded his mother (see Table 11.5). In both cases it is a question of the recognition and ritual murder of a close relation: in *Sémiramis* the audience knows that Ninias has wounded his mother, and that he is about to recognize her; the suspense is mostly spent; in *Iphigénie en Tauride*, on the other hand, we expect the recognition and fear the sacrifice but are uncertain of the outcome.

In the first version of the recognition, the moment in which Orestes recalls his sister's sacrifice at Aulis is set to a literal quotation of the final "tempo primo" section of *Sémiramis*, No. 14. Orestes doubles the violins with his phrase "Iphigénie, aimable sœur! C'est ainsi qu'autrefois tu péris en Aulide," and Iphigenia's entrance with "Mon frère" emphasizes the final cadence from the borrowed passage. What follows is a somewhat diffuse passage of confused and questioning dialog which occasionally doubles melodic fragments in the orchestra related to the final phrases of the *Sémiramis* passage. (See Table 11.6.) It is the priestesses who straighten things out with a brief but emphatic chorus in a contrasting meter (2/4) with a syncopated accompaniment motive.

The second version of this scene, that found in the first libretto, was much shorter (cut by almost twenty bars). The final "tempo primo" section of *Sémiramis* is abandoned, as are the melodic fragments in the orchestra (though the A minor cadence on which Iphigenia enters is retained). Straight obbligato recitative, in which phrases of text are punctuated with chords in the orchestra, allowed the singers more freedom and caused fewer difficulties of coordination between singers and orchestra. Orestes' text at the moment of sacrifice is refashioned: the first clause, "Iphigénie, aimable sœur," which gave away his identity too soon, is cut, and the other revelatory word, "Aulide," is reserved for the end of the sentence. All but one of Iphigenia's interjections are cut, and the passage becomes a brief recitative dialog between Orestes and the chorus of priestesses.

This version of the scene goes by so fast that we can hardly grasp it. Iphigenia comes in with "Mon frère" right on top of Orestes' "Aulide," so we

Table 11.6. *Versions of the recognition/sacrifice scene*

1st version, P1 (ms. Score): Croll, pp. 316–19		3rd version, O (first printed edition): Croll, pp. 266–8		2nd version (first libretto) Croll, pp. 320–1
		I. Barbares, arrêtez, respectez ma faiblesse. Dieux! tout mon sang se glace dans mon cœur. Je tremble, et mon bras plus timide…		
Pr. Frappez!	=	Pr. Frappez!	⎡	Pr. Frappez!
O. Iphigénie, aimable sœur! c'est ainsi qu'autre-fois tu péris en Aulide.		O. Ainsi tu péris en Aulide, Iphigénie, ô ma sœur!		O. O ma sœur! Ainsi tu fus jadis immolée en Aulide.
I. Mon frère!… je me meurs…	=	I. Mon frère!…		I. Mon frère!… je me meurs…
Pr. Oreste! notre Roi!		Pr. Oreste! notre Roi!		P. Oreste! notre Roi
O. Que vois-je?		O. Où suis-je?… se peut-il?…	⎦	
I. Et j'allais l'immoler?		I. Oui, c'est lui, c'est mon frère!		
O. Où suis-je?				
I. Oreste,				
O. Quel mystère?				
I. O mon cher frère!	⎦			
O. Iphigénie, ô ciel! est-ce vous que je vois?		O. Ma sœur! Iphigénie! est-ce elle que je vois?	→	O. Iphigénie, ô ciel! est-ce elle que je vois?

Pr. C'est elle, qu'aux fureurs
  d'un père,
  qu'à la rage des Grecs
  Diane a su soustraire,
  oui, c'est Iphigénie.
I. O mon frère!
O. O ma sœur, oui, c'est vous,
  oui, tout
  mon cœur me l'atteste.

=

I. Oui, c'este elle, qu'aux
  fureurs d'un père,
  qu'à la rage des Grecs
  Diane a su soustraire.
Pr. Oui, c'est Iphigénie!
I. O mon frère!
O. O ma sœur, oui, c'est vous:
  oui, tout
  mon cœur me l'atteste.

] = [

Pr. Oui, c'est Iphigénie.

O. Ah! mon cœur me l'atteste.

I. O mon frère, ô mon cher Oreste!
O. Qui, vous pouvez m'aimer,
  vous n'avez point horreur...
I. Ah! laissons là ce souvenir
  funeste, laissez-moi ressentir
  l'excès de mon bonheur!
  Sans te connaître encor,
  je t'avais dans mon cœur,
  au ciel, à l'univers
  je demandais mon frère,
  le voilà! je le tiens!
  il est entre mes bras!
  Mais que vois je?

] = [indicates that the music is essentially the same in these two passages.

cannot even hear what it is that reveals Orestes' identity. In the final version, found in the first printed edition, Gluck corrects all these problems. He retains the new orchestral texture for the opening, but rewrites Orestes' phrase once again, so that "Aulide" comes at the end of the first line, "Iphigénie" at the beginning of the next, and Iphigenia's "Mon frère" appropriately coincides with Orestes' "O ma sœur." After cutting out some of the questioning phrases (including the melodic reminiscences of the *Sémiramis* passage), Gluck reincorporates most of the end of the first version, but gives most of the priestesses' chorus (minus the orchestral accompaniment) to Iphigenia as recitative. In this version it is the mutual recognition of Orestes and Iphigenia which is the focus of attention – the priestesses, instead of controlling and redirecting the action, speak for us, the spectators, watching breathless as light dawns on the sister and brother.

Gluck seems to have been experimenting here, trying to find the right balance among clarity of exposition, economy of means, moving music, and naturalistic declamation. Modern listeners are sometimes disappointed in this scene – they expect more of a lyric outpouring, a duet at least. Iphigenia has a brief arioso at the end of the scene ("Ah, laissons là ce souvenir"), but she is immediately interrupted by the announcement that Thoas is coming. Gluck's decision to cut the melodic fragments from *Sémiramis* and to rely on recitative suggests that he felt the most authentic way to project emotion in this scene was to allow his singer-actors the freedom to project the accents of speech. The pacing of the act as a whole was also important to him – he wanted a dramatic accelerando leading to the arrival of Pylades, and then Diana, and any pause would have compromised that effect. While we may miss the typical operatic lyrical effusion here, we can admire the dramatist who could dispense with it for the sake of naturalism and pacing.

Gluck's version of this scene is personal, poignant, and immediate. The recognition happens in a moment of privacy between the two central characters, as Iphigenia raises the knife and looks down on the stranger who is so dear to her, and as Orestes peacefully prepares himself for death by thinking of his lost sister. Gluck used the "speaking music" from his ballet to express and arouse in his audience the terror and suspense of the moment just before the recognition, and to focus attention on the intimacy of Iphigenia and Orestes. He struggled with the moment of recognition and acknowledgment, but finally chose traditional obbligato recitative, the most flexible and natural style available to him. The act as a whole has a thrilling sureness of pacing and drive toward the climactic arrivals of Pylades and the goddess.

Although Aulis was the subject recommended by Algarotti and Diderot, it did not become a popular subject for reform opera. In *Iphigénie en Aulide* Gluck and Du Roullet attempted both to fulfill the reformers' program and to please the French public. The success of the work was compromised by the attempt to combine too many aesthetic premises, and especially by the conflict between Racine's drama and prestige and the new purist neoclassicism.

In *Iphigénie en Tauride* Gluck faced no such conflicts, and was able to fulfill his operatic ideals through the judicious use of his experience. De la Touche's tragedy, on which the libretto is based, was written with the new neoclassicism well in mind; it had been approved by the Parisian intellectuals, and satisfies all the requirements of Gluck's neoclassical vision. The subject had also been adopted by the operatic reformers Traetta and De Majo. Gluck chose the drama, selected the most effective scenes from previous treatments, and refined and melded them into a unified whole that revolves around Iphigenia and Orestes. The opening tempest brings Orestes to Tauris while it represents the inner torment of Iphigenia. Orestes' confusion of Iphigenia with Clytemnestra heightens the suspense around the recognition, and it intensifies the relationship between the siblings. The recognition/sacrifice scene focuses on their moment of intimacy. The action is knit together with music from Gluck's own past: music that was neither French nor Italian, music that could depict dramatic action without words – the descriptive overture to an opéra comique and the music from a pantomime ballet. The result was a neoclassical work that has become a classic, a musical drama that was, as Gluck hoped, "propre à toutes les Nations," and to all times.[46]

NOTES

A version of this essay was presented at the National Meeting of the American Musicological Society in 1988.

1 On neoclassicism see Jean Locquin, *La Peinture d'histoire en France de 1747 à 1785* (Paris, 1912; reprinted 1978), pp. 148–9; and Hugh Honour, *Neo-classicism* (Harmondsworth and New York, 1968; 2nd, rev. edn, 1977), especially pp. 21, 32–3, 57–62. Gluck's language echoes that of Winckelmann and the other proponents of neoclassicism, especially the preface to *Alceste*. A facsimile is found in Gerhard Croll and Winton Dean, "Gluck, Christoph Willibald," *The New Grove Dictionary of Music and Musicians* (London, 1980), vol. 7, p. 466; it is translated in Oliver Strunk, ed., *Source Readings in Music History* (New York, 1950), pp. 673–5.
2 See David Grene and Richmond Lattimore, eds., *The Complete Greek Tragedies* (Chicago, 1959).
3 I refer to the first edition of 1730, *Le Théâtre des Grecs* (Paris, 1730), 3 vols. Aulis is found in vol. 1, pp. 1–103; Tauris is found in vol. 2, pp. 3–76. Brumoy's translation was the the most widely known in the eighteenth century, referred to by both Algarotti and Grimm. For Algarotti, see *Saggio sopra l'opera in musica*, in *Saggi*, ed. Giovanni da Pozzo (Bari, 1963), p. 192; for Grimm see *Correspondance littéraire, philosophique et critique*, ed. Maurice Tourneux, 16 vols. (Paris, 1877–82), vol. 3, p. 466.
4 Brumoy, *Le Théâtre des Grecs*, vol. 1, p. 103.
5 See Jean Racine, *Œuvres complètes*, 2 vols., ed. Raymond Picard (Paris, 1950), vol. 1, pp. 687–752. Racine's comments are from the Préface, p. 688.
6 Zeno's libretto is Schatz no. 1484.
7 I have read the libretto for the 1768 revival, Schatz no. 4102. See E. Eugene Helm, *Music at the Court of Frederick the Great* (Norman, Okla., 1960), pp. 66–7 and 153.

8 The scene appears in Algarotti's libretto (to be discussed below). And even though pantomime processions are not a normal part of opera seria, it appears in Verazi's libretto for Jommelli (Rome and Mannheim, 1751), and in Cigna-Santi's conservative libretto set by Bertoni (Turin, 1762) and Franchi (Rome, 1766).
9 See note 3 for Pozzo's modern edition, in which the many editions and translations are listed, pp. 546–57. Selections from an anonymous English translation (1768) are found in Strunk, *Source Readings*, pp. 657–72.
10 Algarotti, *Saggi*, p. 191, note (b).
11 See Jean Locquin, *La Peinture d'histoire*, pp. 180–1; the painting is reproduced in Plate 46 of the 1978 reprint. See also Pierre Rosenberg and Marie Sahut, eds., *Carle van Loo, premier peintre du Roi* (Nice, 1977), p. 78, no. 158; they provide bibliographical citations for the pamphlet war and later literature. The important points of the pamphlet war were summarized and commented on by Grimm in the *Correspondance Littéraire*, vol. 3, pp. 427–31, and by Fréron in the *Année Litteraire*, vol. 6 (October 15, 1757), pp. 316–44.
12 Denis Diderot, *Entretiens sur le fils naturel*, ed. Paul Vernière in *Œuvres Esthétiques* (Paris, 1968), pp. 167–71.
13 Brumoy, *Théâtre des Grecs*, vol. 2, p. 76.
14 I cite the edition in the *Répertoire générale de Théatre Français*, vol. 31 (Paris, 1818), pp. 134–200.
15 Grimm, *Correspondance littéraire*, vol. 3, p. 393 (1 August 1757). Racine's fragmentary plan for an *Iphigénie en Tauride* is found in the *Œuvres complètes*, vol. 2, pp. 965–9. Both De la Touche and Euripides include a fourth character, Thoas.
16 *La Petite Iphigénie, Parodie de la Grande* (Paris, 1768).
17 Ibid., pp. 4–5.
18 Ibid., p. 23.
19 Ibid., pp. 32–3.
20 Gustav Zechmeister, *Die wiener Theater nächst der Burg und nächst dem Kärntnerthor von 1747 bis 1776*, Theatergeschichte Österreichs, vol. 3 (Vienna, 1971), p. 477. The play was also mentioned in the unpublished diary of Zinzendorf in the Vienna State Archives on 25 April 1761. De la Touche's tragedy seems to have aroused public interest in other treatments of the story. In 1762 Paris saw a revival of the old French tragédie lyrique on the subject by Desmarets and Campra, with the music revised by P. M. Berton. Gluck heard reports of it from Durazzo, who had heard of it from Favart. See Charles Simon Favart, *Mémoires et correspondances littéraires, dramatiques, et anecdotiques*, 3 vols. (Paris, 1808), letter of 7 December 1762. I am grateful to Bruce Alan Brown for the references to Zinzendorf and Favart.
21 The libretto is Schatz no. 10393, and it has been reprinted in Howard Mayer Brown, ed., *Italian Opera Librettos: 1640–1770*, vol. 6 (New York, 1979), libretto no. 4. Another version of the libretto was published in Livorno by Coltellini later that year: it is Schatz no. 10393a. A copyist's score, Florence, Biblioteca del Conservatorio di Musica Luigi Cherubini, MS Basevi 306, has been reprinted with an introduction by Howard M. Brown (New York: Garland, 1978). Some scenes from the opera are discussed and edited in Hugo Goldschmidt, *Tommaso Traetta, Ausgewählte Werke*, Denkmäler der Tonkunst in Bayern, series 2, vol. 14: 1 (Leipzig, 1914). The opera was very successful, and revived many times (Florence, 1767; Mantua, 1768; Trent, 1775; Florence, 1776; Mantua, 1777; etc.). For an extended discussion, see Daniel Heartz, "Traetta in Vienna: *Armida* (1761) and

Ifigenia in Tauride (1763)," *Studies in Music from the University of Western Ontario* 7 (1982): 65–88.

22 See Sergio Martinotti, "Traetta, o il musicista di un'impossibile riforma," *Chigiana* 29–30 (1972–3): 350. Gluck wrote a prologue to Traetta's opera for the 1767 performance, and he met Traetta in 1769; see Croll, "Gluck," *The New Grove*, vol. 7, pp. 463–4.

23 The libretto is Schatz no. 5856; I examined the score on microfilm from the Staatsbibliothek Preussischer Kulturbesitz, Berlin. This is not a neoclassical libretto: there are new characters, love triangles, and a final conflagration reminiscent of *Armida* or *Didone abbandonata*. But the music is that of a reform opera: there is lots of obbligato recitative, numerous ensembles, and some pantomime (though there are few choruses and ballets). Algarotti recommends both simplicity and the imperial pomp of ancient theater: Traetta and Coltellini stressed the first, while Verazi and De Majo stressed the second. The Verazi libretto was set twice more: by Carlo Monza, under the title *Oreste* (Turin, 1766); and by Jommelli (Naples, 1771; Schatz no. 4896).

24 Edited by Richard Engländer in *Don Juan / Semiramis: Ballets Pantomimes von Gasparo Angiolini*, Gluck, *Sämtliche Werke*, Abteilung II, Bd. 1 (Kassel, 1966) pp. 77–114 (henceforth Engländer).

25 See Gerhard Croll, "Ein unbekanntes tragisches Ballett von Gluck," *Festschrift zum 70. Geburtstag von Herbert Klein*, Mitteilungen der Gesellschaft für Salzburger Landeskunde, vol. 109 (Salzburg, 1969), pp. 275–7.

26 Gluck mentioned his fears about the production in a letter to Padre Martini of 26 October 1773. "This is assuredly a bold undertaking and there will be serious obstacles, for we must face up to national prejudices against which reason is of no avail." Hedwig and E. H. Mueller von Asow, eds., *The Collected Correspondence and Papers of Christoph Willibald Gluck*, transl. Stewart Thomson (New York, 1962), pp. 45–6 (henceforth *Correspondence*).

27 Both letters are found in translation in Strunk, *Source Readings*, pp. 676–83. They are also found in the *Querelle des Gluckistes et des Piccinnistes: Text des pamphlets avec introduction, commentaires et index*, 2 vols., ed. François Lesure (Geneva, 1984), vol. 1, pp. 1–10 (henceforth *Querelle*). A facsimile of the original edition of Gluck's letter is also found in Christoph Willibald Gluck, *Iphigénie en Aulide*, Tragédie Opéra en trois actes von Marie François Louis Gand Bailli Du Roullet dit Le Blanc, ed. Marius Flothuis, *Sämtliche Werke*, Abteilung I, Bd. 5, Teilband b (Kassel, 1989), p. xxii (henceforth Flothuis).

28 He combines text from the two passages that Diderot had recommended for operatic treatment into one passionate arioso and air. Compare Racine, *Iphigénie*, with Gluck and Du Roullet, Act 3, Scene 6.

29 See Flothuis, Teilband b, p. xxiii.

30 In the letter to the *Mercure de France* cited above, Du Roullet explains: "On a trouvé moyen, sans avoir recours aux machines, & sans exiger des dépenses considérables, de présenter aux yeux un spectacle noble & magnifique."

31 Du Roullet should have "changé le dénouement, & profité de la magie de ce spectacle pour amener plus d'action & de machines dans cette partie." See Flothuis, Teilband b, p. xxiii.

32 *Querelle*, vol. 2, pp. 51–2. See also pp. 68–9.

33 See Patricia Howard, *Gluck and the Birth of Modern Opera* (London, 1963), p. 101; Alfred Einstein, *Gluck* (London, 1936), p. 160; and Croll and Dean, "Gluck,"

p. 465. Gossec, Grétry, and Piccini all wanted to write operas on the subject; see Howard, *Gluck and the Birth of Modern Opera*, p. 101; *Correspondence*, pp. 83–7, 133–4; and Julian Rushton, "'Iphigénie en Tauride': The Operas of Gluck and Piccini," *Music and Letters* 53 (1972): 411–30.

34 *Querelle*, vol. 2, pp. 107–61. See especially p. 121.
35 In a letter to Guillard of 17 June it is clear that he has composed most of the opera; see *Correspondence*, pp. 130–3.
36 See Croll and Dean, "Gluck," pp. 465, 472. Grimm, in reviewing the performance, had this to say about the libretto (*Correspondance littéraire*, vol. 12, p. 250): "Le poëme est le coup d'essai d'un jeune homme, de M. Guillard. Il est vrai que M. le Bailli du Rollet prétend en avoir tracé le dessin, M. le chevalier Gluck l'avoir corrigé et pour ainsi dire refait; de sorte qu'il ne resterait guère à M. Guillard que le mérite de l'avoir rimé."
37 Ibid., "Quoi qu'il en soit, l'auteur ou les auteurs de l'opéra n'ont fait que suivre le plan de la tragédie de Guimond de la Touche."
38 *Querelle*, vol. 1, pp. 427–9; also excerpted in the edition of the opera: Christoph Willibald Gluck, *Iphigénie en Tauride*, Tragédie opéra in vier Akten von Nicolas-François Guillard, ed. Gerhard Croll, *Sämtliche Werke*, Abteilung I, Bd. 9 (Kassel, 1973), p. viii (henceforth Croll).
39 See note 1 for the references to this preface.
40 This was particularly praised at the time. See *Querelle*, vol. 1, pp. 429, 432–3, especially p. 433: "Pour donner á son tableau plus d'énergie & de vérité, M. Gluck le fait précéder par un morceau de Musique d'une douceur d'harmonie & de mélodie qui, en peignant le calme de la Nature, le porte au fond de nos coeurs. Un coup de timbale détruit ce tableau, & change toute la situation: l'orchestre se trouble & frémit sourdement..."
41 *Querelle*, vol. 1, p. 429.
42 Algarotti, *Saggi*, p. 174.
43 8 December 1763; this passage was discovered by Bruce Alan Brown.
44 Croll, pp. vi–vii; translated in *Correspondence*, pp. 130–3.
45 Ibid.
46 *Querelle*, vol. 1, pp. 8–10.

Concerning Mozart

12

The "storm" music of Beaumarchais' *Barbier de Séville*

WALTER E. REX

"Le morceau qui représente un orage a été fort goûté" – so stated the *Almanach musical* of 1776 (p. 46). The "morceau" in question was the incidental music between Acts 3 and 4 of Beaumarchais' *Barbier de Séville* that was performed by the theater orchestra of the Comédie Française, then housed in the Salle des Machines of the Tuileries. The composer of the music, Antoine-Laurent Baudron, was principal violinist of the orchestra, and he would later be called upon to arrange and partly compose the music for the play version of *Le Mariage de Figaro*.[1] The *Almanach*'s words imply something like a musical hit, and so far as is known, this is the first recorded expression of interest, not to say enthusiasm, aroused by any such between-the-acts incidental music at the Comédie Française during the eighteenth century. Usually the music performed by the theater orchestra "qui joue des pièces de symphonie un peu avant la représentation du spectacle, pendant les intermèdes, et entre les deux pièces"[2] fell on deaf ears: no one seems to have listened to it.[3]

Nor, given the long-standing tug-of-war between the Comédiens du Roi and the Opéra, which theoretically held exclusive rights to musical performances,[4] would one have expected them to want any special emphasis placed on what went on between the acts: the Comédiens were lucky enough to get by with the music that was an essential part of the plays themselves – at the finales of comedies, for example, or in Molière's *Bourgeois gentilhomme* and *Le Malade imaginaire*.

Perhaps the excitement registered by the *Almanach musical* over incidental music might have seemed more appropriate for the Comédie Italienne (which of course had merged with and absorbed the Opéra Comique in 1762), and the observation is useful in that it points to a fact about *Le Barbier de Séville* that sometimes becomes obscured by other considerations: Beaumarchais' comedy had begun its professional life as an opéra comique; it had been offered as such to the Comédie Italienne in 1772, and turned down.[5] In short, the comedy we know today is an ex-opéra comique, and, despite the extensive revisions that took place as it was readied for the Comédie Française, the music in Beaumarchais' play remains faithful to its original role, which is to say that it functions not merely as a simple *divertissement* or merely to make a rousing conclusion, as music often did in "regular" comedies of Beaumarchais' time, the author also uses it as a necessary part of the plot itself, an element that furthers the action, just as it would have done in an opéra comique. It might even seem tempting to conclude that the reason the music of Beaumarchais' play attracted such special attention was simply his novelty in transferring to the Comédie Française something of the musical functions traditionally reserved for another institution.

Such a simple conclusion might be easier to reach, were it not for the ghost of the author who is everywhere in eighteenth-century comedy (even in the productions of playwrights like Marivaux, who claimed to dislike him), and who, for the rest, was the main source of inspiration for *Le Barbier de Séville* – Molière, and not only because such comedies as *L'École des femmes* contributed so much to the basic conception of Beaumarchais' plot, but because, particularly in *Le Malade imaginaire*, Molière had genially set the example of how to use music, not simply as *divertissement*, but as an operative element in the development of the action, just as Beaumarchais was to do.

Let us recall, for example, Act 2, Scene 5 of *Le Malade imaginaire*, where the young lover, Cléante, contrives to visit the well-guarded object of his affections, Angélique, while disguised as a music master. He further contrives for both of them to declare the passionate nature of their sentiments, right under hostile Argan's watchful eye, by using double-entendres as they sing "un petit opéra impromptu" which allegedly recounts the pastoral love of a shepherd, Tircis, for a shepherdess, Philis. Here the music was not merely ornament or entertainment, it was the instrument that allowed the hero and heroine to avow their passion directly to one another for the first time. Of course Beaumarchais brilliantly revised and restaged the same scene in *Le Barbier de Séville*, Act 3, Scene 4, in which the Count plays the music-master's assistant, and Rosine sings double-entendres having allegedly to do with the love of a shepherd for a shepherdess, while bored Bartholo's intermittent slumbering affords the amorous couple occasional moments for brief displays of their mutual ardor. Music functions in this scene exactly as it would have done in an opéra comique, but paradoxically Beaumarchais learned his lesson in this connection not so much from the Comédie Italienne or from the Opéra Comique, as from the most hallowed author of the Comédie Française.

As for the ancestry of the musical storm used by Beaumarchais between Acts 3 and 4 of *Le Barbier de Séville*, in one sense there is an *embarras de choix*: for decades in the eighteenth century the Opéra had been staging instrumental musical storms, sometimes with elaborate scenic effects featuring shipwrecks, mountain torrents, or whatever. Campra, Colasse, Marais, and Rameau (to name just a few) had composed famous storms, of which Baudron probably was aware. Instrumental musical storms were also an established part of the traditions of opéra comique: one finds them in the repertoire early in the century, and they continue on down to Beaumarchais' time.[6] In fact, as Bruce Alan Brown was kind enough to bring to my attention, in 1762 the Comédie Italienne staged an opéra comique entitled *Le Roi et le fermier*, the music by Monsigny, the libretto by Sedaine, in which an instrumental musical storm took place between two of the acts, thus anticipating a similar positioning of the storm of *Le Barbier de Séville*. Because this precedent is so close to Beaumarchais' time, it seems worthwhile to consider briefly – as a *point de repère* – how Sedaine and Monsigny intended their storm to function in the dramatic structure of the work.

In Act I of *Le Roi et le fermier*, honest Richard, guardian of the king's hunting grounds, and virtuous Jenny, a shepherdess, are reunited just after Jenny's terrible experience: lecherous Milord Lurewel (the action supposedly takes place in England)[7] had craftily lured her to his castle by coaxing her sheep onto his property, and then, when she followed after, tried to seduce her. Only the interruption of the king's hunt passing by, which Lurewel left off his seductions to join, and a lucky escape from a locked room, had saved her. For the moment the young couple is safe, but Richard is still agitated from his recent emotions (he feared she had forsaken him for Lurewel's wealth), and Jenny, though happy to be reunited with Richard and reassure him of her faithfulness, nevertheless fears for the future: Lurewel is still in possession of the sheep that were to be her dowry, and Richard's mother will never give them permission to marry unless the herd can be recovered. The first rumbles (crescendo – diminuendo) of the brewing storm occur as they sing a duo, sighing sweetly of their happiness at being together and of their past distress:

J: Ah! Richard. Ah! mon cher ami.
R: Ah! que tu m'as coûté de larmes.
J: Quel plaisir de te voir ici.

In a *récitatif obligé* of increasing tension the intermittent storm motifs become more frequent and louder. Richard, seeing the oaks bowing before the wind, compares their furious shaking to his own earlier rage, which had been on the point of getting out of control: he had fully intended to seek out the traitor, take vengeance, and, after gazing one last time upon his beloved, to kill himself. Suddenly the storm is interrupted by a musical hunt, signifying that the king and his entourage are not far away: there are horn calls, then a galloping-horse motif (à la *Guillaume Tell*) played by the violins, and echo effects as the hunt is heard resounding on the mountain slopes (*rinforzando – subito piano*). At last the hunt disperses, but the storm is now fast approaching; Richard's sister runs up to warn the couple to seek shelter, at which point the entr'acte storm begins in somber G minor, a fittingly resonant key for musical storms.

For present purposes it is not necessary to describe the music itself in any detail. This is a rather elaborate piece, with ingenious scoring for the instruments, and employing quasi-melodic material as it imitates various aspects of the storm; one notes too some telling dissonances and harmonic colorings, and the whole leads to a suitably thunderous climax. Indeed the forcefulness of its total effect is quite in keeping with the high-mindedness of this *opéra comique* as a whole.

Nor is the storm being used simply as a dramatic end in itself, and in fact it is the symbolic role of the storm that is most significant in the present context. One finds several layers of meaning: Richard himself compared the storm to the rage he felt at losing the woman he loved, which is to say that the musical storm functions in a rather traditional way as a cosmic amplification of his sentimental distress. But in addition, Richard's imagined loss, in this libretto, has social overtones: the storm also symbolizes his anger and indignation at the great lord who took advantage of wealth and high social station to deprive a simple but honest fellow of the woman he loved. The rage is partly a rage against injustice. Thus the storm gives cosmic amplification not just to the sentimental dimension of the plot, but to Sedaine's timely social message as well. In respect to Jenny, too, the storm seems connected with the danger she had just undergone as she fell into the hands of the lecherous nobleman. Of course later in the play the king (allegedly the English monarch, Henry VIII, but his conduct in this plot suspiciously resembles the legend of Henri IV of France)[8] personally intervenes to make everything all right for the young couple, and in so doing not only sets an edifying example of how a truly virtuous monarch could and should behave, but pays fitting homage to the honor and intelligence of young Richard, who in his uneducated simplicity proves wiser than many courtiers and in essence as noble as any nobleman. The moral stated in the final vaudeville is that although life may have its measure of storm and stress, storms give way to happiness. As one of the minor characters, Rustaut, phrases it:

> L'Orage écrase nos forêts;
> Mais l'orage améne la paix,
> Et de là ton bonheur commence.

Richard agrees in his concluding verse:

> Le chagrin imprime sa trace
> Sur l'Amour et sur sa gaité;
> Aujourd'hui quelle adversité!...
> Viens, ma Jenny, que je t'embrasse.
> Il ne faut s'étonner de rien,
> Il n'est qu'un pas du mal au bien.

In this opéra comique, just as in *Le Mariage de Figaro*, "tout finit par des chansons." Meanwhile the storm has accrued three essential symbolic meanings: the anger of Richard's thwarted passion, his social indignation (in fact this angry blast implies at least a temporary challenge to the injustices of the social system), and thirdly, the travails and hardships of life, which the concluding vaudeville optimistically depicts as being just a step away from happiness. One might note that the first two meanings relate to subjective feelings, whereas the third implies conditions that are objectively given: life, or fate, brings hardships as part of the natural order of things. Finally, though a sentimental storm might have been staged anywhere, a storm with such political overtones was peculiar to opéra comique; in 1762, it would have been unthinkable at the Opéra.

Even though there do not appear to be any explicit musical echoes of this between-the-acts storm in the storm in *Le Barbier de Séville*, one may legitimately surmise that Monsigny's music and Sedaine's libretto would have suggested powerfully the potential of such a between-the-acts device, and to be sure, the storm in *Le Barbier de Séville* is very much anchored symbolically in the dramatic situation of the plot and in the evolving feelings of one of the characters. Perhaps in a curious way it too embodies part of the message of the play. Yet, at the same time, the general effect is quite different, and for a variety of reasons. Let us consider the larger dramatic situation in which the Beaumarchais-Baudron storm occurs.

Past generations of scholars have not really done justice to the third act of Beaumarchais' comedy. They have usually concentrated on the daring of the Count's enterprise, the plight of the lovers, their hairbreadth escapes, and so on, almost forgetting that the main character in this act is not the lovers but Bartholo. Yet even when Bartholo's central importance has been acknowledged, only half of his role, the obvious half, has received its due.[9] No doubt it is true (as all critics have recognized) that Bartholo expends enormous amounts of energy trying to keep the Count out or the lovers apart: in previous acts his efforts in this regard had been orchestrated by a veritable symphony of grating, squeaking, or banging sounds as he turns the key in some lock, or slams some door shut, or brings some shutter down. The sound-effects of this play are those of a Bastille, and in fact, in Bartholo's mind at least, his house had come to resemble a fortress under siege. In Act 3 also, Bartholo will wear himself to exhaustion as he struggles to divine the Count's true motives or out-fox Figaro's maneuvres, in short, to shore up his crumbling defenses and keep the enemy at bay.

But there is a second battle being waged simultaneously by Bartholo, which deserves more attention than it has received: this is an inner struggle, waged in various compartments of Bartholo's psyche, to suppress and keep out of sight an intolerable realization, a thought that he is determined at all cost to prevent from showing itself or coming into being, and this effort will absorb just as much energy, and cause just as much stress, as the first. The reasons he found it essential to keep this intolerable thought out of sight would have been instantly understandable to moralists in the French tradition, such as Diderot, and especially La Rochefoucauld, because the key factor in Bartholo's motives was that potent species of vanity known as *amour-propre*. "On avale à pleine gorgée le mensonge qui nous flatte; et l'on boit goutte à goutte une vérité qui nous est amère," remarks Lui in Diderot's *Le Neveu de Rameau*.[10] And who can forget La Rochefoucauld's immortal pages in which he describes the secret maneuvres of *amour-propre*, comparing its endless agitations, "la succession turbulente de ses pensées et de ses éternels mouvements," to the ceaseless ebb and flow of the sea?[11] Not merely is Bartholo struggling to keep the Count from forcing his way into his domain, but his vanity and self-esteem are also under siege from the intolerable realization, the unthinkable thought, that in fact Rosine finds him utterly odious and desires nothing so much on earth as to escape the necessity of marrying him. This is the truth he will go to any lengths to avoid facing: he will deceive himself, render his mind dull and incapable of understanding, blame others, turn violent – as La Rochefoucauld knew so well, *no* measures are too extreme when a person's *amour-propre* is at stake.

On the other hand *amour-propre* has a battery of devices it can bring into play to avoid thinking the unthinkable. One of the more common strategies occurs in Bartholo's little monolog at the beginning of Act 3. Rosine has just had a temper tantrum, and, for reasons that are at first incomprehensible to Bartholo, she has suddenly refused to take a music lesson from Bazile.[12] But now Bartholo's reflections bring him perilously close to the intolerable truth: he realizes, muttering to himself, that in Rosine's mind Bazile is connected to the preparations for the wedding. Were his thought processes to move just an inch further he would come face to face with the unthinkable idea that her anger is connected to her desire to get out of the hateful wedding. But in the nick of time *amour-propre* comes to the rescue with the soothing cliché that Rosine is behaving just the way women always do: no matter how much one does for them, if one forgets even the smallest thing, there's the devil to pay. The cliché is extraordinarily improbable and irrelevant for the situation he finds himself in, but of course that is not the point. The point is that the strategy pushes the intolerable truth out of sight and shifts the blame onto Rosine.

A second device employed by *amour-propre* for self-defense in this play is the "searchlight device" (to borrow the term devised by Erich Auerbach),[13] which is somewhat similar in its effect to a disease ophthalmologists today refer to as tunnel vision. The device is especially useful in situations that have gotten rather out of hand, where the unwanted truth has emerged so far into the light that it can no longer be sent back underground. As employed by Bartholo at least, the searchlight device narrows everything down and so circumscribes the import and meaning of an event that all the significant implications remain in the dark. A good example occurs just after the opening monologue of Act III, when Bartholo answers a knock at the door and unwittingly lets in the Count, disguised as a (music) student. The Student-Count delivers two staggering bits of news whose implications would be enough to deal a death-blow to Bartholo's *amour-propre* if they were allowed free play: the alleged student relates that the Count, having left his former living quarters, is now on the move, and that Rosine has managed to convey a letter to him. But before Bartholo has time to realize that Rosine may possibly be having a liaison with the very suitor he had been dreading above all others, and in any case that her written communication implies she is conspiring against him with the Count, *amour-propre* leaps to the rescue: the letter she received, shorn of its dramatic import, now dwindles to a mere instrument by which the Count can be slandered, and Rosine brought to heel if she protests against the wedding, which she surely will. The situation, if not exactly solved, is at least off the critical list.

But the most extraordinary device invented by Bartholo's *amour-propre*, a rather dangerous ploy that ought to be brought into play only in direst emergencies, is found in Scene 4. Rosine is about to sing an air about springtime from a work allegedly entitled *La Précaution inutile*, whose title alone (for excellent reasons, of course) has set Bartholo to grumbling. She prefaces the air with some allegorical reflections whose subversive import is so evident it might seem impossible that Bartholo would miss the point. Looking straight at the Student-Count she explains just why she is so happy to be singing about spring:

> ... c'est la jeunesse de la nature. Au sortir de l'hiver, il semble que le cœur acquière un plus haut degré de sensibilité; comme un esclave enfermé depuis longtemps goûte avec plus de plaisir le charme de la liberté qui vient de lui être offerte.

Even though the "esclave" is given in the masculine, surely the allegory is clear enough for any fool to understand. One may note too that this is one of those fascinating moments in the play when political overtones appear out of nowhere, and the plot suddenly and quite gratuitously makes capital from two of the most explosive ideas of this pre-revolutionary era, liberty and slavery. But meanwhile Bartholo's *amour-propre* has been threatened as never before: in her little allegory Rosine had as much as told him he is a tyrant and that she yearns only to be free of him. At first his vanity has recourse to the remedy used before, namely, the soothing cliché:

Bartholo, *bas au comte*: Toujours des idées romanesques en tête.

But he is not going to be let off the hook so easily. The Count, still disguised as a music student, and whom Bartholo thinks he can trust, suggests to him in a whisper:

En sentez-vous l'application?

To which Bartholo replies: "Parbleu!"

Surely the unthinkable thought has become so explicit, there is no possibility of using more clichés or searchlight devices; the usual remedies have run out. The Count's question has put the awful truth squarely before Bartholo with pitiless clarity, once and for all; there is no way around it – whereupon Bartholo sinks into a chair and proceeds to fall asleep! No doubt Bartholo's slumbering is connected to his poor taste in music, which makes him so bored by Rosine's charming air that he can hardly keep his eyes open.[14] But at the same time, his *amour-propre* must have found this *assoupissement* a blessed deliverance from all the stress, especially since, in the ensuing part of the scene, it allowed him to remain blind to the actual love-making of the amorous pair.

This scene owes much to *Le Malade imaginaire* of Molière, as has already been noted, but it is part of a plot that owes still another debt to Molière, in particular to the *École des femmes*, and which must be mentioned at this point. One of the enduring ironies of Bartholo's behavior is a trait shared in common with Arnolphe of Molière's great comedy: Arnolphe is constantly engineering – quite unwittingly to be sure – his own undoing. Every gesture he makes in his self-defense turns to his detriment, so that at the end of the play when he loses Agnès to Horace, his punishment lies not just in his loss, but also in the irony that he himself has brought about the outcome. With Bartholo also, some unlucky star presides over each of his actions, assuring that they will all play against him. In Act 3, it is Bartholo himself who opens the door to the Count, duped by his disguise as a student; it is Bartholo too who falls asleep so that the young couple can indulge in love-making, and it is even he who quite gratuitously suggests to the disguised Count that he give Rosine a music lesson. Whatever disaster befalls him is entirely his own handiwork.

The climactic moment of this act brings together all the elements of the preceding discussion into a single grand conjunction. This occurs when, in Scene 13, Bartholo, thrusting Figaro aside, discovers the lovers conspiring together and overhears the Count admitting that he is playing a false role. When he confronts the couple with their "crime," the Count denies that Bartholo has seen or heard what he has just seen and heard, and remarks that given such "lubies" he doesn't wonder Mademoiselle is reluctant to become his wife. Whereupon the impossible thought bursts out, exploding so loudly, clearly, so explicitly and with so much heart-felt emotion, there simply is no place for Bartholo's *amour-propre* to hide:

> Rosine: Sa femme! Moi! Passer mes jours auprès d'un vieux jaloux, qui, pour tout bonheur, offre à ma jeunesse un esclavage abominable!

Bartholo seems unable to cope with the message he has just heard ("Ah! qu'est-ce que j'entends!"). So Rosine drives the point home again, just to make sure there is no mistaking it:

> Rosine: Oui, je le dis tout haut: je donnerai mon cœur et ma main à celui qui pourra m'arracher de cette horrible prison, où ma personne et mon bien sont retenus contre toutes les lois.

The bastion Bartholo had been so energetically defending with all his locks and bars has been irremediably penetrated, invaded by the enemy, in fact the conspirators are plotting under his very nose; despite all his labors, the unspeakable thought has not only materialized but irrevocably been shouted for all to hear; finally, the disaster was all his own (un)doing: he brought it all on himself. Naturally, given the utter collapse of *amour-propre*'s last defenses, Bartholo has no other recourse but to fall in with the Count's and Figaro's jeering suggestion ("Il est fou. Il est fou, il est fou") and take leave of his senses, calling out for non-existent persons, and finally crying: "Il y a de quoi perdre l'esprit! il y a de quoi perdre l'esprit!" Naturally, too, this is the perfect moment for the stage to darken and Baudron's G minor musical storm to begin (Plates 19a–d).

Perhaps one should state at the outset what Baudron's storm is not going to be. It is not Rossini's tempest in the grand style that even today almost stops the show: Baudron did not have anything like the nineteenth-century orchestral forces that Rossini had at his disposal – clarinets, trombones, etc., not to mention Rossini's special genius for musical storms;[15] Baudron's storm is not even as tumultuous or adventuresome as Paisiello's: indeed in fairness to Baudron one should remember that the orchestra of the Paris Opéra, where Paisiello's *Il barbiere di Siviglia* was eventually performed, was approximately three times the size of the orchestra of the Comédie Française.[16] Nor is

Baudron's storm to be compared to that of Monsigny, even though the latter's orchestra was almost exactly the same size as the one at the Comédie Française;[17] for Baudron's effort was not required to have the impact of a storm in a serious drama whose medium was more essentially musical.

In the context of Beaumarchais' play, the single purpose of Baudron's storm was to provoke mirth, and for this aim virtually the only requirement was that all parts be immediately recognizable as belonging to a storm, and that the climax be reached as effectively, and as efficiently, as possible. Baudron's is a minimalist tempest, and no time is wasted on original effects or on artistic genius. For example, let us consider Baudron's scoring for the flutes, or piccolos (according to the printed version of the score, although not according to the manuscript version). Naturally one cannot expect him to employ the special effects devised by later composers, the Rossinis and Beethovens and so on, for the key mechanisms of more modern instruments. But even accepting the limitations of the flutes and piccolos of Baudron's time, the composer almost never exploits the special colors of which the instruments were capable. Just twice they are allowed innocuous scale passages on their own; in two or three other instances, they double the violins on downward runs; the rest of the time they are employed exclusively to play long notes along with the horns (which are not allowed any independent effects either), whose sole function is to sustain the harmonies and reinforce the dynamics. This storm stresses the basic elements.

What devices would any audience immediately recognize as storm imitations? First of all, sixteenth notes, bowed détaché in the strings, especially when these are done as measured tremolos on held notes, on broken thirds, and as ascending or descending runs up or down the scale. In Baudron's score, sixteenth notes in such combinations are almost incessant. Another feature inevitably associated with storms is the hushed beginning, expecially when combined with sixteenth-note tremolos, such as one finds at the beginning of this piece. Swells (crescendo, sometimes followed by diminuendos, but often breaking off in a brief silence, followed by a *piano* or *pianissimo*) are classic intimations of stormy violence to come, and indeed this piece is full of them: at the beginning the swells are dramatically swift and short, with rising and falling arpeggios, bowed détaché, the texture of the orchestral sound being thickened by the divisi second violins and violas. Soon a rolling, up-and-down, five-note scale pattern (legato) establishes itself as a principal motif. Repeated in rapid succession by all the strings and flutes, it has a cumulative effect as if energy were building up – and in fact the violins do eventually take off, soaring up the B♭ major scale, crescendo, to the high register, *forte*, a held sixteenth-note tremolo B♭, reinforced by the piccolos and dramatically set off by simultaneous rumblings of the rolling motif in the lower strings. Just as precipitously, the violins swiftly descend the scale, back to low unison B♭, which then subsides, breaking into a diminished seventh (here dominant of the subdominant) – the most dramatically charged chord employed in this piece. ("Muss es sein?") For two beats all is silence. Then, in C minor, the rolling

(a) **Plate 19a–d** "Orage," Antoine Laurent Baudron, *Le Barbier de Séville*, Act 4. F-Pn, Réserve F 1124.

(c)

Plate 19 (continued)

motif starts up again, first in hushed *pianissimo* in the flutes, but soon spreading to the strings, after which the entire pattern, just described, repeats itself.

A transition follows, as a series of sequences, *piano*, in measured tremolos with sighing appoggiaturas in the violins over a long pedal on the dominant in the lower strings, horns, and piccolos gives the effect of hovering, suspended, before all the strings descend, still *piano*, to a low D. And now the moment the audience has been waiting for: the low D is held in hushed sixteenth-note tremolos for an entire bar before all the strings start their slow ascent (sixteenth-note tremolos) up the chromatic scale, one beat to each half step until they reach G, which is held for two beats (a telling hint of the tonal orientation of the passage, to be sure), then crescendo, one beat to each note again creeping up the chromatic scale, then a swell mark urges the strings to play still louder as they climb up to the note of the dominant; even more crescendo is asked for, and the unison breaks at last into a dominant chord leading in a grand cadence to the tonic, *fortissimo*, held for several bars, while the lower strings play broken arpeggios driving home the home tonality. This is the climax, the fury of the blast, the moment towards which all the preceding activity had been heading, and although there will be another onslaught of the storm, also in the tonic, it comes in mere *forte*, and is briefer, so that the effect is deliberately post climactic; the storm is already subsiding. Next, the dynamics are marked *smorzando*, while the rhythmic pulse slows from sixteenth notes to eighths, to quarters, and finally to a soft whole-note unison on G at the end.

Abrupt changes in rhythmic patterns and dynamics are another essential feature of storm music, for as everyone realizes, when putting on a tempest, nature is at its most unpredictable. And fittingly enough, not only are there abrupt *piano*s and silences in this storm, but when the music starts up again, the tonality is not in every case the one anticipated. The long chromatic climb up the scale to the climax might, theoretically, have stopped, or gone, anywhere, although in actuality, having begun on the dominant, and rested an extra beat on G, it is heading inexorably towards a cadence on the tonic. This is to say that the unpredictability of this tempest is purest illusion, of course. The piece is no closer to getting out of control than are the harmonies, whose range of keys is as narrow (tonic, dominant, the relative major, subdominant, dominant, tonic) as convention would decently permit.

It is certain that there were stage effects for this storm: one contemporary account described the sky as being "all fiery" (with lightning) and "pouring torrents of water,"[18] and Figaro in the next act speaks of thunder and lightning – in addition to the fact that he and the Count have gotten soaked.[19] The music itself is much less specific about exactly which aspects of the storm are being imitated, and much is left to the imagination: the crescendos with whirring sixteenth notes certainly imply gusts of wind and rain. Low sixteenths in the cellos may suggest thunder. But at the climax, where the storm strikes in its full fury, one is left free to imagine any meteorological effects one wishes: thunder, lightning, wind blasts, cyclones, deluges, or whatever. All the music indicates (and such, of course, is the only point of consequence) is a general cataclysm.

One suspects that if Baudron's "Storm" attracted the exceptional attention attested to by the *Almanach musical*, it was less for the originality of the music than for its skillful compression of essentials, and for genial relation to the plot – especially the witty device of translating Bartholo's crescendo of rage and ascent into madness, into an unexpected transfer to an entirely new idiom, in other words, adding a mock metaphysical dimension to the piece by translating the storms of his mental state into an imaginary universal cataclysm via the disembodiedness of music.

No doubt one finds here something of the same kind of subjective symbolism observed earlier in *Le Roi et le fermier*, though played off in a comic register to be sure. Even so the similarities are quite evident: just as Monsigny's storm had come as a dramatic extension of the young couple's distress, so too in the Beaumarchais-Baudron conception, the whole cosmos is made to resound to the psychological idiocies of Bartholo's *grande crise*.

Might one find implied overtones of social criticism in this storm, even as there had been in *Le Roi et le fermier*? Certainly Rosine's recent outburst had just raised the issues of tyranny and slavery explicitly and with unusual emotional intensity, and this was the last time in the comedy that social issues would appear so prominently. Yet one has to work a little too hard to find deliberately "revolutionary" implications in this storm. Whatever overtones there might be really dissolve into the general mockery of the event.

On the other hand, one aspect of this storm is unique to the Beaumarchais-Baudron conception: the storm as comic revenge *in which the audience participates by sympathetic vibration*. Bartholo has been behaving so horridly for so long; his insensitivity, his unbearable male chauvinism, his tyranny over poor Rosine, whose life has in fact been reduced to a sort of slavery, his raising impediments to the course of true love, all these accumulating unpardonables have reached a critical point where, if there is any justice left in the universe, some sort of retribution should be forthcoming – nor would the spectators really mind if the punishment turned out to be of some grand, cosmic species. And how utterly satisfying, how deliciously pleasing, for Beaumarchais to extend magically the usually sacred boundaries of an act, in order to see that impossible old Bartholo gets copiously rained upon, along (one hopes) with a large dose of the nastiest sort of thunder, wind, and lightning. Next to the happy ending in Act 4, this is probably the most soul-satisfying moment in the entire comedy. Is it stretching symbolism too far to imagine that part of the special appeal of the music lies also in the author and composer having so cleverly spelled out here what in our bones we already knew – that in the deepest sense, Bartholo was all wet?

NOTES

1 See Philip Robinson, "La Musique des comédies de Figaro: éléments de dramaturgie," *Studies in Voltaire and the Eighteenth Century*, vol. 275 (1990), which appeared after the present article was in press.
2 Blondel, *Architecture française* 4 (1754): 30, cited in Henri Lagrave, *Le Théâtre et le public à Paris de 1715 à 1750* (Paris, 1972), p. 75.
3 Though we are not so well documented concerning the audience's activities "pendant les intermèdes," in his *Mémoires* the actor Fleury gave a lively and nostalgic account of what the spectators and some of the "Sociétaires" were doing, while ignoring the music played "entre les deux pièces":

> Le foyer de la Comédie-Française réunissait alors l'élite de la société parisienne. Les grands seigneurs, les gens de lettres, les artistes célèbres, y vivaient à pot et à feu. Tous les soirs, entre la première et la seconde pièce, on était sûr de trouver nombreuse compagnie et compagnie choisie. Chacun y venait porter sa nouvelle, son anecdote, son mot...
>
> Quel bon temps! il fallait entendre Beaumarchais, fin, spirituel, emportant la pièce; Barthe, un peu lent à se mettre en train, mais ne s'arrêtant plus quand il avait commencé; Saurin, le beau parleur de l'assemblée; Favart, lourd, et se laissant mordre par Rochon; Goldoni, venant se chauffer les pieds l'hiver et ne disant rien, double économie d'esprit et de combustible; Fanier, riant pour tout le monde et sur tout le monde; Contat, n'ayant pas encore permission d'être spirituelle pour le public, et se rattrapant au foyer; et Lauraguais, rapportant des mots d'Arnoult, dont elle n'aurait dû être que le prête-nom; et Préville, si bon conteur! et Monvel, au langage si choisi! Dugazon, l'écureuil du théâtre, sautant de chaise en chaise, chifonnant ces dames, puis bondissant sur la table, et là, contrefaisant le montreur de curiosités, crier avec sa pénétrante voix de tête:
>
> "Ecoutez tous, messieurs, mesdames, la fameuse proclamation du général Bourgoyne, c'est une œuvre unique... c'est sur la fameuse guerre du pays lointain, américain, contre le peuple de Francklin. Ecoutez!"

Fleury, *Mémoires*, 2 vols. (Paris, 1847), vol. 1, pp. 156–7.
4 Lagrave, *Le Théâtre et le public*, p. 365.
5 On this incident see Beaumarchais, *Œuvres*, Bibliothéque de la Pléiade, ed. Pierre and Jacqueline Larthomas (Paris, 1988), p. 1295. All quotations from the text of *Le Barbier de Séville* will be taken from this edition.
6 On the French traditions of operatic storms, including a brief characterization of *Le Roi et le fermier*, see Gudrun Busch, "Die Unwetterszene in der romantischen Opera," *Die "Couleur locale" in der Oper des 19. Jahrhunderts*, Studien zur Musikgeschichte des 19. Jahrhunderts, vol. 42 (Regensburg, 1976), pp. 161–6. A few other incidental details will be found in my volume, *The Attraction of the Contrary: Essays on the Literature of the French Enlightenment* (Cambridge, 1987), pp. 117–19, 142.
7 On the plot see Daniel Heartz, "The Beginnings of the Operatic Romance: Rousseau, Sedaine, and Monsigny," *Eighteenth-Century Studies* 15 (1981/82): 175–6.
8 This point is made by Heartz, ibid.

9 A short bibliography of the major studies will be found in Beaumarchais, *Œuvres*, p. 1685. For a complete bibliography, see Brian N. Morton and Donald C. Spinelli, *Beaumarchais: A Bibliography* (Ann Arbor, 1988).
10 Ed. J. Fabre (Geneva, 1963), p. 56.
11 *Maximes*, ed. Jacques Truchet (Paris, n.d.), pp. 133–6.
12 This stormy fit of temper has taken place between the acts, and may be seen as, in some sense, announcing the musical storm to come.
13 *Mimesis: The Representation of Reality in Western Literature* (Princeton, 1968), p. 404.
14 Act 1, Scene 2 of *Le Bourgeois gentilhomme* is also one of the inspirations for this scene.
15 For the rest, Rossini's storm comes later in the action, so that it does not correspond to the moment of Bartholo's fit of madness.
16 According to the *Almanach des spectacles de Paris* of 1776 (recording the previous year's spectacles), among the players of the orchestra of the Opéra were twenty-eight violins (in the modern sense), seven flutes and oboes, eight bassoons, two trumpets, two clarinets, and one percussion, to give just a few examples. The orchestra of the Comédie Française had ten violins (including Baudron), two oboes (doubtless doubling on the flutes), two bassoons, but lists no trumpets, no clarinets, and no percussion – although Mary Cyr has kindly pointed out to me the likelihood that in fact, for a storm such as this, the traditional "tambour" would also have been used.
17 According to the *Almanach des spectacles de Paris*, the Comédie Française orchestra numbered twenty-four, the Comédie Italienne, twenty-five.
18 "Je trouve bien des choses neuves dans votre pièce, et les mœurs, et l'intrigue, et ce tuteur si méfiant et si confiant, ce comte Almaviva, qui, croyant poursuivre une femme mariée, se trouve *empêtré* d'un amour légitime, et le ciel en feu versant des torrents d'eau pour faire dire un bon mot au *Barbier*, et ces plaisanteries sur les Médecins, et cet étonnement d'un personnage [Basile]." *Lettre du Diable à Monsieur de Beaumarchais au sujet du Barbier de Séville* (1775) quoted in Enzo Giudici, *Beaumarchais nel suo e nel nostro tempo: Le Barbier de Séville* (Rome, 1964), p. 425.
19 "Nous voici enfin arrivés, malgré la pluie, la foudre et les éclairs... Nous sommes tout percés" (Act 4, Scene 5). At the beginning of one of the few remaining fragments of Beaumarchais' original opéra comique version one reads the following: "Bachelier le soir, diable la nuit, n'as-tu rien égaré *parmi les flots orageux?*" (emphasis mine), quoted in Giudici, *Beaumarchais nel suo tempo*, p. 351. Although making sense of these fragments remains a thorny, and still largely unresolved problem, this text (assuming it is Figaro or the Count who speaks) at least allows for the possibility that, in the final version, the storm was in fact a left-over from Beaumarchais' earlier opéra comique conception. Pierre-Jean-Baptiste Nougaret, in his extensive and totally malevolent criticism of Beaumarchais' comedy, takes the author to task for inserting a storm which he claims has no legitimate function in respect to the plot. Among other sarcastic comments he exclaims, "O mon frère, mon frère! vouliez-vous d'abord faire un Opéra?" *Le Coup d'œil d'un Arabe sur la littérature française, ou le Barbier de Bagdad faisant la barbe au barbier de Séville Figaro* (London and Paris, 1786), pp. 49–50, quoted in Giudici, *Beaumarchais nel suo tempo*, p. 534.

13

On *Don Giovanni*, No. 2

JOSEPH KERMAN

Edward Dent remarks in *Mozart's Operas* that three factors contribute to make *Don Giovanni* "an opera of a very unusual type." These factors, he says, are a libretto basically resistant to the conventionalities of opera buffa construction; the license that Mozart allowed himself to try experiments in expression and to push every technical device to its furthest limits; and the fact that "owing to external circumstances, he happened at that time to be in a mental condition favorable to a certain emotional expansiveness."[1] These external circumstances are set forth in a very dry passage on a previous page:

> Returning to Vienna in February 1787, Mozart was soon to lose three of those most dear to him within a few months of each other: Count August Hatzfeld, then his father, and lastly Siegmund von Barisani... Hatzfeld, who was the same age as Mozart, was a remarkably good violinist; he had often played in Mozart's quartets, and Mozart is said to have preferred his interpretation of them to all others. It is therefore possible that the two great string quintets, composed in April and May of this year, may have been to some extent connected with his death in the composer's mind. We must, however, beware of jumping to such conclusions as a matter of course, otherwise we may be tempted to suppose that the death of Leopold Mozart on 28 May was the direct inspiration of the *Musical Joke* dated 14 June.

What is Dent trying to say here, or trying not to say? He suggests that Mozart's quintets may have been connected with the death of Hatzfeld, but says nothing about the *quality* of this music to support the suggestion. On the other hand, it is implicitly the quality of the *Musical Joke* that argues against its being a memorial to Leopold. In fact, the Quintet in G minor feels like a response to tragedy, and the *Musical Joke* has recently been shown to have been planned and half-written as early as 1785.[2] Prior to this demonstration, however, Wolfgang Hildesheimer among others had reversed Dent's argument and claimed that Mozart's *Musical Joke* was indeed a response to the death of his father – a mocking response. With or without Dent's invitation, we will do better to look for such "connections" in *Don Giovanni*.

Why deny, minimize, fudge, or evade the fact that children are greatly affected by the death of fathers? In 1913, when *Mozart's Operas* was published, Dent was already a programmatic modernist, and one of two prominent subtexts in his book was the demystification of the opera by Mozart that the romantics had taken most to heart. (The other subtext was the canonization of

Idomeneo. The main text, a stunning campaign to bring Mozart back to the stage, is still heart-warming to contemplate, eighty years later.) Dent was particularly dismissive of E. T. A. Hoffmann's vision of Donna Anna as superwoman drawn ineluctably toward the masculine life force; in reaction to this, perhaps, the view he himself formed of Anna was practically abusive. She is "self-absorbed and aloof" and "a thoroughly unpleasant young lady"; "we cannot expect her to reveal her true self in any duet [sic] or trio," declares Dent, writing her off as any kind of real force in the drama. He could never see Anna's trauma on the discovery of her father's still-warm body as an adequate motive for the opera's action – in Daniel Heartz's words, "the driving force that unites the work and propels it to the inevitable catastrophe."[3]

In this Dent has been followed by a number of other critics. I believe Mozart thought otherwise, and I also believe he knew that if the motive was going to stick, he was going to have to project it especially strongly. Composing Da Ponte's libretto, he understood its problems as well as any commentator who has pointed them out after the event. Don Giovanni, since his actions are by definition unchanging and unchangeable, is not really the stuff of drama; the drama that can be teased out of Don Juan materials is the "chase" drama of his pursuit. Dent praised Da Ponte for his skillful arrangement of this – Anna's somewhat late discovery of the murderer's identity, the accelerating pursuit of Giovanni by two, three, five human and finally one superhuman figure, plus a crowd of devils. But there was a difficulty. Anna provides the impetus for the basic action, but because of her sex and social status she cannot take an active role in it. All the more important, then, to project her initial impetus in the most vivid, extreme, extravagant form.

To appreciate Mozart's insight as a dramatist is not, however, to minimize his responses as a man – responses which, unless he was the weird automaton imagined by Hildesheimer, enabled the realization of his dramatic vision. It is easy enough to identify with strong situations in a play, a movie, or an opera that mimic one's own pressing affairs even when one is just attending it. When one is actually writing it, such identification cannot be easy to shake off. Surely the composer's identification with situations in the libretto fueled the emotionality of his musical settings of them. Sensitized as we have become to the likelihood of Oedipal feelings on Mozart's part, we may think of the scene in which the Commendatore is killed and Don Giovanni responds in stupefaction. Titillated by rumors of Mozart's profligacy, we may think of the cemetery scene in which Giovanni's ribald joking is rebuked by the ghostly father. Familiar as we are with Leopold's nagging letters, we think of the Statue's repeated "Pentiti" in the Act 2 finale, and Giovanni's "No," and then his positively *Almavivesca* cascade of "No's" immediately afterward, leading (as with Almaviva) to utter defeat.

The dullest of us can hardly avoid thinking of the recitative and duet, No. 2, "Ma qual mai s'offre, oh Dei" – "Fuggi, crudele, fuggi!", in which a child confronted by the death of a father recoils, keens, and collapses, revives, hallucinates, and then shrieks for relief, for relief through revenge. Certainly

Don Giovanni, No. 2 Recitativo e Duetto

ANNA	Ma qual mai s'offre, oh Dei, spettacolo funesto agli occhi miei! Il padre, padre mio, mio caro padre!	ANNA	Fuggi, crudele, fuggi! lascia ch'io mora anch'io, ora ch'è morte, oh Dio, chi a me la vita diè. [stz. 1]
OTTAVIO	Signore…		
ANNA	Ah l'assassino mel trucidò. Quel sangue, quella piaga, quel volto, tinto e coperto dei color di morte. Ei non respira più; fredde ha le membra… Padre [mio, caro padre], padre amato… io manco, io moro.	OTTAVIO	Senti, cor mio, deh senti, guardami un solo istante, ti parla il caro amante, che vive sol per te. [stz. 2]
		ANNA	Tu sei… perdon, mio bene, l'affano mio, le pene… Ah il padre mio dov'è? [st. 3] [line 11]
OTTAVIO	Ah soccorete, amici, il mio tesoro! Cercatemi, recatemi qualche odor, qualche spirto, ah, non tardate … Donn' Anna, sposa, amica, il duol estremo la meschinella uccide.	OTTAVIO	Il padre…lascia, o cara, la rimembranza amara: hai sposo e padre in me. [st. 4]
ANNA	Ahi!	ANNA	Ah! vendicar, se il puoi, giura quel sangue ognor.
OTTAVIO	Già rinviene; datele nuovi aiuti.	OTTAVIO	Lo giuro agl'occhi tuoi, lo giuro al nostro amor. [st. 5]
ANNA	Padre mio…	INSIEME	Che giuramento, oh Dei! Che barbaro momento! Fra cento affetti e cento vammi ondeggiando il cor. [st. 6] [line 21]
OTTAVIO	Celate, allontanate agli occhi suoi quell' oggetto d'orrore. Anima mia, consolati, fa core.		

On Don Giovanni, No. 2

Ex. 31 Mozart, *Don Giovanni*, close of Introduction (No. 1) and beginning of Duet (No. 2)

this is a number in which technical devices are pushed to their furthest limits, as Dent says – to the limits of expressivity and violence. It is the most extreme piece in the opera.

Extremity in the musical setting of this number must have been encouraged by an extreme feature of the opera's total form. (Or to put it another way that does not imply any kind of causality, the extremity Mozart wanted to project in this number, or found himself projecting, fell in with his plan for the opera as a totality.) The beginning and the end of *Don Giovanni* are bound together by large composite musical units which echo one another, as is well known. The overture runs into the Act 1 introduction, which is itself linked – in a most radical way – across a passage of simple recitative to the following accompanied recitative and duet for Donna Anna and Don Ottavio. Then the Act 2 finale features a whole network of musical recollections of the opening unit, some of them obvious (one might almost say lurid) and others quite subtle.

For all the originality of the Act 2 finale – the insertion of opera hits played by Don Giovanni's *Tafelmusik* band, the nature and the development of the Statue's music, the final fugato – it is possible to feel that Mozart was even more visionary in his composition of the opening unit. In ascending order of boldness, there is the modulating bridge from the overture to the introduction; the introduction closing on the dominant of a key other than that of its (or the overture's) beginning; and the motivic link between the introduction and the accompanied recitative (all three descending semitones at the end of the introduction – not only the treble A♭–G – are resumed at the beginning of the recitative; see Ex. 31).[4]

To be sure, Mozart provides the recitative and duet with its own number, No. 2, thus giving it a certain sub-auditory claim to autonomy. But the fact that the number was linked to the continuous overture and introduction as a single unit, in however radical a fashion, seems to have offered him the license to treat it with unusual freedom. It is as though the duet, in particular, were not a free-standing number, with certain requirements or at least expectations associated with its genre, but the concluding section of an ensemble. Freedom, violence, extremity: Mozart was never more violent than in this operatic number (unless perhaps in "Fin ch'han dal vino").[5] As a depiction of trauma in action, it is painful to witness. We are almost grateful to be released from it by Donna Anna's collapse.

Thus the recitative, beginning with an agitato introduction built around those semitones, develops into what must be Mozart's most radical page of free-floating chromatic harmony. The chromaticism becomes particularly dizzy at the points where Donna Anna examines the corpse ("quel sangue, quella piaga, quel volto") – the upward chromatic sequences here are almost Tristanesque – and where Don Ottavio calls for the smelling salts ("qualque spirto, ah non tardate"). However, Mozart establishes a central point of orientation for all this instability. When Anna faints at the end of her long speech in the recitative ("io moro!") she sings the word "moro" on the notes B♮–A as a half cadence in D minor. When she returns to this word in the first phrase of the duet ("lascia ch'io *mora* anch'io"), she sings the same two notes to make essentially the same cadence. There is still much varied chromaticism to come in the duet, but the step B♮–A (6–5 in D minor) stands out as its epitome or focus.

As for the duet, the first remarkable thing about it is the shock of its opening on a syncopated half-note beat, *senza ritornello*. This number emerges implosively but seamlessly out of the recitative. The second remarkable thing about it is that nearly half of its text is never repeated. One can see that Mozart would have wanted to hurry past Anna's initial distraught outburst, where she seems to hallucinate and mistake Ottavio for her father's murderer ("Fuggi, crudele, fuggi!") – she herself apologizes for it in line 9 – and dwell first on her poignant questioning in line 11 ("Ah il padre mio dov'è") and then on the matter of the oath. Still, this is ruthlessly compressed, "dramatic" writing. The first three textual units of the duet, lines 1–4, 5–8, and 9–10, are never heard again, and neither are the musical ideas they are set to.

So we had best listen to them especially hard the first time. The duet's implosive opening deploys what another era would have recognized as a classical second mode formula, d a f e d a. And as Daniel Heartz has remarked, this formula is projected so strongly here that we can scarcely miss its recurrence at later points in the opera: at the Maskers' entry in the Act 1 finale, and in Anna's speech during the Act 2 sextet.[6] Given Mozart's instinct for economy, it may very well be that he plotted these recurrences as compensation for his frugality in the duet.

The second text-music idea that is never repeated, the response to Anna's outburst by Ottavio, is bland enough; but it is worth noting Ottavio's sensitivity to Anna's state of mind. This is indicated by his adoption of the running eighth-note figure that accompanied her unsteady last words. Characteristically, his version of the running figure cancels Anna's distinctive descending semitone. It is also worth noting how Ottavio's immediate responses to Anna's "io moro!" in the recitative and to "mora anch'io!" in the duet clinch the parallelism between the two points. His good-hearted if somewhat limited supportive action is launched each time from an A minor chord undercutting the A major chord of the half cadence. In the recitative, he offers assistance, and in the duet, consolation. Ottavio takes charge, or tries to, by moving to the dominant key.

(In the duet Ottavio doesn't make his move until five bars after Anna has reached her "mora anch'io" cadence – though during those five bars she remains on the same harmony. By this time she is almost ready to faint once again, to judge from her static harmony, irresolute phrase structure, and halting vocal line.)

As Ex. 31 reminds us, Ottavio's harmonic move (V of D minor to A minor) has been foreshadowed by the ending of the introduction (V of F minor to C minor). This C minor is the point from which the accompanied recitative has picked up and moved through various keys to D minor, the key of the duet. The progression from C minor to D minor was a resonant one for Mozart, which Daniel Heartz has discussed on a number of occasions. A classic case is within Electra's D minor aria "Tutto in cor vi sento" from *Idomeneo*, also in the aria's link to the following C minor chorus, "Ah! Numi, pietà!" In *Don Giovanni*, Anna's beautiful speech in the Act 3 sextet also moves from D minor to C minor. Most shattering of all, no doubt, is the way this same progression is encapsulated in the Statue's two brief pronouncements in the graveyard.

The third never-to-be-repeated musical idea in the duet is Anna's second speech, in response to Ottavio ("Tu sei... perdon, mio bene"). His words seem to have had their effect, for she signals her readiness to accept the consolation he offers; this we understand when she accepts his B♮, the one note in *his* key of A minor best designed to exorcize *her* B♭. And when Anna then returns to B♮ on the words "mio bene" – intensified by a new root below it, G, and an expressive auxiliary above it, G–A♭–G – this musical gesture goes far to belie her reputation as an unusually chilly character.[7]

But the ending of her speech restates, a little obscurely, the cadence associated with "moro" and "mora"; the step B♭–A is now reinterpreted as 4–3 in F major. At this point the orchestra cuts in and lifts the obscurity, as an expressive new violin motif singles out the notes B♭ and A once again, or rather, three times, on three downbeats.

It is now, as Anna questions pathetically after her father (line 11) and Ottavio renews his proffered solace (stanza 4), that the music first repeats itself (freely) and begins to cohere – only to crack open almost at once with a return of accompanied recitative for the first oath (stanza 5). To which the characters respond with an awe-struck, awe-inspiring stretta (stanza 6). Although at this point almost the whole of this stretta remains over the dominant, it counts as a stable element, only the second such element in the whole duet. Then to conclude the duet, the music for the oath and the stretta are freely repeated.

Predisposed as we are to formal models derived from instrumental music, we may feel inclined to hear stanza 1 as a "first theme," stanza 2 as a modulating bridge, stanzas 3–4 as a second group in the mediant, the first oath as a sort of development section, touching on iv and VI, and the first stretta as a recapitulation in the sense of a resumption of the opening tonality. Then the second, more fervent oath plus the extended stretta would be heard as an enhanced repetition of the second large division in sonata form, namely the development plus the recapitulation.

Yet in instrumental forms such repeats are, precisely, purely formal. Here the point is surely that the second oath is a real second event, and one of some dramatic import. Anna insists on the oath's being reaffirmed. Her trauma is already turning to obsession. That obsession drives the opera's essential action.

The stretta is composed much more intensely than usual in Mozart arias and ensembles, even those in the minor mode (of which there are not many). The first part of the stretta features accentuation that is unusually subtle even for Mozart, resulting in a single twenty-two-bar period whose mood is half gloom and half nervous energy.[8] A brooding augmentation of the music for line 21, "Fra cento affetti e cento," precipitates a new climactic sonority:

> The powerful Neapolitan sixth to tonic progression elaborates the tonal climax of the opening duet for Anna and Ottavio, and one is tempted to hear it as the crux of her personal tragedy. From the duet it was taken over as the climax of the slow minor section of the Overture (which was written last). Related to this is the music for the uncanny return of the Commendatore as the stone guest. Here, as always, Mozart marshalled his most potent resources and deployed them to utmost dramatic advantage.[9]

The Neapolitan harmony is in 6/4 position, so what stands out is the progression B♭–A in the bass. Line 21, with its hyperbole, its grandiloquent inversion, and its brutal vowel pattern was probably meant by Da Ponte parodistically; it is taken from a Metastasio text that Mozart had actually set to music twenty years earlier.[10] Mozart was in no mood for levity here, however.

As for the stretta's second part or extension, which consists of smaller units, its effect is still hectic, first of all because of the irregular phraseology –

‖: phrase a   phrase b   :‖ orchestral postlude
5 bars × 2   6 bars × 2   6 bars (= 2+2+2)   6 bars

– and secondly because of highly-wrought syncopated harmonic action involving B♭. In phrase a, the violas sustain an off-the-beat B♭ in bar 4, resolving via A to D at the cadence – an already disruptive effect that is echoed and much heightened in phrase b. Here B♭ juts in earlier, in the third bar; clashes retrospectively with a B♮ introduced even earlier to initiate a syncopated rising sequence; and is prolonged by violent means for two and a half bars before resolving.

The syncopated, dissonant sequence rising up the melodic minor scale gives this music a startling, almost Beethovenian vehemence. By now the pitch B♭ – derived ultimately from Anna's "moro" and "mora" – is acting like a loose irritant, floating almost free of its resolution (see Ex. 32). Finally, when the stretta straightens out into two-bar cadential units, one of them moves de-

On Don Giovanni, No. 2

Ex. 32 Mozart, *Don Giovanni*, No. 2

ceptively to B♮ in the bass, once again – now *on* the beat. This simple, indeed stereotyped, move is excellently strong here.

Tracing chromatic steps like 6–5 in a Classical minor-mode piece is bound to make a scrupulous analyst uneasy. It feels like taking candy from a baby. Still, there is something more than ordinarily obsessive about the chromaticism of this particular minor-mode piece. Even Ottavio's music is touched by it – most obviously, in his response to Anna's faint in the recitative, and in his second response to Anna in the duet (stanza 4). Ottavio is so affected by Anna's downward step B♭–A at the words "l'affanno mio, le pene," and by the orchestral motif that silhouettes that step, that his new consolatory couplet is swamped by descending chromatics.

Gerald Abraham remarks on "the hard edge on Ottavio's voice (intensified by the harmony) at 'Lascia o cara, la rimembranza amara' – he is trying to master his own feelings."[11] There is nothing in the music to suggest that Ottavio will not be a strong *sposo e padre* to Anna, much to suggest that he will be a sympathetic one in the literal sense of the word.

Chromaticism seeps into Ottavio's music on less obvious occasions, too. These are occasions when he repeats a short passage of music and varies it – and in the variation the music becomes more chromatic. A case in point is stanza 4:[12] originally his first downbeat ("hai *spo*so e padre in me") on a vii^4_3 chord in F major is prepared by two bars arpeggiating a ii^6_5 chord (bass B♭), then in the repetition the preparation expands to four bars and admits a half-step inflection (B♭–B♮–B♭). The repetition (reaffirmation) of his oath, too, involves extensive chromatic incursions (see Ex. 33).

267

Ex. 33 Mozart, *Don Giovanni*, No. 2

Nowhere else in the opera does Ottavio betray this penchant for chromatic detail – except at certain moments in "Dalla sua pace." Did Mozart, coming back to the opera in 1788, realize that chromaticism was after all one of Ottavio's strong suits? Ottavio's reputation for blandness does not take into account this capacity of his for sympathetic chromatic resonance. One does not begrudge him his bonus aria.

If a string quintet may grieve for a dead friend, *Don Giovanni* may grieve for a dead father, and it is vexing that Dent does not come out and say so. Although *Don Giovanni* was contracted for in January or February 1787, some months before Mozart had any inkling that Leopold was ailing (letter of 4 April), the best estimate is that the libretto was not yet finished when Leopold died, on 28 May. Mozart set the libretto at a time when his father's death was very much on his mind.

Another death comes to mind in connection with *Don Giovanni* – to our collective mind, if not to Mozart's: that of the Chevalier Gluck. It was in November of 1787, maybe six weeks after Mozart had gone to Prague for the *Don Giovanni* premiere, that the old gentleman took a glass of wine with his wife, against doctor's orders, and presently suffered his final stroke. (Such, at least, is the legend memorialized by the well-known painting variously attributed to Georg Weikert, Vienna's fashionable portraitist, and Barbara Krafft, best known to musicians for her posthumous portrait of Mozart. Later research suggests that Gluck reached for the schnapps at a dinner party when his wife had left the room for a moment. See Plate 20.) Gluck was of course inseparably associated with the Don Juan legend. Mozart must have thought of his celebrated ballet if only to reject it as a model or an influence.

No pages of *Don Giovanni* seem to be modeled on specific Gluck compositions, as so many pages of *Idomeneo* are, and at least one page in *Die Zauberflöte* – Tamino's cavatina, with its echo of Gluck's last publication, the Klopstock songs of 1786. But the spirit of the older composer has often been evoked in connection with the Commendatore's music, both in the graveyard and at Don Giovanni's dinner, and I am certainly not the first to sense in the

On Don Giovanni, *No. 2*

Plate 20 Barbara Krafft or Georg Weikert, painting of Gluck with his wife Marianne. Vienna, Museum der Stadt Wien.

recitative and duet, No. 2, Mozart's complete and perfect internalization of Gluck's severe musico-dramatic ideal, as well as something of his method. Abert traced the rising chromatics at Ottavio's "Cercatemi, recatemi qualche odor" to a characteristic device of Gluck's and was reminded of Gluck by the rhythm – "hard as steel" – of Anna's "Fuggi, crudele, fuggi!" The dramatic flexibility of the recitative, Abert opined, would have been impossible without Gluck's example. When Anna returns with Ottavio, writes Abraham, "there follows a great scene (for once) in the manner of Gluckian *opera seria*."[13]

Mozart had helped himself liberally to *Alceste* in *Idomeneo*, but there can be a question about his full artistic grasp of Gluck's manner in some of the scenes that are the most obviously indebted. Whatever one thinks about this, the mastery of that manner displayed in the great Act 1 recitatives "Ma qual mai s'offre, oh Dei" and "Don Ottavio, son morta!" is beyond dispute.[14] *Don Giovanni* as a whole does not feel anything like Gluck – of course not; Gluck may have made the Don Juan theme his own, but all of Mozart's characters some of the time, and most of them all of the time, come from a completely different operatic universe. Yet portions of *Don Giovanni* can be seen as a private tribute to Gluck that is no less moving, one may feel, than Mozart's public tribute to Haydn in the opus 10 string quartets.[15]

NOTES

1. Edward J. Dent, *Mozart's Operas: A Critical Study*, 2nd edn (Oxford, 1947), pp. 146, 144–5.
2. Alan Tyson, *Mozart: Studies of the Autograph Scores* (Cambridge, 1987), ch. 15.
3. Daniel Heartz, *Mozart's Operas* (Berkeley and Los Angeles, 1990), p. 202.
4. This point must be familiar to Mozartians, but I never encountered it in print prior to Julian Rushton's analytical essay in his Cambridge Opera Guide (*W. A. Mozart: Don Giovanni* [Cambridge, 1972]).
5. On "Fin ch'han dal vino," see my essay "Reading Don Giovanni," in *The Don Giovanni Book*, ed. Jonathan Miller (London, 1990), pp. 108–25.
6. *Mozart's Operas*, p. 204.
7. "Music that utterly refutes the idea of the unloved bridegroom," according to Abert; see Hermann Abert, *Mozart's Don Giovanni*, trans. [from the 1924 biography] Peter Gellhorn (London, 1976), p. 68. Abert is at his best in his account of the recitative and duet.
8. "Not merely, as Abert points out, an outburst of vengeful feeling but rather of half-terrified excitement." Gerald Abraham in *The Mozart Companion*, ed. H. C. Robbins Landon and Donald Mitchell (Oxford, 1956), p. 296.
9. Heartz, *Mozart's Operas*, p. 205.
10. "Fra cento affanni e cento," K.88, an aria from *Artaserse*: see Abert, *Mozart's Don Giovanni*, p. 69.
11. *Mozart Companion*, p. 296.
12. Abert notes that the hard rhythms of Anna's "Fuggi, crudele" and "lascia ch'io moro" are recalled by Ottavio's "Lascia, o cara, la rimembranza amara" – "a deeply poetic move." *Mozart's Don Giovanni*, p. 68.
13. *Mozart Companion*, p. 296.
14. Incidentally, the contrast between these Gluckian Act 1 recitatives and Anna's more traditional Act 2 recitative "Crudele!" – "Ah no, mio bene!" speaks to the psychological change in this character over the course of the opera. But that is a question for another time.
15. Some of the above material was first presented at a colloquium on "Music and Biography: The Case of Mozart," held at Rutgers University in 1984. I should like to record my thanks to Professor Ellen Rosand, then of Rutgers, in connection with that event.

14

Leopold II, Mozart, and the return to a Golden Age

JOHN A. RICE

The reorganization of Viennese musical theater initiated and supervised by Emperor Leopold II in 1791 represented in some respects a return to musical conditions that prevailed in Vienna during the 1760s.[1] As such, Leopold's reorganization can be seen as one aspect of his efforts to return, on a political and social level, to the stability and values of the past, to establish, as imperial propaganda put it, "a new Golden Age."

Mozart did not play a prominent role in Leopold's reorganization. Yet he was by no means isolated from it. His last two operas, while not commissioned by Leopold, were nevertheless influenced by the emperor's policies. Leopold's return to the past had the indirect result of encouraging Mozart, in *La clemenza di Tito* and *Die Zauberflöte*, to turn to his own musical past. Musical parallels between these operas and works composed between 1779 and early 1781 suggest that Mozart, whether consciously or not we cannot know, turned to the music of this period in particular for inspiration during 1791.

That parts of *La clemenza di Tito* and *Die Zauberflöte* are closely related to *Idomeneo* was noticed as early as 1798. Friedrich Rochlitz, first editor of the *Allgemeine musikalische Zeitung*, pointed to some of these parallels, arguing that Mozart showed his fondness for *Idomeneo*

> by taking several of its ideas as the foundation – or even more than just the foundation – in some of his best later works. Compare, for example, the overture to *Idomeneo* with that to *Tito*, or the incomparable scene "Volgi intorno lo sguardo, o sire" in *Idomeneo* with the equally outstanding finale of Act I in *Tito*, the moving aria of the first, "Se il padre perdei," with the aria "Dies Bildnis ist bezaubernd schön," and the Andante of the aria "Zum Leiden bin ich auserkoren" in *The Magic Flute*; and so forth. He has been reproached for this, I believe unjustly. Mozart could rightfully make use of his earlier work thus, not only because it was so magnificent, but also because, as long as he lived, it lay hidden, like buried treasure.[2]

But *Idomeneo* is only one of several works that Mozart wrote between 1779 and 1781 containing music remarkably close to that in *La clemenza di Tito* and *Die Zauberflöte*.

Despite many disappointments and frustrations, the period between Mozart's return to Salzburg from Paris in 1779 and his decision to settle in Vienna in 1781 was of great artistic and personal excitement and satisfaction.

These years saw the composition of the Posthorn Serenade, the Coronation Mass, the Symphony K.338, the final version of the choruses and incidental music for *Thamos*, the Symphonie Concertante for violin and viola and, most important of all, *Idomeneo* itself.[3] Mozart's letters from Munich express unmistakably that with *Idomeneo* he had reached a point of professional fulfillment. Emperor Leopold's attempt to return to a Golden Age of Viennese music thus found a parallel in Mozart's musical return, in the last months of his life, to a period of his life that we might describe as a personal and musical Golden Age.

Coming to power in February 1790, at a time of crisis and revolution, of uncertainty and instability, Leopold had to offer the Habsburg Monarchy hope for a future in which the values of the past were reestablished. The political rhetoric surrounding Leopold's various coronations reflects the emperor's goal with its constant reiteration of the idea of a return to a Golden Age. *Redeunt Saturnia regna*: "The Golden Age returns." These words, from Vergil's *Eclogues*, decorate a portrait of Leopold published as the frontispiece to the *Journal von und für Deutschland* (Vienna, 1791). A eulogistic commentary on Leopold's reign, Joseph Sartori's *Leopoldinische Annalen* (the propagandistic character of which suggests that it was published at the instigation of the imperial court), begins with the same idea: "Germany has embarked on the new Golden Age."[4] The idea is expressed visually in an engraving made to celebrate Leopold's coronation at Frankfurt (Plate 21).

The sunrise at the right seems to promise a future filled with light and warmth. The poem below ends:

> Jauchzet, meine teutschen Brüder,
> Goldne Tage winken euch!
>
> Rejoice, my German brothers:
> Golden days are in store for you!

The ideology of a return to the Golden Age found its way into discussions of Leopold's musical patronage. Early in Leopold's reign an anonymous writer acknowledged in the *Musikalische Korrespondenz der teutschen filarmonischen Gesellschaft* that the emperor had done little to further the state of music during the first months of his reign; but he looked forward to the musical fruits of Leopold's future patronage:

> once the enormous burdens of statesmanship that lie on his shoulders are reduced to minor difficulties, once he has bestowed golden peace on his dominions, then too will we have a new Golden Age of music.[5]

Fully aware of the theater's potential as a political symbol, Leopold used it skillfully. During his first year in power he pointedly ignored the theater, as a way of projecting the image of a sovereign too busy with the affairs of government, too weighed down by "the enormous burdens of statesmanship," to dabble in such trivial matters. Sartori conveyed this image in his *Leopoldinische Annalen*:

Leopold II, Mozart, and the return to a Golden Age

Plate 21 "Vivat Leopoldus Secundus," allegorical engraving by I. C. Berndt in celebration of Leopold's coronation as Emperor, 1790. Frankfurt am Main, Historisches Museum.

> One could easily imagine that a ruler who entered his hereditary dominions at a time of the greatest confusion had a great deal of work ahead of him. But he showed immediately the greatest diligence and ceaseless labor in affairs of state. For several months after his arrival in Vienna he took no part in public amusements. Except for the audiences he granted, no one saw him in public.[6]

Lorenzo Da Ponte remembered: "Leopold, absorbed in the most important affairs, had no time to devote to the frivolities and intrigues of the theater."[7]

Leopold's efforts to keep the Habsburg Monarchy from sliding into chaos began to show signs of success in mid-1790. He managed to suppress a rebellion in the Austrian Netherlands by cleverly playing the two revolutionary parties against each other, and effectively blending concessions with firmness. He extracted the Austrians from a costly and unpopular war with the Turks. With the signing of the Convention of Reichenbach on 27 July 1790 he came to an understanding with the Prussians, who had earlier contemplated supporting rebellious nobility in Hungary. Leopold also put dynastic affairs in order by arranging marriages between three of his children, including his eldest son Francis, and three offspring of his brother-in-law and sister, the King and Queen of Naples. Leopold's coronations as Holy Roman Emperor in Frankfurt in September 1790 and as King of Hungary the following month in Pressburg, with all their pomp and magnificence, presented Europe with tangible evidence

273

that the emperor's policies were working, that his hard labors were paying off. In a New Year's greeting from his brother Ferdinand, Governor of Milan, Leopold could have the satisfaction of seeing the accomplishments of his first year neatly summed up:

> Peace obtained for the Monarchy, the Imperial crown again secure, the Netherlands subdued, the entire Monarchy and especially the Hungarians pacified, the enthusiastic and deserved love for the Sovereign excited and awoken in all his subjects by acts of justice and beneficence, the marriages of the two archdukes and that of the archduchess arranged at Naples; in sum, a new order of things both within and without the affairs of the Monarchy; these are the accomplishments that have marked the first year of Your Majesty's glorious reign.[8]

Ferdinand applauded Leopold's establishment of "a new order of things." But he could just as easily have seen in Leopold's success a return to an old order.[9] Leopold reversed several of Joseph's most important reforms, including his reorganization of the tax system and his commutation of feudal dues (by which Joseph had required the landed nobility to accept cash rent from its tenants and had abolished the hated robot, the institution that forced peasants to pay their rent with labor on the nobles' land). Leopold relaxed Joseph's restrictions on the Catholic Church and its ceremonies, including Joseph's restrictions on the performance of music in church.[10] He allowed representatives of the privileged Estates to assemble in various parts of the monarchy and to submit lists of grievances to the central government in Vienna. With these and other policies Leopold moved backwards towards a pre-Josephinian status quo, a process made palatable, perhaps, to some of those who might otherwise have opposed it by Leopold's promise of a new Golden Age.

Success on the political and military fronts encouraged Leopold to turn to the theater, just as the anonymous correspondent to the *Musikalische Korrespondenz der teutschen filarmonischen Gesellschaft* had hoped. The emperor's appointment of a Musikgraf (court music director) in January 1791 marked a critical turning point in the direction of the Viennese musical theater, from a laissez-faire policy of continuity with the Josephinian past to a policy of change in which Leopold played a crucial role. The office of Musikgraf had been vacant since 1775, that is, since the period of Joseph's own theatrical reorganization, which resulted in the founding of his Nationaltheater for the performance of German spoken drama a year later.

Leopold announced his decision to appoint the Moravian nobleman Count Wenzel Ugarte as Musikgraf in a letter to Obersthofmeister (Chief Steward) Prince Starhemberg dated 25 January 1791. Starhemberg, jealously guarding the prerogatives of his office, and suspicious that Leopold wanted to run the court theaters through Ugarte, wrote to the emperor, reminding him that the Musikgraf, when the position had been occupied, had always been subordinate to the Obersthofmeisteramt. Starhemberg's fears were well founded. Leopold returned Starhemberg's letter with the following note in the margin: "Musikgraf Count Ugarte will indeed be under the direction of the

Obersthofmeister; but in matters concerning the direction of the theater he will be under my authority alone."[11]

By appointing Ugarte to the newly revived position of Musikgraf, Leopold took responsibility for the running of the court theaters out of the Oberstkämmereramt (Chamberlain's Office), to which it had been entrusted by Joseph, kept it from falling into the hands of the Oberthofmeisteramt, and put himself more in touch with day-to-day decision-making at the court theaters. The appointment of Ugarte was consistent with other policies that reversed Josephinian reforms in that it looked to the past. It called to mind immediately, in a government bureaucracy obsessed with precedents, the previous holders of the office of Musikgraf during the 1760s and early 1770s (to whom Starhemberg referred in his letter) and the conditions of the court theaters during their tenure.

Having taken control of the court theaters through Ugarte, Leopold moved them quickly from the state in which Joseph had left them. Expenditures increased dramatically from the levels that Joseph had maintained. Leopold largely abandoned the sophisticated, complex opera buffa style associated with Joseph and championed by the composers – Mozart, Salieri, and Martin y Soler – who benefited from Joseph's patronage. He introduced new genres, new librettists, new singers, and even considered building a new theater. But here again, novelty meant a return to the past. In introducing Italian serious opera to Vienna, Leopold returned to a genre for which Vienna had once been famous. In assembling an Italian ballet troupe in the Burgtheater, Leopold must have reminded the Viennese of the 1750s, 60s and 70s, when leading Italian and French dancers made Vienna one of Europe's centers in the cultivation of the pantomime ballet. Leopold grew up at the Viennese court during the 1750s and 60s, years that saw the performance of Gluck's *Orfeo*, the Viennese operas of Traetta, the ballets of Hilverding and Angiolini – truly a Golden Age in Viennese musical theater. He may well have intended his theatrical reorganization of 1791 to remind the Viennese of the glories of their musical past and to communicate to them, through the symbolism of the theater, the success of his efforts to establish a new Golden Age in the political sphere.

In a memorandum to Musikgraf Ugarte dated 27 July 1791, Leopold gave detailed instructions concerning repertory, personnel, and administration of the court theaters. In addition to prompters, singers, actors, and librettists, Leopold mentioned several composers. Mozart, who was probably hard at work on *La clemenza di Tito* for the Emperor's coronation as King of Bohemia, less than two months away, is not among them:

> The [soprano Irene] Tomeoni can, since she pleases the public, be engaged for two years with an addition of 100 ducats to her present [annual] salary; likewise her husband [Pietro Dutillieu] can be engaged for two years with 300 ducats [annual] pay as composer of opera and ballet...
>
> Kapellmeister [Antonio] Salieri will, as of 1 November [1791], certainly remain at the post he now occupies, but he will at the same time be relieved

of the direction of the theater; only [Joseph] Weigl, and when he is indisposed, [Ignaz] Umlauf, will have to remain, but only to accompany, without any say in the distribution of roles or [in the management of] the troupe.[12]

With the fall of Lorenzo Da Ponte and the soprano Adriana Ferrarese (the first Fiordiligi), both essential members of the comic troupe during Joseph's last years and both dismissed in early 1791, around the time that Leopold began to assert his authority over theatrical matters; with the court's increasing reliance on operas, serious and comic, imported from Italy; and with Leopold's decision to award the (apparently new) position of "Opern, und Ballet Komponist" to the husband of his new prima buffa Irene Tomeoni, Mozart could hope for few major commissions from the court. And he received none. *Così fan tutte*, brought to the stage of the Burgtheater a few weeks before Joseph's death, was Mozart's last operatic commission from the court. A performance of *Figaro* in February 1791, just before Da Ponte's dismissal, was the last performance of a Mozart opera given in the court theaters before the composer's death in December of that year. The effect of Leopold's reorganization on the repertory of the court theaters outlived both Mozart and Leopold: it was not until 1798 that one of Mozart's opere buffe was performed again in the court theaters.[13]

Yet the situation Mozart faced in 1791 was more complex than a simple rejection by the court and by the Emperor. Mozart's operas were not singled out for exclusion from the repertory. Most of the operas that enjoyed success in Vienna during the 1780s, whether they were by Salieri, Martín y Soler, Paisiello, or Mozart, were spurned once Leopold's reorganization began to take effect. Martín's operas may serve as an example. *Una cosa rara* was a staple of the Burgtheater repertory from the time of its premiere in 1786 until 1790. In February 1791, just as Leopold's reorganization was getting under way, *Una cosa rara* was dropped from the repertory, to be revived only in 1794. The same happened to Martín's *L'arbore di Diana*: performed sixty-six times between 1787 and early March 1791, it vanished from the Burgtheater repertory during Leopold's reorganization, to be revived in German translation only in 1802. Martín's operas as well as Mozart's were replaced, for the most part, by opere buffe imported from Naples. Guglielmi's *La pastorella nobile*, first performed in Naples in 1788, was performed more often than any other opera buffa in Vienna during Leopold's reign. The absence of Mozart's operas from the court theater repertory from early 1791 until near the end of the 1790s was part of a reaction against Josephinian opera buffa in general that characterized Leopold's theatrical policies.

Mozart continued to occupy the prestigious post of court composer, which meant that he was in a good position to observe Leopold's theatrical reorganization. The court paid him an annual salary of 800 gulden and left him free to accept commissions from other sources, a freedom of which Mozart took full advantage in 1791. The works that resulted from these commissions were not the direct result of Leopold's policies, but it is unlikely that he would have written them if Leopold had not launched his reorganization of Viennese musical theater.

Exactly when Mozart began his collaboration with Emanuel Schikaneder on a German opera for the suburban Theater auf der Wieden is unknown.[14] Mozart's heavy musical output during January, February, and March 1791 – dominated by many sets of dances for Carneval balls, as well as the Quintet in E♭, K.618, dated 12 April – makes it unlikely that he could have done much work on *Die Zauberflöte* before the middle of April; at the same time the fact that he completed an aria for Franz Gerl, who would later create the role of Sarastro, on 8 March suggests that Mozart's involvement with members of Schikaneder's troupe had already started to solidify by early March. In June he was certainly at work on the opera, which was substantially complete by July, when Mozart entered it in his thematic catalog. He probably began work in March or April, completing the bulk of the opera during May and June.

The beginnings of *Die Zauberflöte* thus almost certainly followed shortly after the beginning of Leopold's theatrical reorganization, and may well have roughly coincided with one particular aspect of that reorganization: the end of Da Ponte's nine-year tenure as poet to the court theaters in March 1791. This conjunction of events has not received the attention it deserves. Da Ponte, inextricably tied up with Josephinian opera and all that it stood for, was also one of Mozart's most important links with the court theatrical establishment; it cannot be only coincidence that around the time of Da Ponte's dismissal Mozart, whose operatic production since 1786 had consisted entirely of opere buffe with librettos by Da Ponte, turned to another literary collaborator, another theater, another operatic genre, and a libretto in another language.

The normal run of operas presented by Schikaneder's troupe were composed by minor musicians unconnected with the imperial court. Neither Kapellmeister Salieri nor Vice-Kapellmeister Umlauf wrote any such operas, although both had experience writing German opera for the court theaters. That Mozart, who had written no operas for Viennese theaters other than the court theaters since his arrival in Vienna and had written no full-length opera in German since *Die Entführung aus dem Serail*, decided to write a German opera for Schikaneder's troupe may well have been a reaction to Leopold's theatrical reorganization, his dismissal of Da Ponte, and his apparent preference for operas imported from Italy to those written especially for the Viennese opera buffa troupe.

Die Zauberflöte represents on one level Mozart's declaration of independence from the court theaters; but on another level it reflects Leopold's reorganization, and in particular his establishment of an opera seria troupe in the Burgtheater. The Italian aspects of *Die Zauberflöte* are often overshadowed by discussions of its importance as a forerunner of German Romantic opera. The playbill and the libretto for the original production called *Die Zauberflöte* a *grosse Oper*. This term was also used to refer to opera seria; Mozart himself had used the term for *Idomeneo*.[15] A report in the Berlin *Musikalisches Wochenblatt* referred to Leopold's plans for the performance of "italiänische grosse Opern" for which castrati had been engaged; the reference is clearly to Leopold's reintroduction of opera seria to Vienna.[16] That *Die Zauberflöte* was described by its promoters as a *grosse Oper* encourages one to look for evidence that Leopold's revival of Italian *grosse Oper*, which was being organized at the same time as *Die Zauberflöte* was being composed and produced, had some influence on Mozart's opera.

The playbill advertising the premiere of *Die Zauberflöte* is decorated with a banner that reads "K. K. priv. Wiedner Theater," meaning that the theater operated under license of the imperial royal court; a shield inscribed "L. II" and topped with a crown refers of course to Leopold himself. These symbols serve as a reminder that Schikaneder's troupe was not completely independent of the court and its theatrical reorganization.

One way in which the emperor exercised control over the Theater auf der Wieden was by including its programs in his "Frey Spektakeln." Leopold ordered that the theaters of Vienna open their doors free of charge on 13, 14, and 15 December 1791, with all expenses to be covered by the court. The main reason for this generosity was doubtless Leopold's eagerness to show off his new ballet and opera seria troupes, which had made their debuts only a few weeks earlier. But Leopold's largesse on this occasion extended even to the Theater auf der Wieden, where *Die Zauberflöte* continued to enjoy its extraordinary first run, a week after its composer's death. Joseph Bauernfeld and Schikaneder, as managers of the Theater auf der Wieden, received 750 gulden (250 a day) from the court in exchange for their participation in the Frey Spektakeln.[17] By including *Die Zauberflöte* in the Frey Spektakeln, Leopold managed to co-opt Schikaneder's troupe and Mozart's opera into his own theatrical program.

Leopold seems to have assumed that he could freely use Schikaneder's singers in his own opera seria troupe. This, at any rate, is suggested by a remark made by the emperor in the memorandum of 27 July 1791 to Musikgraf Ugarte. Leopold ordered that Franz Gerl, the first Sarastro, be used in the roles of the high priest and the ghost of Nino in one of the opere serie that were to be presented in the court theaters, Alessio Prati's *La vendetta di Nino*:

> The bass Gerl who sings in Schikaneder's theater is to be questioned about when he will apply himself as much as is necessary to the learning of the Italian language, so that he can be used in the [court] opera, and he will in the meantime be able to be used in the opera *La vendetta di Nino* as the high priest and the ghost.[18]

These are rather vague instructions, apparently leaving Ugarte the option of casting a singer other than Gerl in the roles specified by the emperor. If Gerl was indeed engaged to sing in Leopold's opera seria troupe, he must have been very busy between 6 January and 11 February 1792 (during which time *La vendetta di Nino* was performed nine times in the court theaters),[19] juggling priestly roles in Prati's *grosse Oper* and Mozart's.

But Gerl did not have to move to the Burgtheater to find music and musical

Leopold II, Mozart, and the return to a Golden Age

Ex. 34 a. Sebastiano Nasolini, *Teseo a Stige*, Chorus of Priestesses, bars 3–6
   b. Mozart, *Die Zauberflöte*, Aria with Chorus, "O Isis und Osiris," bars 17–20

drama reminiscent of opera seria. His prayer to Isis and Osiris in *Die Zauberflöte* resembles in its dramaturgy some of the *preghiere* of late eighteenth-century opere serie; one of its musical ideas is close to the music sung by the priestesses of Diana in Sebastiano Nasolini's *Teseo a Stige*, the opera in which Leopold's opera seria troupe made its debut on 24 November 1791 (see Ex. 34a–b and Plate 22).

The Queen of the Night and her music take us into another part of the world of serious Italian opera. The extraordinary coloratura, the high tessitura, the dramatic power of this music were, in all probability, completely new to the suburban operas produced by Schikaneder. How could Mozart have conceived such music, and such a musical personality? He may well have found inspiration in his own music, music written much earlier but revived in 1791 in connection with the performance of excerpts of an opera seria in Vienna.

In April 1791, during the period in which *Die Zauberflöte* was probably taking shape, excerpts of Paisiello's *Fedra* were performed in the Burgtheater as part of a Tonkünstler-Sozietät concert. The playbill for the concert shows that a symphony by Mozart opened the concert and that three soloists took part

279

Plate 22 Playbill announcing the debut of Emperor Leopold's opera seria troupe in Sebastiano Nasolini's *Teseo a Stige*, 24 November 1791. Vienna, Nationalbibliothek, Theatersammlung.

in the performance of *Fedra*: "la Sigra. Lang" is the soprano Aloysia Lange, née Weber, Mozart's sister-in-law; "il Sigre. Calvesi" is the tenor Vincenzo Calvesi; "il Sigre. Nenzini" is the tenor Santi Nencini, a member of the Burgtheater troupe from 1790 to 1792.

The singers who took part in the performance of excerpts of Paisiello's serious opera may have hoped to signal to Leopold their abilities in this genre and their eagerness to be part of his soon-to-be-assembled opera seria troupe. If this was their goal, at least one of the singers achieved it. Although Lange had been a member of the court theaters during the 1780s, she was not in them at the time of the Tonkünstler-Sozietät concert. But she did enter imperial employment later in 1791, receiving a monthly salary of 150 gulden from 1 November. That Leopold engaged her specifically to sing opera seria is known from a report in the Berlin *Musikalisches Wochenblatt* dated 20 October 1791: "Madame *Lang*, who has earned a reputation on numerous tours of Germany as a skillful and interesting singer and was engaged previously at the National Theater in Vienna, has now been engaged again, with a yearly salary of 400 ducats, for the *grosse Oper*."[20]

Leopold II, Mozart, and the return to a Golden Age

The aria that Lange sang in the Tonkünstler-Sozietät concert was not by Paisiello but, according to the playbill, by Mozart, who wrote it for her six years earlier as a substitute aria for Anfossi's *Il curioso indiscreto*.[21] "No, che non sei capace di cortesia, d'onore," K.419, is a bravura aria that explored the limits of Lange's voice. Brilliant but somewhat cold, it is performed today justifiably less often than the other aria that Mozart wrote for Lange to sing in Anfossi's opera, "Vorrei spiegarvi, oh Dio."[22] Perhaps the coldness has something to do with the aria's text, and with Mozart's feelings for Lange, with whom he had been passionately in love a few years before he wrote it, and who had rejected him. In the aria Clorinda berates her lover:

> No, che non sei capace
> Di cortesia, d'onore
> E vanti a torto un core
> Ch'arde d'amor per me.
> Vanne: t'aborro ingrato,
> E più me stessa abborro
> Che l'ho un istante amato
> Che sospirai per te.

(No, for you are incapable of courtesy or honor, and falsely boast of a heart that burns with love for me. Go, ingrate; I abhor you, and I abhor myself more for having loved you for an instant, for having sighed for you.)

Clorinda's hostility to her lover and the self-contempt she expresses so vehemently remind one of Mozart's feelings about himself and Lange. "I acted like a fool with Lange," he wrote to his father (16 May 1781), "but who is not a fool when in love? Indeed I loved her truly, and even now I feel that she is not a matter of indifference to me."[23] Later that year he called Lange "a false, malicious person and a coquette" (15 December 1781).[24] Because Mozart made this comment in the course of a letter whose principal motive was to give his father a good impression of Lange's sister Constanze, we have to view his characterization of Lange with some skepticism. But it seems clear that his feelings about her were still strong, or, as he had put it so delicately to his father a few months earlier, that she was "not a matter of indifference" to him; exactly what Mozart's feelings about Lange were, and how they changed as he became closer to Constanze, is not so easy for us to guess. As is surely true with Clorinda, the passion with which Mozart criticized Lange to his father may have disguised a passion of quite another sort that Mozart, now that he had become involved with Constanze, would have wanted to hide from himself as well as from his father. Did the vivid poetry of "No, che non sei capace" bring these feelings closer to the surface, causing Mozart to set it to music as if he were speaking to the "false, malicious person," to the "coquette" for whom he wrote the aria?

In 1791 Mozart had an opportunity to write two bravura arias for another of his sisters-in-law, Lange's sister Josepha Hofer, who evidently had a voice

Ex. 35 a. Mozart, "No, che non sei capace," K.419, bars 47–50
b. Mozart, *Die Zauberflöte*, "O zitt're nicht, mein lieber Sohn," bars 91–4

similar to Lange's. Her character, at least as Mozart saw it, resembled Lange's as well. Just before describing Lange as "false" in a letter of 15 December 1781, he used the same word to describe Josepha: "The eldest is a lazy, gross, false person, and as cunning as a fox."[25] Hofer created the role of the Queen of the Night. Lange's singing of "No, che non sei capace" in April 1791 may have suggested to Mozart some aspects of the Queen of the Night's vocal characterization. (That the Tonkünstler-Sozietät program opened with a symphony by Mozart increases the likelihood that Mozart attended the concert or took part in its preparation.) In his music for Hofer Mozart exploited her voice in much the same way as he used Lange's in "No, che non sei capace."

The Queen of the Night's compass is similar to that of Lange's aria; the Queen must go only a half-step beyond Lange's high E. The coloratura is of a similar breathtaking kind. Lange's first coloratura passage reaches a cadence by way of an ascending scale in sixteenth-notes. In the first of her two arias in *Die Zauberflöte* Lange's sister sang a similar passage (Ex. 35a–b). Comparison of the two cadences reveals richer craftsmanship in the later one. Mozart's approach to the $^6_4$ harmony by way of ii^6 in *Die Zauberflöte* is an improvement

Leopold II, Mozart, and the return to a Golden Age

Ex. 36 a. Mozart, "No, che non sei capace," K.419, bars 1–5
b. Mozart, *Die Zauberflöte*, "Der Hölle Rache," bars 88–93

over the analogous bar in "No, che non sei capace," where the G-major harmony preceding the $^6_4$ chord weakens the effect of the arrival of G major three bars later. By shifting the violins off the beat and keeping the cellos and double basses silent in the following bar Mozart subtly enlivened the drum bass and allowed Hofer's coloratura to shine more clearly than her sister's could in the earlier aria.

The dramatic climax of "Der Hölle Rache" arrives just before the end, with the Queen's threefold command "Hört!", the orchestra responding fortissimo (this is the only aria in the opera with trumpets and drums). Mozart here came very close to the beginning of Lange's aria, where her thrice-repeated "No" is answered by the full orchestra (with trumpets and drums) almost exactly as is the Queen's "Hört!" (Ex. 36a–b). In neither case is the repetition of the monosyllabic word part of the poetry; it was Mozart's idea, as it was, apparently, elsewhere in *Die Zauberflöte*, the whole of which is characterized by a large number of words sung three times, usually monosyllabic, and often at the beginning of numbers: "Du, du, du"; "Wo? wo? wo?"; "Wie? wie?

Ex. 37 a. Mozart, *Thamos, König in Ägypten*, No. 2, bars 1–3
b. Mozart, *Die Zauberflöte*, Overture, bars 1–3

wie?"; "Nie, nie, nie"; "Nein, nein, nein"; "still, still, still"; "bald, bald, bald"; "Triumph, Triumph, Triumph"; "Dank, Dank, Dank"; "Papagena! Papagena! Papagena!". The fact that not a single number in *Figaro*, *Don Giovanni* or *Così fan tutte* begins with a word sung three times may cause one to wonder why Mozart used this particular technique so often in *Die Zauberflöte*. Lange's performance of "No, che non sei capace" in April 1791 suggests a possible explanation.

Mozart's masterstroke at the end of "Der Hölle Rache" is not the simple transposition of an idea from C major to D minor. It is the transformation that he brought about by moving from the third degree to the flat sixth, rather than to the fifth, as in "No, che non sei capace." No matter how often one hears this passage (and even if one has never heard the earlier aria) one is led by musical logic to expect, after D and F, A. But the Queen sings a terrifying B♮ instead.

Mozart may have been aware of the special quality of this moment. Seyfried[26] recalled that as Mozart lay dying he imagined he heard the Queen of the Night singing, of all notes, the B♮ at the end of "Der Hölle Rache":

> On the evening of 4 December M. lay delirious, imagining he was attending *Die Zauberflöte* in the Theater auf der Wieden; almost his last words, which he whispered to his wife, were, "Quiet, quiet! Hofer is just taking her top F; – now my sister-in-law is singing her second aria, 'Der Hölle Rache'; how strongly she strikes and holds the B♮: 'Hört! hört! hört! der Mutter Schwur!' – ".[27]

Ex. 38 a. Mozart, *Thamos, König in Ägypten*, "Ihr Kinder des Staubes," bars 88–95
b. Mozart, *Die Zauberflöte*, Quintet, "Hm, hm, hm," bars 196–203

There are other ways in which *Die Zauberflöte* shows Mozart looking to his past. Schikaneder was an old acquaintance, as Daniel Heartz has pointed out,[28] and *Die Zauberflöte* itself has connections with the late Salzburg years. It shares its Egyptian setting and its atmosphere of priestly solemnity with the choruses and entr'acte music for *Thamos*, for which Mozart made revisions, and apparently composed some new music, in Salzburg in 1779. Alfred Einstein called *Thamos* the "springboard" for and a "distant ancestor" of *Die Zauberflöte*; but neither he nor Branscombe, who showed how the text of *Thamos* served as source for *Die Zauberflöte*'s libretto, sufficiently emphasized the musical connections.[29] Einstein alluded to the three solemn chords with which the first orchestral movement of *Thamos* (in C minor) begins as a precursor of the three chords that announce the beginning of *Die Zauberflöte* (in E♭); he might have made the connection stronger by noting the almost identical rhythms with which the three chords are proclaimed in both contexts (Ex. 37a–b).

The simple homophonic style that Mozart used so often in *Die Zauberflöte* is also common in *Thamos*, especially in the several episodes for soloists within the choruses. The final chorus looks forward to *Die Zauberflöte* in passages like the one in Ex. 38a, with its simple, symmetrical phrase structure, its harmony (especially the suspension at the cadence), melody (2–5–1 at the cadence), and the breaking of words between syllables. The farewell from the first-act quintet comes to mind (Ex. 38a–b).

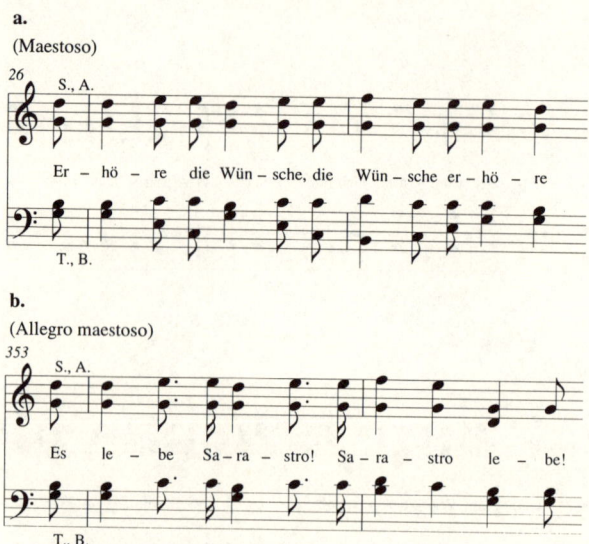

Ex. 39 a. Mozart, *Thamos, König in Ägypten*, No. 1 Chorus, "Schon weichet dir," bars 26–7
  b. Mozart, *Die Zauberflöte*, Finale, Act I, bars 353–4

The opening chorus of *Thamos* features a short, declamatory phrase that Mozart used again, in the form of an off-stage choral interruption, to introduce Sarastro (Ex. 39a–b). In both passages Mozart inverted the words as he repeated them, giving them a quasi-biblical character. The only difference in voice-leading results from the older Mozart's avoidance of first-inversion chords in which the bass doubles the treble. This and dotted rhythms give the later acclamation more energy and incisiveness than the earlier one, helping it, when sung off-stage, to be heard clearly in the auditorium.

Mozart may have heard his music for *Thamos* in September 1790, less than a year before he wrote *Die Zauberflöte*, during the festivities surrounding the coronation of Leopold II at Frankfurt. The theatrical troupe that presented Karl Martin Plümicke's play *Lanassa* at Frankfurt often included Mozart's *Thamos* music in their performances of *Lanassa*, and they may have done so at Frankfurt.[30]

Just as *Die Zauberflöte* can be interpreted as both a reaction to and at the same time a reflection of Leopold's transformation of Viennese musical theater, Mozart's other opera of 1791, *La clemenza di Tito*, can be seen as an indirect product of Leopold's theatrical reorganization. Emperor Joseph's dislike of opera seria (and perhaps also his unwillingness to pay for it) meant that opera seria was rarely performed in Vienna during the 1780s. Leopold's reintroduction of opera seria to Vienna in 1791 represented an important part of his theatrical program. The aristocratic members of the Bohemian Estates who commissioned *La clemenza di Tito* to celebrate the coronation of Leopold as King of Bohemia must have been aware of Leopold's intentions, since many of them had residences in Vienna and close connections with the court. Certainly they would not have commissioned such an opera for Leopold if Leopold's theatrical tastes had been similar to Joseph's.

It should not be surprising to find in Mozart's *La clemenza di Tito* traces of his previous opera seria. Sesto's first aria, "Parto, ma tu, mio," reminds one of Idamante's first aria, "Non ho colpa, e mi condanni," both in its dramatic context and in its musical details. Sesto has just been scolded by his beloved; as he leaves to start the insurrection against Tito he manages to collect his dignity. Mozart reacted to this dramatic situation with music that recalls what he wrote for another primo uomo in a similar situation ten years earlier. In Idamante's aria, also in B♭, the hero expresses a mixture of passion and dignified defensiveness similar to Sesto's.

Several elements occur in the first two bars of "Non ho colpa" (Ex. 40a) that reappear in Sesto's aria, which has the same orchestration with the exception of the solo clarinet part that replaces the two orchestral clarinets in the earlier aria. A B♭ arpeggio for full orchestra in octaves, simple and noble, provides the opening for both arias, ascending for Idamante, descending for Sesto (Ex. 40b). The second bar of "Non ho colpa" introduces two more ideas, a chromatic ascent in thirds that might allude to the lover's unfulfilled desires,[31] and a sinuous line in the first violins. In Sesto's aria Mozart used a similar chromatic ascent in thirds at bar 8 (Ex. 40c); later, in the Allegro, he extended it into a lyrical idea in the bass (Ex. 40d). The violin line also reappears in "Parto," but transformed, combined with an orchestral effect that was of particular interest to Mozart during 1791: the solo clarinet and its combination with full orchestra, an interest revealed not only here but in "Non più di fiori," with its concertante bassett horn, and the Clarinet Concerto. The connection with "Non ho colpa" is clearest at bar 18. Mozart did not start his clarinet solo with material from "Non ho colpa," but as he spun the beautiful melody out, he casually, and probably unconsciously, wrote again what he had written a decade earlier (Ex. 40e). Sesto's great aria is rooted in Mozart's past; but at the same time the clarinet solo, which, as Heartz has pointed out, includes passages almost identical to passages in the Clarinet Concerto,[32] helps us recognize it as a product of Mozart's last year.

The overture of *La clemenza di Tito* looks to Mozart's past as well, and to exactly the same part of the past. Most of the thematic material is related to works written between 1779 and early 1781. Mozart's opening gesture, a splendid, majestic C major chord and a leap down two octaves to middle C (Ex. 41a) recalls a fondness for such downward leaps at the beginning of works that Mozart showed between 1779 and 1781. The Concerto for Two Pianos in E♭ (probably composed early in 1779), the Posthorn Serenade in D (3 August 1779), and the overture to *Idomeneo*, also in D (January 1781), all begin with similar gestures. Closest of all to the overture to *Tito* is the opening of the C major Symphony K.338 (Ex. 41b, August 1780), which shares with the overture not only the brilliant opening C major chord and the two-octave leap to middle C, but also the unison slide from G up to C and the dotted rhythms

Concerning Mozart

Ex. 40 a. Mozart, *Idomeneo*, "Non ho colpa," bars 1–4
b. Mozart, *La clemenza di Tito*, "Parto, ma tu, ben mio," bars 1–3
c. Ibid., bars 8–9
d. Ibid., bars 68–70
e. Ibid., bars 18–19

that follow (played by the brass in the symphony, by full orchestra in the overture). From this athletic opening Mozart went on to a triadic ascent close to the one that opens the overture to *Idomeneo* (Ex. 41c), but with the rather staid rhythms of the *Idomeneo* passage replaced by the livelier rhythmic pattern played by the brass in the symphony.

Mozart's second theme is close to an idea in one of his last Salzburg church compositions, the *Vesperae solemnes de confessore*, K.339, composed in 1780. The choice, whether conscious or not is impossible to tell, is apt, in this overture that celebrates the coronation of a great ruler. Mozart's second theme resembles a melody from the closing movement of the Vespers, the Magnificat: his setting of the words "Et exultavit spiritus meus Dominum" (Ex. 42a–b).

The beautiful counterpoint that predominates in the development of the *Tito* overture also looks to the past. The jagged line tossed back and forth between first and second violins in ascending sequence and later transferred to the bass is similar to one used in a very similar way (tossed back and forth between parts and repeated in descending sequence) in the first movement of the Posthorn Serenade (Ex. 43a–b). Mozart's use of this material is more interesting in the overture, where he incorporates within the polyphonic fabric a fragment of the overture's first theme (in the bass) repeated in sequence.

Yet the overture to *La clemenza di Tito* is much more than a nostalgic reminiscence of old material and old-fashioned form. Heartz has demonstrated that it incorporates many of the opera's most characteristic rhythmic and harmonic features.[33] The overture looks forward to the opera just as it looks back to the *Idomeneo* years. The opera, while glorifying the Habsburg dynasty and the tradition of enlightened absolutism that kept it in power, also alludes to the forces of revolution that were threatening to bring that dynasty down. Performed before Leopold and his court on 6 September 1791, *La clemenza di*

Ex. 41 a. Mozart, *La clemenza di Tito*, Overture, bars 1–4
    b. Mozart, Symphony in C, K.338, 1st movement, bars 1–4
    c. Mozart, *Idomeneo*, Overture, bars 2–7

Tito spoke allegorically both to the sovereign and to his subjects. The burning of the Capitoline at the end of the first act may well have been understood in 1791 as a frightening symbol of the violence with which the Bastille had been attacked just two years before.

    Just as the opera as a whole deals with human passion, suffering, and destructiveness within a framework of majestic celebration, so the overture uses the festive music of Mozart's last Salzburg years as a foil with which to set off the darker colors of the development. The development, although it builds on material also used by Mozart in the Posthorn Serenade, is completely different

Ex. 42 a. Mozart, *Versperae solemnes de confessore*, Magnificat, bars 6–7
b. Mozart, *La clemenza di Tito*, Overture, bars 30–3

in character from the serenade and from the rest of the overture. The somber E♭ chord with which it begins announces the exploration of more serious issues: the majestic formality of the exposition gives way, in the development, to the tragic. If the opening material of the overture and the "Et exultavit" theme can be said to reflect the ideals of Leopold's reign, a return to the grandeur and stability of the past, to a Golden Age, then the development can be said to reflect the more dynamic reality of the present, full of anxiety and instability.

The parallels drawn in this study between the music that Mozart wrote during the late 1770s and early 1780s on the one hand and in 1791 on the other should not be understood to mean that traces of Mozart's late Salzburg music cannot be found in works that he wrote in Vienna before 1791. The music that Mozart wrote during his last years in Salzburg served the composer as a source of ideas for many Viennese works, and not just those of his last year. But Mozart's reliance on Salzburg works in 1791 seems to have been on an order of magnitude quite different from anything to be found in music composed before 1791.

Nor should the parallels cited here be taken to mean that Mozart's last two operas were in any way old-fashioned when performed in 1791. In *Die*

Ex. 43 a. Mozart, Posthorn Serenade, 1st movement, bars 26–8
b. Mozart, *La clemenza di Tito*, Overture, bars 71–6

Zauberflöte Mozart embraced the new possibilities of Viennese magic opera with enthusiasm and great originality. *La clemenza Di Tito* was, in Heartz' words, "the most modishly up-to-date work that he left."[34] Inspired by the past, Mozart's operas looked to the future: *Die Zauberflöte* to German Romantic opera, *La clemenza di Tito* to opera seria of the early nineteenth century, the period in which it achieved its greatest popularity. This same paradox is characteristic of Leopold's theatrical reorganization. Leopold returned to genres associated with Vienna's past. But in bringing opera seria and ballet back into the mainstream of Viennese musical culture, and in bringing to an end the great era of Josephinian opera buffa, Leopold helped to shape Viennese theater in ways that would be felt well into the nineteenth century.

Just before returning to Salzburg after his trip to Paris, Mozart wrote to his father: "I cannot bear Salzburg or its inhabitants – I mean native-born Salzburgers" (8 January 1779).[35] And yet during those last years in his native city and in his father's house the future still looked bright, and the present, stable and comfortable even if somewhat constricting, was filled with the composition of brilliant music. It was to this Golden Age that Mozart returned in 1791. Badgered by illness and debt, neglected by a patron whose approval he valued highly, Mozart poured all his energy into his final masterpieces. He may have found solace in the spring and summer of 1791, probably without realizing what he was doing, by turning in his music back to Salzburg, to a happier past.

NOTES

1 For a more detailed discussion of Leopold's theatrical reorganization see John A. Rice, "Emperor and Impresario: Leopold II and the Transformation of Viennese Musical Theater, 1790–1792," Ph. D. Dissertation, University of California at Berkeley, 1987.
2 Daniel Heartz, *Mozart's Operas*, (Berkeley, 1990), p. 341, quotes Rochlitz (his translation is used here) and comments: "He might have added that Sesto's 'Parto' (No. 9) echoes several elements in Idamante's 'Non ho colpa' (No. 2), and that the postlude of Pamina's 'Ach, ich fühl's' resembles a passage in *Idomeneo*... Particularly astute on Rochlitz's part is his detection of a minor-mode passage in Ilia's aria 'Se il padre perdei' (No. 11, mm. 33–39) that was transferred to the Queen of the Night's first aria (No. 4, mm. 40–44), which shows that he knew well the three operas in question."
3 Neal Zaslaw, *Mozart's Symphonies: Context, Performance Practice, Reception* (Oxford, 1989), entitles the chapter dealing with Mozart's last years in Salzburg "Salzburg (III): Serfdom (1779–1780)." The word "serfdom," obviously intended figuratively, is nevertheless misleading. The idea of serfdom is inconsistent with the degree of freedom allowed Mozart by his employer, freedom that made it possible, for example, for Mozart to accept the commission for *Idomeneo*. More important, it is inconsistent with the brilliance, splendor, and originality of much of the music that Mozart wrote during this period. Certainly the Symphony in C, K.338 (to cite just one example) cannot have been the product of serfdom in any sense of the word.
4 "Das goldene Alter beginnt in Deutschland zu reisen." [Joseph Sartori], *Leopoldinische Annalen*, 2 vols. (Augsburg, 1792–3), vol. 1, "Vorbericht".
5 "Allein ich denke, wenn einmal die Riesengebürge von Staatsgeschäften, die auf seinen Schultern liegen, werden zu Sandhügeln abgeebnet seyn, wenn er seinen Staaten den geldnen Frieden wird wieder geschenkt haben, daß alsdann auch das goldene Zeitalter für die Musik eine neue Periode bei uns habe wird." "Auszug eines Schreibens aus Wien vom 5ten Jul. 1790," *Musikalische Korrespondenz der teutschen filarmonischen Gesellschaft* (28 July 1790), cols. 27–31.
6 "Mann konnte sich leicht vorstellen, daß ein Regent, der wie Leopold seine Erbstaaten in der größten Verwirrung antrat, ein schweres Stück Arbeit vor sich hatte. Er zeigte aber gleich die größte Thätigkeit und rastlose Beschäftigung in seinen Regierungsangelegenheiten. Durch einige Monate nach seiner Ankunft in Wien nahm Er an öffentlichen Belustigungen keinen Antheil. Außer den erheilten Audienzen sah man Ihn niemal im Publikum." Sartori, *Leopoldinische Annalen*, vol. 2, p. 223.
7 "Leopoldo, occupato da faccende importantissime, non avea tempo di badare alle frivolezze ed imbrogli del teatro." Lorenzo Da Ponte, *Memorie*, 2nd edn, 3 vols. (New York, 1829–30), vol. 1, p. 115.

8 "La Paix procurée a la Monarchie, la Couronne Imperiale fixée de nouveau, les Pais-bas reduit, la Monarchie entiere et surtout les hongrois tranquillisés, l'Entousiasme du juste amour pour le Souverain exité et reveillé dans tous ces sujets par les actes de justice et de bienfaisance, les Mariages des deux archiduques; et celui de l'archiduchesse fixé a Naple enfin un nouvel ordre de chose aux dedans qu'aux dehors des affaires de la Monarchie, sont les objets qui ont marqué cette premiere année du Glorieux regne de V. M." Letter of Ferdinand to Leopold, 21 December 1790, Vienna, Haus-, Hof- und Staatsarchiv (henceforth abbreviated HHStA), Sammelbände, Kart. 19.

9 On Leopold's retreat from Josephinian reforms see Ernst Wangermann, *From Joseph II to the Jacobin Trials*, 2nd edn (London, 1969), where it is convincingly argued that Leopold made many of his concessions with the aim of preserving the most important reforms implemented by Maria Theresa and Joseph.

10 John A. Rice, "Vienna under Joseph II and Leopold II," in *The Classical Era*, ed. Neal Zaslaw (Englewood Cliffs, N.J., 1989), pp. 126–65 (159–60).

11 "Der Graf Ugarte als Musikgraf wird zwar unter dem Obersten Hofmeister stehen; in dem aber was die Theater Direction betrifft hat her lediglich von Mir allein abzuhangen." Marginal note by Leopold on a letter from Prince Starhemberg to Leopold, HHStA, Obersthofmeisteramt, Akten 1791, Nr. 165. The same series of documents includes Leopold's letter to Starhemberg announcing the appointment of Ugarte. Both letters are reproduced in Rice, "Emperor and Impresario," pp. 364–9.

12 Die Tomeoni kann, da sie dem Publico gefällt, auf 2. Jahre mit einer Zulage von 100.# zu ihrer itzegen Besoldung, wie auch ihr Mann, als Opern, und Ballet Komponist, mit 300.# Gehalt eben auf 2. Jahre engagiret werden...

Der Kapellmeister Salieri, wird a 1ma 9^{bris} zwar bey dem, was der dermalen bezieht, verbleiben, aber von der Theater direction gleichfalls dispensiret werden, bey welcher der einzige Veigel und wann diser verhindert seyn sollte, der Umlauf zu verbleiben haben wird, bloß zu accompagniren, und ohne jedoch etwas weder in der Austheilung deren Rollen noch bey der Trouppe zu sagen zu haben.

"Entwurf zu einer Allerhöchsten Resolution über den Vortrag des Musikgrafen v. Ugarte in Theatersachen," Vienna, HHStA, Handbilleten-Protokoll, 78b, Fol. 197r–202r. The document is published in Rice, "Emperor and Impresario," pp. 371–80.

13 These data and those in the following paragraph are derived from Franz Hadamowsky, *Die Wiener Hoftheater (Staatstheater) 1776–1966* (Vienna, 1966), vol. 1.

14 For a careful discussion of the chronology of the composition of *Die Zauberflöte*, see Peter Branscombe, *W. A. Mozart: Die Zauberflöte* (Cambridge, 1991), pp. 67–86.

15 Daniel Heartz, "Mozart and His Italian Contemporaries: 'La clemenza di Tito,'" *Mozart-Jahrbuch 1978/79*, pp. 275–93 (276). Writing from Munich during the production of *La finta giardiniera* (18 January 1775), Leopold Mozart used the terms "opera buffa" and "grosse Opera" to distinguish his son's comic opera from Antonio Tozzi's *Orfeo ed Euridice*.

16 "Wien, den 26ten Oktober. Ausser dem deutschen Theater und der italiänischen Opera Buffa, sollen auch italiänische grosse Opern hier aufgeführt werden. Es sind dazu einige Castraten aus Italien verschreiben worden." *Musikalisches Wochenblatt* (Berlin, 1791), p. 62.

17 According to an entry in HHStA, Rechnungsbuch 1791, p. 71.

18 "Der Bassist Gerl so im Schikanederisch. Theater singt wird zu vernehmen seyn wann er sich so viel als nöthig aus die Erlernung der italienisch. Sprache verlege, auf daß er bey der Opera verwendet werden könne, und er wird einsweilen bey der opera la vendetta di Nino als Hoher Priester und Schatten gebraucht werden können."
19 Hadamowsky, *Die Wiener Hoftheater*, p. 131.
20 "Madame *Lang*, die sich durch öftere Reisen in Deutschland als eine fertige und interessante Sängerinn bekannt gemacht hat, und ehedem schon beim National-theater in Wien engagirt war, ist nun wieder mit 400 Dukaten jährlichen Gehalts für die grosse Oper angenommen." *Musikalisches Wochenblatt*, p. 62.
21 According to the Köchel catalog, 7th edn (Wiesbaden, 1965), p. 455, a manuscript in the Gesellschaft der Musikfreunde, Vienna (Sign. IV 7751), contains four excerpts from Paisiello's *Fedra* featuring the characters named in the playbill together with Mozart's aria "No, che non sei capace." This manuscript presumably represents the contents of the Tonkünstler-Sozietät concert of April 1791. Since the excerpts are preserved in the order in which they occur in Paisiello's opera, we can assume that Lange sang Mozart's aria in place of Paisiello's "Tu pagherai la pena" (Act 2, Scene 11).
22 Lange seems to have preferred "No, che non sei capace," however. Not only did she sing it in 1791, it was still in her repertory in 1795, when she included it in a concert that she gave with her sister Constanze in the Leipzig Gewandhaus. See Otto Erich Deutsch, *Mozart: Die Dokumente seines Lebens* (Kassel, 1961), p. 419.
23 "bey der ⟨Langin⟩ war ich ein Narr, das ist wahr, aber was ist man nicht wenn man ⟨verliebt⟩ ist! – Ich liebte sie aber in der that, und fühle daß sie mir noch nicht gleichgültig ist –" Wilhelm A. Bauer, Otto Erich Deutsch, and Joseph Heinz Eibl, eds., *Mozart Briefe und Aufzeichnung*, 7 vols. (Kassel, 1962–75), vol. 3, p. 116. The words in angled brackets are in cipher in Mozart's manuscript.
24 "die Langin ist eine falsche, schlechtdenkende Personn, und eine Coquette." Ibid., p. 181.
25 "die Älteste ist eine faule, grobe, falsche Personn, die es dick hinter den ohren hat." Ibid., p. 181.
26 The dependability of Ignaz von Seyfried's reminiscences of Mozart's last year have been recently called into question by Peter Branscombe, *W. A. Mozart: Die Zauberflöte*, pp. 70–1, yet very little of what Seyfried said has been contradicted by other evidence; and the specificity of much of his information gives one the feeling that he was often telling the truth.
27 "Am Abend des 4ten Dec: lag M: schon im Fantasien, u: wähnte im Wiednertheater der Zauberflöte beizuwohnen; fast die letzten, seiner Frau zugeflüsterten Worte waren: 'Still! still! jetzt nimmt die Hofer das hohe F; – jetzt singt die Schwägerinn ihre zweyte Arie: "Der Hölle Rache"; wie kräftig sie das B anschlagt, u: aushält: "Hört! hört! hört! der Mutter Schwur!" –.'" Ignaz von Seyfried to Georg Friedrich Treitschke, in Deutsch, *Dokumente*, p. 472. English translation in Otto Erich Deutsch, *Mozart: A Documentary Biography*, trans. Eric Blom, Peter Branscombe, and Jeremy Noble (Stanford, 1965), p. 556.
28 *Mozart's Operas*, pp. 255–6.
29 Alfred Einstein, *Mozart: His Character, His Work* (New York, 1945), pp. 450–2; Branscombe, *W. A. Mozart: Die Zauberflöte*, pp. 18–20.
30 Köchel, 7th edn, p. 353.

31 See Heartz' provocative interpretation of Mozart's "sudden chromatic surges upwards" in *Mozart's Operas*, pp. 210–15.
32 Ibid., p. 329.
33 Ibid., pp. 318–41.
34 Heartz, "Mozart and his Italian Contemporaries," p. 292.
35 "ich schwöre ihnen bey meiner Ehre daß ich Salzburg und die ihnwonner |: ich rede von gebohrnen Salzburgern :| nicht leiden kann; – " *Mozart Briefe und Aufzeichnungen*, vol. 2, p. 536.

Epilogue

15

From fairy tale to opera in four moves (not so simple)

RICHARD TARUSKIN

Though I mean no disrespect to either, I seem to have a habit of linking Mozart and Prokofieff.[1] A genuine point of congruence between the two was transient involvement with the work of Carlo Gozzi (1720–1806), the Venetian theatrical fabulist. In both cases, the composer's interest was stimulated by a theatrical collaborator. In Mozart's case it was Schikaneder, at whose request he took time out from *Idomeneo* in 1780 to compose a recitative and aria for insertion into Gozzi's *Le due notte affannose*, which Schikaneder gave in German as *Peter der Grausame, oder Die zwei schlaflosen Nächte*.[2] It was a minor work, and now it is lost. But Schikaneder's own plays and libretti had many Gozzian resonances, too, *Die Zauberflöte* included. Some have been mentioned.[3] This paper will add a couple *en passant*.

Prokofieff's involvement with Gozzi went much further, though it was less direct. His opera *The Love for Three Oranges* is indebted, for its title and for the general outlines of its plot, to Gozzi's celebrated *fiaba* of 1761. It is, to be precise, an adaptation of an adaptation of Gozzi. But Gozzi's work was itself an adaptation. With each telling the tale became further encrusted with theatrical artifice and literary doctrine, even as the tellers advertised simplicity. The end product of this peculiar gestation, composed in New York by a Russian for performance in Chicago in French, was a prescient little exercise in the irony we take for granted in Modernist theater. So cozy and familiar are its distancing tactics by now that it is hard to recapture their strangeness, or to appreciate the archness of the composer's demurrer: "They found mockery and challenges and grotesques in my *Oranges*, while all I had done was write a merry show."[4] Behind the comic mask lay an icy countenance, a foretaste of the ban on all pathos that would dominate European art between the wars in the name of a reimagined, vicariously restored "eighteenth century." Never before, and never again, was Serge Prokofieff so clearly ahead of his time.

Yet a review of the successive adaptations of the oranges tale – something that has not yet been undertaken in any detail – will uncover considerable precedent in back of Prokofieff's brash modernity: not only the tradition of the tale itself, and not only the tradition of the commedia dell'arte on which Gozzi drew, but an immediate, local, and very characteristic precedent in St. Petersburg theatrical circles. Prokofieff's great success was in integrating music into an already existing compound of verbal text and miming. His comedy

Epilogue

subsists in the interaction between sight, sound, and word. "The punch lines of his jokes can come in any one of the three elements," America's leading Prokofievite has written, echoing the comment of an astonished critic that *The Love for Three Oranges* "scarcely makes even lunatic sense if not both heard and seen."[5] That is already enough to justify opera as a genre, which is more than many a fine composer has managed to do.

The parable of the three pieces of magic fruit and the prince who finds his true love inside one of them shows up in literature for the first time in 1634, as part of the earliest printed collection of European folk and fairy tales, *Il pentamerone*, subtitled *Lo cunto de li cunti* (The Tale of Tales), by Giambattista Basile, Conte de Torrone, who is believed to have collected its contents in Crete and Venice.[6] Written in the Neapolitan dialect, the collection was published over half a century before Perrault brought out his *Mother Goose*. Like Boccaccio's *Decamerone* (or the *1001 Nights*, or the *Canterbury Tales*), Basile's *Pentamerone* was organized around a running situation that motivated all of the stories it contained.

In this case the motivating device was a fable of a king with an unhappy daughter, Zoza, who never laughed. After trying all kinds of conventional pills to purge Zoza's melancholy without success, the king orders a large fountain of oil to be set in front of the palace gates, thinking that when the oil ran down the street it might cause some accident to amuse her. What finally gets Zoza to laugh is a mishap suffered by an old witch, who immediately places a curse on the princess for mocking her. The poor girl is forced on a quest for a handsome prince, Taddeo, whom she almost manages to discover and wed. But she is outsmarted at the last moment by a black slave girl named Lucia, who marries the prince in Zoza's place.

Through a series of ruses, in which she is aided by a trio of benign fairies, Zoza arouses in Lucia an insatiable appetite to hear stories. The Prince commands that the ten best storytellers in the kingdom be brought before him, and bids each tell one story a day for the next five days. The *Pentamerone* consists of the stories they tell, of which "The Three Citrons" (Le tre cetre) is the very last. The tale parallels Zoza's own story in such uncanny fashion that it frightens Lucia into admitting her treachery. She is executed and Zoza's quest is consummated.

The tale of the three citrons, which brings about this resolution, concerns a prince named Ciommetiello who, under a delusion, seeks a princess "the color of blood and cheese." He finds her in the third of three citrons given him by an ogress in a distant country to which his quest had led him. (All three citrons contained fairy princesses; the first two disappeared when the prince did not give them water in time.) The prince leaves the fairy princess to wait while he travels home to fetch her a bridal gown, whereupon a black slave girl – yes, her name is Lucia – frightens the princess off with a hair pin and takes her place. Lucia is duly crowned queen when the surprised but dimwitted Prince Ciommetiello is crowned king. The fairy princess, meanwhile, turns herself

From fairy tale to opera

into a dove, flies to Ciommetiello's kingdom, manages to have herself retransformed into a citron and thence into a maiden once more, exposes her rival, and reclaims her groom.

This harmless if not quite inoffensive dual fancy began its bizarre career as a theatrical hobbyhorse in the middle of the next century, when an impoverished Venetian aristocrat named Carlo Gozzi declared war in the name of art on Carlo Goldoni and Pietro Chiari, the reigning local dramatists. They were complementary figures, rivals: Goldoni was the virtuoso of bourgeois realism, Chiari a specialist in lofty melodrama. What united them was contempt for the antiquated freak show known as commedia dell'arte, which together they had almost succeeded in killing off. To Count Gozzi, resolute upholder of the older tradition, Goldoni and Chiari were but the two faces of a single plebeian coin: "commonplace and transparent inanities on the one hand, inanities sonorous and oracular upon the other."[7]

In his *Memorie inutile*, published near the end of his eighth decade, Gozzi tells us how Goldoni, master of "those vulgar scenes from life" that were polluting the taste of Venetian theatergoers, responded to his critic's sallies. Meeting Gozzi at the bookstore where the latter sold his diatribes and slanders, Goldoni opined that "it is one thing to write criticisms, another thing to compose dramas which shall fill the public theaters with enthusiastic audiences." Whereupon Gozzi boasted that he could put Goldoni and all his cohorts out of business by dramatizing the merest fairy tale in the very manner they despised most, that of the slapstick comedy of masks.[8]

And so he did. Within a year of the first performance of Gozzi's *L'amore delle tre melarance* – "The Love of the Three Oranges," as he retitled it – by Antonio Sacchi's commedia dell'arte troupe in the 1761 carnival season, Goldoni had to flee Venice for Paris. Over the next several years Gozzi produced nine more theatrical "fables" – including such other operatic familiars as *La donna serpente* (Wagner, *Die Feen*), *Turandot* (Busoni, Puccini, not to mention Weber's incidental score to Schiller's translation) and *Il re cervo* (Henze, *König Hirsch*) – and singlehandedly revived the moribund commedia. For a couple of decades he was regarded everywhere in Europe as the wonder of the theatrical world. Dr. Johnson's crony Joseph Baretti placed him second only to Shakespeare.[9]

Unlike the later *fiabe*, *The Love of the Three Oranges* was just a scenario for commedia dell'arte improvisation, not a fully written-out script. Although Gozzi's memoirs, as well as the preface to the play, seem to imply that its source was just a bedtime story everyone knew, we can tell that Gozzi relied on Basile. His plot actually conflates the tale of the three citrons with that of Princess Zoza, Basile's linking tool. His prince-protagonist Tartaglia, like Zoza, is a melancholic who cannot laugh, and who is both cured (inadvertently) and cursed (deliberately) by a witch who suffers a mishap as a result of the fountain gag (in Gozzi's version there are two fountains: one spouting oil, the other wine, both rancid – Goldoni and Chiari again). It is the peculiarly humiliating

301

curse that determined Gozzi's strange title: the witch condemns the prince to fall in love with three oranges – "three particular oranges, not just any oranges" – and chase them to the distant corners of the earth. It is only when the oranges are opened that Tartaglia's love-object becomes human(oid).

Because he was adapting Basile's tales to the conventions of the commedia dell'arte, Gozzi had to make room in his version for a large number of traditional masks. Tartaglia himself was one. Others included Pantalone (cast as an adviser to the king), the lusty wenches Smeraldina and Brighella (cast as servant henchmen of Tartaglia's enemies, Smeraldina taking over the role of the black slave girl), and, of course, Truffaldino. The last-named, a species of Arlecchino, was the mask worn by Antonio Sacchi himself, and figures as a major character in every one of Gozzi's *fiabe*. In *The Love of the Three Oranges*, Truffaldino is the jester who first tries to cure Tartaglia's melancholia, then accompanies him, Sancho Panza fashion, in his quest. During the heyday of Gozzi's popularity in Germany, the Tartaglia-Truffaldino pair provided Schikaneder with a model for Tamino and Papageno in another theatrical quest fable that, thanks to Mozart, has eclipsed the fame of its prototype. (In *Il re cervo* Truffaldino is actually a bird-catcher.)

As for Gozzi's witch, she is the ubiquitous Fata Morgana, who figures by name in a number of Basile's Neapolitan tales. She is provided with a benign counterpart, the magus Celio, who helps Tartaglia gain his objective. The two rival supernaturals – cf. Sarastro and the Queen of the Night – are the only characters for whom Gozzi provided fully written-out speeches in the scenario, and here is where the literary satire most obviously shows through. Fata Morgana's bombastic "Martellian" verses parody Chiari, while the folksy Celio is Goldoni's surrogate. Erudite burlesque reaches its height in a little set piece in Act 2 – Gozzi called it the "quarrel trio" (contrasto in terzo) – in which three masked characters, plotting against Tartaglia, fall into a dispute about dramatic values. Clarice declares her preference for "tragic performances, in which you find characters hurling themselves from windows or turrets without breaking their necks, and similar miracles" ("Idest Opere del sig. Chiari," Gozzi duly notes in parentheses); Leandro plumps for comedies of manners ("Idest Opere del sig. Goldoni"); Brighella, the author's stand-in, pleads for "the improvised comedy of masks, an innocent popular diversion."

"Oh, what a lot he's given me!" wrote Vsevolod Meyerhold to a friend who had made him a gift of Gozzi's works in 1912.[10] The great director (1874–1940) had already been trying for some years to resurrect the art of theatrical improvisation, having become as disgusted as Gozzi had been with the dual debasement of the theater by purveyors of vaulting melodrama or petty naturalism. By the next year he had instituted a veritable academy of histrionics all'improviso in his St. Petersburg studio, where his friend Vladimir Solovyov gave practical demonstrations of commedia dell'arte techniques and taught them to Meyerhold's pupils. So carried away were the two of them with *The*

Love of the Three Oranges, the most elaborate document ever printed of the commedia dell'arte in action, that (together with a scholarly co-conspirator named Konstantin Vogak) they adapted it for performance in Russian. A performance was planned for October 1913, but it did not take place since the collaborators could not get a composer to join them at the time. ("I've grown cool toward Strauss," Meyerhold wrote Solovyov, as if he could have had the celebrated German for the asking. "We need a Frenchman. Or else one of the latest Russians.")[11] In the 1914–15 season Meyerhold staged the piece, without music, at the Tenishev *gimnaziya* in St. Petersburg. As an official employee of the imperial theaters, he had to do his experimental work under a pseudonym, for which purpose he appropriated the name of E. T. A. Hoffmann's Doctor Dapertutto. So central had Gozzi and his scenario become to "Dr. Dapertutto's" aesthetic program that Meyerhold launched a little magazine to propagandize his ideas, called it *Love for Three Oranges; or, Doctor Dapertutto's Journal* (*Lyubov' k tryom apel'sinam, zhurnal Doktora Dapertutto*), and published his translation in the first issue (January 1914).[12]

Meyerhold and his collaborators took Gozzi's "quarrel trio" as their jumping off point. It grew enormously in their conception to become, both temporally and spatially, the frame of the entire play. The spatial frame was to consist of twin turrets on opposite sides of the stage, housing a collection of clowns representing aesthetes of differing and antagonistic persuasions. The action was to commence with a parade, in which the actors portraying the aesthetes – divided into camps of "Realistic Comedians" (*bytovïye komiki*) and "High Tragedians" (*sugubïye tragiki*) – would enter duelling with quills. The fight was to be broken up by a trio of Cranks (*chudaki*). One, restraining the comedians, shouts: "We are fed up with your wares, contemptible farce-mongers, these four- and five-act comedies without any content at all, but with the inevitable pistol shot at the end!" Another, holding off the tragedians, thunders: "We are bored to death with plays that have such a load of dreary philosophy and such a dearth of healthy laughter, to say nothing of stagecraft!" The third, pointing at the audience, was to say, "Look – they are waiting there for some actors who can show them the real thing!" The battle, thus joined, would continue in an undertone (and with frequent eruptions) throughout the play; the aesthetes' constant comment on the action, and their strenuous exhortations to the actors, would furnish the temporal frame.

Meyerhold's *Lyubov' k tryom apel'sinam* was one of the very earliest applications of the illusion-destroying "art as art" gimmickry that would within a couple of decades become a Modernist cliché. What makes it historically so significant is the clarity of its descent from a cynical eighteenth-century aristocratic model. Even if Prokofieff had never set it, Meyerhold's response to Gozzi would have been a prime document of the nascent Modernist manner and its sources.

Thanks to Prokofieff it is much more than a document. He and Meyerhold met in late 1916 at the Petrograd apartment of Albert Coates, the English

Epilogue

conductor, who then headed the conducting staff for opera at the Mariyinsky (later the Kirov) Theater. Coates was then organizing the production of an iconoclastic (though in Russia not unprecedented) opera-in-recitatives the twenty-five-year-old composer had written to a libretto he had drawn himself from Dostoyevsky's novella *The Gambler*. Meyerhold, then a staff director at the Maryinsky, recognized in Prokofieff the "new Russian" he had been looking for, and offered on the spot to take over the direction of *The Gambler* from an older regisseur who was finding it unmanageable.

This collaboration did not materialize: the February Revolution of 1917 put an end to plans for producing new operas in Petrograd that season. It was only the first of many aborted collaborations between Meyerhold and Prokofieff, who over the next twenty-three years embarked on many joint ventures yet never saw a single one of them through to performance. What might have been a comedy of errors abruptly turned to tragedy in 1939, when the director was arrested and condemned weeks before the slated premiere of their final collaborative project, the opera *Semyon Kotko*.

After the Bolshevik coup in October, Prokofieff decided to emigrate to the New World by way of Siberia and Japan. Disappointed yet still taking a hopeful long view, Meyerhold "gave Prokofieff the first issue of our journal *Love for Three Oranges* on the very eve of his departure for America," as he wrote Solovyov, meanwhile "exhorting him to write an opera on our scenario. He said, 'I'll read it on the boat.'"[13] Prokofieff arrived in San Francisco with some notes toward a libretto in hand. (He was a man of real literary gifts, as anyone knows who has read his autobiography.) Having secured a commission from Cleofante Campanini, the director of the Chicago Opera, who had wanted to produce *The Gambler* but was unable to obtain the materials from revolutionary Petrograd, the composer went to work on the opera early in 1919, and delivered it on the first of October. It took more than two years before the work achieved production, owing in the first place to Campanini's sudden death, but in the second to Prokofieff's impossible demands (he insisted on compensation for the delay in implementing the contract). Mary Garden, who took over the directorship of the Chicago company, finally agreed to the composer's terms, and the opera was given under his baton on 30 December 1921, with Nina Koshetz in the role of Fata Morgana.[14] Its enormously successful Soviet premieres took place in 1926 (Leningrad, Academic Theater – the former Maryinsky – with Ivan Yershov as Truffaldino) and 1927 (Moscow, Bolshoi Theater under Golovanov, with Nadezhda Obukhova as Clarice and Antonina Nezhdanova as Ninetta). These triumphs – coupled with the fiasco in the West of his next opera, *The Fiery Angel* – played a significant part in persuading Prokofieff to come home to Russia in the 1930s.

Compared with Meyerhold's scenario, the opera shows a bit of streamlining. The character Brighella is eliminated; the protectors of the oranges (a gate, a rope, a dog, and a cook) are reduced to just the cook (modeled in Prokofieff's score after the male-voiced witch in *Hänsel und Gretel*, and equipped with a threatening ladle). Only one reference to the old Venetian disputes survives in the libretto, and it is probably unwitting: Leander, plotting with Clarice to worsen the Prince's hypochondria (Act 1, Scene 3), recommends a diet of booming "Martellian verses." The composer made other minor alterations as well: Ninetta, the fairy princess, is briefly turned before Prokofieff's denouement not into a dove but, more incongruously, into a rat; the Act 1 card game between Fata Morgana and Celio (a notorious dramaturgical stumbling block) was entirely Prokofieff's idea.

The biggest change, though, was the hugely expanded role accorded the Greek chorus of on-stage spectators – the very thing Meyerhold and his colleagues had already so notably expanded from Gozzi's little "quarrel trio." To Meyerhold's Comedians, Tragedians, and Cranks (the latter numbering three in thescenario, ten in the opera), Prokofieff added groups of "Lyricists" (*Liriki*), forever demanding "romantic love, moons, tender kisses," and "Empty Heads" (*Pustogolovïye*), bent on "entertaining nonsense, witty double entendres, fine costumes." In this way he thought to cover every possible sort of hackneyed operatic situation – what in Russian is still called *vampuka* after a famous grand-opera lampoon first produced at a St. Petersburg cabaret in 1909 – and the sort of taste that demanded it. Prokofieff's Comedians, Tragedians, Lyricists, and Empty Heads butt in whenever the action approaches one of their pet stereotypes to egg it on, in the process puncturing whatever mood they were abetting.

The Cranks, eager to foil all factions (but particularly the Tragedians), do more than that. They actually intervene in the plot, Pirandello-fashion (but before Pirandello!), change its course, and utterly destroy all stage-illusion. It is they, not the Prince, who come up with the water that saves Ninetta's life. It is they, not Celio, who abduct Fata Morgana to one of the onstage towers and enable the good sorcerer to transform the giant rat back into the fairy princess in time for the wedding. The play, literally, is their plaything. (And art, so the composer implies, is ours.)

Notwithstanding its sublimated eighteenth-century inspiration, Prokofieff's *Love for Three Oranges* deserves recognition as one of the first harbingers of a true twentieth-century aesthetic. Like *The Gambler*, it is cast in what Prokofieff called a "declamatory" style; but ("taking the American temper into account," as he put it in his autobiography[15]), the composer provided a few more obviously lyrical moments cast in fugitive rounded forms (though the great love duet seemingly promised and musically anticipated in the desert scene is foiled when the Lyricists break into a distracting paean in praise of love duets), and there are a couple of diverting, now famous, instrumental showpieces (the march in Act 2, the scherzo in Act 3).

The musical style derives from Rimsky-Korsakov's *Golden Cockerel* by way of Stravinsky's *Petrushka*: its nub and essence is the exploitation of the harmonic possibilities of paired triads with roots a tritone apart. These harmonies function variously as a cadential succession (as in the opening announcement, in the Prologue, of the start of the show), as a vertical

Epilogue

"polychord" (at moments of horror; e.g., the curse music in Act 2, Scene 2) or as the governors of a bipolar tonal plan (as in the Act 3 scherzo).

When the temporarily forgotten opera was given its earliest postwar revivals (especially the Ljubljana revival of 1956 that traveled to the Holland Festival and was recorded there),[16] it was the presciently multileveled, distanced action that amazed. Musicians were struck, moreover, by the mutually validating affinity between the ironically detached, constantly interrupted antics on stage and the idiosyncratically discontinuous structure of the score.[17] Unlike many modern classics, moreover, it is easy to like: it was one of the early epitomes of a revolution in taste that cultivated hygienic belly laughs to replace the neurasthenic wheezing of prewar decadence, a therapeutic to counteract late Romanticism's gangrenous grandiosity. The emblematic moment, just as it was for Gozzi, is the scene of the hypochondriac's cure: at the sight of Fata Morgana's knobby knees and withered behind, Tartaglia goes into gales of laughter, represented in the music by a little set piece over an ostinato – and with the Prince's "ha-ha-ha-HA," an inevitable parody of the opening unison in... need I say what? Now that the Modernist tradition has itself gone as puffy and decadent as the opere del sig. Chiari, perhaps it is time once again to avail ourselves of Prokofieff's buffered multivitamins.

NOTES

As a tribute to my colleague Daniel Heartz I offer a counterpart to chapters 1, 6, and 13 of his recent collection, *Mozart's Operas* (Berkeley and Los Angeles, 1990). Like those, this essay was originally written on commission from an opera house and published in its program magazine (*English National Opera Programme* [December 1989]). It has been revised and expanded, and lightly annotated, for its appearance here.

1 See "Tradition and Authority," first given as a talk at the symposium, "Performing Mozart's Music," in the Juilliard Theater, Lincoln Center, New York, on 24 May 1991, and published in *Early Music* 20 (1992): 311–25.
2 "Warum, o Liebe, treibst du jenen grausamen Kurzweil – Zittre, töricht' Herz und leide," K.365a; see Heartz, *Mozart's Operas*, p. 256.
3 E.g., by Edward Dent in *Mozart's Operas: A Critical Study*, 2nd edn (London, 1947), p. 222n.
4 Serge Prokofieff, "Avtobiografiya," in Semyon Isaakovich Shlifshteyn, ed., *S. S. Prokof'yev: Materialï, dokumentï, vospominaniya*, 2nd edn (Moscow, 1961), p. 177.
5 Malcolm H. Brown, review of Serge Prokofieff, *L'Amour des trois oranges*, opus 33, *MLA Notes* 39 (1982–3): 468; Donald Mitchell, "Prokofieff's 'Three Oranges': A Note on its Musical-Dramatic Organisation," *Tempo* no. 41 (1956): 20.
6 The editions I consulted were *Il Pentamerine* [sic] *del cavalier Giovan Battista Basile; overo, Lo cunto de li cunte, trattenimento de li piccerille di Gian Alesio* (Naples, 1697), and *Il Pentamerone; or, The tale of tales, being a translation by Sir Richard Burton...from Giovanni Battiste Basile* (New York, 1943).
7 *Useless Memoirs of Carlo Gozzi*, trans. John Addington Symonds (London, 1962), p. 168.
8 Ibid., p. 181.

9 Ted Emery, "Carlo Gozzi in Context," Introduction to Carlo Gozzi, *Five Tales for the Theatre*, trans. Albert Bermel and Ted Emery (Chicago, 1989), p. 1.
10 To S. S. Ignatov, 14 March 1912; V. E. Meyerhold, *Perepiska* (Moscow, 1976), p. 143.
11 Meyerhold, *Perepiska*, p. 154.
12 I am indebted to the Lilly Library of Indiana University for a photocopy of this bibliographical rarity, procured with the kind assistance of Malcolm H. Brown.
13 Letter of 18 February 1926; Meyerhold, *Perepiska*, p. 388.
14 Prokofieff, "Avtobiografiya," pp. 166ff. In the midst of rehearsal, Prokofieff recalled, when he was having difficulties making himself understood, one of the choristers shouted to him from the stage, "Why are you struggling with English – half of us here are Russian Jews!" (p. 170).
15 Prokofieff, "Avtobiografiya," pp. 164–5.
16 The recording was issued in America on Epic records (4 SC-6013).
17 See the article by Donald Mitchell cited in note 5.

Index

Abert, Hermann, 270n7–8, 270n12
Abos, Girolamo, 218
Abraham, Gerald, 267
Adorno, Theodor, 76, 88n56
Aeschylus, 220
aesthetic(s), 8, 15, 35, 57, 68, 94, 189, 201, 217, 221, 236, 303, 305
affections, 93, 227
Agricola, Johann Friedrich, 219
Algarotti, Francesco, 91, 93, 219, 221, 223, 227, 236, 239n23
allegory, 249
Altick, Richard, 63–4, 80n5
amateurs, 49–52
Amory, Thomas, 28–9, 40n13
amour-propre, 247–50
ancient music, cult of, 2, 45–52; versus modern music, 58n6
Anfossi, Pasquale, 127, 281
Angiolini, Gasparo, 2, 189–92, 196–201, 205, 207, 210, 212–13, 215–16, 223, 228, 275
antiquity, 46, 196, 214n22
Arcadia, 23–33, 36–41
Arcadian reform, 126
aria (air), 8, 30, 33–5, 95–102, 119–26, 129, 138–41, 199, 221, 248–9, 265, 286–7; borrowings, 2, 97, 125–6, 142–50, 156–7, 169–87, 174; cavatina-cabaletta, 153; continuo, 144; da capo, 140, 144, 147, 157–8, 160–2, 164–5; dal segno, 140, 166; *di bravura*, 281–4; exit, 140; in ballet, 205; modified da capo, 155; *preghiere*, 279; rondo, 174; stretta in, 265–7; vengeance, 159; with action, 121–2, 125–6; with chorus, 195; with obbligato, 144; with *pertichini*, 126, 129; with recitative, 126–7, 157–8; without exit, 122, 128, 140; *see also* ariette; cavatina; coloratura; ritornello; vaudeville
ariette, 8, 140, 155, 157, 186
arioso, 97, 120–1, 123, 126, 140, 147, 152, 155, 158, 160–1
Aristotelian precepts, 7, 12, 93
Armide (Armida), 32–3, 127–8
audiences, 1–2, 7–11, 13, 15, 46, 48–9, 51, 57; for ballet, 189, 191; for *Der Freischütz*, 70–4; for opera seria, 92, 119, 120, 126, 227; for phantasmagoria and panoramas, 61–8, 71, 75, 80n5; French, 223–5, 236–7, 257n3; taste of, 135, 138–9; Venetian, 301
Auerbach, Erich, 248
Aureli, Aurelio, 218
Avison, Charles, 49

Bach, Johann Samuel, 32, 35
ballet, 2–3, 75, 119, 123–5, 128–9, 221, 227, 239n23; actions (scenario), 191; borrowings, 225; *en action*, 199, 208; finale, 201; Gluck's *Zéphire et Flore*, 189–216; reform, 189; troupe (Burgtheater), 275, 278; *see also* choreographer; dance; *divertissement*
Ballière de Laisement, Denis, 199
Baretti, Joseph, 301
Barlocci, Giovanni, 218
Baroque, 92, 99, 135
Basile, Giambattista, Conte de Torrone, 300–2
Bâton, Charles (le jeune), 115
Baudron, Antione-Laurent, 243, 247, 250–2, 257
Beaumarchais, Pierre-Augustin Caron de, 3, 243, 247, 252, 257, 258n4, 259n18–19
Becker, Wolfgang, 70, 84, 86, 88

308

Index

Beethoven, Ludwig van, 49, 54, 252; *Fidelio*, 73, 76, 86n39
Benserade, Isaac de, 214n28
Berlioz, Hector, 75
Berton, Pierre Montan, 218, 238n20
Bertoni, Ferdinando, 179, 186, 219, 238n8
Bianchi, Francesco, 127–9
bienséance, 198
Blondy, Michel, 199
Boccaccio, Giovanni, 300
Bodin, Pierre and Louise, 216n38
Bononcini, Giovanni, 59n26; *Serse*, 2, 135, 139–52, 155–9, 161–2, 167
Boquet, Louis-René, 110–11
borrowing, *see*, aria; ballet; dramatic; musical; overture; recitative
Botticelli, Sandro, 12
Boyce, Dr. William, 53–4
Branscombe, Peter, 285
Bruce, Marinda, 28–9
Brumoy, Le Père, 220, 222
burlesque, 302
Burney, Dr. Charles, 43–6, 54–8, 60; on Handel, 138, 144–5, 153–5, 160, 164, 168, 187
Burney, Edward Francesco, 2, 46–7, 49–57, 59n14
Burney, Fanny, 58n4
Busoni, Ferruccio Benvenuto, 301
Byrd (Birde), William, 49

Caffarelli, *see* Majorano, Gaetano
Cahusac, Louis de, 106
Caldara, Antonio, 121, 218, 220
Calvesi, Vincenzo, 280
Calzabigi, Ranieri de', 91, 189, 207, 210, 223
Campanini, Cleofante, 304
Campra, André, 218, 238n20, 244
Capece, Carlo, 218
Carducci, Giosuè, 13
Carl Theodor, Palatine Elector and Duke of Bavaria, 120
Casanova, Giovanni Giacomo, 213
Caspar, Franz von, 70, 83n26
Castiglione, Baldassare, 14
Castle, Terry, 80n4
castrati, 139, 278

Cavalli, Pietro Francesco, 2, 135, 138, 140, 167n27
cavatina, 122–9, 140, 144, 158–9, 164, 229
Cecilia, Saint, 48, 56
ceremony, 94
Český Krumlov, 192, 195, 200
Champée, Bonifacius Carl, 192, 214n20
Chatsworth, Duke of Devonshire, 25
Chiari, Pietro, 301–2, 306
chiaroscuro, 212
Chodowiecki, Daniel, 29, 38
Chompre, Pierre, 196–7, 213n15–16
choreographers, 197, 210; choreography, 205, 210, 214n22
chorus, 30, 94–5, 119–21, 123, 128–9, 140, 173, 221, 229, 233, 236, 239n23, 265, 285–6; coro, 103, 157; da capo, 94; French, 2, 105–18; gestures of, 110–12, 115; Greek, 305; stage action of, 106, 112–13; with solo, 102–3, 285
Chrysander, Friedrich, 167n9
Cigna-Santi, Vittorio Amadeo, 127, 219, 238n8
cities: Berlin, 67, 71–4, 77, 221; Chicago, 304; Dresden, 70–1, 74, 77; Florence (Florentine), 8–9, 12–13, 16, 18, 127, 129; Hamburg, 31; Hannover, 33; Karlsruhe, 73; Leipzig, 67; London, 62–3, 67, 73, 135, 168–70, 178, 180; Ljubljana, 306; Milan, 120, 125, 127–8; Mannheim, 119–20, 122, 126–7, 223; Mantua, 8, 18; Moscow, 304; Munich, 120, 128, 272; Naples (Neapolitan), 127–9, 302; Paris (Parisian), 62–3, 67, 75, 105–15, 122, 125, 179, 185, 195, 198, 217, 250, 292; Parma, 121, 126; Prague, 169–70, 173, 178; Rome, 23; Saint Petersburg, 200, 299, 302–3, 305; Salzburg, 285, 290–3; Stuttgart, 119, 126; Turin, 127; Versailles, 105, 198; Vienna (Viennese), 74, 122, 126, 128, 178, 186, 189, 191–2, 200, 205, 207, 210, 223, 227, 271–93; Venice, 7, 9, 17–18, 127–9, 139
Classical, 26, 32–3, 92, 212; drama, 94, 220, 223; musical style, 99, 267

309

Index

Clubb, Louise, 11, 15, 17
Coates, Albert, 303–4
Cody, Richard, 13, 15, 17
Coletti, Agostino, 218
Collasse, Pascal, 109–10, 215n28, 244
Colloredo, Hieronymus, Archbishop of, 149
coloratura, 147, 152–3, 183, 282
Coltellini, Marco, 128, 219, 223, 239n23
comedy, 11, 15, 243–4, 247, 249, 257, 303; of masks, 302; operatic, 141–2, 299–300
commedia dell'arte, 299, 301–3
conductor, *see maestro di cappella*
continuo, 105, 157, 165
copyist, 168, 183, 192
Corelli, Arcangelo, 45, 48–9
Corneille, Pierre, 93, 121
Correggio, Niccolò, 12
costumes, 95, 108, 110, 191
Crown, Patricia, 50, 52, 56, 59n14
Crusius, Siegfried Lebrecht, 38
culture, 126; educated European, 13–15, 74–6; French, 223; middle class, 61; popular, 2, 13, 61–4, 68, 74–6

Daguerre, Louis, 75, 80n5
dance, 7, 33, 51, 117n28, 120, 212, 221, 224
  forms: chaconne (ciacona), 97, 103, 205; gigue, 98, 144, 161, 165; minuet, 95, 102–3, 165, 168, 173–8, 196; passepied, 102; sarabande, 98
  movements, instrumental, 94–5, 144, 196
  rhythms, 144
dancers, 105, 113, 191, 197–8, 200, 205, 208, 210
Danchet, Antoine, 128, 218
Da Ponte, Lorenzo, 141, 261, 273, 276–7
deus ex machina, 220, 224
death, 23–4, 27–8, 31, 33, 39, 65; staged, 123-7–129
Defoe, Daniel, 56
De la Touche, Guimond, 219, 222, 225, 227–8, 237, 238n20
Della Viola, Gian Pietro, 12

demonic (demons), 48–9, 65, 70–3, 77–8, 113; *see also* devil
dénouement, 224, 305
Dent, Edward J., 1, 162, 260–1, 263, 268
De Sanctis, Francesco, 10
Desmarets, Henri, 218, 238n20
devil, 48–9, 56, 73–4, 77, 261
Didelot, Charles, 200
Diderot, Denis, 24, 221, 223, 236, 239n28, 247
divertissement, 33, 113, 199, 208, 215n28, 224, 243–4
divine intervention, 224–5
Doni, Giovanni Battista, 10–11
drama, Greek, 217–22; spoken, 3, 7, 224–5, 299
dramatic, action, 225, 227, 261; borrowings, 225; gestures, 110; symbolism, 247, 261; tension, 225
dramaturgy, 9, 92, 97, 99, 103, 126, 196, 279, 305
Du Bos, Abbé, 26, 28, 29, 32, 36–7, 39, 40n13
Du Boullay, Michel, 197, 199
Duché, Joseph François, 218
duet, 3, 30, 35, 122–5, 128, 139, 144, 147, 155, 157, 162, 166, 186, 261–9, 305; with *pertichino*, 123
Duparc, Elizabeth (Francesina), 163, 165
Durandi, Jacopo, 127
Durazzo, Count Giacomo, 215n36, 223, 238n20; Collection, 191, 205, 214n24
Du Roullet, Bailli, 219, 223–5, 236, 239n30–1
Dutillieu, Pietro, 275

eighteenth century, 1–3, 25, 29, 39, 105, 220, 243, 299, 303, 305
Einstein, Alfred, 285
Enlightenment, 1, 24, 29, 35, 140, 222
ensemble, 126, 128–9, 140–1, 221, 239n23; action in, 122–6; of fluctuating personnel, 122–7; of opposition, 155; *see also* duet; finale; quartet; quintet; sextet; trio
Eszterházy, Prince Paul Anton, 213n19
ethics, 94, 217

310

Index

Euripides, 217-18, 220-1, 223-4, 227-8

fairies, 7, 300
Favart, Charles Simon, 199, 210, 215n36, 222, 225, 238n20
favola (fabula), 12, 17; *boscareccia*, 11; *(fiaba)*, 299, 302; *pastorale*, 11-12; *see also* folk tale
Faustus, Dr. 48, 55-6
Favier, Jean, 200
Ferdinand, Archduke of Austria, Governor of Milan, 274
Ferrarese, Adriana, 276
Ficino, Marsilio, 12, 13, 15
finale, 2, 76, 95, 103, 128, 201, 261, 263; action, 123-5, 127
Fleury, N., 258n3
Flud, Dr. Robert, 52
Fogliazzi Angiolini, Maria Teresa, 191, 197-8, 205, 208, 213n17, 216n38
folk tale, 68, 300
Foppa, Giuseppe, 128
Förtsch, Johann Philipp, 166
Foucault, Michel, 12, 18
Fragonard, Jean-Honoré, 212n4
Francesina, *see* Duparc, Elizabeth
Franchi, Carlo, 219, 238n8
Francœur, François, 198
Frankfurt, 67, 286
Frederick II, Emperor of Prussia, 221
Freud, Sigmund, 13
Frugoni, Carlo Innocenzo, 126-7
Furies, 227, 229
Fuzelier, Louis, 199

galant, 189, 191, 196, 199, 210, 212
Galuppi, Baldassare, 169, 187n8, 188n19, 219
Gamerra, Giovanni de, 128
Garden, Mary, 304
Gasparini, Carlo Francesco, 142
Gellert, Christian Fürchtegott, 35
Geminiani, Francesco, 45, 48-9
Genest, Abbé, 215n28
George III, King of England, 43
Gerl, Franz, 277-8, 295n18
ghosts *(Erscheinungen)*, 62, 64-7, 70, 72, 74-6, 77, 79, 82n13, 83n24, 222, 227, 229, 261

Giardini, Felice, 168
Gillray, James, 51
Giordani, Giuseppe, 127, 218
Giovannini, Pietro, 130n30
Girelli, Antonia Maria, 186
Gluck, Christoph Willibald, 1-2, 33-4, 91, 94, 104n10, 119, 125-6, 129, 189, 217, 268
  ballets: *Les Amours d'Alexandre et de Roxane*, 205; *Citera assediata*, 210, 216n39; *Don Juan*, 207, 227, 268-9; *Iphigénie*, 223; *Sémiramis*, 212, 223, 225, 229-33, 236; *Zéphire et Flore*, 189-216
  borrowing from Handel, 168-88
  model for Mozart, 268-9, 270n14
  operas: *Achille in Sciro*, 203, 215n33; *Alceste*, 119, 227, 269; *Antigono*, 179; *Armide*, 203, 224; *Le Cadi dupé*, 196; *La caduta de' giganti*, 180; *La clemenza di Tito*, 169, 178-9; *La contesa de'numi*, 179; *Cythère assiégée*, 196; *Demofoonte*, 168-70, 186; *Echo et Narcisse*, 224; *La Fausse esclave*, 180, 183, 186, 188n25; *Le feste d'Apollo*, 179; *L'Île de Merlin*, 227; *Iphigénie en Aulide*, 196, 217, 219, 224-5; *Iphigénie en Tauride*, 179, 186, 217, 219, 224-37; *Issipile*, 169, 173-9; *Le nozze d'Ercole e d'Ebe*, 179; *Orfeo ed Euridice*, 212, 215n33, 223, 227; *Orphée et Eurydice*, 179, 196; *Paride ed Elena*, 223; *La Rencontre imprévue*, 196; *Semiramide riconosciuta*, 178; *Telemaco*, 179; *Il trionfo di Clelia*, 195-6
Goethe, Johann Wolgang von, 31, 61, 72, 83n27
Golden Age, 3, 23-4, 45, 271-5, 291-2
Goldoni, Carlo, 3, 258n4, 301-2
Goldsmith, Oliver, 172
Galovanov, Nikolay, 304
Gossec, François-Joseph, 240n33
Gothic, references, 46, 48, 52-3; novels, 63, 65
Gounod, Charles, 74-5
Gozzi, Carlo, 299, 301-3
Graun, Carl Heinrich, 219, 221

311

Index

Gresset, Jean Baptiste, 37
Grétry, André, 240n33
Grimm, Friedrich Melchior von, 113, 222–3, 225, 238n11, 240n36–7
Gropius, Carl Wilhelm, 71–2, 83n27, 85n36, 87n48
ground bass, 158, 160–1
Guarini, Giambattista, 10–11, 25, 31
Guercino, Giovanni, Francesco, 23–5, 28, 37–8, 39n2
Guglielmi, Pietro, 127–8, 276
Guillard, Nicolas-François, 219, 225, 229, 233
Gumpenhuber, Philipp, 200

Hagen, Oskar, 166
Handel, George Frideric, 1–2, 43–6, 49, 51–2, 55, 57–60
  Gluck borrowing from, 168–88
  instrumental music, Concerto Grosso in B♭ opus 6, no. 7, 158
  operas: *Admeto*, 156, 160; *Agrippina*, 135, 140, 145, 160; *Alcina*, 156; *Alessandro*, 180, 183, 185; *Arianna, in Creta*, 168, 170, 173–8, 187; *Berenice*, 144, 156; *Faramondo*, 142, 165; *Giulio Cesare*, 135, 164, 173; *Giustino*, 140; *Orlando*, 162; *Partenope*, 135, 145; *Riccardo Primo*, 164; *Serse*, 2, 135–67; *Tamerlano*, 142
  oratorios, odes, cantatas: *Alexander's Feast*, 144; *Athalia*, 162; *Clori, mia bella Clori*, 144; *Israel in Egypt*, 145; *Saul*, 162, 164, 167n15
  sources and editions, 164–6
Hasse, Johann Adolf, 95–6, 103–4, 145, 169
Hatzfeld, Count August, 260
Hawkins, Sir John, 45, 52–3, 55–7
Haydn, Franz Joseph, 49, 126, 130n20
Heartz, Daniel, 1, 3, 92, 116n1, 8, 118n32, 264–5, 285, 287, 292, 293n2, 296n31
Hegel, Georg, 17
Henze, Hans Werner, 301
Herz, Joachim, 166
Hildesheimer, Wolfgang, 260–1
Hiller, Johann Adam, 33, 35, 38

Hilverding, Franz, 190, 197–201, 205, 210, 214n24, 215n36, 275
Hirsch, E. D., 13
Hofer, Josepha, 281–4, 295n27
Hoffmann, E. T. A., 72–3, 83n27, 86n42–4, 261, 303
Hogarth, William, 24, 50
Horace, 220
Hortschansky, Klaus, 179
humanism, 10, 24

imagery, 55–6
incidental music, 243
intermèdes, 215n28, 243
intermezzo, 160
introduzione, 125, 127–8, 225, 263
Iphigenia (Ifigenia), 2, 217–40
irony, 249–50, 299, 306

Jacobi, Johann Georg, 32
Johnson, Dr. Samuel, 301
Jommelli, Niccolò, 33, 119–21, 123, 130n5, 169, 188n19, 219, 238n8, 239n23
Joseph II, Emperor of Austria, 286

Kaufmann, Angelika, 29, 40n13
Keate, George, 29–31, 35, 37, 39, 41n14
Keats, John, 141
Keiser, Reinhard, 42
Kelly, Michael, 2, 186
Kerll, Johann Kaspar, 173
Khevenhüller-Metsch, Johann Joseph, 190
Kind, Friedrich, 70–1
Kircher, Athanasius, 62, 65
Koshetz, Nina, 304
Kron, Wolfgang, 86n43

Lampe, Frederick, 56
Landi, Stefano, 219
Lange (Weber), Aloysia, 280–4, 295n21–5, 295n20–7
Laujon, Pierre, 113, 199
Laval, Michel Jean de, 112–13
Legrand, Claude, 128
Leo, Leonardo, 188n19
Leopold II, Emperor of Austria, 3, 271–80, 286, 292

Index

Lessing, Gotthold Ephraim, 24
Lewis, M. G., 65
Lichtenstein, Hinrich, 77
lieto fine (happy ending), 30, 126, 257
Lobe, Johann Christian, 84n33, 85n35
Locke, John, 59n22
Lonsdale, Roger, 53
Lorenzo the Magnificent, 12
Lucretius, 220
Lully, Jean-Baptiste, 116n3, 189, 196–7, 199, 214n28; *Alceste*, 105, 107, 117n12–13; *Amadis*, 108–10; *Armide*, 110–11, 117n18, 224

mad scene, 229
madness, 54–5, 257
madrigal, 11, 56
maestro di cappella, 52
magic, 7, 13–16, 18, 19n25, 82n12; Dr. Faustus, 55–6; opera, 291
Maisak, Petra, 41n14
Majo, Gianfrancesco de, 122, 219, 223, 227, 229, 237, 239n23
Majorano, Gaetano (Caffarelli), 163, 165
Marais, Marin, 244
Marchand [probably not Louis], 215n28
Marchesini, Maria Antonia, 149, 165, 186
Marivaux, Pierre Carlet de Chamblain de, 244
Martin y Soler, Vicente, 275–7
Martini, Padre Giovanni Battista, 239n26
Mattheson, Johann, 187
Mayerhofer, Gottfried, 83n26
Mazzoni, Antonio Maria, 218
melodrama, 73, 301
Merighi, Antonia, 163, 165
Metastasio, Pietro, 2, 11, 58n5, 93–4, 104, 119, 121, 123, 138, 140, 168–70, 185, 221
Meyerbeer, Giacomo, 75–6
Meyerhold, Vsevolod, 302–5
Micheli, Benedetto, 218
Milton, John, 215n34
mime, 7, 16; *see also* pantomime
Minato, Niccolò, 138–40, 161, 165
Mingotti, Regina, 168, 186
Mirandola, Giovanni Pico della, 13

modernist, 299, 303, 306
Molière, Jean-Baptiste Poquelin, 243, 249
Moncrif, François, 198
Mondonville, Jean Joseph, 186; *Titon et l'Aurore*, 114–15, 199
Monsigny, Pierre Alexandre, 244–5, 247, 252, 257
Montagnana, Antonio, 163, 165
Monteverdi, Claudio, 1, 8–10, 141
Monticelli, Angelo Maria, 183
Monza, Carlo, 218–19, 239n23
morality, 25, 39, 217, 220, 222, 246
moralizing, 23–39
morals, 92, 212; instruction in, 30–1, 35, 39; effect of music on, 51
Moretti, Ferdinando, 128, 131n30
Mortellari, Michele, 130n14
Mozart, Constanze, 281
Mozart, Leopold, 260–1
Mozart, Wolfgang Amadeus, 1–3, 49, 73, 140–1, 271–2, 275–93; and Prokofieff, 299
  instrumental works: Clarinet Concerto, 287; Concerto for Two Pianos in E♭, 287; *Musical Joke*, 260; Posthorn Serenade, 272, 289–92; Quintet in E♭, (K.618), 277; Quintet in G minor, 260; String Quartets, Opus 10, 269; Symphonie Concertante for Violin and Viola, 271; Symphony in C (K.338), 272, 287, 293n3
  operas: *La clemenza di Tito*, 92–3, 271, 286–92; *Così fan tutte*, 135, 276, 284; *Don Giovanni*, 3, 85n39, 260–70, 284; *Die Entführung aus dem Serail*, 35, 277; *La finta giardiniera*, 294n15; *Idomeneo*, 35, 128, 268–9, 271–2, 277, 287–90, 293n2–3, 299; *Mitridate, rè di Ponto*, 127; *Le nozze di Figaro*, 3, 76, 276, 284; *Thamos, König in Ägypten*, 272, 284–7; *Die Zauberflöte*, 268, 271, 277–9, 282–7, 291–3, 299, 302
  sacred works: Cornonation Mass, 272; Vesperae solemnes de confessore (K.339), 289, 291

313

Index

murder, 233
music criticism, 105, 107; and Burney, 43–5
music, power of, 13–14, 33, 51; dramatic meaning in, 94–103
musical, borrowings, 225
  characterization, 144–63
  chromaticism, 144, 264, 267–8, 286
  culture, 292
  discourse, 91–4
  effects, 157, 201–5, 221, 245, 282–4; harmonic, 305; modal 174; *see also* Neapolitan harmony
  fashion, 45–6, 48, 51, 53
  forms: binary, 155, 161, 201, fugue, 173; rondo, 174, 201; rounded binary, 173; sonata, 265–6; *see also* aria, chorus, dance, overture
  genre: cantata, 144; canzona, 173; march, 305; scherzo, 306; siciliano, 144, 150, 157; sinfonia, 155, 161; sonata, 94; symphony, 243; *see also* opera, overture
  rhythm, 143, 147; cross-, 155
  symbolism, 95–103, 245–6, 250–7, 264–8
  taste, 43–6, 49, 52–3, 55, 57, 306
  texture: antiphonal, 105, 147, 157; contrapuntal, 178–9; fugal, 95; fugato, 263; imitative, 178
  tonality, layout, 142; relationships, 95–103, 163; symbolism, 264–8
Myon, Charles Louis, 215n29
mythology, 214n22
mythological subjects, 9–15, 17, 32, 120, 126, 129, 196–7; judgment of Midas, 52–4, 56–7

nature, 249; idealized, 24–5; imitation of, 8, 16, 20n28, 227
naturalism, 236, 302
Neapolitan harmony, 150, 152, 157, 266
Nencini, Santi, 280
neoclassicism, 217, 221, 225, 236–7, 239n23
Neoplatonism, 13–18
Nicolai, Friedrich, 40n12
nineteenth century, 2, 63, 67–8, 74, 292

Noverre, Jean-Georges, 199, 205, 212, 228
Nugent, Thomas, 26, 28

Obukhova, Nedezhda, 304
occult, 14–15, 17
Oeser, Adam Friedrich, 31, 35, 38
Oettermann, Stephan, 63, 67, 80n5, 81n6, 82n17, 88
opera, Baroque, 135; cohesion in, 2; comic, 33, 135; conventions, 135; dramatic relevance in, 2; French, 223, 227; Franco-Italian synthesis in, 119–29; German, 277; monologue in, 248; prologue of, 305; reform in, 2, 7; Romantic, 293; scene complex in, 122, 125–6, 128; serious, 2–3; Venetian, 140; Voltaire on, 7; *see also* aria; ariette; arioso; audiences; ballet; castrati; cavatina; chorus; ensemble; finale; *introduzione*; overture; recitative; reform; stage; theater
opera companies: Comédie Française, 63, 243–4, 251, 258n3; Comédie Italienne, 222, 243–4; Comédiens du Roi, 243; Opera of the Nobility (London), 170; *see also* theaters
opera (Oper, opéra), genre of: ballet, 105, 189, 214n28; buffa, 160, 260, 275–7, 292; comique, 3, 69, 71, 179, 190, 192, 196, 199, 210, 237, 243–4, 246; giocosa, 140; grand, 305; grosse, 277–80; pasticcio, 97, 168–9, 178, 186; serenata teatrale, 190; seria, 2, 92, 100, 140, 195, 220–1, 238, 269, 277–80, 286, 292; tragédie en musique, 105; tragédie lyrique, 189, 217, 238n20; tragédie-opéra, 196
orchestra, theater, 243, 259n16
orchestral effects, 94–100, 105, 147–50, 155–7, 163, 186, 251, 256
orchestration, 156, 161, 178, 251, 286–7
Orlandini, Guiseppe, 218
Orpheus, 9, 11–18, 48
Oulibicheff (Ulibishev), Alexander, 85n39
overtures (sinfonias), 35, 91–104, 119–22, 125, 161, 165, 168, 173, 201,

205, 263, 266, 287–90; borrowings, 2, 155–6, 179, 227, 237; French, 99
Ovid, 9, 11–12, 15, 197, 199, 214n28, 220

Paisiello, Giovanni, 128, 276, 279–80, 295n21; *Il Barbiere di Siviglia*, 3, 250
Panard, Charles François, 199
Panofsky, Erwin, 14, 23, 26, 29, 39, 40n3
panorama, 63, 65, 67–8, 80n5, 81n17, 82–3, 87n46
pantomime, 56, 70, 113, 119–20, 125, 128, 173, 238n8, 239n23; ballet, 205, 207, 223, 225, 229, 233, 237, 275, 299; *see also* mime
parody, 96, 196, 199, 223, 306
Pasqualigo, Benedetto, 218
Pasquini, Giovanni Claudio, 218
passions, 94, 141
Pastor fido: Guarini, 11, 25; subject, 33, 39
pastoral, 224, 244; effects 201
pastoral subjects, 1, 10–12, 15–17, 19n13, 27–8, 32, 39, 48; style, 35, 95, 99–103, 189–212, 244–5; *see also* shepherds
pastorale héroïque, 199
patronage, 3, 43–5; patrons, 31, 49, 85n38
Pergolesi, Giovanni Battista, 104, 188n19
Perrault, Charles, 300
Petriconi, Hellmuth, 40n5
phantasmagoria, 61, 63–9, 71–6, 80, 83–8; in opera, 73–6, 85n39, 87n46, 87n54; instruments for, 66
Picart, Etienne, 26
Piccinni, Niccolò, 188n19, 240n33
Picque, Abbé, 215n28
Pignolet de Montéclair, Michel, 105
Pirrotta, Nino, 8–10, 12, 15
Plümicke, Karl Martin, 286
poetics, 92–3
Poggioli, Renato, 18
Poliziano, Angelo, *Fabula di Orfeo*, 12–13, 15, 18
Porpora, Nicola, 170, 218

Porta, Nunziato, 218
Postel, Christian, 166
Poussin, Nicolas, *Et in Arcadia ego* 2, 23–4, 26–7, 29–30, 32, 36–7, 39–41
Powers, Harold, 138, 141, 150
Prati, Alessio, 128, 278, 295n18
Priestman, Brian, 166
Prokofieff, Serge, 1, 3, 299, 303–7
Puccini, Giacomo, 1, 155, 301
Pulli, Pietro, 188n19
Purcell, Henry, 53, 161

Quaglio, Lorenzo, 128
quartet, 123, 128
Quinault, Philippe, 110, 189, 196, 214n28, 224
quintet, 121, 285; instrumental, 260

Racine, 120, 218, 220–4, 236
Rameau, 105–7, 186, 244; *Castor et Pollux*, 111–13, 117n25; *Les Indes galantes*, 115, 199–200; *Hippolyte et Aricie*, 116n1; *La Princesse de Navarre*, 111–12; *Le Temple de la Gloire*, 111
Rasoumoffsky, Count, 49, 55
realism, bourgeois, 301, 303; dramatic, 9–10; in *Der Freischütz*, 71–3; in panorama and phatasmagoria, 68; theatrical, 79n1, 85n38
Rebel, Françios, 198
recitative, 119, 126, 155, 164; accompanied, 97, 139, 144, 221, 263–5, 267; as sung speech, 9–12, 15, 17; borrowings, 142; obbligato (récitatif obligé), 33, 120–2, 125–6, 128, 143, 221, 233, 236, 239, 245, 263–5, 267–8; programmatic, 121; simple, 107, 126, 229, 263
reform, opera, 2, 7, 217, 221–3, 227, 236–7, 239n23; theatrical, 196, 201, 210, 212, 221, 227
Renaissance, 1, 13–14, 16–18, 23
Reutter, Georg von, 218
Reyer, Ernest, 74
rhetoric, 10, 54, 91–3; in ballet, 208
Riccarelli, Guiseppe, 168–9, 186
Riccoboni, Francesco, 106

Index

Richardson, Samuel, 24
Rimsky-Korsakov, Nicolay, 305
Rinuccini, Ottavio, 9, 12–13, 15
ritornello, 144, 148, 157, 165
Riva, Pietro, 218
Robertson, Etienne-Gaspard, 62–6, 76, 80n4, 81–2, 87n54
Rochefoucauld, La, 247–8
Rochlitz, Friedrich, 293n2
rococo, 33, 212
Rolland, Roman, 12–13
Romanticism, 306
Rosand, Ellen, 7
Rossini, Gioacchino, 1, 48, 59n15, 250, 252, 259n15
Rossmässler, Johann August, 38
Rousseau, Jean Jacques, 186, 199, 223–5
Roy, Pierre-Charles, 215n29
Royal Society of Musicians, 180, 186–7

Sacchi, Antonio, 302
Sacchini, Antonio, 123, 188n19
sacrificial scenes, 120, 220–3, 229, 233, 237
Salieri, Antonio, 125, 275–6
Sallé, Marie, 199–200
Sammartini, Giovanni Battista, 179–186
Sannazaro, Jacopo, 23–4, 31, 40n3
Sarti, Giuseppe, 131n30, 218
Sartori, Joseph, 272
satire, 46–57, 302
Sbarra, Francesco, 7
Scarlatti, Alessandro, 1, 142, 161, 168–9, 186
Scarlatti, Domenico, 218
scenario, dramatic, 225, 229, *commedia dell'arte*, 301–3
Schidermair, Ludwig, 33–4
Schikaneder, Emanuel, 277–9, 284, 295n18, 299, 302
Schiller, Johann Christoph Friedrich, 61, 301
Schinkel, Karl Friedrich, 68, 71–2, 80n5, 83–5, 87–8
Schmittbauer, Joseph, 33–6
Schönbrunn Palace, 200–1
Schünemann, Georg, 61, 83n26, 84n34
Schwarzenberg, Prince Joseph Adam von, 192

Sedaine, Michel-Jean, 244–5, 247
Sertor, Gaetano, 127, 128
seventeenth century, 1, 7–8, 17, 138, 140
sextet, 265
Seyfried, Ignaz von, 284, 295n26–7
shepherds, 10–11, 26, 28–30, 32, 38, 75, 244–5; *see also* pastoral
Sheridan, Richard, 173
Silvani, Francesco, 121
singers, 162, 168–70, 178, 183, 186, 276, 304
social criticism, 246, 257
society, English, 44–6, 50–1; German, 66, 71–4, 76; Italian, 126; Parisian, 75–6; Russian theatrical, 303–4
Socrates, 16
Soden von Saßanfart, Count Julius Freiherr, 32–3, 35–7, 39, 41n18
Sografi, Antonio, 129
Solovyov, Vladimir, 302–3
Sophocles, 220
spectacle, 121, 123–8
stage, action, 71, 122; directions, 173; layout, 105, 303; setting, 71–3, 77–8, 80n5, 85n39, 95, 191; *see also* theatrical effects
Stampiglia, Silvio, 138–40, 165
Stanhope, Philip Dormer, Fourth Earl of Chesterfield, 50–1
Stanley, John, 44
Starhemberg, Prince, 274
Starzer, Joseph, 190, 198, 200, 205, 210, 215n36
Steefel, Laurence, D., Jr., 40n6
Steglich, Rudolf, 140
Sterne, Laurence, 32
storm, music, 3, 121–2, 125, 225–7, 244–6, 250–7; and stress, 246
Stravinsky, Igor, 305
Striggio, Alessandro, 17

Tallis, Thomas, 49
Tarchi, Angelo, 128, 218
Tartini, Giuseppe, 48
Tasso, Torquato, 11, 23–5, 28, 31, 40n5
Tebaldeo, Antonio, 12–13
Tesi, Vittoria, 178
theater, French Classical, 93; improvised, 302; musical, 217;

popular, 72–3; upper class, 72; Viennese court, 286
theaters: alla Scala, 120, 125, 127; auf der Wieden, 277–8; Bayreuth, 73; Bolshoi, 304; Burg (National), 190, 205, 223, 274–6, 279–80; du Château de Choisy, 107; King's, in the Haymarket, 168–70, 178, 180; Kirov (Maryinsky), 304; Opéra (Académie Royale de Musique), 2, 105, 113, 243, 246, 250
theatrical, effects, 70–4, 77–9, 83n27, 119–20, 299; fables, 301; lighting, 71, 84n35, 87n46, 244; organization (Viennese court), 274–7; *see also* costumes; reform
Theocritus, 11
Thrale, Hester Lynch, 45, 60n34
Tielker, Johann Friedrich, 82n21
Tommeoni Dutillieu, Irene, 275
Tonkünstler-Sozietät, 279–81
Tozzi, Antonio, 294n15
Traetta, Tommaso, 116, 121–2, 126–7, 188n19, 219, 223, 227, 229–31, 275
tragedy, 15, 141, 189, 217, 222–3, 302–3; tragic ending, 30, 121, 126–7
Trial, Jean-Claude, 215n30
trio, instrumental, 201; vocal, 123–5, 261, 302–3
Twining, Thomas, 46
Tye, Christopher, 49

Ugarte, Count Wenzel, 274–5, 278
Umlauf, Ignaz, 276

Van Loo, Carle, 221
vaudeville, 186, 199, 246
Verazi, Mattia, 2, 119–31, 238, 239n23

Vergil, 11, 31, 212, 221; *Eclogues*, 23, 272
verisimilitude, 7–10, 15–16
Villati, Leopoldo de, 219, 221
Vinci, Leonardo, 2, 96–9, 104, 145, 188n19
visual arts, 1, 14; engraving, 2, 38; painting, 2, 23–39, 197, 221; sculpture, 197, 217; watercolor, 46
Vivaldi, Antonio, 2, 48–9, 99–104
Vogak, Kostantin, 303
Voltaire, François Marie Arouet de, 7, 114, 189

Wagner, 7, 73–4, 85n35, 87n47, 92
Walker, Adam, 82n14
Walker, D. P., 14–15
Walsh, John, 168–9
Weaver, Robert, 130n30
Weber, Aloysia, *see* Lange, Aloysia
Weber, Carl Maria von, 74, 301; *Der Freischütz*, 61, 72, 77–8, 80n5, 84, 86–7, 92; Wolf's Glen Scene, 2, 61, 64–7, 69–71, 73–4, 76, 84–5
Weigl, Joseph, 276
Weisse, Christian Felix, 26, 35–9
Wieland, Christoph Martin, 40n12
Wild, Doris, 40n8
witch(es), 65, 302
Woelfl, Joseph, 48
Yates, Frances, 14, 18
Yershov, Ivan, 304

Zaslaw, Neal, 116
Zeno, Apostolo, 120, 138, 218, 221
Zinzendorf and Pottendorf, Count Carl, 200, 227, 238n20
Zuccarelli, Francesco, 29